D0205929

JUSTIFICATION

NOMOS
XXVIII

NOMOS

Lieber-Atherton, Publishers

New York University Press

NOMOS XXVIII

Yearbook of the American Society for Political and Legal Philosophy

JUSTIFICATION

Edited by

J. Roland Pennock, *Swarthmore College*

and

John W. Chapman, *University of Pittsburgh*

New York and London: New York University Press · 1986

Justification: Nomos XXVIII
edited by J. Roland Pennock and John W. Chapman
Copyright © 1986 by New York University
Manufactured in the United States of America

Library of Congress Cataloging in Publication Data
Main entry under title:

Justification.

   (NOMOS ; 28)
   Includes index.
     1. Political ethics—Addresses, essays, lectures.
2. Justification (Theory of knowledge)—Addresses,
essays, lectures.   3. Law—Philosophy—Addresses, essays,
lectures.   I. Pennock, J. Roland (James Roland),
1906–   . II. Chapman, John William, 1923–
III. Series: Nomos; 28.
JA79.J87   1985   172   85-13811
ISBN 0-8147-6595-5

CONTENTS

CONTRIBUTORS

KURT BAIER
Philosophy, University of Pittsburgh
MICHAEL D. BAYLES
Philosophy, University of Florida
RICHARD DAGGER
Political Science, Arizona State University
J. PATRICK DOBEL
Public Affairs, University of Washington
JAMES S. FISHKIN
Government and Philosophy, University of Texas at Austin
GERALD F. GAUS
Philosophy, The Australian National University
MARTIN P. GOLDING
Philosophy and Law, Duke University
AMY GUTMANN
Politics, Princeton University
BARBARA BAUM LEVENBOOK
Philosophy, North Carolina State University
FRANK I. MICHELMAN
Law, Harvard University
JEFFRIE G. MURPHY
Philosophy, Arizona State University
FELIX E. OPPENHEIM
Political Science, University of Massachusetts at Amherst
J. ROLAND PENNOCK
Political Science, Swarthmore College
MARGARET JANE RADIN
Law, University of Southern California
JEFFREY H. REIMAN
Philosophy and Justice, American University

CHRISTOPHER H. SCHROEDER
  Law, Duke University
THOMAS A. SPRAGENS, JR.
  Political Science, Duke University

PREFACE

The American Society for Political and Legal Philosophy held its 28th annual meetings on December 27th and 28th, 1983. Meeting in Boston with the American Philosophical Association (Eastern Division) on that occasion, its topic was "Justification, in Ethics, Law, and Politics." The principal papers were presented by Kurt Baier, Frank I. Michelman, and James S. Fishkin. As is the custom of our Society, each paper was commented on by representatives of the other two disciplines represented in the Society and, in this case, by the topic of the meetings. These commentators were Felix E. Oppenheim and Margaret Jane Radin for Baier's paper, Amy Gutmann and Jeffrey H. Reiman for Michelman, and Barbara Baum Levenbook and Christopher H. Schroeder for Fishkin. All of these papers appear in this volume, in revised form and, in the case of the commentators, sometimes considerably expanded and even made into independent essays, as they were encouraged to do if they so desired. To make the volume representative of even more points of view, the eight other essays were written for this volume.

Part I deals with justification in ethics. Kurt Baier leads it off by arguing that the only morality we can justify is that which "we can in reason want or ever demand of one another, in the sense that it would be contrary to reason not to satisfy these wants or demands." Both intuitionism and consequentialism are plausible. The latter can be proved correct if, and only if, "we can develop suitable conceptual machinery for amassing the empirical data which would enable us to tell which changes in our moral principles would bring us closer" to the ideal (i.e., justifying the objectionable features, such as the imposition of sanctions) and whether the gain is worth the cost.

Felix E. Oppenheim is not persuaded. He holds that Baier's definition of morality, in ruling out self-interest, is defective. Self-interest itself may be a morality, as exemplified by elitism. He rejects Baier's value cognitivism, and holds that it is not possible to make a rational decision between mutually incompatible basic moral principles. "In this sense," he concludes, "there can be no justification in ethics." (32)

Margaret Jane Radin finds the use of rational unanimity by Baier, Rawls, and others unsatisfactory; it doesn't fit the real world. The law makes use of a device for developing a second-best theory of justice that, in her view, is more practicable: "risk-of-error rules." They may not solve the intellectual problem, she admits, but in both moral and legal practice they provide "at least an antidote to too-great faith in ideal theories of justice."

Michael D. Bayles concludes this Part by arguing for the importance of mid-level principles in the process of justification. The traditional classification into act-theories and rule-theories is too narrow. When principles conflict, subordinate ("mid-level") principles come to the rescue. They make it possible for people with quite different strategies of choice and fundamental norms to reach agreement. Moreover, "because many principles can be justified by most plausible theories, one can be more sure of their correctness than one can of theories." (65)

Part II, "Justification in Law," opens with Frank I. Michelman's tussle with himself and with Duncan Kennedy (as a representative of the Critical Legal Studies [hereinafter CLS] school of thought) about the contradictions that both of them find in liberal legal theory. Agreeing with Kennedy about the existence of the contradictions, Michelman concludes that they need not lead to discouragement or disillusionment with liberalism. Rather, they reflect the nature of man himself, in whom the resulting tensions give to life "much of whatever it has of life and meaning."

The second essay in this Part, by Christopher H. Schroeder, is really a comment on James S. Fishkin's lead-off paper in the next part, and for that reason readers may wish to read Fishkin before considering Schroeder's contribution. Yet, as will appear, the latter is logically placed in its present position. Schroeder, agreeing with Fishkin about the crisis of liberal theory and the consequent need to lower our expectations with respect to what it can accomplish, extends the argument and applies it to the writings of the CLS school. He finds that something similar to Fishkin's "minimal objectivism" is acceptable and provides an answer to the charges made by the CLS advocates. In fact, he argues that one can already find within mainstream scholarship the elements of a nonabsolutist liberalism.

In the succeeding essay, Martin P. Golding offers a modest attempt to rescue judicial objectivity by suggesting that justification in law may differ from philosophical justification. It has a social component, but that feature does not give it the extreme relativism that might be the consequence in other contexts. The values that may properly enter into a judicial decision are not personal predilections; "they must have some purchase on the community to which they are addressed."

Jeffrie G. Murphy's concern in his essay, "Rationality and Constraints on Democratic Rule," is specifically directed at the justification, by courts, of "fundamental rights." He finds the usual justification of this concept, including reliance on the notion of "compelling state interests," singularly unconvincing. If anything is to be salvaged it must be "something considerably less ambitious than what we get from such writers as Dworkin and Rawls." (160) At the same time he finds value skepticism (exemplified by Alasdair MacIntyre and Paul Brest) self-destructive. He has hopes of finding the answer, soon.

Amy Gutmann tackles the problem of justifying the authority of judges, not by contending that it differs from that of legislators, but by arguing that the two groups share a "unity of moral labor," and that each of them can justify their actions without reliance on "legalism" by using a contextualist approach. In this way she believes it is possible to evade the criticisms of CLS.

In the last contribution to this section, Jeffrey H. Reiman takes still another path to justify the liberal theory of legal justification. Taking issue both with Kennedy and with Michael Sandel, he denies the existence of any inevitable contradiction between rights and community. On the contrary, rights (and justice) provide for any society—even a benevolent one—a backdrop of rules.

Part III moves to the problem of justification in politics, beginning with a paper by James S. Fishkin. He finds that liberalism is confronted by an as-yet-unmet challenge that threatens both its intellectual foundation and its practical legitimacy. The challenge arises out of the variety of moral decision rules provided by differing metaethical theories, a consequence of which is that the ethical foundations of liberal democracy rest upon sand.

Fishkin obviously touched a sensitive nerve, for no fewer than four of our contributors, including one of the editors of the volume, take issue with his conclusion, each in a different way. First, Barbara Baum Levenbook finds logical fallacies in his argument, arising out of ambiguities in some of his terms—especially the phrase "rationally unquestionable." Another of his points, the "unforseeability argument," demands so much by way of proof, she contends, that it becomes an argument for complete skepticism, supporting doubts about such propositions as "the sun will rise tomorrow."

Gerald F. Gaus develops a cautious and (from the point of view of one who would briefly summarize it) complicated argument to the effect that a theory of subjective value does not undermine liberalism, and further that subjectivists are committed to a form of argument that is "liberal-like" and requires them to develop public justificatory theories "to demonstrate that proposed political arrangements advance the well-grounded values of each and every citizen, whatever they may be." (263)

Richard Dagger enters the fray by directly supporting a particular type of metaethical theory as providing the proper foundation for democratic theory. He defends a rights-based theory as opposed to utilitarianism, answering objections commonly raised against rights-based theories, using the right of personal autonomy as the starting point.

J. Roland Pennock's intervention at this point takes a dual tack. First, he contends that the legitimacy of liberal democracy or any political system is not in fact threatened by the average person's desire for philosophical assurance. Further, the link between metaethics and normative political theory is less firm than Fishkin supposes; indeed, it is tenuous at best. As an example of how he believes political justification should proceed, he sets forth an argument in support of the democratic ideal that, like Dagger's, relies heavily upon an argument from autonomy, which in turn, Pennock contends, is founded upon certain facts about the nature of man.

The last two chapters in this final Part were not written with Fishkin's essay in view. First, J. Patrick Dobel, after discussing the numerous constraints to which all political justification is subject, argues that it is inherently contextual (reminding us of Gutmann's position), but it must make maximum use of principles. Whether the latter are deontic or consequentialist is of no importance so long as they are arrived at from a neutral or disinterested point of view, generating "duties incumbent upon all rational humans." (319) He remarks that this must be "ineluctably unsatisfying from a philosophical point of view," (317) to this extent placing himself in agreement with Fishkin.

Finally, Thomas A. Spragens, Jr., searches for and believes he finds in contemporary philosophy of science the tools for a rehabilitation of "practical reason" as providing the means for political justification. He does not expect to find certitude by this method, his strategy being rather to show that certitude has "seeped out of scientific justification as well." The materials for political justification are not genuinely "theoretical;" they will be prudential in the sense of "conducing to the human good," including what is fitting and proper as well as what is useful and agreeable.

Enough by way of foretaste of the fare we hope will be found enjoyable as well as profitable. It remains only for the editors to extend their thanks: to the contributors; to Hugo Bedau, who chaired the committee that arranged the program for the meetings of which this volume is an outgrowth; to Despina Papazoglou who skillfully sees us through the Press, and to our editorial assistant, Eleanor Greitzer, whose praises she wearies of hearing us extol.

J.R.P.
J.W.C.

PART I

JUSTIFICATION IN ETHICS

1

JUSTIFICATION IN ETHICS

KURT BAIER

1. The Requirement of Justification

Morality seems to parallel the law in that it requires us to arrange our lives so that we could always morally justify ourselves if necessary. Behaving in a morally unjustifiable way brings moral sanctions, such as condemnation and disapproval. This seems pernicious, for if taken seriously it must invite caution to the point of timidity, destroy spontaneity, and generally discourage enterprise, venturesomeness, and innovation. Hence this requirement to justify oneself morally in order to avoid moral sanctions would, itself, seem to call for justification. Quite apart from the threatening vicious regress, this latter justification is surprisingly hard to produce. Should we, then, with the Nietzscheans, throw off the chains of morality?

I shall argue that, if we begin by assuming, with commonsense, that the practice of imposing moral sanctions on people who behave in morally unjustifiable ways must itself be justifiable, then we have a clue about the proper content of morality. My thesis is that the guidelines of morality point to behavior that would satisfy what we can in reason want or ever demand of one another, in the sense that it would be contrary to reason not to satisfy these wants or demands. I then claim that a mo-

I am greatly indebted to Annette Baier, Don Hubin and Mark Singer for helpful comments on earlier versions of this paper and to Roland Pennock and John Chapman for innumerable editorial improvements.

3

rality with that content and only such a morality can be justified.

But first a few words about ethics. Like "physics" or "economics," "ethics" is the name of both a discipline and its subject
matter. Its core is normative questions about what is, directly or
indirectly, under our control, such as, what to do, what to believe and feel, what attitudes to take, what tastes to cultivate,
and what character to build.

The broadest conception of ethics regards it as dealing with
all normative questions: not only questions of how one ought
to act, but also of what sort of person one ought to be and of
what one ought to believe, sometimes called "the ethics of belief." At the other end of the range, the narrowest conception
takes ethics to be concerned only with those normative questions that are *moral,* in a somewhat narrow sense[1] about which
there is a great deal of dispute among moral philosophers. Here
I am concerned primarily with moral justification, in that sense.

2. Varieties of Justification

I begin with two distinctions. The first is based on two different justificanda, namely, individual performances and social
practices. Thus one type, let us call it performance justification,
comprises justifications of one's own or someone else's actions
or character either to oneself, to another individual, or to society, in response to an actual or envisaged accusation or unfa-
vorable judgment. If someone's performance is justified, then a
negative response to it or him is inappropriate; otherwise it is
appropriate. Performance justification is an important step in
the social practice of determining the proper response to certain types of behavior.

The second type, practice justification, comprises justification
of an institution, social activity, or practice. It is given *to* members, ideally *all* members, of a society that already has or con-
templates creating that institution.[2] This consists in showing that
everyone has adequate, perhaps compelling, reason to want that
social activity, institution, or practice continued, and no one has
adequate reason to oppose it. If it is shown to be justified, then
everyone has adequate reason to work for its suitable modification or abolition, and no one has adequate reason to regard

its rules as authoritative precepts. Hence, ultimately, all justification is, to all members of society. Individuals may be required, by a social practice, to justify themselves, but in order for that requirement itself to be justified, all members of society must have adequate reason to accept the practice that imposes that requirement.

The second distinction is between two types of performance justification, which I shall call "exculpatory" and "probative." It is based on the different kinds of negative response that are appropriate when some individual's action is shown to be unjustified. Let us begin with the probative. Someone's act is probatively justified if he did correctly or well what he did or if, though he did not do it correctly or well, he employed, with the required care, the available guidelines for doing it.

For a wide variety of activities society instructs its members how to do them well or correctly. Two ideas underlie most of them. One is that such guidelines enable all or most to perform better than if they had to perform without their assistance. The other idea is that it will be in the interest of many to know how well others perform. They may therefore wish to monitor one another's performance and appraise it, so that where it falls below an acceptable standard, they can if they want to take whatever reasonable *self-protective* measures they deem appropriate. Thus, people are judged fools, simpletons, credulous dupes, boors, louts, and so on, if they persistently perform poorly.

Adequate performance is optional, that is, not obligatory. We have no claim on others that they improve their performance if it has fallen below the desired standards. We are all perfectly free to perform as well or poorly as we please, and our fellows are equally free to monitor our performance, appraise it, and respond so as to safeguard their interests. So, most of us prefer, in a variety of mutually advantageous enterprises, such as hiring for jobs or inviting to a party, those of our fellows who are favorably appraised in respect of the relevant activities and excellences. Of course, although both the performance itself and monitoring, appraising, and responding to it so as to safeguard our interests are things we are morally free to do or not to do as we please, these practices and responses will put pressure on us to meet the expected standard, or (where that is appropriate) to "(probatively) justify ourselves," that is, show that we have performed up to that standard, when we learn or suspect that we have been judged unfavorably. But again, if we do not want to, we *need not* change our behavior or justify ourselves probatively. Still, we have good reason to do so, for others are free to take self-protective measures that will tend to affect us unfavorably. Hence, although the aim of these self-protective measures is merely to protect the interests of their users and not to put pressure on others to perform correctly, they will influence people to do so, and can therefore be regarded as "self-protective pressures."

In contrast, exculpatory justification is associated with a different kind of pressure, which I call "corrective." If a person is exculpatorily justified, then he is *in the clear* with others. They have no *complaint* or *claim* against him. Suppose he has failed, without exculpatory justification, to discharge an obligation or duty or responsibility—to meet a deadline, to grade his students' papers, or to keep up with the latest work in his field—then those to whom he has that obligation may *insist* that he perform accordingly or, if that is no longer possible, that he suitably make up for it. He is not then entitled to tell them to mind their own business, as he would be if they insisted that he not be so foolish, or so boorish, and so on. If one has an exculpatory justification for failing to do something then one is immune to corrective pressure. This pressure involves two things: (1) Unlike merely self-protective pressure its aim really is to influence people to conform to the relevant social guidelines; (2) the person lacking exculpatory justification is not free to persist in his deviant behavior at the cost of the imposed burden. Punishment is corrective pressure; shunning an ill-mannered person is not. If one lacks exculpatory justification, one is open not merely to two kinds of pressure, corrective and self-protective; one is, furthermore, *not morally free,* as one would be if one merely lacked probative justification, to persist in rule-breaking. If one lacks "prudential" exculpatory justification, one is perfectly free to continue behaving foolishly at the cost of being known and treated as a fool.

The difference between self-protective and corrective pressure is not that one is an individual, the other a social response: parental punishment is an individual response, legal punishment a social response, yet both are corrective pressures. Nor is the difference in degree of severity. Parking fines may be punishment, hence corrective pressures, but they are less severe than not being considered for a job, which may be a self-protective pressure against incompetents. What makes the pressure corrective is not the likelihood of success in "correcting" (reforming) the person, but the purported availability of a (practice) justification for imposing pressure *with the aim of reform*. How severe corrective pressures should be depends on many factors, of which aptness to achieve reform is only one. Chopping off the right hand for stealing or castration for sexual offenses may be effective, but objectionable on other grounds. Taxes, though often burdensome, are neither self-protective nor corrective pressures. They differ from the former in that their aim need not be to change the taxed behavior. Import duties on cars have that aim, cigarette taxes usually do not. And they differ from corrective pressures in that they do not imply that people are not free to persevere in their behavior.

But do moral sanctions really involve or amount to corrective pressures? Do we not reserve this kind of pressure for legal sanctions? If we ignore a moral guideline, is not the strongest appropriate response moral disapproval or condemnation, perhaps supplemented by appropriate self-protective measures? I do not think so. Morally condemning someone implies that he has violated some moral guideline and that he was not morally free to do so even at the cost of the penalty. But then the pressure exerted by moral disapproval and condemnation is corrective pressure. It is unlike refusing to associate, which leaves one morally free to choose, although because it weights it, one's choice is not free.

But is not moral disapproval and the like too weak to amount to insistence? To this there are two replies. The first is to reiterate that whether it amounts to insistence or not, the moral sanction is corrective pressure because a person is *not morally free* to choose the immoral conduct weighted by the sanction. If he chooses to do it, having shouldered the burden does not suffice to put him in the clear. The moral community should receive him back in good standing, but only if he has learnt his lesson, which means that he is now willing to conform to the guidelines. If he says, "I have paid my debt to society, I can now start all over with my next killing and raping spree, for which in due course I will again willingly pay my debt to society," then he is not yet morally in the clear. Corrective pressure has not done its moral work; the moral community need not receive him back in good standing. If there was a miscarriage of justice and the wrong man has borne the moral sanctions, they are not an advance payment morally licensing him to commit his penalty's worth of wrongs.

The second reply is more important and more complex. Nothing about the moral enterprise prevents it from employing severe sanctions. In fact, in so far as the legal sanctions are morally justified, they also serve as moral sanctions. Whatever corrective pressures the legal system legitimately brings to bear, it does so in the name of morality. Where a society has a morality, it regulates (among other things) what people may *demand* of one another and conversely what demands of others they *must* comply with, on pain of having "the social force" used against them. This is so whatever level of organization the social force has achieved. A society may have a morality without having a legal system, for it may have no institutionalized judiciary and legislature.[3] Enforcement may not have risen above custom. Even where a society is a legal as well as a moral order, as ours is, and where morality bestows on the legal system the right and duty of enforcement—perhaps the sole right and duty—it does so conditionally on law heeding morality. Even when there are legislators as well as courts, law still *purports* to work within the principles of morality. Of course, law goes beyond morality, in the sense of regulating matters, such as vehicular traffice, on which morality has nothing to say, except that there should be uniformity. It also may occasionally run counter either to conventionally accepted or to sound morality, but then, we believe, the law deviates from what it ought to be and such deviations should be corrected at the earliest opportunity. The respect we pay to law depends very much on its having institutions, such as the electoral and constitutional control of legislators, which ensure a continuous "moralizing" of its content. Legal positivists have rightly claimed that the law as it ought to be conforms to the requirements of morality, but that is only half the story: the law also always should embody such moralizing institutions, to ensure that deviations from what it ought to be are corrected as swiftly as possible. Of course, such

institutions will not be perfect and so what the law actually requires may well occasionally run counter to morality, in spite of
its built-in moralizing institutions. Nevertheless, it is desirable
that the law be respected. It therefore ought to deserve our respect and so ought to have moralizing institutions. If they work,
by and large effectively, to move law in the direction of what it
ought to be, then this explains why legal *requirements* will by and
large be morally obligatory.[4] For this reason, we ought not to
and I believe in fact do not call a coercive rule system a legal
order unless it has such moralizing institutions working sufficiently well to put the burden of proof on those who would claim
that they were not morally obligated to obey a certain law.

If this is true, then it establishes a connection between law and
morality that is considerably stronger than that asserted by Hart.[5]
For it is institutionally, not merely evolutionarily, guaranteed.
But is is still weaker than that claimed by pure natural law theorists.[6] In short, our morality confers on law the sole right and
duty to impose the severe (coercive/corrective) pressures in
support of some of its own guidelines (our laws), but our morality does so only because and to the extent that our law embodies moralizing institutions, such as the constitution and the
legislature, thereby ensuring the continued conformity of our
laws at least to the community's deepest and least doubtful moral
convictions. Law's monopoly of these strongest sanctions does
not imply that they do not belong in morality. What it shows is,
rather, that morality can justify the use of the legal machinery
for imposing them in preference to other (pre-legal) methods
of imposition, as long as the ultimate judgment of what is to be
enforced is not relinquished by morality.

3. The Bases of Moral Justification

Morally justifying a person, whether oneself or another, consists in showing that he has tried as best he could to act in accordance with the requirements of morality. But what are these
requirements? And can they justify the practice of imposing
moral sanctions on those who cannot show that they have met
or tried to meet them?

3.1. Commonsense morality. The man in the street relies for an
answer to moral questions on commonsense or conventional

morality that offers a set of guidelines, for example, the Ten
Commandments. Of course, commonsense morality contains
more than a short code. Like grammar, it is far richer and subtler than these explicit precepts, rules, and principles. We learn
much of commonsense morality by extrapolation from other
people's moral judgments and performance, by developing our
own moral principles, and in many other ways, which shape our
moral sensibility or *savoir faire*. With their aid we can give immediate answers to moral questions without first needing, or
indeed being able, to spell out the principle(s) by reference to
which we have settled the case in hand. However, in justification, these nonexplicit lessons are less readily employable. One
may perhaps get by with the question, What else would you have
done in my place? but this cannot clinch one's case. To show
that we are justified, we need to make explicit the principles we
actually have or could have applied in our deliberation. For
whether we are justified or not depends on their soundness and
on how well we have applied them.

Even where we can cite conventionally accepted principles, this
need not carry conviction with the person *to whom* we are justifying ourselves, for he may doubt or reject them. As far as performance justification (justifying a person) is concerned, such
doubts can be ignored. For we cannot demand of one another
that we live by principles other than those accepted by commonsense morality. But we can and do argue with one another
about the merit of the currently accepted principles. We are then
engaged in a practice of justification. Commonsense morality
seems to have only a rather feeble response to such a doubt or
rejection. I would guess that for most people the most plausible
answer would still be that we must accept these principles because they embody God's commandments. But, as has often been
said, this seems to be a question-stopper rather than an answer.

Alas, moral theory has not done significantly better than
commonsense morality. It certainly has not impressed us sufficiently to supersede commonsense the way science has. We throw
out commonsensical beliefs when a scientific discovery requires
it, if only because so much of today's commonsense is simply
yesterday's science. Moral theorists cannot expect cumulative
advance. New moral insights (or fads) don't usually come from
moral theorists but from people with quite different gifts.

Many factors have contributed to this feature of moral theory. We are unclear about what, if anything, are the aims and data of ethics, and how they bear on theory. Consequently, instead of being dominated by a single "paradigm," replaced only when a better one appears, the field is always occupied by a number of paradigms, each continually refined and spawning more and more complex subtypes, few of which are ever decisively refuted. Indeed, what counts as refutation for some, e.g., that the theory has moral consequences which would be rejected by commonsense morality, would be calmly accepted by others as the inevitable and indeed desirable result of moral progress. Consequently, the number of rival theories tends to increase rather than diminish. Admittedly, commonsense morality does not provide a clear, unambiguous, and well-grounded method for "validating"[7] our moral opinions, but moral theory has done worse. It has provided, not indeed a single better method, but a set of competing methods, such as utilitarianism or contractarianism, that are no less open to question than commonsense itself. Moral theorizing, far from helping settle moral disagreements, adds new ones.

We must look not for a method by which moral disagreement might be resolved, for we already have a large number of candidates, but for a way of determining which among methods for validating our moral opinions is the right one. What we are looking for is something analogous to what has been called a "vindication."[8] In the natural sciences, we can vindicate the hypothetico-deductive method because we can say with reasonable clarity what it is, and that its use accomplishes their ends better than any other known method.[9] Unfortunately, at this level, too, we are stymied in ethics, because the goals themselves are in contention. Even if that disagreement could be settled, we would still have to "exonerate"[10] these goals. But that raises a serious problem. Justification of the moral enterprise is formidably difficult, for it appears to have at least two aspects that, at any rate at first sight, are objectionable, hence call for justification, but seem incapable of being justified.

3.2. Morality, rationality, and self-interest. One of these problematic aspects is the assumption that the requirements of morality may come into conflict with self-interest. Thus, it may be in one's best interest but immoral to keep the change the grocer returned by mistake, to kill the uncle whose fortune one will inherit or to blackmail the senator whom one has photographed in a compromising situation. This raises the serious problem of whether it can always be rational to do what is morally required if, as is very widely believed, it is *always rational* to do what is in one's best interest. Our problem is even more serious if, as is also believed though not quite as widely, it is *never rational* to do what runs counter to one's best interest. As Bishop Butler put it, "Let it be allowed, though virtue or moral rectitude does indeed consist in affection and pursuit of what is right and good as such, yet that, when we sit down in a cool hour, we can neither justify to ourselves this or any other pursuit till we are convinced that it will be for our happiness, or at least not contrary to it."[11]

It is natural, then, to take the line, as many philosophers do,[12] that whether it is rational to be moral must be a contingent matter. They think of morality as an activity that, by its linguistically correct definition, has certain desirable ends, such as "the maintenance of liberty and justice and the defeat of inhumanity and oppression,"[13] and of rationality as the maximization of the satisfaction of one's own preferences or concerns or interests. As a result, being moral will be rational if and only if the attainment of the specifically moral ends occupy a suitable position in the hierarchy of one's own preferences. Questions about the rationality of one's preference structure itself and the soundness of the definition of morality enshrined in our language are not allowed. On this view, a person bent on amassing as many as he can of what he considers the good things in life, in whatever way this affects people he does not care about, can perhaps be shown that this would at times involve doing what is, as we say, *morally wrong.* However, if he does not care about that either, then he has no reason at all, let alone compelling or even adequate reason, not to do it. The best one can do on this view is to try and show that he does not *really* prefer what he thinks he prefers. But it seems, at least to me, that there is every reason to believe that in many cases we shall fail. So a person may find himself in situations in which whatever he does will be either rationally or morally justified but not both. What then should he do?

This seemingly unanswerable question may lead us to reject

this view and to maintain, as Sidgwick does,[14] that it must always be rational to be moral, or even, as Hobbes and Kant do, that it must always be contrary to reason to be immoral. We are thus confronted by an inconsistent triad: Proving the rationality of some conduct to someone consists in showing him that it would be for his good; compelling moral considerations sometimes require us to do things quite irrespective of whether doing them would be for our good; moral considerations could not require this unless one could be shown that acting from them was rational, whereas ignoring them was not. It seems that no single one of these propositions can be true if the other two are, yet it also seems that we cannot in reason abandon any of them.

3.3. Justifying corrective pressures. The second problematic aspect are the implications (sketched in section 2) of the moral requirement that we always act so that we can morally justify ourselves or else suffer moral sanctions. For then, we must add to the troublesome question Why be moral? the equally troublesome Why ascribe to society the right or duty to use corrective pressure to get its members to be moral? If some persons have adequate reason not to be moral, getting them to be moral is as arbitrary and oppressive as getting one set of people to satisfy the preferences of another set at the expense of their own.

The enforcement implications of moral obligation could themselves be justified only, it seems, if no one *ever* could have adequate reason to be immoral, but that would seem not to be the case. Even that requirement is insufficient if paternalism is ruled out. For then society does not have a right, let alone a duty, to force people to do something, say, to give up smoking just because they have adequate or compelling reason not to smoke. If society is to have that right or duty, there must be something about immorality that calls for stronger measures than does mere contrariety to reason.

To solve these problems, we need two things: an escape from our inconsistent triad (section 4) and a suitable hypothesis about the nature and function of the moral enterprise (section 5). To be suitable, this hypothesis would have to exonerate the function of the enterprise. That function would have to enable us to make a rational choice among rival moral theories and so vindicate the one chosen. And the general moral principles derived from the vindicated theory would have to settle moral

disagreements by validating one of the opposing moral judgments.

4. Morality and Rationality

Our first problem is to escape from this inconsistent triad. The
problem is to conceive of rationality and morality in such a way
that morality need never be contrary to reason, immorality never
in accord with it. Fortunately, we can do this simply by drop-
ping the currently popular conception of rationality with its
substantive thesis that rationality *consists in* always doing what
one has worked out with adequate care to be in one's best interest, or best promotes one's happiness, or maximally satisfies
one's preferences, and the like. We must replace it by the more
formal, more cautious, and more plausible thesis that it consists
in performance *according to reason,* where that means *according
to the balance of reasons.* This admits that considerations of self-
interest and the like are indeed reasons, but is silent on whether
they are the only or the paramount reasons. It thus allows that
moral considerations may also be reasons and that they may
sometimes or always override self-interested reasons when they
come into conflict, as we commonly believe.

5. The Nature and Function of the Moral Enterprise

My hypothesis is this. The moral enterprise is that part of the
enterprise of practical reason[15] that tells us what it is (or is not)
according to reason for us to do in response to what others want
of us. Moral questions arise when someone has adequate self-
anchored reason[16] to want to do something, but someone else
has adequate self-anchored reason to want *him* not to do it. Thus,
Jones may have adequate self-anchored reason to want to kill
Smith, Smith not to want Jones to do so. Moral considerations
then determine whose wants should be frustrated or modified.
Such considerations really are reasons if and only if it is in accordance with reason to follow them. Since they are supposed
to adjudicate in cases of conflicts of self-anchored reasons, they
must from their nature be capable of *overriding* them. Suppose
we say that killing is morally wrong. The person who had adequate self-anchored reason to want to kill loses out by this ad-

judication. His self-anchored reasons have been overridden by a compelling moral reason.

But can any considerations really be reasons overriding self-anchored reasons and especially those of self-interest? Can it really always be in accord with reason to be moral and always contrary to reason to be immoral? I shall try to make a case for this without any further changes in our conception of rationality and reason beyond those already introduced in section 4. However, my conclusion holds only if the following three conditions are satisfied: (1) Moral questions must be said to arise only in certain sorts of situations, similar to those now often called Hobbesian; (2) there must be a functioning social order operating with suitable social and individual pressures; and (3) moral answers must be taken at least to purport to satisfy a criterion of soundness, that is, rational acceptability.

5.1. Situations giving rise to moral questions. The central ones are those now often called Hobbesian or Prisoners' Dilemma (PD) situations.[17] They are situations of interaction in which the general acceptance of "independent" self-anchored considerations as the only or the supreme reasons for action has suboptimal outcomes for the persons involved. Considerations are independent if someone regards them as recommending a course of action *whatever others do.* The outcomes are suboptimal by comparison with suitable "interdependent," that is, coordinated behavior. Whatever the other does, *each* prisoner in PD does best by confessing, but *both* do better if they coordinate their behavior and refuse to confess. It is typical of the outcome of Hobbesian situations that there are two quite different self-interested reasons for not cooperating. One is the fear of gaining less or even losing if one cooperates while the other players one-sidedly fail to do so. The other is the hope of gaining even more by failing to cooperate. Let us call these the Assurance and Sacrifice problems, respectively.[18]

5.2. Social pressures and the assurance problem. The suboptimal outcomes of independent self-interested reasoning in Hobbesian situations, the possibility of improving things for all by universal compliance with cooperative, adjudicative guidelines, and the presence of the Assurance and Sacrifice problems suggest that there is adequate, if not compelling reason for everyone to bring into, or maintain in, existence a social order that makes coordinative guidelines available and ensures general conformity by suitable social sanctions. If this were right, then we would have justified the existence of a coercive social order that provides coordinative solutions for Hobbesian situations and solves the Assurance and Sacrifice problems for people who accept only self-anchored considerations as reasons for action. It would explain why even those who acknowledge only self-interested considerations as reasons must concede that institutions that sometimes coerce them into acting contrary to what they have compelling independent self-interested reasons to do, can be rationally justified to them.

However, this does not show that it is always according to reason to be moral, let alone always contrary to it to be immoral. Hobbes's famous argument, that although immorality may turn out to have been in one's interest, the risks involved in being caught are such that one can never in reason expect that it will so turn out, notoriously fails. Hobbes's rational egoists are in an insoluble dilemma. They must undermine the very conditions on which the solution of their Assurance and Sacrifice problems depends. On the one hand, each has compelling reason to support a coervice social order to solve his Assurance Problem (to deter *others* from being immoral). On the other hand, each continues to have compelling reason to minimize *his own* sacrifices. Therefore no one has adequate reason to obey moral precepts if contravening them is in his interest or satisfies his preferences and if he can reasonably expect to do so with impunity. Hence each has compelling reason to work for a perfectly efficient, omniscient and incorruptible police state—something like the Christian supernatural world order. For only in such an order are the certainty and severity of punishment so great that it would always be imprudent for anyone to infringe its rules. But at the same time he has compelling reason not to do so, since the costs of maintaining such an order will probably be greater than the gains and since he must fear that he will be a member of an oppressed and exploited class with no hope of remedy. And, he has compelling reason to try to change the law so that it benefits him more than it currently does, and, where he cannot change it, to subvert it by corrupting officials to bend it in his favor. Similarly, officials have strong reason to accept, indeed to invite, bribes for such favors. Hobbes cannot therefore give a coherent account of how Rational Egoists would solve the Assurance and the Sacrifice problems.

5.3. Equitability. Hobbes's solution thus has two major flaws. One is to define reason so that it can never be in accord with it to do what one has adequate reason to think will not be in one's best interest. He overlooks that in the situations, whose peculiarities he himself had noticed, everyone has adequate reason to think it in his best interest to live under a coercive social order in which conflicts of interest are authoritatively and uniformly settled by rules generally and, if but only if equitable, *rightly* regarded and treated *as reasons overriding self-anchored and especially self-interested considerations.* There is thus no need to show, as Hobbes tried, that even in these cases, complying with these rules cannot be in accordance with reason unless one has adequate reason to think that it will be in one's best interest.

The second flaw is that, because he had not seen the need for equitability, he was blind to the importance of the enormous moral differences between the various possible "solutions" for Hobbesian situations.

Imagine that most men are by inclination polygynous and opposed to polyandry, whereas most women incline to monogamy. Suppose also that freedom of choice would have suboptimal outcomes. A case could then be made for general acceptance of the fact of someone's being "married" to someone else as an overriding reason not to attempt to enter into an intimate relation with him/her even if he/she had adequate or compelling self-interested reason to do so. But this still leaves open the question how many women a man should be allowed to "marry," that is, "remove from the sexual market," whether he should be allowed to divorce any of them, how many men women should be allowed to marry, and so on. Even though all or most of such solutions may be improvements over freedom of choice, it may well be that not all people have equally strong reason to favor the specific arrangement selected by their social order. The question then arises whether everyone has compelling or even adequate reason to accept that solution as providing a reason which overrides compelling or even adequate reasons of self-interest.

There is a further problem. Circumstances may be such that some people have adequate reason to *support* a certain social institution yet lack adequate reason to *follow* its directives. Suppose several middle-class white males have applied for a position. The guiding principle is that the best-qualified applicant gets the job. Suppose also that the interests of those filling and those seeking the job as well as those eventually served by the chosen occupant of the position are best promoted if that principle of selection is followed. It seems then that everyone has compelling self-interested reason to support not only the practice of competition for jobs and candidate selection by some principle, but also this particular principle. Yet, when the decision is finally made, *it* (considered by itself) will probably run counter to the interests of all or some of those rejected. Nevertheless, each has the strongest self-interested reason he can in reason demand for accepting the selection (considered as the outcome of this practice), even though he may also have compelling self-interested reason to subvert the decision (considered by itself), by, say, offering a bribe to the selecting official or by giving one if invited to do so. In this case of conflicting reasons, the less-qualified candidate would be acting contrary to reason, it seems to me, if he offered a bribe. For he would be acting contrary to a consideration (that the successful candidate was properly selected by a practice of selection based on a certain principle) which he has the strongest self-interested reason he can in reason demand to recognize as a reason *overriding* his conflicting and compelling reason of self-interest.

Now consider the following variation. One of the candidates is a black whose job qualifications are inferior, but in all probability would not have been so if he had not been excluded on racial grounds from all schools that could have taught him the required skills. He does not then have the strongest self-interested reasons he could in reason demand for accepting the outcome of the selection procedure. Since he was the victim of discrimination, he could in reason demand modification of the selection procedure so as to compensate for the discrimination. Of course, the currently accepted selection procedure may be preferable from his point of view to any politically feasible alternative. He may, therefore, have compelling self-interested reason to support it against the proposed alternatives—"separate but equal" is preferable to "separate and unequal"—but he does not have compelling self-interested reason to *conform* to its outcome. Unlike his white competitors, he may have adequate reason to take the job if offered even though he is not the best qualified. In the first version of this case, the selection is sound; conforming to it is, therefore, in accordance with reason for every candidate, winning or losing, even if it goes against his best interest. For, as we said, going against one's best interest is not *tantamount to* being against reason. When everyone affected has the strongest self-interested reason he can in reason demand for accepting a principle or rule as an overriding reason, then it is in accordance with reason for everyone to set the overriden self-interested reasons aside. In the second version (involving the black), it is in accordance with reason for him to support the continuation of the selection procedure but not necessarily to conform to a particular ruling that goes against his best interest, for since he was discriminated against, he does not have as good reason as he can in reason demand for accepting the outcomes of this selection procedure.

Since good job performance is in the interest of all those concerned and since job performance hinges on job qualifications, everyone concerned has an interest in getting jobs filled on the basis of qualifications, provided everyone has an opportunity to acquire them. Those who have had this opportunity, therefore, cannot claim that they are not bound to accept job selections based on the principle of qualification. One could not escape being bound by decisions based on this principle unless the principle ignored, as it does in the case of the black, a prior discrimination which unfairly disadvantaged one in the competition for the job.

The case of the black job candidate shows that one may have compelling reason to support the use of a principle for resolving a Hobbesian situation, yet not have compelling (or even adequate) reason for conforming to a resolution based on that principle. The explanation is that one does not have as good reason as one could in reason demand for accepting resolutions based on that principle as reasons overriding those of self-interest. As far as I can see, this is the only justification for the claim that one does not have compelling reason to conform to a resolution of a Hobbesian situation based on a principle that one has compelling self-interested reason to support.

What, then, is the strongest self-interested reason one can in reason demand? It is one no less strong than anyone else's, that is, an equally strong one. Why can't it be stronger? Because, to justify the method, we must jusfity it to *everyone,* and that involves showing to everyone that he has reasons no less strong than the next man's. For if one person had stronger and another weaker reason to support the method, then there would be arbitrary discriminations between different individuals, but that would be contrary to reason.

And what is it for two people to have equally strong self-interested reason to accept an adjudication? It is for each of them to have adequate reason to consider it more likely that there will accrue to both *the same* most favorable balance of gains over losses if this guideline rather than any of the other ones envisaged or none is accepted by all. It is clear that in the Prisoners' Dilemma, the precept "Don't confess" would be the only sound moral solution. By contrast, in the case of, say, "Thou shalt not kill," there are many possible solutions, any of which might conceivably be sound.

To determine what is a sound solution, we need to answer two difficult questions, one theoretical, the other empirical. The theoretical concerns the range of beings whose interests are to be morally protected and so taken into account: normal adults; humans that need support, e.g., the sick, children, the aged, fetuses; perhaps also all or some animals, possibly plants. The indubitable nucleus unquestionably consists of normal adults, because they bear the essential duties and responsibilities whose discharge constitutes moral protection for others and involves sacrifices on the part of the duty-bearers. We may see reason to extend protection to others who, like children and fetuses, are essential to the continuation of the moral order or to those, like the sick and aged, whose fate everyone must expect to share. It gets progressively harder to justify to duty-bearers the burdens involved in extending protection beyond this primary group.

The second question concerns the favorable balances that will result from these alternative specifications, say, that *all* killing is wrong, or only all killing of humans, or all such killing *except* in self-defense, or in war, or in euthanasia or in abortion and so on. To settle this question, we need to know a lot about the consequences of these alternative solutions and how they are to be assessed as balances of gains over losses when compared to alternatives.

To sum up: I offered an account of the nature and function of the moral enterprise. It is part of the enterprise of practical reason and deals with certain interpersonal questions, namely, which of the things that others want of us is in accordance with reason for us to satisfy, and which not to satisfy, especially when they are incompatible with our own wants. I argued that this must be a social enterprise, not only in the sense that society must make available public guidelines to be followed by every-one who wants to act in accordance with reason but also that society must see to it that everyone follows them, and that those who do fare no worse than those who do not. I said that such use of social pressure or even force can be rationally justified to everyone, though only if the guidelines purport to satisfy a cer-tain criterion of soundness, if the community is concerned to discover whether they are sound, and if it is prepared to change them in the direction of greater soundness when suitable changes can be brought about. I argued that the criterion of soundness is the principle of equitability because, if and only if the guide-lines satisfy it, has everyone as strong self-interested reason as he can in reason demand for wanting such enforced guidelines, and no reason for saying that he lacks compelling reason to fol-low them himself.

6. Implications for Moral Theory

(Normative) moral theory, as opposed to theory of morality (which occupied us in the first five sections), aims at the im-provement of currently accepted conventional or commonsense moral principles and precepts, much as the natural sciences aim at the advancement of knowledge. My theory of morality im-plies that commonsense moral principles and precepts purport to satisfy a criterion of soundness, namely, the principle of equitability. They may, however, fail to do so, in which case they do not provide everyone with compelling reasons to accept them. The task of moral theory is therefore to develop the empirical data and the methods with the help of which we can discover whether the principles and precepts of a given moral order do or do not satisfy that criterion of soundness, and if they do not, how they would have to be changed to do so.

It may be helpful to look at a few simplified models of the structure and function of moral theory that, though not the work of specific authors, are representative of major types. My theory of morality should vindicate one of these types and reject the others.

6.1. Intuitionism of principles. On this sort of view (e.g., Sidgwick or Ross, but not Prichard), in ethics nothing is analogous to observation or apprehension of particular moral facts; particular moral judgments can be arrived at only by seeing what general moral principles apply to the case in hand. These general principles, in turn, are incapable of being empirically supported. Nevertheless, we need not uncritically accept the currently favored principles of commonsense, for these are not necessarily what we would accept if we brought our powers of moral apprehension more closely to bear on the issues. For in these matters, it is difficult to see clearly, because our vision tends to become clouded by interest, prejudice, ignorance of relevant facts, and the like.

6.2. Moral scientism. On this sort of view (which has been more often sympathetically expounded than actually embraced),[19] moral theory is closely parallel to scientific theory. For moral theories can be confirmed and disconfirmed, like scientific ones, on the basis of moral observation, which is not of course observation by a special moral sense or faculty, but is noninferential and immediate opinion formation about particular cases, based directly on sensory perception. In observing a group of hoodlums setting a cat on fire just for the fun of it, we also see, in the same way, that this is morally wrong. Both our natural and our moral seeing is theory-laden, each carrying the theoretical ballast of the relevant theories. The general moral principles and the theory from which we have derived them may come into conflict with our moral observations and are then disconfirmed by them, as in the natural sciences. Of course, in both domains, we sometimes retain our theory in the face of contrary data, e.g., when we have reason to doubt our data.

6.3. Consequentialism. This accords with Intuitionism that there is no moral perception of particular moral facts; that moral judgments can be arrived at only by subsumption under the relevant general principles. And it agrees with Moral Scientism that these general principles can be empirically confirmed or disconfirmed. However, empirical evidence becomes relevant in a more indirect way and only with the aid of a suitable ideal. The relevant empirical data are the consequences of the acceptance of or the conformity with, alternative moral principles, and they are made relevant by the extent to which these consequences bring the relevant lives closer to that suitable ideal. We are, of course, most familiar with this type of theory from hedonistic egoism and utilitarianism. Even those two advocate different ideals and consider different lives relevant, egoism only the agent's, utilitarianism all lives affected. Other consequentialist theories may differ even more widely.

If my theory of morality is sound, then we must reject Moral Scientism as entirely unhelpful, since it draws a parallel where none exists. In the natural sciences, theories serve to extend our knowledge and understanding of nature, and the basis for preferring one theory over another is mainly its greater predictive power, for that demonstrates its greater power to give us knowledge of the sort we want. Not so in ethics. Moral theory does not aim at raising our power to predict what moral observations various individuals will make, for two main reasons. The first is that we cannot accept moral observation. We must agree with Intuitionism and Consequentialism that particular moral judgments can be arrived at only by subsumption under general principles. Particular moral judgments are not merely theory-laden, they are entirely theory-generated. The observation that the sun is now rising in the east is theory-laden, and indeed laden with a false theory. But the newer and better theory denying that the sun moves round the earth has to explain why it *appears* to rise. Although we cannot perhaps formulate this stubborn datum in a wholly theory-free way, we may find one that is neutral as between the two theories, e.g., the position of the sun and the observer are changing relative to each other, and the two rival theories then give different explanations of *that* same datum. If I try to stop a person from jumping out of a window in his 25th-story apartment because I think it is wrong for him to do so, and if I come to change my mind about the wrongness of suicide, there may well be no datum left to explain. His suicide may no longer even appear wrong to me. And if it still does, this will be so only because I still believe in some other moral principle, say, one's duty to one's family or one's society and so on, that would forbid suicide.

The second has to do with the evidential status of particular moral judgments. If all people had the same moral observations in every particular case, the best explanation might well be that the principles on which they base their judgments are sound. But since disagreement in ethics is a fact of life, which cannot be disposed of (as in perception) by selecting standard (moral) observers whose observations are properly regarded as normal, and divergent observations as deviant or abnormal and therefore not evidence, that the best explanation of their variations in observation cannot throw any light on whose theory is the better. What is the "best" explanatory theory of these observations and their divergence therefore need not concern itself with, nor allow us to infer, what is the best moral theory.

Intuitionism and Consequentialism are both plausible. The choice between them depends on whether we can formulate an ideal that will justify the moral enterprise with its prima facie objectionable characteristics, such as putting pressure on people to conform, and whether we can develop suitable conceptual machinery for amassing the empirical data which would enable us to tell which changes in our moral principles would bring us closer to that ideal, and whether the gain is worth the cost. If the answer is yes, we should develop a consequentialist moral theory. Otherwise we will have to make do with Intuitionism.

NOTES

1. I have in mind something like J.L. Mackie's "Morality in the narrow sense:" "In the narrow sense, a morality is a system of a particular sort of constraints on conduct—ones whose central task is to protect the interests of persons other than the agent and which present themselves to an agent as checks on his natural inclinations or spontaneous tendencies to act." *Ethics* (New York: Penguin Books, 1977), p. 106. But I disagree with some of the implications Mackie draws from this description, e.g., that moral considerations in this narrow sense are not "necessarily finally authoritative with regard to our actions" (ibid., p. 107).

2. Don Hubin raised the objection that a practice justification could be given to members of another society. This is true and important. But it should be noted that if the society is truly independent, not a colony or satellite or other dependency, then the members of the other society cannot *demand* such a justification, cannot impose sanctions if it is not forthcoming, and so on. Members of different societies need not justify themselves to one another nor do they owe one another a justification of their practices and institutions. Perhaps as different parts of the world become increasingly interdependent, a moral world order will come into being. Meanwhile, members of different moral orders can, of course, justify themselves to one another, though they may find that, to be persuasive, they will have to do so in terms of the principles and practices prevalent in the moral order of the recipient of the justification. If that order is very different, they may have trouble justifying their behavior both to members of their own and the other order. The problem may be even greater when they try to justify their institutions and practices to one another.

3. H.L.A. Hart, *The Concept of Law* (Oxford: Clarendon Press, 1961), chapter V, section 3.

4. If legal systems have built-in moralizing institutions, then it will be natural to think that legal requirements are necessarily morally obligatory, that they are the same as legal obligations. It is, however, misleading to think, with Natural Law theorists, that legal requirements are necessarily morally obligatory and are therefore (necessarily) legal obligations, in the sense in which promises (contingently) give rise to promissory obligations, for it is misleading to think of the law as a *part* of morality. It is equally misleading to treat all legal requirements as legal obligations, even those that do not give rise to moral obligations, as if "moral," "legal," "promissory," "parental," "filial," marked different *senses* of "obligation," rather than different *grounds* giving rise to the same kind of moral tie. What legal positivists can talk about are legal requirements. To call them legal obligations is to move, without warrant, from the descriptive to the normative.

5. Hart, *Concept of Law,* chapter IX, section 2, pp. 189–195.

6. It is worth pointing out that St. Thomas himself was not a Pure Natural Law theorist in the Legal Positivists' sense. The famous section "Whether Human Law Binds Man in Conscience" makes quite clear that Thomas is interested in the conditions under which law is morally obligatory and not those under which an ordinance is to be *called* a law. He simply did not have that latter question in mind, or else he could not have said in the same paragraph that

"laws may be just or unjust," that "laws are unjust . . . by being contrary to human good" and also "Such are acts of violence rather than laws." He simply had no consistent view on whether such acts were not laws at all or were laws but unjust. What mattered to him was to show that they were not *binding*, even if they were laws.

7. Herbert Feigl, "De Principiis Non Disputandum . . .?," in *Philosophical Analysis*, ed. Max Black (Englewood Cliffs, N.J.: Prentice-Hall, 1962).

8. Feigl, "De Principiis," pp. 113–116.

9. For a different view, see e.g., Paul Feyerabend, *Against Method* (Atlantic Highlands, N.J.: Humanities Press, 1975).

10. This is not a felicitous choice, but I can think of no better one. So I have followed James H. Fetzer, *Scientific Knowledge* (Dordrecht, Holland: D. Reidel, 1981), pp. 179 ff., where the question is clearly explained.

11. Bishop Butler, *Sermons*, sermon 11, para. 20.

12. Most recently Philippa Foot, in her much-discussed paper, "Morality as a System of Hypothetical Imperatives," *Philosophical Review* v. 81 no. 3 (July 1972).

13. Foot, "Morality as a System," pp. 305–326.

14. Sidgwick, *The Methods of Ethics,* concluding Chapter (London: Macmillan, 1922).

15. For further details, see my paper, "The Social Source of Reason," *Proceedings and Addresses of the American Philosophical Association* 51, no. 6 (August 1978); "Rationality and Morality," *Erkenntnis* (1977); "Moral Reasons and Reasons to be Moral," in *Values and Morals,* ed. A.I. Goldman and J. Kim (Holland: D. Reidel, 1978).

16. Self-anchored reasons are based on the agent's preferences. If I prefer that your interest be served rather than mine, I have a self-anchored reason to set aside my own interest in preference to yours. Self-interested reasons are a subclass of self-anchored ones. They are those based on the agent's self-favoring distributive preferences. For details see my paper "Moral Reasons and Reasons to be Moral," (cited in note 15 above, especially sections 12–14.

17. For a marvellous treatment of these much-discussed cases, see Derek Parfit, "Prudence, Morality, and the Prisoner's Dilemma", *Proceedings of the British Academy* (1979), pp. 539–564.

18. For a more detailed discussion, see A.K. Sen, "Choice, Orderings and Morality," in *Practical Reasons,* ed. Stephan Korner (New Haven: Yale, 1974); and my paper "Rationality and Morality," *Erkenntnis* (1977), pp. 197–223.

19. Cf. Gilbert Harman, *The Nature of Morality* (New York: Oxford

University Press, 1977), especially chapter 1. See also Nicholas Sturgeon, *"Morality Explanations"* in David Copp and David Zimmerman, eds., *Morality, Reason and Truth* (Totowa, N.J.: Rowman & Allanheld 1984.

2

JUSTIFICATION IN ETHICS: ITS LIMITATIONS

FELIX E. OPPENHEIM

Kurt Baier has provided thoughtful arguments for the justifiability of ethical principles. Yet I remain skeptical. I question Baier's definition of morality, his conception of rationality, and his underlying metaethical view.

1. MORALITY

Baier contrasts self-interest with morality. But self-interest is itself one of various moral points of view. Egoism must be distinguished from altruism and benevolence (in J.S. Mill's sense) and utilitarian views may conflict with deontological moralities such as justice as fairness. Accordingly, there are incompatibilities, not between "self-interest" and "the requirements of morality," but between the moralities of egoism and, e.g., the moral obligation to pursue the common interest. That concern for the public good should always override self-interest is itself just *one* ethical principle.

This is not just semantic quibbling. One form of egoism has been predominant in political ethics, namely elitism (in the broadest sense), the view that it is right for a privileged group—social, ethnic, religious, national—to promote its own interest, and morally obligatory for the rest to serve that interest.

Throughout history, exploited groups have endorsed the norms of their overlords as their own "slave morality."[1]

I would therefore not speak of "the requirements of morality," nor of *a* "common sense or conventional morality," (9–10) nor even of a given society having "a morality." (8) In our society, a representative democracy, ethical disagreement on such issues as abortion, the death penalty, civil disobedience, and foreign policy is widespread. So I would interpret Baier's question "Why be moral?" as: Why adopt a nonegoistic morality and why act accordingly? And the further question "Why ascribe to society the right or duty to use corrective pressure to get its members to be moral?" (13) covers two issues: To what extent does society have the moral right to translate any moral code into positive law rather than the duty to leave its members free to adopt their own? And what is the basis for a particular principle such as equality of opportunity? The question "whether it is rational to be moral" then means: Is there a particular moral code that can be rationally justified?

2. RATIONALITY

This leads me to Baier's conception of rationality. While there are various moral codes, there is only one set of criteria of rational choice, roughly, basing one's action on sound inductive and deductive reasoning. But contrary to Baier, it seems to me that actions can be said to be rational only with respect to some *given* ultimate goal—*any* given goal. This does not mean that rationality is concerned only with means to ends. Failure to act rationally may consist, not only in the choice of inefficient means, but also in selecting incompatible ends, utopian goals, or acting contrary to one's real preferences, or incorrectly combining probabilities and utilities, and so on. Given *any* goal, it is in principle possible to decide which of several alternative courses of action is the most rational under the circumstances. One can give sound advice on how to invest, give to charity, or rob a bank.

For these reasons, I adopt the view that Baier rejects, "that whether it is rational to be moral must be a contingent matter." (12) First of all, as mentioned before, acting self-interestedly may be in accord with the person's morality. Doing so is then both rationally and morally justified (contrary to Baier). In the light of Adam Smith's "invisible hand," producers who efficiently maximize profits act morally as well as rationally. When self-interest and morality conflict, we must distinguish: Someone primarily committed to some nonegoistic morality acts rationally by acting "morally" (in Baier's sense) rather than self-interestedly. Hence it is not "always rational to do what is in one's best interest." Saint Francis acted rationally as well as morally when he gave his wealth to the poor—against his self-interest. But it is not "always rational to do what is morally required" either. Someone who values his own self-interest more highly than some moral principle or who disregards moral considerations altogether acts rationally by acting for his or her own good. One sometimes goes about rationally doing what one considers morally wrong. I do not agree that "proving the rationality of some conduct to someone consists in showing him that it would be for his good." Rather, it consists in showing him that it is consistent with his ultimate goals, be they moral (according to whatever ethical principles) or nonmoral.

Accordingly, it would be rational for the less qualified job applicant to let the better qualified be hired, provided *his* "guiding principle is that the best-qualified applicant gets the job." (18) But suppose he values the principle of preferential treatment for some minority (to which he himself may or may not belong) more highly than efficient job performance. It would then be rational for him to oppose the criterion of ability as well as its particular applications (contrary to Baier).

If Jones, the would-be killer in Baier's other example, and Smith, the prospective victim, both consider killing morally wrong, and if that is their highest principle, then it is indeed the case that Jones's "self-anchored reasons have been overridden by a compelling moral reason." (15) But suppose that Jones, a member of some national liberation organization, aims at dramatizing his cause and considers it therefore morally right to kill Smith: Is there a compelling reason that overrides Jones's own moral reason for wanting to kill Smith? A similar argument applies to what Baier says elsewhere: "A slave in a slave society would surely not *rightly* regard the coercive rules concerning slavery as reasons to act as they require him. He would surely act in accordance with reason if he tried to escape."[2]

Trying to escape would not be rational if he accepted the kind of slave morality mentioned above.

Similar considerations are relevant to prisoners' dilemma situations. If I am self-interested, and others are also, it is indeed rational for me to accept the authority of a government capable of coercing practically everyone to comply with its enactments, including myself. But I do not see that "justification of an institution . . . consists in showing that everyone has adequate, perhaps compelling, reason to want that social activity, institution or practice continued." (4) If I belong to a privileged group, it is in my best interest to support a regime that effectively protects these privileges and imposes all burdens—e.g., for the production of public goods—on the majority it exploits; but the latter may have compelling reasons to overthrow that regime. (I am of course not assuming here Rawls's hypothetical original position where institutions are chosen behind a "veil of ignorance.")[3] Only if I am committed to the ethical principle of equitability—"that each person should be prepared to do his part in a practice that is mutually beneficial"[4]—will it be rational for me to favor egalitarian institutions that *everyone* has self-interested reasons to support, and to cooperate even when I have the opportunity to free ride with impunity.

3. METAETHICS

These examples raise the more fundamental question whether there is a rational way of deciding between conflicting moral points of view. Here, Baier does not deal explicitly with metaethical problems; but elsewhere, and implicitly also here, he takes a value-cognitivist position. When he uses expressions such as "sound morality," "acting morally," "why be moral?" he evidently means to refer to one particular morality, the "principle of equitability," and to imply that *this* ethical principle is objectively valid. If these moral norms could be rationally justified, it would indeed follow that it is both normal and rational to comply with them.

For reasons I cannot present here, a "rational choice among rival moral theories" (13) in the sense of metaethical theories, leads me to noncognitivism.[5] Accordingly, actions can be rationally justified only with respect to some given moral principle. Only if we are morally committed to the principle of cooperation is it then true that "compelling moral considerations sometimes require us to do things quite irrespective of whether doing them would be for our good." Of Baier's "inconsistent triad" I consider the second true under the conditions mentioned, but the first and third false. If I am committed to egalitarianism, school segregation is immoral as well as irrational. On the basis of the dominant morality of South African whites, this policy is rational and right. Given any consistent normative standards, justification in ethics is possible and necessary. But I do not believe that one can decide rationally between conflicting intrinsic values. Thus, actions and policies are justifiable on the basis of "those shared notions and principles thought to be already latent in commonsense."[6] But we must specify: commonsense as understood in Western liberal democracies. However, the most crucial ethical issues arise between individuals and groups or cultures not sharing the same "commonsense" views. I do not believe that it is possible to decide rationally between incompatible intrinsic valuational systems and basic moral principles. In this sense, there can be no justification in ethics.

NOTES

1. For an apt illustration, see G.T. di Lampedusa, *Il Gattopardo* (Milan: Feltrinelli, 1958); English ed., *The Leopard* (New York: Pantheon Books, 1960), chapter 3.
2. Kurt Baier, "Moral Reasons and Reasons to Be Moral," in *Values and Morals*, eds. A.I. Goldman and J. Kim (Dordrecht, Holland: D. Reidel 1978), p. 245.
3. John Rawls, *A Theory of Justice* (Cambridge.: Harvard University Press, Belknap Press, 1971), p. 12 and passim.
4. B. Barry and R. Hardin, eds., *Rational Man and Irrational Society?* (Beverly Hills, Ca.: Sage Publications, 1982), p. 380.
5. A recent formulation of this position: "But whereas we can test a prediction against the independent course of observable nature, we can judge the morality of an act only by our moral standards themselves." W.V. Quine, in Goldman and Kim, *Values and Morals*, pp. 37–46, at p. 43.
6. John Rawls, "Kantian Constructivism in Moral Theory," *The Journal of Philosophy* 77 (1980: 515–572, at 518.

3

RISK-OF-ERROR RULES AND NON-IDEAL JUSTIFICATION

MARGARET JANE RADIN

This chapter addresses the salience for legal theory of a distinction between morally justifying individual acts and morally justifying a practice or institution. In a well-known article, John Rawls offered this distinction as a method of avoiding some notorious difficulties of utilitarianism.[1] A practice, such as punishment, may be justified by rule-utilitarianism, and then actions falling under it are justified simply by appeal to the practice. Kurt Baier's distinction between performance justification and practice justification[2] bears an important similarity to Rawls's two kinds of rules: namely, that individual actions or performances are justified simply by appeal to social practice—the prevailing moral guidelines—and it is the practice that must be substantively justified. When we ask whether what someone did was right or wrong, we are to ask only whether the act fits within prevailing practice. Normative analysis is reserved for scrutiny of prevailing practice, not the individuals who conform to it. Justification is bumped up from the particular to the general, from the individual to the collective.

In this bifurcated mode of analysis we must justify legal practices, but those whose actions conform to them are automatically deemed justified. Presumably this goes both for the law-abiding citizens who obey legal rules and for the functionaries (police, judges) who implement coercive sanctions against those who do not. So far so good, perhaps.[3] But justifying a practice means justifying its application to a continuing stream of individuals. Focusing on the systematic nature of practices has important consequences for legal justification because it helps us remember that the system is imperfect. So if we wish to pursue this mode of analysis, practice justification needs special elaboration and qualification in light of the difficulties of actually determining when someone is in fact not act-justified because her act is not within the relevant practice, hence justifiably incurs sanctions.[4]

One may suppose, whatever one's normative style or metaethic, that a strong and certain justification is required when serious invasions of important individual interests, such as liberty, are the sanctions. Maybe is not good enough. One possible ground for requiring certainty of justification in these circumstances—the one I suggest below—is the traditional Kantian *Grundnorm* of respect for persons. Yet systematic application of norms in the circumstances of uncertainty, which is the daily business of the legal system, makes strong justification for legal actors problematic. A main thesis of this chapter is that the risk of error in applying otherwise seemingly acceptable norms to many individuals may undermine their justification. From this two conclusions follow. Practice rules that are formulated without taking account of the risk of error in application are likely to be unjustified and in need of modification or reformulation. And the fact that practice rules dealing explicitly with risk of error are pervasive in our moral/legal discourse undermines modes of moral theorizing that start by postulating an errorless ideal world.

To elaborate, I shall first mention some problems of knowing whether or not someone is act-justified. These will be by way of recounting some well-known kinds of difficulties that create uncertainty. Next I shall mention legal practices—here called risk-of-error rules—responsive to uncertainty. Then I shall consider the implications for practice justification and the use of ideal theory.

How, then, does one find out whether an act is within a practice, so as to conclude that the actor is justified? Obviously we must at minimum be able to define the act, determine that it occurred, define the practice, give an adequate account of what it means for an act to be "within" (or "falling under") a practice, and determine that the act in question does so. In attempting to carry out this agenda we run into deep philosophical problems.

Consider the problem of knowing what has occurred in the natural world, the problem of evidence or post-diction. Some of the difficulties that create uncertainty are the fallibilities of perception, the problem of description of events, and the problem of causal inference. These are code words for philosophical quagmires. And we have just begun. For we need to know more than physical facts; we need to know whether they are a human act. There is no easy answer to Wittgenstein's famous question, "What is left over if I subtract the fact that my arm goes up from the fact that I raise my arm?"[5] Now, let us suppose that there is a practice rule that it is wrong for someone to knock down someone else. What are the difficulties in the way of knowing whether A knocked B down, so that A is morally/legally blameworthy? The actor could have been A′ who might have resembled A under the circumstances. (Perhaps to the witness "they all look alike.") A's movement might not have been the cause of B's fall. (B might have independently tripped.) A's movement might not properly be the act of A (caused instead by independent physical forces); A's movement, if her act, might not properly be described as knocking someone down (perhaps an act of arm-waving instead).

Even if we know B's fall is properly regarded as caused by the act of A, and the act is properly regarded as knocking B down, for moral/legal blame our practice usually requires even more detailed "internal" knowledge—of what the law calls the mental element. When the act of A causes the death of B, it is homicide. Not all homicides are murder. Our practice says that to be a murderer one must kill while intending to kill and without any of the recognized justifications or excuses such as self-defense or insanity.[6] What is intentionality and how do we observe that someone was in a particular intentional state at the given time? What is sanity and how do we observe that she was sane?[7] Though of course we must and do make these observations in the normal course of everyday life, their underlying uncertainty—or rather their inherent imprecision—has greater moral significance when they are relied upon to justify legal consequences.

The requirement that there must be intent to kill for a homicide to be murder also should remind us that moral/legal rules seem to come with attached standards of effort to comply. The question is what kind of effort constitutes compliance with a moral/legal command like "Thou shalt not kill." The choices form a continuum. Certain stopping places along it—how do we observe "where" they are?—have acquired names in the law: intent, recklessness, negligence, strict liability.[8] Philosophers who speak of justifying a simply stated practice rule (like "It is wrong to knock someone down") ignore an important complexity of moral practice. The rule (1) "It is wrong to knock someone down even if you were trying to avoid doing so" requires a different justification from the rule (2) "It is wrong to knock someone down on purpose"—and so with the intermediate gradations. Should rule (1) be considered a different rule from rule (2)? Or are they the same rule with different standards of care attached to it? Either way we choose to speak, two things are apparent. First, standards must be substantively justified along with prescriptive rules themselves. Second, the difficulty of knowing when someone is to be deemed not to have complied with the relevant standard is a further serious difficulty in the way of determining whether someone's act is unjustified. One of my teachers, Michael H. Shapiro, made sure his students saw this problem by asserting, "The difference between gross negligence and negligence is seven."

Still another difficulty in the way of certainty of justification and blame is the least philosophically interesting but perhaps the most important. Contrary to the assumptions in ideal theories of justice, we have reason to believe that overworked, misguided, stupid, and corrupt lawyers and judges do exist, as well as lying clients and witnesses. They will bring about wrong decisions.

What are we to make of these thickets of philosophical and practical difficulties rendering act-justification problematic? The crucial fact is that the law goes on in spite of them, blaming and exonerating people, awarding and levying damages, etc. The law must operate in a non-ideal world.[9] Amidst uncertainty, ambiguity, fallibility, and error the law goes on adjudicating while philosophers argue over the foundations of fact and value that are necessary to make adjudication possible. Police, prosecutors, and judges cannot really find out with certainty how to apply a practice rule to defendant X. Nor can they know whether the rules they are imperfectly implementing are really justified. This being so, the one thing legal actors do clearly know in making moral judgments—for example, that defendant X deserves ten years in prison—is that they make mistakes.[10] Some people who are not act-justified get off and some who are do not.

Because error in the systematic context seems more certain than the judgments the system produces, the law is sensitive to risk of error in many ways. What comes most readily to mind for the nonlawyer is the system of appeals. My concern here is broader. I wish to consider the way the law's sensitivity to risk of error has generated the kind of rules I call risk-of-error rules. These are rules responding both to the possibility of error in formulating practice rules and in applying them. Risk-of-error rules are themselves moral practice rules.

Rules responsive to risk of error in applying practice rules to specific cases come easily to mind. Take the rule that criminal punishment cannot be imposed unless one is guilty beyond a reasonable doubt. One is to be deemed act-justified if it is only reasonably probable that one is in fact not act-justified. This means one is to be deemed *not* a murderer if it is only reasonably probable that one *is* a murderer. The beyond-a-reasonable-doubt rule allocates risk of error away from the accused and toward the accuser. It tilts the scales so that most errors will go one way, to avoid most of the errors against the accused that would otherwise occur in the normal course of events. It is a moral rule: "It is *better* to let ten guilty people go free than to let one innocent person suffer." Perhaps it is useful to think of it as a second-order practice rule, since it operates on a class of first-order or substantive practice rules, the rules defining criminal conduct. Alternatively, as with the standard-of-care rules, we could think of it as being an implicit part of each and every rule of criminal justice. Either way we choose to speak, its importance in moral/legal practice is clear.

If we pursue the manner of speaking that characterizes the

reasonable doubt rule as a second-order rule, we can see it as delineating a practice of allocating the risk of error in making performance judgments under a class of first-order rules, like "Stealing is wrong." There are other classes of first-order rules, like "Someone who steals deserves fitting punishment," and "Twenty-five years in prison 'fits' the crime of stealing." These too could have corresponding risk-of-error rules, like "Err in the accused's favor on what constitutes fitting punishment."

The second-order rule on reasonable doubt is one of a family of rules assigning burden of proof or persuasion. Another in this family is the rule in ordinary civil tort cases that in order for the victim to recover damages the trier of fact must find it more likely than not (i.e., greater than a fifty-fifty chance) that a negligent act of the alleged injurer caused the victim's injury. That rule seems to reflect a social commitment to risk error against the victim to a slightly greater degree than against the alleged injurer.

Sensitivity to risk of error also influences the level of generality of legal practice rules. Some specific practice rules, such as the "per se" condemnation of price-fixing in antitrust law, are supposed to leave the judge nothing to do but decide whether what someone did comes within the meaning of the rule, for example whether a trade association's activities are properly described as price-fixing. It is supposed to follow automatically that the act is unjustified. Another type of legal approach (sometimes called a standard), such as the "rule of reason" approach to nonprice restraints in antitrust law, asks the judge to evaluate the conduct in each case, that is to judge whether the conduct was good or bad, reasonable or unreasonable with respect to much more general practice rules, the law's general goals. All fields of law exhibit both rules that are applied (more or less) "per se" and rules that are applied (more or less) case-by-case. The rule that Miranda warnings must be given automatically in every case of custodial interrogation is of the first type, while the rule that warrantless searches are illegal where someone had a reasonable expectation of privacy is of the second.

Evaluation by applying standards seems to fit less readily into the bifurcated act/practice model of justification than does evaluation by blanket rules, because when the judge is asked to evaluate individual conduct on a case-by-case basis it seems she is asked to do more than merely decide whether someone's act is within a practice. Case-by-case evaluation does not seem as mechanical as this model of act-justification would have it. In fact, the difference seems to be only one of degree. A similar type of evaluation is also necessary in the case of blanket rules, to determine whether the individual's case ought to be deemed to be within the rule. Under the price-fixing per se rule, a judge is not supposed to consider whether the case before her might be allowed as beneficial price-fixing, but her reasoning about the goodness or badness of the challenged business activity will help her decide whether the activity is properly called price-fixing at all. Act-justification is not as automatic as the model would have it even under specific blanket rules.

I bring this up here not merely to qualify the distinction between justifying a practice and justifying an act falling under it by showing that the categories shade into each other, although they do, but rather primarily to point out that risk of error is an important factor governing whether a blanket rule or a case-by-case rule is chosen. Each type of rule generates its own problem in application. Blanket rules are both over- and under-inclusive with respect to their underlying ground. The rule that contracts signed by someone under 18 are void will invalidate contracts signed by responsible 17-year-olds and validate contracts signed by immature 19-year-olds. Case-by-case rules result in apparent unequal treatment or inconsistency. Judge A may find a reasonable expectation of privacy where Judge B would not. As with the blanket rule, some decisions will be wrong; in addition, although the individual treatment is morally attractive, the appearance of inconsistency smacks of arbitrariness. Which kind of rule is chosen depends on which kind of problem is worse under the circumstances. From this perspective the Miranda rule rests on the judgment that it is better to force police to give warnings in cases where the defendant is in fact not in danger of coerced confession than to risk infringing a defendant's right against coerced confession because of erroneous police judgment on the matter. Similarly, the per se rule against price-fixing risks error against cases of beneficial price-fixing, because of the judgment that there are very few if any of them, so that these errors are outweighed by the expected inconsistency, that is, the expected validation of cases of bad price-fixing, plus the cost and confusion that would be caused by case-by-case examination under the rule of reason. On the other hand, because of the importance of the individual interest at stake and because of our social commitment to risk error against the government in criminal cases, a blanket rule decreeing execution for all murderers has not been permitted. Rather, respect for the individual requires that murderers' desert is to be evaluated on a case-by-case basis. The idea is that a mandatory execution rule risks executing some who do not deserve it, and this risk will be less if each murderer's desert is individually evaluated.[11]

Another prominent response in legal discourse to risk of error is a family of second-order rules known as standards of review. They regulate the attitude courts are to take when asked to invalidate legislation or the decisions of administrators and lower courts. A state law that arguably infringes free speech, for example, is much more readily found unconstitutional than one that seems to deal with merely economic matters. This reflects a social commitment to risk error against individual rights or interests more readily in economic activity than where free speech might be involved. The "higher" standard of review does two things: it requires the court to deem that the questioned law does impinge on individual rights if it might; and it requires the government to have an especially strong justification if the law is to stand. The "lower" standard of review, in circumstances where errors against core individual rights and interests are not involved, directs courts to presume that legislation is justified absent a strong showing to the contrary. The commitment to risk error against the government—and majority rule—in cases involving core individual rights and interests can be viewed as justified by a *Grundnorm* of respect for persons. That is, if respect for persons requires some such guarantees as the Bill of Rights enumerates, it also requires that the government not administer its affairs so as to "chill" persons from attempting to act upon those rights, and it also requires that the government not override those rights without a strong and certain justification.[12]

Now we can see how risk-of-error rules govern formulation of substantive rules as well as their application. The risk-of-error rules embodied in standards of review apply to invalidate statutes or judge-made rules (first-order practice rules) as well as their application to specific cases. The risk that a first-order rule itself is wrong may seem to reflect a different uncertainty than the various problems of application, but I think it is illuminating to consider them together. The risk that the rule is wrong is simply the risk of moral error in creating a practice rule. The philosophical aspect of the risk is just the contested nature of moral and political theory; the practical aspect of the risk is the imperfection of the legislative and judicial processes. These are parallel to the philosophical and practical difficulties that cause uncertainties of application.

To see how taking risk of error into account may render a practice unjustified, take the "25-years-for-stealing" rule. In light of a more general rule of punishment—"the punishment must fit the crime"—we may be unsure whether 25 years in prison fits the crime or is too harsh. If there exists a risk-of-error rule telling us not to risk too-harsh punishment (perhaps qualified: at such-and-such a level of seriousness of sanction; at such-and-such a level of uncertainty about what is really deserved) then we must reformulate our first-order 25-year-rule. To take another example, our current practice rule is that some murderers deserve execution.[13] Perhaps this is right in ideal retributivist theory. But it is possible to argue—and I am convinced[14] — that a risk-of-error rule derived from a more general rule on punishment renders this practice rule unjustified in our world. The more general rule on punishment is, "Punishment must respect persons, where that entails both individual desert and equal treatment." This more general rule encompasses the general rule mentioned previously, that the punishment fit the crime, which addresses the issue of desert. In the case of the death penalty, act-justification for the executioners under the current practice rule, which requires singling out which murders are bad enough, is sufficiently uncertain, and the inevitable errors, wrongly killing people, are sufficiently grave, that to risk these errors against those accused and found guilty of murder constitutes disrespect for persons. Thus the general rule of respect for persons requires that we not permit the level of risk of erroneous execution that our current practice rule does permit.

How are risk-of-error rules justified? What is their bearing on the general methodology of justification? The method of justification used in the argument just mentioned falls back on a more general rule we assume is justified, respect for persons. It asserts that the proposed risk-of-error rule more clearly obeys the rule of respect for persons that does the disputed first-order rule that someone can deserve to die for some crime or the inherently uncertain particular judgment that this defendant deserves to die. Similarly, I think the guilt-beyond-a-reasonable-doubt rule and many of the others can be viewed as resting on respect for persons.

I shall not undertake to argue how the more general rule on respect for persons may be justified since this is not the occasion for a review of Kantian moral philosophy. A rational unanimity procedure such as Baier's could presumably generate practice rules of this very general form.[15] In Rawls's roughly parallel procedure the rational agents in the original position arrive at a very general primary rule of equal liberty. A rational unanimity argument could perhaps generate risk-of-error rules too. It would ask the postulated rational agents how seriously in real life they could in reason take the practice rules they would unanimously agree to in their postulated original position. But the ideal nature of the rational unanimity procedure seems somehow at odds with the non-ideal circumstances that create the need for risk-of-error rules, because the ideal procedure implicitly declares these circumstances unnecessary for thought about justice. Risk-of-error rules relate to the world of mistakes, irrationality, misinformation, prejudice, and evil. The ideal observer does not make mistakes. There is no gap between creating an ideal theory of justice and imagining it implemented by an ideal observer. But in our world there is a gap. The risk-of-error rules tell us not, or at least not always, to seek the ideal observer's judgment on individual acts, because so to judge *everyone's* acts, knowing we do make mistakes, must harm some people in ways we cannot morally countenance. Thus the risk-of-error rules seem irreducibly social and dynamic as well as non-ideal. They relate to the performance of a system as a whole. They relate to the performance of everyone as well as to the performance of each, and to the performance of the judges as well as the judged.

So risk-of-error rules are part of a non-ideal, second-best theory of justice. They play out "ought implies can" on a systematic basis. Whether they can in fact be justified by an ideal procedure—assuming wholly rational beings, perfect information, etc.—seems to me unlikely. At least it seems that a rational unanimity procedure would lead to a regress on the issue of risk of error in the first-order rules: What in rationality would we agree to do because we may be wrong about what in rationality we would agree to do? What in rationality would we agree to do because we may be wrong about *that?* And so on. To take risk-of-error rules as central in systemic justification seems to me to undermine the usefulness of the methodologies of ideal theory. In my view this is the philosophically interesting thing about them.

Since I do not possess a full-blown non-ideal theory of justice, I shall conclude, perhaps anticlimatically, by pointing out how the methodology of rational unanimity seems indeed to be undermined by the problems exponents such as Baier see as lying in the way of using it to determine which moral practices are justified. Baier's ideal procedure consists in showing that everyone has reason to want a practice and no one has adequate reason to oppose it. (Or that all members of society have adequate reason to accept the practice. Or that everyone has adequate reason to believe each will get the same most favorable balance of gains over losses by accepting one guideline rather than another.) He presents the Hobbesian choice situation as the only one in which moral questions may be said to arise. He then discovers two problems in finding a sound—equitable—solution to a Hobbesian choice. There is the "theoretical" question of what is the range of beings whose interests are to be morally protected and so taken into account; and there is the "empirical" question of what favorable balances will result from each possible cooperative solution to a Hobbesian dilemma.[16] Both of these problems undermine rational unanimity as a method of generating or justifying moral practices.

I do not see what theory one might use to answer Baier's "theoretical" question, in considering extending moral protection to the insane, animals, and the environment. It cannot be a question of *moral* theory as he defines it, because animals and plants are not involved in Hobbesian choices, nor are they, or the insane, involved in practical reason or rational response to interpersonal demands. Likewise, none of them was invited to the meeting in the original position. This "theoretical" problem undermines the methodology of rational unanimity. We cannot use the methodology to describe the moral universe for us, but it seems clear that the constitution of the moral universe is a moral issue that our methodology ought to be able to deal with.[17]

Furthermore, if only human beings, perhaps only reasonable human beings, constitute the moral universe, we still need to know who they are. This vagueness might be used to support a relativist view of ethics. For, if we say, as in one of Baier's formulas, that a practice is justified when "all members of society" have adequate reason to accept it,[18] then what is justified morally might vary from society to society, both historically and among different nations today. Perhaps what is justified morally might vary from group to group within a nation, if the nation could be understood to be more than one society. On the other hand, if we say, as Baier more often does, that a practice is justified when "everyone" has reason to accept it,[19] who is "everyone?" If "everyone" means timeless rational abstract persons, then perhaps we have here a species of contract theory like Rawls's that aims to establish an objective ethics. But perhaps not, if "everyone" does mean "all members of society" or all humans alive today with their particularities and limitations. Rational unanimity procedure, it seems to me and others,[20] begs crucial questions about the nature of persons and community and about whether they are historically contingent.

Baier's "empirical" question about what favorable balances will result from various possible cooperative solutions in Hobbesian choice situations also raises and skirts the issue of objectivity. If the question is empirical, does that mean that the balance varies from time to time and place to place, so that ethical justifications come and go? Or is the balancing supposed to be an abstract universalized procedure that does not countenance mutability?

These philosophical problems are crucial for law. It greatly matters which entities have moral claims in legal adjudications. The problem is far more pervasive than the attention given to euthanasia, abortion, and involuntary commitment suggests. The original position does not seem to help us decide whether we may experiment on animals, kill them for their skins, raise them in pens to eat them. The extent to which human property-holders and governments are morally free to manage and control natural resources is bound up with the question whether there are moral interests in the environment itself that must be taken into account. It also matters whether ethics has an objective basis. Some species of ethical objectivity seems necessary if one wishes, as I do, to reject the positivist separation of law and ethics and at the same time leave open the possibility of the rule of law.[21] It seems that using the format of rational unanimity procedure, or of ideal theory in general, makes it too easy to submerge, but not dissolve, real dilemmas of ethics—like the theory of the person and of community, the subjective/objective dichotomy, the problem of ignorance and evil, the role of history and culture. Taking notice of the significance of risk-of-error rules cannot create the philosophical matrix that is wanting here. Acknowledging their role in our moral and legal practice is at least an antidote to too-great faith in ideal theories of justice.

NOTES

1. John Rawls, "Two Concepts of Rules," *Philosophical Review* 64 (1955): 3.
2. Kurt Baier, "Justification in Ethics," in this volume.
3. Like Stanley Cavell, I am somewhat uncomfortable with this bifurcated approach to morality in general, although it is illuminating if not pressed too far. See his *The Claim of Reason* (Oxford: Oxford University Press, 1979), pp. 292–312. I am uncomfortable as well with the large terrain covered by the term "rule" in the present chapter, but I have no handy terminology to indicate how the particular fades into the somewhat general (rules?), the more general (standards?), and the very general (principles?).
4. The terms "practice-justified" and "act-justified" are introduced by Baier, "Justification in Ethics," to mark the distinction between the two types of justification.
5. Ludwig Wittgenstein, *Philosophical Investigations* (New York: Macmillan, 1958), section 621.
6. Actually, the criminal law is more complex. The felony-murder rule does away with the intent requirement in some circumstances, in some jurisdictions. So does manifestation of a "depraved heart." But we need not here elaborate the law of homicide.
7. See Michael Moore, *Psychiatry and Law: Rethinking the Relationship*

(Cambridge: Cambridge University Press, 1984), chapter 6; see also Stephen J. Morse, "Crazy Behavior, Morals and Science: An Analysis of Mental Health Law," *Southern California Law Review* 51 (1978): 527.

8. These stopping places also have substations. "Intentionally" can mean purposely or merely knowingly with respect to the proscribed state of affairs; gross negligence might lie between recklessness and negligence; negligence can be subjective or objective, depending upon whether our judgment takes into account the actor's particular limitations such as below-average eyesight or intelligence.

9. I use the term "non-ideal world" to highlight the assumptions of theories that assume away those difficulties. By a non-ideal theory of justice I mean one that would take into account the uncertainties, errors, and complexities of real life and practice. The term is intended to contrast with the term "ideal theory" used by John Rawls in *A Theory of Justice* (Cambridge: Harvard University Press, 1971), p. 9.

10. I assume it is recognized that legal actors do make moral judgments. It is hard to escape that conclusion at least in the straightforward case of a statute or rule directing a judge to decide whether punishment is deserved, whether fiduciary trust has been violated, or what is in the best interests of a child. This is not to say that legal positivists do not try to escape it. Holmes "often doubt[ed] whether it would not be a gain if every word of moral significance could be banished from the law altogether." Oliver Wendell Holmes, Jr., "The Path of the Law," *Harvard Law Review* 10 (1897): 464. I would go further and claim that the legal and moral are never separate realms, though there is not space for that argument here. Also, in order to make sense of the notion of mistake it must make sense to speak of right and wrong—one cannot hold a truly skeptical metaethics. There are very few true skeptics in the legal world; most lawyers and judges think it sensible to argue about right and wrong, if only on the issues of following historical tradition or precedent.

11. See notes 12 and 13 below and accompanying text.

12. The Supreme Court has recently arrived at an approach that specifically considers risk of error when a standard of proof is challenged under the due process clause. ("[I]n any given proceedings, the minimum standard of proof tolerated by the due process requirement reflects not only the weight of the private and public interests affected, but also a societal judgment about how the risk of error should be distributed between the litigants." *Santosky v.*

Kramer, 102 S. Ct. 1388, 1395 (1982).) This and other cases make clear that "higher" standards are mandated by threatened infringements of individual rights or of liberty. But in most legal fields risk-of-error rules exist but have not been made explicit. The beyond-a-reasonable-doubt rule itself was not explicitly recognized as constitutionally required until *In re Winship,* 397 U.S. 358 (1970). In *Addington v. Texas,* 441 U.S. 41, 424 (1979), it was characterized as a rule requiring that "society impos[e] almost the entire risk of error upon itself."

13. The Supreme Court holds that execution for murder is not unconstitutional if it is imposed under statutes mandating guided discretion for the sentencing judge or jury. Both too little discretion and too much discretion are unconstitutional. In addition, a death sentence is unconstitutional if statutory guidelines are not employed by the state courts in such a way as to execute consistently only those murderers whose crimes are bad enough to be clearly distinguishable from ordinary first-degree murder. *Godfrey v. Georgia,* 100 S. Ct. 1759 (1980); *Lockett v. Ohio,* 438 U.S. 586 (1978); *Gregg v. Georgia,* 428 U.S. 153 (1976).

14. See Margaret Jane Radin, "Cruel Punishment and Respect for Persons: Super Due Process for Death," *Southern California Law Review* 53 (1980): 1143.

15. Baier, "Justification in Ethics."

16. Baier, "Justification in Ethics."

17. Rawls's "reflective equilibrium" seems to be prior to the original position and in fact a method of arriving at the constitution of the original position. As such it seems a more satisfactory moral methodology than starting with a rational unanimity procedure. Perhaps it renders the original position superfluous. See, e.g., Ronald Dworkin, "The Original Position," in Norman Daniels, ed., *Reading Rawls* (New York: Basic Books, 1974), p. 16.

18. Baier, "Justification in Ethics."

19. Baier, "Justification in Ethics."

20. See, e.g., Michael J. Sandel, *Liberalism and the Limits of Justice* (Cambridge: Cambridge University Press, 1982). Rawls in his Dewey Lectures comes to grips with the problems of objectivity, historical circumstances and the theory of the person. John Rawls, "Kantian Constructivism in Moral Theory," *The Journal of Philosophy* 77 (1980): 515.

21. A species of objectivity is apparently needed for "the rule of law, not of people;" that is, for consistent nonarbitrary treatment of individuals and groups. Cf. Frank Michelman, "Justification in Law," in this volume. For the ethical skeptic who wishes to affirm the

rule of law, some way must be found to insulate law from the arbitrariness of ethics, so the separation of law and ethics becomes important. This has seemed to be the motivation of some legal positivists. Some members of the "Critical Legal Studies" movement, discussed in Michelman, have enthusiastically debunked the notion of neutral principles separate from politics or ethics. They seem to think this automatically knocks out the rule of law. But it does not, unless the rule of law is defined as synonymous with such neutral principles, or unless ethics itself is necessarily arbitrary, subjective, just a matter of preference, etc. So far this assumption has seemed implicit in much "CLS" writing, yet this isolationist view of ethics is contrary to the communitarian spirit of their enterprise. A renewed interest in varieties of objectivity, or in dissolving the subjective/objective dichotomy, seems to be on the horizon for those who deny the separation of law and ethics. See, e.g., Thomas Nagel, "The Limits of Objectivity," in S. McMurrin, ed., *The Tanner Lectures on Human Values*, vol. 1, p. 75 (University of Utah Press, 1980), pp. 77–139; Hilary Putnam, *Reason, Truth and History* (Cambridge: Cambridge University Press, 1981); Richard Rorty, *Philosophy and the Mirror of Nature* (Princeton: Princeton University Press, 1979).

4

MID-LEVEL PRINCIPLES
AND JUSTIFICATION

MICHAEL D. BAYLES

Ethical theories are often classified as "act" and "rule" theories. In act theories, a fundamental norm is used directly to evaluate particular actions; in rule theories, a fundamental norm is used to justify rules, and particular acts are evaluated by reference to the rules. Usually applied to utilitarianism, this classification also applies to deontological theories. Although Kant thought that the Categorical Imperative justifies rules, one can treat it as a fundamental norm for evaluating particular actions.

Here I will argue that both act and rule moral theories—ethical, political, and legal—are too simple. Instead, four levels or types of moral statements should be recognized: fundamental norms, mid-level principles, rules, and particular judgments. Mid-level principles play, or should play, an important role in many justifications of rules and particular assessments. Many writers use these principles, often without appreciating their role. They are appreciated most in legal theory, occasionally in political theory, and hardly at all in ethical theory. I consider how mid-level principles can be justified, how they can be used to justify rules and particular judgments, and why they should be used in moral theories.

Before I turn to these matters, mid-level principles need to be distinguished from fundamental norms, rules, and judgments. A "fundamental norm" is often called a supreme principle of ethics (or politics or law). The principle of utility and Kant's Categorical Imperative are examples in ethics. Kelsen's *Grundnorm* is one in legal theory.[1] A moral theory can have more than one fundamental norm; John Rawl's theory of justice has three—the liberty, fair equality of opportunity, and difference principles.[2] A fundamental norm is simply one that, within a theory, cannot be justified by appeal to a higher norm, although there can be arguments for one rather than another norm. Mid-level principles are subordinate to fundamental norms, and their justification usually refers, directly or indirectly, to a fundamental norm. Hence, mid-level principles are not as general as norms, although they can be quite general: for example, that freedom should be respected.

A theory need not have a fundamental norm. It might consist of a decision procedure for choosing mid-level principles. One might object that in this case all the principles justified by the decision procedure are fundamental norms. However, there is a logical difference between the way fundamental norms and principles operate. Fundamental norms do not conflict, but principles can. Thus, with the priority rules, Rawls's principles cannot conflict with one another and are fundamental norms, whereas W.D. Ross's prima facie duties can conflict and need to be weighed and balanced against one another and thus are principles.[3] Weighing and balancing of conflicting principles also helps distinguish them from rules.

The distinction between principles and rules has been much discussed in legal theory. My account essentially follows Ronald Dworkin's.[4] (1) Rules apply in an all-or-nothing way while principles do not. Although two conflicting rules may appear applicable to a case, in the end only one of them can be applied. For example, one cannot apply rules of both contributory and comparative negligence to a case. When rules so conflict, one of them is deemed invalid or an exception is made to it. (2) Principles have a weight that rules do not. Because several conflicting principles can apply to a situation or type of situation, they must be balanced or weighed against one another. As only one of conflicting rules is applicable, rules are not so weighed or balanced.

Weight is not to be confused with importance. Both rules and principles can have varying importance. For example, the rule against perpetuities is more important than a rule prohibiting transference of property on Sundays. Similarly, a principle of freedom of contract is more important than a principle that an agreement will be interpreted against the party who wrote it. Because a less important principle can outweigh a more important one on some occasions, the concepts of weight and importance are not identical. Importance has to do with effects on society's structure—its institutions and the relations among its members. Weight has to do with the force or stringency of a principle.

Some scholars do not accept this distinction between principles and rules, and my comments are certainly not sufficient to change their minds. Critics often claim that principles are simply general rules. Perhaps this is often true in ordinary discourse, but it is not claimed that the distinction corresponds to ordinary usage. Rules can, of course, be quite general; "Lying is wrong" is usually treated as a general rule with a number of exceptions. One can, however, treat it as a principle by regarding it as a prima facie duty. In any case, the argument for the recognition of mid-level principles does not require the logical distinction. Most critics recognize that general rules (principles) can have weight and be balanced against each other.[5] In effect, they deny the characterization of rules, not that of principles. Consequently, most of the subsequent arguments about the use of principles in justification remain valid if one treats the distinction as only one of generality and admits that general rules (principles) can be weighed and balanced against one another.

Mid-level principles are easily distinguished from particular judgments. Moral judgments referring to one and only one event, case, action, and so on are particular judgments. They can, of course, be universalizable or imply general rules or principles. Mid-level principles (and rules), however, always refer to classes of persons, events, cases, actions, and so on. They need not be universal, but they must be general. No legal principles are universal, because they all refer to a specific temporal period or physical location; they are all confined to the jurisdiction of the legal system, whether that is determined by a geographical area or unique population (as in nomadic tribes).

1. Justification of Mid-Level Principles

Justification of mid-level principles depends on the moral theory or fundamental norm involved. In general, a principle is justified by being shown to encapsulate a moral consideration important for the theory. But other considerations might be relevant, so use of a principle does not provide a conclusive evaluation by that theory. Privacy is an important consideration for many theories, but other considerations can also be relevant. Because theories differ in the way they embody important considerations, perhaps the best way to show how principles can be justified is to look at a few representative theories.

Justification of mid-level principles is perhaps most easily illustrated with utilitarianism, even though no contemporary exposition of utilitarian theory explicitly acknowledges them. A class of actions, such as truth-telling, has consequences promoting happiness. Thus, on a utilitarian view, there is a good reason to do the actions—tell the truth. Or, one can note that something, say, punishment, usually has negative effects on human well-being. One then has a principle against it. One can even treat specific types of effects on well-being as constituting special considerations—considerations of justice.[6] The effects of the use of punishment as a deterrent might support a principle of justice outweighing that against punishment.

This account of utilitarian justification of principles illustrates an important point: mid-level principles can be of different levels of generality. Because punishment causes suffering, utilitarians have a general principle against it. But because punishment of innocent people produces more unhappiness (increased fear and uncertainty) than punishment of guilty persons, utilitarians can justify a special principle against punishment of innocent people which has more weight than the general principle against punishment. Utilitarians can still hold that in very special circumstances the harm involved in punishing innocent people can be outweighed by other principles.

At this point, one might think that utilitarian principles are merely rules of thumb. However, they differ in both their meaning and use. Rules of thumb are statistical statements about the overall correctness or incorrectness of conduct. A rule of thumb might state that 90 percent of the time promises ought to be kept. Rules of thumb are not used in hard cases, because the question is whether the case falls in the 10 percent of exceptions; instead, the fundamental norm is applied directly. If application of the fundamental norm shows that in a hard case a promise should not be kept, then the rule of thumb has no force.

Principles are not statements, even statistical statements, of the overall correctness or incorrectness of actions. Instead, they refer to considerations that must be weighed or balanced against one another. Thus, they always have force. The principle against punishment has force even when it is outweighed by other considerations, otherwise reasons would not be needed to justify punishment. When one uses principles, one does not, even in hard cases, revert to a fundamental norm. Principles have a status similar to rules in rule theories. The application of a fundamental norm is always mediated through them. Nonetheless, even though relevant, the consideration embodied in a principle might not be very significant in some situations.

Justification of principles in rights-based theories differs significantly from utilitarian justification. Rights-based theories, such as those of Ronald Dworkin and Alan Gewirth, have abstract rights—to equal concern and respect or to liberty and welfare.[7] Principles in these theories specify the basic ones, picking out important elements of concern and respect or liberty and welfare. For example, in Gewirth's theory, principles could embrace various liberties—freedom of religion, speech, and so on. These rights, as he notes, can conflict with each other and with welfare rights. One must then weigh these rights against one another, and they function as principles.

A right-based theory might escape the use of considerations (principles) that have to be weighed against one another, but none of the major theories do so. First, such a theory must have only one right as a fundamental norm. Once two rights are recognized as fundamental, it is possible for them to conflict. Second, although Dworkin's theory, for example, is based on only one fundamental right, that right is so vague and abstract that it must be operationalized by concrete rights that can conflict. A right to a fair trial can conflict with freedom of the press. Third, it has been suggested that one can develop a rights theory with many rights each so qualified that they do not conflict.[8] However, this proposal explicitly concerns rules rather than principles. More importantly, the qualified rights arise from a prior weighing of goals, which is likely to involve principles. In short, the harmony of rights emerges from a balancing of goals, so it does not obviate the need for principles to construct the set of harmonious rights.

Justification of principles on a Rawlsian theory uses both the rights and utilitarian methods. The liberty principle can be used to generate principles as in a rights-based theory. The principle specifies that everyone has a right to the most extensive system of equal basic liberties.[9] In using this principle, a number of comparisons or weighings is necessary, for some liberties play a more significant role in achieving the most extensive system of liberties. For example, freedom of speech might be more significant than others, both because of its importance for self-respect and because its exercise is less likely to interfere with the exercise of other liberties than is, say, liberty of action. Consequently, to achieve the most extensive set, liberties must be balanced with each other. As liberties in the set can conflict, they must be weighed and balanced in establishing rules and settling particular cases.

A utilitarian type of justification pertains to the difference and fair equality of opportunity principles. Justification of mid-level principles by the difference principle differs from utilitarian justifications only by concern being restricted to effects on the least advantaged instead of everyone. Thus, one might justify a principle against sales or value-added taxes, because they harm the least advantaged more than others. Similarly, the fair equality of opportunity principle might justify a principle favoring universal free education as important for producing fair equality of opportunity. Nonetheless, other principles could outweigh this principle; for example, it might compete with funding adequate medical care. With both the difference and fair equality of opportunity principles, mid-level principles can be justified as picking out types of conduct that promote or reduce the well-being of the least advantaged or fair equality of opportunity.

Recognition of mid-level principles might help defeat one of the main criticisms of Kantian ethical theory. Kant suggested that application of the Categorical Imperative to a particular action would justify a universal rule, for example, against suicide or lying.[10] Many critics contend that different rules result depending on how one describes an action (states the maxim of the action). This difficulty might be alleviated if one viewed application of the Categorical Imperative to an action's description as establishing a principle instead of a hard and fast rule. From a maxim of lying whenever it is to one's advantage, one could derive the principle that lying is wrong. As a principle, "lying is wrong" does not imply that all instances of lying are wrong. Instead, it provides a consideration to be weighed against other principles, as when a would-be murderer asks where an intended victim is hiding. The description of an action always omits features that might be present and morally relevant in some instance of lying. Granted, this approach is not a correct interpretation of Kant, but it shows how principles might be used by a Kantian moral theory.

My purpose here has not been to derive any specific principles or to provide correct interpretations of the theorists discussed. The former is irrelevant to my metaethical concerns, and the latter would be inconsistent with the claim that theorists have generally failed to recognize and use mid-level principles. That is, Kantian and utilitarian theorists have at most used fundamental norms, rules, and particular judgments. Instead, I have tried only to show how principles might be justified by different types of theories. Although it has not been proven that one can justify them with all theories, enough has been said to indicate that it is possible with the most common moral theories.

2. Justification by Mid-Level Principles

Mid-level principles can be used to justify rules or particular judgments. Before examining how that is so, it is worth considering further the different levels of principles. One can roughly arrange fundamental norms, mid-level principles, rules, and particular judgments as a hierarchy from the most general to the least general and as steps or levels in justification. However, this perspective does not do full justice to their relations.

First, mid-level principles can be of various degrees of generality. Justification can thus go from one principle to another. For example, a principle of autonomy might be justified by the Categorical Imperative, and then be used to justify a principle of political freedom. More specifically, one might justify a special principle of freedom of speech. One can be even more specific. The U.S. Supreme Court historically did not hold that freedom of speech is as strong for advertising as for other types of speech, and, of course, obscenity has been denied any free speech protection.[11] One still has questions about how freedom of speech in its core applications is to be balanced against other principles. The clear and present danger test is a principle indicating the general weight to be assigned to freedom of speech against other considerations. Note that the clear-and-present-danger test is not deduced from a higher level principle, because it must take into consideration more than one principle; that is, it specifies a balancing of freedom of speech against other considerations. Such a basic comparative principle cannot be deduced.

Second, some rules can be more general than some principles. Principles and rules are not distinguished by their generality but by whether they apply in an all-or-nothing way and can be weighed. Consequently, some rules, such as that of contributory negligence, can be quite general. If one distinguishes rules and principles by the greater generality of the latter, then this point does not apply. Nevertheless, so long as one weighs and balances conflicting rules, the rest of the discussion will apply. One might contend that one does not weigh and balance rules, only the considerations supporting them. But in that case, the supporting considerations are principles.

Third, not all justifications of particular judgments need involve rules. One can justify them directly by principles. Rules with the logical features specified in the first section are not appropriate for all situations. Rules can be formulated only when the considerations represented by principles do not conflict (which is very rare) or are almost always affected in the same way. The case of *New York Times Co. v. Sullivan* illustrates how conflicting principles can be brought to bear to formulate a rule.[12] This was a libel action filed by an elected commissioner of Montgomery, Alabama, against *The Times* and several signatories of an editorial advertisement criticizing actions in Montgomery against civil rights demonstrators. The primary conflicting principles were freedom of the press for *The Times* and protection of reputation for Sullivan. The court recognized that the press requires a greater latitude in discussing public than other matters. That is, freedom of the press is a more significant concern in public than in private affairs. Moreover, public persons at least implicitly consent to being the subject of criticism. Thus, the Court required a higher standard (actual malice—intentional or reckless rather than negligent misstatement) for libel actions by public officials and figures than for actions by ordinary citizens. The rule takes into account differences in the effect on and importance of freedom of the press concerning public as opposed to private persons. A rule is possible, because these differences generally correspond to an empirical classification—public persons.

Often the considerations in conflicting principles do not balance the same way in an empirically identifiable class of cases. For example, one can rarely formulate a rule about patients who should be allowed to die, because there is no empirical classification that generally corresponds to the distinction between those who should and should not be treated. Treatment decisions require balancing several principles such as the likely value of continued life to the patient, the burdens on others, the patient's past wishes, if any, and the availability of scarce resources (triage). A balance between them rarely corresponds to a medical classification of cases. Sometimes it does, and one can then make rules, such as not treating anencephalic infants. Otherwise, the balancing must be done for each individual case.

A similar process often occurs in the law. One can contrast *Sullivan* and the Supreme Court's handling of other matters, such as capital punishment. In determining whether capital punishment is appropriate, one can establish rules permitting it for only some crimes. However, because many principles are involved and no one uniform empirical classification distinguishes defendants for whom capital punishment is appropriate from those for whom it is not, the Court has adopted a factorial approach.[13] That is, several factors to be balanced and weighed against each other are specified. In effect, some possibly conflicting principles are enunciated. Whenever one finds a factorial approach used, principles rather than rules are being applied to reach particular judgments. One can, of course, have a rule stating that these factors must be considered, but that amounts to a meta-rule requiring that one decide on the basis of specific principles. Thus, this legal situation differs from the ethical one in that the principles are required by a rule. In effect, a standard with many subfactors is being applied.

In the common law, as opposed to ethics and politics, one cannot avoid the use of rules. That is, whenever principles are applied to a particular case, a rule results in law, but it need not in ethics. The decision to allow a particular patient to die does not establish a rule even though the decision is universalizable. This difference is due to the use of precedent in common law systems. If a judge applies principles to a case, then a rule of the case results. The rule has weight for future cases; there is an institutional expectation that it be followed. To decide differently in a similar case, a judge must do more than show that the previous decision was bad; the judge must show that overcoming that bad precedent outweighs the commitment to precedent. By contrast, if a physician thinks that a previous treatment decision was incorrect, the physician need not overcome any institutional expectation that a similar decision be made in this case. "I was wrong before" is always a sufficient reason for acting differently in ethics, but not in law.

Rules are not finalities. When rules are formulated, not all the possible situations that can arise are considered. In short, what James Fishkin calls the problem of unforeseeability always accompanies rules.[14] They cannot be formulated so as to cover all possible exceptions. However, the cases that contain unforeseeability problems almost always involve particularly acute and unusual conflicts of established principles. One is much more likely to face a case that requires a new rule or an exception to an old one than a case that requires a new principle. Indeed, the logical structure of principles—their not being all-or-nothing and having weight—prevents their being overturned by such cases. Nonetheless, changing social conditions or unusual situations can call for development of a new principle. The principle of privacy is essentially a twentieth century development generated by a few cases. If one operates with a broad set of principles, unforeseeability is much less of a problem than if one deals with only fundamental norms and rules.

Mid-level principles do not admit of lexical ordering. In disparate situations, the considerations represented by principles can be involved to differing degrees. The invasion of privacy is significantly less in fingerprinting and photographing arrested persons than in entering their homes to garner evidence, even though the latter might be more effective in apprehending criminals. So one cannot say the principle of privacy always outweighs that of law enforcement, or vice versa. It is usually only in quite specifically defined contexts that one principle almost always takes precedence over all others, and when that occurs a rule can be formulated.

To summarize, mid-level principles can be used to justify other mid-level principles, rules, or particular judgments. Sometimes, though rarely, only one principle need be appealed to—all others are irrelevant. Usually several conflicting principles are relevant. One must then examine how much the considerations (values, rights) embodied in principles are affected, and then weigh and balance the principles accordingly. If an empirical classification demarcates a difference in the balancing of the principles, that is, can distinguish cases in which the considerations are uniform, then a rule can be formulated subject to revision in future unforeseen cases. If an empirical classification does not exist, then a rule cannot be formulated. One can only make a judgment about the particular case.

3. WHY USE PRINCIPLES?

One reason for using principles is that they alleviate problems of justification noted by James Fiskin.[15] He divides ethical theories into three types of objectivism and four types of subjectivism. Objective theories are divided into absolutism, rigorism, and minimal objectivism. Absolutism involves the claim that judgments are inviolable and rationally unquestionable; rigorism drops the claim that judgments are rationally unquestionable; and minimal objectivism contends only that judgments can be supported by considerations that anyone should accept. Because principles are violable, they cannot be used in absolutist or rigorist theories that require inviolability.[16] Of course, justifications of principles can appeal to inviolable, perhaps rationally unquestionable, fundamental norms. However, if fundamental norms are applied by principles, for practical purposes violable norms are used. One can also omit fundamental norms and justify principles directly from a strategy of choice. I have elsewhere used that approach.[17] The point here is that even if one does adopt a fundamental norm, one should still use mid-level principles in justifying rules and particular judgments.

Fishkin raises two central problems with attempts to justify liberalism internally, that is, that "depend on a characterization of morality or the moral point of view."[18] Contractarian and ideal observer views, for example, provide strategies or decision procedures for choosing principles that characterize the moral point of view. The jurisdiction problem is that one does not have a basis for choosing between these various strategies of choice, so liberalism and its doctrines cannot have a conclusive foundation.[19] Moreover, even if one could settle on a strategy of choice, the moral standards it supported would still be subject to the problem of unforeseeability mentioned above. That is, any principles or rules established would be subject to revision due to unforeseen exceptions and problems. Consequently, moral justification is always inconclusive.

Mid-level principles help alleviate both of these problems of justification. In the previous section, it was shown that the use of principles rather than rules decreases the problem of unforeseeability, because hard cases rarely call for new principles. Principles also help avoid Fishkin's jurisdiction problem or the inability to justify a strategy of choice. Showing this requires an indirect argument.

Justification always involves justifying something to someone. Although we speak of justifying things to ourselves, usually one justifies something to another person. Moreover, except for justifications of fundamental norms, a justification must appeal to some standard—fundamental norm, principle, or rule. If the person to whom one is giving a justification does not accept that standard, then the person will not accept the justification. One must then try to justify that standard. Failure ensues if no appeal is ever made to a standard the other person accepts.

It is important to distinguish practical and logical justification. A logical justification is one in which a claim is supported by logically appropriate reasoning using correct premises. A practical justification is one that the person to whom it is addressed finds satisfactory. ("Justification" is here being taken to be a "success" word. The activity of justifying need not be successful; one can try but fail to give a justification.) These two types of justification do not necessarily go together. A logical justification can fail to persuade and be a practical justification. Contrarily, a practical justification need not be logically coherent or compelling. This latter possibility is significant for the use of principles. In daily life, people try to give practical justifications, and the attempts to do so are evaluated by people's conceptions of what constitutes a logical justification. That is, people accept reasons offered as justifications if they think the reasons constitute logical justifications.

Justification can go from the less to the more general—from particular judgments to rules to principles to fundamental norms—or from the more to the less general. Moral theorists almost always follow the latter approach. They argue for a fundamental norm, then perhaps for principles or rules, and finally for particular judgments. In ordinary life, however, most practical moral justification, especially in ethics, goes from the less to the more general. A particular action or decision is questioned or challenged, and a person attempts to justify it by appealing to rules, principles, or fundamental norms. Or a rule is questioned, and one tries to justify it by principles or fundamental norms. In this practical justification, one need not justify standards that are accepted by those to whom the justification is addressed. The regress to more general reasons is limited. Even when justification goes from the more to the less general, if there is agreement on a statement general enough to justify the point in question, one need not appeal to a more general one. If there is agreement on the rule to be used to make a particular judgment, one need not appeal to the principles supporting that rule. Trial court judges can usually simply state the relevant legal rules without appealing to principles to justify them. Thus, practical justification involves justifying something to another person who accepts the judgment or rule as logically supported by more general standards that person accepts.

Principles help obviate Fishkin's problem of alternative strategies of choice justifying different fundamental norms, because agreement on principles exceeds that on fundamental norms or strategies of choice. If a particular judgment or rule can be shown to follow from mutually accepted principles, then it is practically justified, even if the disputants disagree about the norms that support or justify the principles. If people agree about

principles and what follows from them, their differences about
strategies of choice or norms make no practical difference. The
difference is only logical, not practical. Consequently, to the extent there is agreement on principles, liberalism can survive an
ultimate pluralism of stategies of choice and fundamental norms.

The question is whether more agreement is possible on principles than on strategies of choice and norms. This issue might
be addressed by empirical research. I suspect one would find
more disagreement than many people think exists, but less than
Fishkin seems to believe exists. Nonetheless, the question is not
necessarily what the average person believes, but what people
who have seriously examined the questions believe. In any case,
I can only suggest by examples that people holding quite different strategies of choice and norms agree on principles. In
political theory, utilitarians and Rawlsian contractarians agree
on a principle of freedom of speech. Kant and Mill both gave
strong agruments for such a principle. So here is one important instance where people with radically different approaches
agree. A few other such principles might be mentioned: majoritarian voting with universal suffrage, punishment of crime, a
principle of privacy, and nondiscrimination on the basis of race
and sex. In ethics, one could list the wrongness of homicide, an
obligation to keep promises, disapproval of widespread paternalism, and the requirement of informed consent to bodily
touchings (medical treatment, sexual intercourse).

One must distinguish between the core applications of principles or rules and the hard cases. Moral theorists focus on hard
cases, such as difficult appellate court decisions. However, most
behavior in society falls in the core cases. Most trial court cases
center on factual disputes rather than legal (moral) ones. Even
the cases that go to trial are a small subclass of disputes, for most
suits are settled without a trial, and most legal disputes are settled without the initiation of a suit. Ethics is much the same.
Most of the time consent to medical treatment is clearly necessary and obtained. Politics may be different simply because we
do not call an issue a political one unless there is significant disagreement.

The rare, hard cases involve borderlines, complex factual situations, or new and unforeseen situations. Those cases that are
hard because of complex facts do not raise difficulties for moral

theory, unless one unrealistically expects a theory to provide a clear answer to every question no matter one's lack of knowledge about the situation.[20] Only the borderline and unforeseen cases raise moral issues. Resolutions of them often hinge on small differences of weight assigned to principles. These differences in turn can depend on the justification of the principles—whether utilitarian, rights-based, Rawlsian, or whatever. Moral theorists focus on hard cases because they are highly contentious and have important implications for theories. But a steady diet of hard cases often creates moral myopia; theorists cannot see the distant forest of easy cases, only the few nearby trees of hard cases. They come to believe that everything is highly contentious and subject to doubt. Skepticism, subjectivism, and doctrines such as legal realism result.[21] These doctrines often say more about the visual acuity of the observer than the characteristics of the observed.

The greater agreement on principles and core cases than on strategies of choice and fundamental norms has an important epistemic base. Suppose there are ten different moral theories, and seven of them support principle P although they assign somewhat different weightings to it vis-à-vis other principles. The other three theories justify three different principles for the types of situations to which P applies. Given equal a priori probabilities of each theory being correct, then there is a 70 percent probability of principle P being correct. There is a seven times better chance of P being true than any given theory. A similar conclusion follows for the core cases or rules justified by the principle.

Two related objections might be made to this argument. First, it might be said that there is no reason to assume the theories are equiprobable. Second, there is an unlimited number of possible theories most of which would not justify a given principle. However, the claim in the first objection undermines the second and strengthens my argument. One might claim that in the absence of information, one cannot assume equal probability of alternatives. This is a debatable point of probability theory. However, one is not in a condition of no information. Arguments can and have been given for the various theories. Over the centuries, only a few have survived as plausible contenders that need to be seriously considered.[22] Even among those that remain, some are more plausible than others; for example, egoism is at least somewhat less of a contender than sophisticated versions of utilitarianism or Rawls's theory. To return to the example in the previous paragraph, often the three theories that do not justify principle P will be less plausible than the others. Suppose, for example, they each have only a 5 percent probability of being correct. Then principle P has an even greater probability of being correct, 85 percent rather than 70 percent.

One must distinguish between objectivity and certainty. The lesser certainty ascribed above to moral theories than principles and core particular judgments need not imply a lesser objectivity. Objectivity obtains when intersubjective standards exist for evaluating claims. These standards need not be sufficient to ensure that one of several competing claims can be shown to be more correct than the others. A standard might eliminate two of five competing claims but be unable to distinguish between the others. For example, the requirement of logical consistency can sort moral theories into those that are and are not logically consistent. It thus provides an objective basis for judging between moral theories, without providing a reason for preferring one consistent theory over another. So long as some such standards exist, the choice between theories is not purely arbitrary or subjective. One might view this process as using filters to remove some incorrect theories. Unfortunately, some of the filters for moral theories are difficult to use, for example, that a theory not rest on false empirical assumptions. Consequently, the best one can say is that some theories appear more likely than others to pass through the filter.

Besides the greater agreement on and certainty of principles than on fundamental norms and strategies of choice, principles also provide practical advantages in moral reasoning. First, they help focus attention on concrete problems. Fundamental norms are often too abstract to aid in directly focusing on the moral difficulty in situations. Being told to act to produce the greatest average net good or by a maxim one can will as a universal law does not pick out the moral problems of government funding of abortions or capital punishment. Principles of respect for conscience, government responsibility for health, deterrence, not punishing the innocent, and so on are more helpful.

A second and related advantage is that principles help avoid overlooking important considerations. Principles incorporate the important moral concerns of a theory (or group of theories). For example, in applying a utilitarian fundamental norm, it is often easy to overlook a consequence that is significant for happiness. A set of principles presents important considerations and reviewing them will make one look for certain factors. Of course, one can forget to consider a principle, but it is often easier to keep a few principles in mind and to refer to them than to analyze ab initio the various consequences of a particular action without any guidance except to consider effects on happiness. Rights principles also provide more guidance than simply considering liberty and welfare or whatever.

Third, the use of principles can save much time in practical justification. A reference to the principle of freedom of speech may be all that is necessary to justify a particular judgment. It might take considerably more time to provide a justification by applying the Categorical Imperative, not to mention having to justify that to a utilitarian who nonetheless accepts a principle of freedom of speech. People in everyday life appear to use mid-level principles, otherwise few practical justifications would ever occur. Only moral theorists try to give complete, logical justifications. Mid-level principles at least partially explain why moral theorists make such little difference in the practical world; their differences are simply often not practically relevant.

4. Conclusion

I have argued for the use of mid-level principles in ethical, political, and legal theory. Mid-level principles indicate what a theory takes to be important moral considerations. They can be used and justified by the major moral theories. In turn, principles can be used to justify other principles, rules, and judgments. Justification by principles is not a deductive process, because conflicting principles must often be weighed and balanced against one another, and that process is not a deductive one. The use of principles in justification can weaken, but not necessarily eliminate, Fishkin's concern with unforeseeability and disputes over strategies of choice. Because many principles can be justified by most plausible theories, one can be more sure of their correctness than one can of theories. Their use in justification of rules and particular judgments can also have the practical advantages of focusing attention, preventing omission of important considerations, and saving time. Ordinary moral reasoning appears to use mid-level principles, and moral theorists should use them too.

NOTES

1. Hans Kelsen, *General Theory of Law and State,* trans. Anders Wedberg (New York: Russell & Russell, 1961, original ed. 1945), pp. 115–17.

2. John Rawls, *A Theory of Justice* (Cambridge: Harvard University Press, 1971), p. 302. Rawls states his view as having two norms, but it is preferable to treat the difference and equality of opportunity principles as two, since they are logically independent. One can, of course, also treat Rawls's theory as having only one norm, the general principle of justice (see p. 62).

3. W.D. Ross, *The Right and the Good* (Oxford: Clarendon Press, 1930).

4. Ronald Dworkin, *Taking Rights Seriously* (Cambridge: Harvard University Press, 1977), pp. 22–28. The concern in the text is with Dworkin's distinction between principles generically and rules, not that between principles and policies.

5. See Joseph Raz, "Legal Principles and the Limits of Law," *Yale Law Journal* 81 (1972): 823–54.

6. See T.L.S. Sprigge, "A Utilitarian Reply to Dr. McCloskey," in *Contemporary Utilitarianism,* ed. Michael D. Bayles (Garden City, N.Y.: Doubleday & Co., Anchor Books, 1968), pp. 267–69.

7. Dworkin, *Taking Rights Seriously,* pp. 180–83, 272–78; Alan Gewirth, *Reason and Morality* (Chicago: University of Chicago Press, 1978), p. 64. Dworkin's fundamental norm is the right to equal concern and respect, whereas Gewirth's is the Principle of Generic Consistency and the right to liberty and welfare are the most general principles.

8. S.C. Coval and J.C. Smith, "Rights, Goals, and Hard Cases," in *Justice, Rights, and Tort Law,* ed. Michael D. Bayles and Bruce Chapman (Dordrecht: D. Reidel, 1983), pp. 239–68.

9. Rawls, *Theory of Justice,* p. 302.

10. Immanual Kant, *Groundwork of the Metaphysics of Morals,* trans. H.J. Paton, in *The Moral Law,* 3rd ed. (New York: Barnes & Noble, 1956), pp. 89–91, Akademie pages 421–423.

11. See *Valentine v. Chrestensen,* 316 U.S. 52, 62 S.Ct. 920, 86 L.Ed. 1262

(1942) (distribution of handbills); *Roth v. United States,* 354 U.S. 476, 77 S.Ct. 1304, 1 L.Ed.2d 1498 (1957).

12. *New York Times v. Sullivan,* 376 U.S. 254, 84 S.Ct. 710, 11 L.Ed. 2d 686 (1964).
13. *Gregg v. Georgia,* 428 U.S. 153 (1976).
14. James S. Fishkin, *Beyond Subjective Morality: Ethical Reasoning and Political Philosophy* (New Haven: Yale University Press, 1984), pp. 111–19; idem, "Liberal Theory and the Problem of Justification," (1983 photocopy) p. 29.
15. Fishkin, *Beyond Subjective Morality* and "Liberal Theory."
16. Fishkin, *Beyond Subjective Morality,* pp. 15–17; Fishkin, "Liberal Theory," pp. 2–4.
17. Michael D. Bayles, *Principles of Legislation* (Detroit: Wayne State University Press, 1978).
18. Fishkin, "Liberal Theory," p. 11.
19. Fishkin, *Beyond Subjective Morality,* pp. 89–111; Fishkin, "Liberal Theory," pp. 26–27.
20. Fishkin notes the weaker expectation that an ethical theory determine answers to any (every) moral problem. But even people with that expectation do not expect a theory to determine an answer without adequate information, although I suspect some of Fishkin's interviewees were confused about this. I also agree with Fishkin in rejecting even the weaker expectation. See Fishkin, *Beyond Subjective Morality,* pp. 61, 134–35.
21. As Fishkin well elaborates in *Beyond Subjective Morality,* unrealistic expectations also play a major role.
22. See also Rawls, *Theory in Justice,* pp. 122–23.

PART II

JUSTIFICATION IN LAW

5

JUSTIFICATION (AND JUSTIFIABILITY) OF LAW IN A CONTRADICTORY WORLD

FRANK I. MICHELMAN

1. Introduction: Adjudication, Justification, and Justifiability

The scheme of topic assignments for this volume implies that justification may be a different matter "in" law than "in" ethics or politics—and thus, that law, politics, and ethics may each be a realm distinct, which is not to say insulated, from the other two. Yet it is endlessly controversial whether there really are or ought to be these distinctions.

Is there a standpoint from which to engage the controversy that is, in some obvious way, distinctly that of law? It is the work of the judge, more so than that of the legislator or the speculative legal theorist or critic, that is most readily distinguished from that of both the moralist and the politician. So we shall for present purposes understand "law" as *adjudication,* the activity of judicial decision.

In the purest and most elementary conception, judges' work is the disposition of live disputes among identified parties by a specific award of the matter in dispute to one party or another. Judges produce socially potent arbitral decisions about specifically who must (or need not) do (or suffer) specifically what. It is this arbitral use of power that demands justification.

71

Justification presupposes justifiability—presupposes, then, that adjudication is a rationally determinable activity, one that critical reason can judge in practice as rightly or wrongly, well or poorly done. Required is what Ernest Weinrib nicely calls "an intelligible connection between legal controversy and its resolution."[1] But intelligence is protean, and the question of the relations among reason, logic, morals, and law[2]—hence of the proper forms and terms of judicial justification—remains (perhaps forever) open.

That question is not exactly the issue here, for I shall be more concerned with justifiability (and so with intelligibility) than with justification. The order of business is as follows: First, I shall recall one familiar standard for judicial justification, that of legalism. Second, I shall describe a certain attack on the legalist standard, one coming out of the school of thought known as critical legal studies (CLS). Third, I shall suggest that while the CLS critique does gravely threaten legalism as a form of justification, it does not attack the *justifiability* of adjudication as deeply as both some friends and some enemies of CLS appear to believe. Fourth, I shall take note of connections between the legalist view of justification and certain morally attractive features of the notion of legal rights, and raise some questions about whether the CLS critique of legalism warrants abandonment of that notion, as some CLS writers seem to urge.

2. Legalist Justification

We have been accustomed to think that the intelligible connection between legal controversy and its resolution is—or must be, if at all—provided by a body of norms, a *law* that is both general ("abstract," "impersonal") and rationally determinable in its applications to factually defined cases. Straightforwardly, to furnish *legal* justification for a decision is to show that the decision is according to law. Although it has no fully settled meaning, the notion of decision according to law does—supposing that such a thing can exist at all—seem to imply some minimal requirements. One is that of an intelligible and coherent normative idea distinct from the case in question. The notion of decision *according to* law implies *comparison* of the case with some external standard[3] that in some degree constrains or points to one or another decision, if it does not fully determine the outcome. The external norm must have *some* prescriptive force. Hence while it need be neither simple, nor apparent, nor fixed, it must, as finally grasped, be internally unified, not multifarious and contradictory.

From this primary implication of decision according to law flow two others germane to my theme: (1) A case in course of decision must undergo *interpretation* and *analysis* by which its raw empirical representations are rendered into a standardized version, cast into categories corresponding to the vocabulary—necessarily categorical—of the external norm. (2) Decision according to law involves generalization over cases, a course of reasoning in which the instant case is assimilated to an at least somewhat general class of cases, to which the categorically framed external norm can then be applied with prescriptive force.

A further primary implication of the notion of decision according to *law* is that judges are more the organs than the originators of decision. (For many, that will understate the limits of the judge's role.) The very notion of law connotes both something that transcends individual deciders as well as individual decisions, and also something that binds deciders, as it binds decisions, together. The judge is to invoke as justification a standard that not only is generally and categorically framed, drawn not just from the instant case and applicable to all relevantly similar cases; but also is public, drawn from the same sources, by the same methods, as other judges use.[4]

3. A Critique of Legalism: The "Fundamental Contradiction"

I am going to call "legalist justification" or "legalism" the specific understanding of the justification of judicial decision as appealing to some categorical prescriptive idea ("the law") distinct from both the case and the judge.[5] Since "legalism" and "legalist" these days are epithets—especially when appearing in company with "liberal"—I should say right off that I am interested in the defense of positions that I regard as partaking both of legalism and liberalism, though I largely concur in the critique of legalism I'm now about to relate.

Suppose you think that people's attitudes toward their social situations, their relations with others, are comprised, always and necessarily, of a duality of opposed impulses—like separation versus union, or freedom versus order. You further think that this oppositional experience is directly reflective, or indeed constitutive, of the human self; the very structure of personality. This opposition of impulses, as you understand it, cannot be stabilized nor can its outcome in non-actual particular situations be reliably foreseen. The opposition does not prevent you, in particular concrete circumstances, from deciding what is in your interest, or what you want, or even (let us hazard) what is right. It does place pitfalls in the way of trying to govern your actions towards others, over the course of a lifetime or even for very long at all, by abstract maxim or precept. For, according to your perception, if you profess to rise very far above the concrete particulars of cases as you successively experience them in the continuing course of deciding what to do, you will often be guilty of one or another sort of misdeed: You act according to your maxim, but in so doing betray your actual, situated conviction about the prudent, or good, or right thing to do; or, under pressure of this dissonance, you start generating and accumulating contradictory maxims so that after a while you always find one available to agree with your situated conviction. It follows that strong pretension to a legal order of decision according to abstract rule must issue in miscarriage and betrayal of one or another kind (or more probably a mixture of both kinds): either the illusion of ruledness cloaking moral (or "political") choice, or wrongheaded decision according to inapt rule.

That, in summary, is the situation portrayed by some contemporary critics of legalism. Its most elaborate statement is by Duncan Kennedy in "The Structure of Blackstone's Commentaries."[6]

According to Kennedy, legalism, or what he calls "rights-consciousness," arises in response to a "fundamental contradiction" of values at the core of everyone's experience. Put most generally, the contradiction is our sense that "relations with others are both necessary to and incompatible with our freedom"—and not only to and with our freedom, but to and with our identity and even our existence. The following passage from Kennedy's Blackstone article has become—deservedly—a classic reference in the CLS literature:[7]

Others (family, friends, bureaucrats, cultural figures, the state) are necessary if we are to become persons at all—they provide us with the stuff of ourselves and protect us in crucial ways against destruction. Even when we seem to ourselves to be most alone, others are with us, incorporated in us through processes of language, cognition and feeling that are, simply as a matter of biology, collective aspects of our individuality. Moreover, we are not always alone. We sometimes experience fusion with others, in groups of two or even two million, and it is a good rather than bad experience.

But at the same time that it forms and protects us, the universe of others . . . threatens us with annihilation and urges upon us forms of fusion that are quite plainly bad rather than good. A friend can reduce me to misery with a single look. Numberless conformities, large and small abandonments of self to others, are the price of what freedom we experience in society. And the price is a high one. Through our experience as members of collectives, we impose on others and have imposed on us hierarchical structures of power, welfare, and access to enlightenment that are illegitimate, whether based on birth into a particular social class or on the accident of genetic endowment.

The kicker is that the abolition of these . . . structures . . . appears to imply such a massive increase of collective control over our lives that it would defeat its purpose. . . . If one accepts that collective norms weigh so heavily in favor of the status quo that purely "voluntary" movement is inconceivable, then the only alternative is the assumption of responsibility for the totalitarian domination of other peoples' minds—for "forcing them to be free."

Even this understates the difficulty. It is not just that the world of others is intractable. The very structures against which we rebel are necessarily within us as well as outside of us. We are implicated in what we would tranform, and it in us. This critical insight is not compatible with that sense of the purity of one's intention which seems often to have animated the enterprise of remaking the social world. . . .

At the level of political belief, we think that "the goal of individual freedom is at the same time dependent on and incompatible with the communal coercive action that is necessary to achieve it." This fundamental contradiction, says Kennedy, underlies every legal problem. And he explains the idea of rights as an intellectual construct designed to "mediate" or "deny" "our painfully contradictory feelings about actual relations between persons in our social world."

Kennedy asks us to consider a parable with three characters: "a weak person, a strong person, and the state." Weak's feelings towards Strong are contradictory, since Weak both needs Strong for the "good fusion" of help, trade, conversation, recognition, and stands to be oppressed, destroyed, or harmfully neglected by Strong. Weak wants The State to use its force to control Strong to just the point of allowing for good fusion and not bad, but without The State itself starting to dominate Weak like another Strong. Given this set of goals, says Kennedy, "the extreme complexity of social and political relationships makes it difficult to decide exactly what The State may and may not do." Rights are supposed to respond to this difficulty, by telling us both how The State is to protect Weak from Strong and how Weak is to be protected from The State. Believing in rights, one need no longer be torn or immobilized by contradictory feelings toward others: one can envision both good private relations with one's neighbors on the basis of respect for rights, and good public relations with all one's fellow citizens in the common enterprise of defining and protecting rights.

This process of "mediation," as Kennedy portrays it in legal thought, takes the general form of dichotomous schematizing, designed to let us "deny the contradictory state of our feelings by asserting that there is a proper place for collectivism, and that that place can be determined by the rational analysis of the content of legal rules."

Legal lines and categories organize our intellectual space, allowing and inviting us to classify each case of human interaction according to which aspect of the fundamental contradiction it presents to view. A simple example is provided by the legal line, crucial in the law of nuisance, between "reasonable" and "unreasonable" interference with other people's use or enjoyment of their land. We are enabled to regard each case as an instance of *either* one *or* the other of two general types: the type in which collective intervention is needed to *vindicate* individual freedom (someone is threatening or violating someone else's right—the defendant's glue factory unreasonably impairs the neighbors' freedom of residential use of their property— plaintiff should win), or the type in which intervention would *violate* freedom (all have been freely acting within their rights— the plaintiffs are unreasonably trying to get the court to stop the defendant from conducting an inoffensive veterinary practice—defendant should win).

In this instance, of course, it doesn't take much coaching to see that the line of "reasonableness" is only a restatement, not a resolution, of the conflict—and of the fundamental contradiction, now appearing as our constant, impossible wish for a regime that would give us all both more liberty and more protection against the liberties our neighbors take. Kennedy's thesis is that despite all the lawyers' games and tricks, the contradiction will out—will reappear in both fragments of whatever class, whatever difference, whatever atom or hair, we split; or else in the boundary between them.

For further illustration of the convolutions and field-reversals in legal thought, wrought by the contradictory impulses toward freedom and order, individuality and collectivity, consider some First Amendment phenomena:

- The perceived "paradox," as Carl Auerbach (following Karl Popper) called it, that "suppression may sometimes have to be the means of securing and enlarging freedom."[8]

- The parallel, if converse, Marcusian paradox of "repressive tolerance."[9]

- Roberto Unger's proposal[10] for a "super-liberal" constitution, "a structure of no-structure" founded on certain fundamental rights including the right ("destabilization right") to demand at any time the disruption and dismantling of any and all established (and thus possibly frozen) institutions and social practices.

Auerbach thought his paradox licensed the observation that, in fact, "in suppressing totalitarian movements a democratic society is not acting to protect the status quo, but the very same interests which freedom of speech itself seeks to secure—the possibility of peaceful progress under freedom." He further thought it justified the conclusions, not only that "the First Amendment is part of the framework for a constitutional democracy and should, therefore, not be used to curb the power of Congress to exclude from the political struggle those groups which, if victorious, would crush democracy and impose totalitarianism" but also that "whether in any particular case . . . Congress should suppress a totalitarian movement should be regarded as a matter of wisdom for its sole determination." Paradox indeed!

Marcuse's paradox is parallel with Auerbach's insomuch as both propose partial reversals of the usual valences on free speech and suppression, arriving thence at defenses of suppression for the sake of the greater freedom. Yet for our purposes it is not without interest that Auerbach and Marcuse would have disagreed much about what should count as totalitarianism and what as democracy, and in crucial cases surely would have applied their categories to opposite effects.

Moreover, not even Unger's super-tolerance can easily overcome the internally oppositional—hence hugely indeterminate—structure of impulses represented by these typically sophisticated views about free-speech law. It didn't take long for commentators to see a parallel enigma in "super-liberalism:" "[The] 'structure of no-structure' cabins the social fighting it is intended to facilitate. . . . [D]estabilization rights could not be relied upon to demand the dismantling" of *that* structure.[11]

The critical thesis is a strong one. It speaks of "contradiction," not just "tension" or "ambivalence," meaning thus to insist that the resultant element of arbitrariness in law is pervasive and inescapable—not manageable, for example, by fracturing social life into sub-realms with individualistic rules and principles for one and socialistic ones for another.[12] This insistence is grounded both in lawyers' experience and in theory—in the observations that (1) the problem of separation vs. union arises within "every form of social life," including family, neighborhood, work, trade, and politics; (2) the problem is of "the essence" of "law as law is commonly defined," since "there simply are no legal issues that do not involve directly the problem of the legitimate content of collective coercion;"[13] and (3) law as such aspires to coherence and consistency even *across* the various departments and relations of social life.

The pervasive and "contradictory" character of the duality of impulses may be especially clear when we consider its bearing not just on on the law's contents but on its methods as well.

Plainly enough, to do the work of mediation, the idea of rights has to be convincing both at the level of general statement and at the point of specific application. It therefore requires, Kennedy says, two supports: (1) "an explanation of how there could be a consensus about who has what rights," and (2) "a theory of judicial role, that is, . . . of how a rights-enforcing state can avoid foundering on the biases of the people [he means judges, not the police] who do the actual enforcing." Lacking either one of these, we would also lack reason to prefer The State's tender mercies to those of neighbor Strong.

Liberal legalism has, Kennedy says, worked out two general approaches to the problem of providing the needed supports. One, toward which we incline when taking a comparatively "confident and expansive view of reason," is the natural law view of rights as emanations of reality and judges as rational elaborators of the connection; while the other, toward which we incline when feeling more skeptical about the power of reason to generate consensual answers to tough problems of social conflict, is the legal positivist view of rights as products of an agreed-upon legislative procedure and judges as rule appliers.

Either approach must solve both of the two problems—that of consensus on what and whose the rights are, and that of confidence in their enforcement—if it is to confirm the idea of a regime of rights as a solution to the fundamental conflict of freedom and order. The natural-law approach would solve the first problem, that of consensus in principle, by using "rational reflection on human nature and the structure of social life [to] tell us what rights we have;" and would solve the second, that of credible enforcement, by appealing to a special technique of

legal analysis to reveal one or another decision as "the necessary implication . . . of abstractly formulated rights for [a] particular case." The positivist approach would solve the consen-
sus-in-principle problem by shifting the focus of attention from
substance to procedure; that is, by seeking agreement on rules-
of-the-game for lawmaking, a kind of agreement that may often
seem obtainable when consensus on the content of the rules is
not; and would solve the credible-enforcement problem by
casting legislative output in the form not of broad principles but
of situation-specific rules telling judges exactly when to inter-
vene (and to keep still in situations for which no such rule has
been provided).

There are noteworthy structural relations between these two
standard approaches—the naturalist and the positivist—to the
solution of the standard problems of liberal law. One is that both
are riven by internal conflict between the demands for abstraction and for concreteness in legal norms. The strategy of the
naturalist approach is to translate consensus, thought to be perhaps obtainable at the highest abstract level of propositions about
"human nature" and "the structure of social life," into specific
legal decisions that are broadly acceptable. It seems to be the
very high level of generality at which the starting propositions
are to be cast that invites hope of consensus at that level. Yet
that same abstraction is what also invites the devastating Legal
Realist expose of the impotence of method to derive, from vapid
generalities like voluntarism, equality, or—perhaps most fa-
mously—J.S. Mill's distinction between self-regarding and other-
regarding acts, convincing answers for humanly concrete legal
disputes. The strategy of the positivist mode is to prevent judicial dictatorship by hemming in the judges with situation-specific rules, validated by their having emerged from a pure or
ideal—unchallengeably fair, impartial, non-dictatorial—legislative procedure. Yet if the procedure speaks otherwise than
through the language of general, impersonal, categorical rights,
how may it be defended before those who doubt its fairness or
neutrality, in conception or in practice? What, finally, can guarantee and confirm the procedure's purity, other than its abiding by the universalistic forms of the Rule of Law, which notoriously fall short of giving answers to concrete social disputes?

So there is parallelism between the naturalist and positivist approaches but that is not all. In another perspective, the two approaches represent the two poles of the fundamental contradiction. It's not, though, that each approach represents one pole but rather that each represents both. From one standpoint, the naturalist approach represents a "good fusion" (as Kennedy would say) of human universality and common ends, everyone having (and acknowledging that others have) the same rights because everyone shares the same nature; while the positivist approach represents a "bad fusion" of domination, of conflict decided (but not dissolved) by contest of power. From a converse standpoint, the naturalist mode represents a "bad fusion" of victor and vanquished, one person standing fast on his rights and the other having to submit no matter how awful the consequences; while the positivist mode represents a good fusion of persons together trying to work out their conflict. Neither the duality of the naturalist and positivist modes, nor their parallel internal conflicts, nor their switching valences vis-à-vis each other, Kennedy would say, is any more eradicable from our thought and our practice than is the fundamental contradiction itself, of which they may be understood as manifestations.

If you hear the ring of truth in this kind of critique, if you are struck by the reality and depth of the fundamental contradiction and captured by the vision of its ubiquity in legal discourse, then you must also see this discourse as radically disunified. The more firmly one thinks that all legal imagination is shaped, all legal rationalization driven, by repulsion from the fundamental contradiction—which (one also thinks) is unalterably *there*—the more firmly must one predict, with Kennedy, that "for any given factual conflict of rights, the doctrinal structure will offer a choice of categorization, [and] the techniques of reasoning that are supposed to tell us which choice to make will themselves reproduce that choice at another level."

Finally, the tale, as told by Kennedy, is one of mystification and moral self-betrayal, as well as disunity: a tale of contradiction so deep and painful that it not only prevents stable resolutions of the conflicts of social life at any level above that of the concrete particular dispute, but also prompts the invention of thick intellectual machinery to block daily vision from the painful fact of *choice,* to let it seem that social outcomes flow neutrally from arrangements according to nature or consensus, when really there is nothing to do but take sides; which means, if we insist on generalized, categorical answers in the form of rights, sometimes taking sides against our morally divided selves.

4. Assessing the Damage

4.1. *What Motivates Legalist Justification: Why Justifiability Matters*

I think the constitutive personal experience Kennedy describes—of the constant opposition of separatist and collectivist impulses—is true of us, and that it reverberates in legal life and thought in much the way he claims. Must I then give up belief in the intelligibility and justifiability of judicial decision?

By way of prelude to considering whether, and how, adjudication may remain open to rational, critical appraisal, despite the contradiction thesis, we need to take a brief look at motivations for favoring that particular form of judicial justification—which is indeed endangered by the thesis—that I have called legalist. My treatment of this vast and deep subject will be cursory and conclusory, but perhaps plausible enough to sustain what follows.

In what may fairly be called a standard account, the demand for legalist justification is apparently responsive to a perceived problem about judicial authority. The problem begins with the observation that judges typically are not electorally accountable, as legislators and executive officials are. Of course one sees the point of this deliberately contrived judicial shelter from the winds of popular passion, or from the particularistic demands of the powerful. Still, the question looms: Why obey the judge, if the judge is just "a naked power organ?"[14]

If judges making rules or dictating outcomes were as free as legislators of external discipline—that is, apart from the electoral check—but were also, unlike legislators, free of the electoral check as well, then they would be naked power organs whom no one, it is said, would have good reason to obey and possibly no one would obey. Adjudication that no one obeyed, or that no one had good reason to obey, would be an absurd exercise in futility or fraud. So if adjudication is not to be absurd, futile, or fraudulent, it must, according to the view I am now describing, be distinguishable in some way from legislation. Legalist justification—the holding of judges accountable to norms at least partially external to themselves[15]—is proposed as the way.

This account of our attachment to legalism suffers from both a somewhat gratuitous puzzlement about judicial authority and a stilted notion of accountability.[16] Let us for a moment stipulate that a judge *is* a power organ "naked" of accountability either to electorate or to general and enduring external principle. We should remember that the reality and even the possibility of legalist justification have been under sharp and sustained attack in this country for sixty years and more, and yet the attackers, so far as I know, have not advocated abolition of the courts or even of their power to set aside statutes as unconstitutional.

Why not? Well, surely one could think that there had better be court-like institutions and judge-like officers just because there are going to be conflicts and disputes and most of us, much of the time, are going to feel that arbitration by someone supposedly chosen for practical wisdom, and free of direct interest or personal bias, is safer or better than constant recourse to the contest of raw power, whether between the parties directly or their legislative champions. So thinking one could further think— I am hardly the first to think such things[17]—that those arbitral institutions and officers will legitimate themselves, will act non-tyrannically, just insofar as their decisions and reasons strike enough others as fair, prudent, within the bounds of tradition and expectation, and generally apt to the project of helping us live together in decency and relative peace. Our safeguards against judicial tyranny, then, would lie not only in practices other than judicial self-justification by reason—practices like inter-governmental (interbranch) checks and informal public and peer reaction—but in forms of judicial explanatory or argumentative discourse other than the quasi-syllogistic form of legalism.

4.2. Nihilism, Pragmatism, and Justifiability

The thesis of the fundamental contradiction is, I have said, a strong one. It is not just a continuation of "old" Legal Realist harping on the relativity of doctrine to context, or on the need for particularization of judgment to circumstance. Nor is it guilty of the "logical positivist error" ascribed by J.R. Searle to post-structuralist intellectual fashion, that of thinking that "unless a distinction can be made rigorous and precise it isn't really a dis-

tinction at all." Thus the trouble it makes cannot be cured by
Searle's prescription: a grown-up acceptance of ambivalence,
complexity and approximation, and of the truth that a "condition of the adequacy of a precise theory of an inderterminate
phenomenon [is] that it should precisely characterize that phenomenon as indeterminate; and [that] a distinction is no less a
distinction for allowing for a family of related, marginal, diverging cases."[18]

Searle's cure will not work on the opposed-impulses thesis
precisely because the thesis is—at least in its bearing on law, given
what law is[19]—one of *contradiction,* not just one of complexity,
imprecision, or relativity to context. Robert Gordon (as usual)
has put it well:[20]

> [CLS] . . . carries the claim of law's indeterminate relation
> to social life a significant step further [than the Legal Real-
> ists carried it]: the same body of law, in the same context,
> can always lead to contrary results. This is because law is
> indeterminate at its core, in its inception, not just in its ap-
> plications: because its rules derive from structures of thought
> (collective constructs of many minds) that are fundamen-
> tally contradictory. . . . Since the fundamental contradic-
> tion has never been (perhaps can never be?) overcome, le-
> gal structures represent unsuccessful and thus inherently
> unstable mediations of the contradiction: over time, there-
> fore, they will tend to become unglued and therefore to
> collapse.

So Kennedy and Gordon want us finally to grow up and put
away the entrancing idea of an adjudication both determinate
and universalistic, strongly constrained by rights that are nota-
bly abstract or by principles that have much enduring generality. They are saying both that judges can't possibly, and so don't
actually, do it that way and that we all should stop hoping that
they do or can.

Does it follow—as apparently supposed by those who attack
their stance as "nihilist"[21]—that a judge confronting a case can
do no better than try to apprehend the case in all the fullness
of its unique concoction of concrete particulars, intuit which
decision would best comport with the judge's personal "poli-

tics," and sing out the answer; and that the rest of us can do no better as critics of the decision than to assess whether the judge's politics appear to comport with our own? That response seems to me quite wrong, much as Richard Rorty finds his anti-pragmatist wrong to think that if judgments cannot be held to a test of correspondence with objects (because of skeptical failure of belief in the existence of the objects) then "we have no hope of rationality, but only taste, passion, and will."[22] The thesis of a fundamentally disunified body of law does not, so far as I can see, necessarily deny any of the following:

- That lawyers and judges are rightly expected to "think" as well as "look"—to deal with cases cognitively, by argument, persuasion, rational reflection, and public explanation.

- That lawyers and judges are rightly expected to typecast the problems and parties before them; to render their cases knowable and discussable by having them represent classes of problems and parties that are either found in or constructible out of existing stocks of types and taxonomies of which legal (like other) discourse is made—inevitably submerging, in the process, much of any case's concrete particular uniqueness.

- That lawyers and judges may rightly think and argue about their typified cases using normative formulations—of rule, principle, and policy—drawn from a pre-existing stock either whole and ready-to-use or as the makings of a new or revised formulation.

- That social life displays structural features and systemic regularities of the kinds that make policy analyses sometimes worthwhile; that a legal decisionmaker can sometimes reliably have and usefully invoke systemic knowledge in gauging the consequences of alternative decisions; or that the decider should regularly try to appraise cases in a policy-analytic perspective.[23]

This is not to say that in fact no strain of irrationalism exists anywhere within the CLS camp.[24] It is to say that belief in an insuperably disunified *corpus juris* is not in itself a totally—I don't think it is even a partially—irrationalist position. It disables neither argument nor deliberation, nor places judicial decision beyond possibility of explanation. (It is after all a crucial point about "the fundamental contradiction" that it is a form of order, not chaos. It signifies not random confusion—as such ineffable, indescribable, unexaminable—but a formation of thought that can be named, perceived, cognized. And while surely there is nothing potentially enabling about the coming to consciousness of random disorder (entropy is the loss, not the gain, of energy), appreciation of a hitherto denied contradiction can be emancipatory.[25]

What the disunity thesis does appear to disable is the Rule of Law, if by that we mean the strong separation of legal decision from the "politics"—from the responsible agency—of the judge. The thesis is that:

- The law's available stock of stories and taxonomies into which judges can typecast their parties and problems is—must be, given what we are and what law is supposed to be—always multiple, looking toward opposite decisions, and leaving the judge to choose (or to perceive, but by a non-necessitated *act* of perception) which of the case's concrete particulars are classificatory and which others will be submerged and lost to consciousness.[26]

- The law's formulary of rules, principles, and policies potentially applicable to any case in usually duplicitous, leaving the judge to decide which of the contrarily applicable sets to invoke, perhaps by way of the same act by which the judge decides—or perceives—which of the available legal stock stories[27] the case represents.

- No matter how acute the judge's systemic knowledge and policy-analytic prophecy, the law will not *give* the judge the "objective function" required for decision about which systemic train of events to trigger, or which way to deflect an onrushing train. That is just what the judge has to decide, by deciding which body of normative material, from the available contradictory bodies, is to govern the case under decision.

But from this openness it does not follow that argument, reason, reflection, and explanation are foreign to judicial work. To see that judicial reason cannot be reducible to inductive/ deductive method is not to rule out judicial reason. The good judge might be like Rorty's pragmatist, searching for what Robert Cover calls a "line of human endeavor that brings [vision and reality] into temporary or partial reconciliation,"[28]—a reasoner, but a searching reasoner who has outgrown "the common urge to . . . find something ahistorical and necessary to cling to;" who declines appeal "to something *more* than the ordinary, retail, detailed, concrete reasons which have brought one to one's present view;" and for whom, accordingly, "the pattern of all inquiry . . . is [conversation and] deliberation concerning the relative attractions of various concrete alternatives."[29]

In sum, what the contradictory-law thesis excludes is not judicial reason but judicial scientific positivism. It excludes judicial abdication to a legal logical necessity supposed to stand between the case and politics—"shift[s] the focus of our vision from a stage where social and professional prejudices wear the terrible armor of Pure Reason to an arena where human hopes and expectations wrestle naked for supremacy."[30]

5. Post-Critical Rights?

The evidence is strong—sometimes to the analytic eye, more generally to the listening heart—of some unease among the critics of legalism. Not all seem enthused by the idea of truly lawless or rightsless judging. Why so?

Consider: To doubt that legalist justification is an indispensable support of either the social function, or of the stability, or even—at least in any simple and direct way—of the moral legitimacy of adjudicative institutions is not to conclude that the ideal of decision according to law is pointless or valueless. Other important values have often been associated with the ideal: democracy, for one (in the formal sense of popularly legislated law); regularity, for another (in the sense of predictable, consistent, and unbiased administration of public force); and, for some of us above these two, equality.

From Kant[31] to Rawls[32] and Dworkin,[33] liberal jurisprudence has dwelt on the connections between equality and rights,

and between rights and legalism. But though equality stands well
at CLS, legalism and rights are in trouble there—legalism for
reasons we have reviewed. In what remains of this essay, I examine briefly some reasons advanced by critical legal scholars
for attacking or disparaging "rights consciousness" and begin
to suggest why one may think that the notion of rights in some
form must nevertheless persist as an ideal of law and politics.

5.1. Rights, Equality, and Abstraction

5.1.1. Equality. In egalitarian liberal legal thought, the idea
of rights represents acknowledgment of the claims of humanity
universally resident in each person, prompting the vision of a
consistently principled and binding law. For egalitarians, some
such idea seems irrepressibly coupled with the belief that there
are forms of treatment that human beings, as such or as commonly (if historically and contingently) situated, require of each
other as conditions of self-realization in and through the company of others, and as conditions of effective membership in
the company.[34]

That belief may well co-exist with the fullest appreciation of
the "fundamental contradiction." We can see that social life must
engage the conflicts within our natures in ways that cannot be
definitively and permanently resolved, and yet find it possible
to think deliberately and argue persuasively about which requirements are more urgent, within the conditions and commitments of a given historical moment or social context. (Op-
pressiveness in the social context, or "false consciousness," may
complicate or endanger the effort, but will not make it pointless.) Insofar as the situations we identify are common, actually
or potentially, to all or to many, that dimension of commonality
will be one to which our answers must be responsive. And won't
the answers, then, or some of them anyway, look suspiciously
like rights?

5.1.2. Abstraction. But how can we maintain any notion of
rights, essentially involving abstraction of norms from the ultimate particularity of cases, in the face of critical exposure of
the linkage between legal abstraction and adjudicative arbitrariness, irresponsibility, and mystification? No doubt we cannot,
without some way of limiting the critique of legal abstraction.
But that there is—must be—some such limit seems true by vir-

tue of what law is (if it is anything), including its intimate tie to language.

Consider these remarks by Joseph Singer in an important work of critical legal scholarship: [35]

> The loss of belief in a determinative, objective legal logic should not undermine the sense that we can make rational choices. The reality is quite the opposite. We must in any case make the choices we have always made, but we do it consciously, without the illusion that choices are made for us by a reified logic. The *logic of rights* is a human invention whose purpose is to preserve us from the notion that we must make political and moral choices. To make conscious choices, it is necessary to realize that we are making a choice. To choose wisely, we must know who gains and who loses from the concrete legal rules and what values are thereby preserved or undermined. Once we know everything that is involved in the decision, and we have not arbitrarily constricted the alternatives available to us, then we make a choice. Those decisions may be difficult and painful, but making choices is what human beings do. . . .

Singer is cautioning against the mystifying abstraction (and reification) [36] of legal rules. But just how thoroughly particularized and concrete can we imagine legal decision might become?

Let us try to take seriously Singer's own diction. What does it mean to *choose* (as opposed to, say, just reacting or behaving), or for choice to be *rational?* What is the object (or process) that qualifies choice as *moral* or *political?* What is a *value*, that a judicial choice might preserve or undermine one? What is a *concrete rule?* Who is the "who" that wins or loses? Who is the chooser? (Who is *we?*) How are "we" supposed to function without a common language? What is it, finally, that we are to be conscious *of* when we choose consciously?

The point of my queries is that it is not the whole truth that "making choices is what human beings do." For (at least for one who speaks of choosing rationally and wisely) that cannot be all we do. There is no choice without reflection nor reflection without knowledge, including self-knowledge (here I follow Sandel); [37] no knowledge without language, no language without categories; and one might as well, or as ill, have said that reflecting, conversing, or categorizing is what human beings do.[38] Non-tyrannical and adjudication would, it seems, have to be a process of conversation (argument) and recognition, hence of reason, as much as of choice.[39] Of course, from these observations about law and language (or law and thought) nothing follows affirmatively about either the value or the necessity of a legal discourse in which rights are salient. All that follows is that no critique of legal abstraction can preclude rights from law without precluding law itself. The positive motivation for "rights consciousness" remains to be supplied from substantive ideas of political morality—from liberal equality, perhaps, or from a rather different sort of "value" to which I now turn.

5.2. Rights and Radical Goals: Liberation and Solidarity

Critical legal scholars argue that rights express a certain pathology of human relationship and political practice. Rights are operative only in and through "rights consciousness," and rights consciousness is, according to this view, a form of self-abuse—one might say of self-imprisonment, in the dual sense of the immurement of selves by walls of rights, and of compulsive obedience to reified abstractions of rights and law. Thus, for critics, rights represent both moral error and congnitive confusion. A short, step-by-step review of this critique will disclose (once again, for this is no original discovery) at the core of rights-consciousness a "value"—an idea about human personality—that helps explain and justify the commitment of belief to the two, related ideas that people must have rights and that adjudication must be justifiable, hence intelligible.[40]

5.2.1. Atomization and Antagonism. Karl Klare has written of the moral (or, as he might prefer to call it, the ideological or political) failure of rights discourse. He charges the idea of rights with support for a distortedly one-sided, asocial vision of human nature and freedom, said to be contained in the very idea of the dependency of freedom on the rights of individuals. Rights-consciousness, as thus critically viewed, is at the core of what C.B. Macpherson has called a "political theory of possessive individualism."[41] In this rightsy vision, freedom appears "as either the escape from community [Klare presumably has in mind here a model such as a person's right to exclusive possession of land or to familial privacy], or the prudent, limited participation in community solely to achieve narrow, instrumental ends [here he is thinking of something like a person's right to municipal services equal to those others receive]." Klare says rights-consciousness has available only these two reponses to the question of "the moral evaluation of the institutionalization of community power:" either a libertarian notion of government as necessary evil, in which "rights exist for the purpose of shielding the individual from the unauthorized exercise of . . . power;" or a welfare-state view in which "rights are conceived as entitlements to participate in the advantages flowing from the exercise of . . . power." What is excluded, then, is "the possibility of conceiving human freedom as self-expression and growth in and through community."[42]

Taken as description of actual, recent liberal experience with legal rights, Klare's analysis is telling. But what if taken—as I think it was intended—as a theoretical claim about the inherent tendencies of rights discourse? Why should rights be necessarily atomizing and alienating? A right, after all, is neither a gun nor a one-man show. It is a relationship and a social practice, and in both those essential aspects it is seemingly an expression of connectedness. Rights are public propositions, involving obligations to others as well as entitlements against them. In appearance, at least, they are a form of social cooperation—not spontaneous but highly organized cooperation, no doubt, but still, in the final analysis, cooperation.

5.2.2. Alienation, Reification, and False Necessity. Rights critics will rejoin, first, that "highly organized" fatally understates the case; and, second, that the actual experience of rights is one of antagonism, not cooperation. Morover, they will strengthen their case by offering a theoretical connection between these points, which they might put this way: The regime of rights as we daily live it is at best a degenerate relic of cooperation, so remote— in time, form, or logic—from any cooperative origins as to have become an essentially involuntary, coercive, alien force. In place of organization the critical eye sees mystification; in place of cooperation, the reified state. Thus, according to Peter Gabel and Paul Harris,[43]

The appeal to rights inherently affirms that the source of social power resides in the State rather than in the people themselves. . . . By granting new rights that seem to vindicate the claims of the individuals and groups asserting them, the State can succeed over time in co-opting the movements' more radical demands while "relegitimizing" the status quo through the artful manipulation of legal doctrine. . . . The point is not simply that rights-consciousness inherently implies the necessity of social antagonism (since rights are normally asserted against others). It is that this very way of thinking about people involves a bizarre abstracting away from one's true experience of others as here with us existing in the world. An alternative approach to politics based on resolving differences through compassion and empathy would presuppose that people can engage in political discussion and action that is founded upon a felt recognition of one another as human beings, instead of conceiving of the political realm as a context where one abstract "legal subject" confronts another. . . .

Another telling rendition of modern experience with rights and legality, yet again one finds missing a side of the experience, and so the argument seems incomplete. Indeed, one may fairly complain of this passage, standing by itself, that it lacks the ironic appreciation of dialectical complexity and the cunning of reason, including within one's own thought, that is the glory of critical method. The passage seems to commit the sin of false necessity in the very act of ascribing it to rights-consciousness, reifying[44] rights-consciousness as it claims rights-consciousness reifies rights, law, and state. It does so by attributing to all the rest of us a factitious positivistic idea of the state. To think that rights discourse reinforces submissiveness to foreign powers is to think that everyone but you imagines, and can only imagine, the state to be something other than us;[45] as (we noted above) to think that a law placing much stock in notions of right must be oriented toward the separated rather than the socially situated aspect of the self is to overlook that a right, however much it may be a claim to respect as a distinct person, is, equally fundamentally, a claim grounded in human association.[46]

Now, critique has a response to the sort of liberal anti-posi-
tivist show I've just put on, namely, the critical account of the
liberal legal alternation between positivistic and naturalistic
moods, on which I have already approvingly reported.[47] "What
is the form of a right," critique will ask, "if not that of a premise in a binding proposition supposed to pre-exist and govern
concrete cases? And are there not implicit in that very form the
alienation and false necessity of which we complain—the pro-
jection of political choice onto a reified other? If the other be
not the state, then it is nature; if not the categorical imperative
of law-abidingness[48] then some other supposed furniture of the
world or fixture of the human condition. One way or another,
rights are a form of distancing men and women from the experience of political power and moral responsibility."

Good questions, strong points; yet still they evade an issue,
and still they seem fraught with offense against critical method.
The passage I quoted from Gabel and Harris betrays a remark-
ably "liberal"[49] dualization of the world and of vision: rightsy
atomistic antagonism opposed to rights-ridded empathic community. And if that is unfair as directed against an isolated passage, still the critique of rights, as I have recounted it thus far,
seems lacking in dialectical sensibility. It does not seem to recognize that the "fundamental contradiction" is *a contradiction* in
the full Hegelian sense: that connectedness, even communion,
among persons requires the existence of *persons;* that persons
are as essentially several as (I join in insisting) essentially connected and communal; and that persons in their connected or
communal severalty require kinds of social respect that, just in
order to be the requisite kinds, *must be theirs by right,* publicly
recognized as such. I suppose the critique of rights can succeed
by denying one or more of the propositions in that series; but
who is willing? Peter Gabel seems steadfast in denying the last
one.[50] But the best short statement I know of the point I am
after is, oddly, Duncan Kennedy's:[51] "Embedded in the rights
notion is a liberating accomplishment of our culture: the affirmation of free human subjectivity against the constraints of
group life, along with the paradoxical countervision of a group
life that creates and nurtures individuals capable of freedom."

5.2.3. Temporality. Unanswered (at least by me) remains the
problem of abstraction *coupled with pre-commitment,* which is of

the essence of both rights and the rights critique.[52] Unanswerable it will remain by anyone who shares the critical vision of the constitutive unstable duality of human impulses toward others.[53] The lesson of Duncan Kennedy's heroic, mind-numbingly meticulous exposé of Blackstone's system[54]—a system spectacularly successful in its day—is that no constructive effort is or can be proof against deconstruction. What does not follow is that we ought to—or even can—give up constructive effort, any more than the fact of death argues against the persistence and repetition of life. We die, we live, we waste, we build, and what else is new? Rights like buildings need duration to be serviceable. Perhaps rights like life depend for their meaning on the occasional intimation of their immortality. What we need is a theory of rights immortal, but for not too long.[55] This is what Roberto Unger now seems to be attempting.[56] Life's lesson, if not Blackstone's, is that it's not impossible.

6. Conclusion

That there is something like the fundamental contradiction deeply written into us, and that it results in a radically disunified legal discourse, is the truth as I understand it. Yet good critics have to think the possibility that the idea of the fundamental contradiction, no less than that of rights though doubtless in a different way, can, if we let it, mystify and paralyze.[57] Duncan Kennedy's diagnosis of liberal legal pathology rests on the claim that the contradiction is, for us, an experience fearful and painful. That is not how it seems to me. I think the contradiction is my friend; nay, my self. I think that liberal thought has always contained some understanding that it was there, constituting the most important tensions of human existence and thereby giving life much of whatever it has of value and meaning.[58] If so, then the liberal experience confirms, not denies, that the experience of a somewhat autonomous law can exist among humans quite in touch with the dualistic constitution of their own selves.

NOTES

1. Ernest Weinrib, "The Intelligibility of the Rule of Law," paper presented at the Conference on the Rule of Law, York University (Osgoode Hall), April, 1983.
2. See, e.g., David Lyons, "Justification and Judicial Responsibility," *Calif. L. Rev.* 72 (1984): 178.
3. In speaking of the standard as "external," I mean only that it is not considered to reside wholly in the case, to be obtainable by contemplation of the case alone, or to be applicable, once produced, only to the case. Yet the case in its novelty may play some part in the production of the standard.
4. This is not to say that the judge, any more than the case, is excluded from participation in eliciting the standard, but only that the judge in so doing may not act in total disregard of the public sources and methods.
5. David Lyons calls "legalistic justification" "the doctrine . . . that judicial decisions are justified when they are required by law." Lyons, "Justification and Judicial Responsibility."
6. Duncan Kennedy, "The Structure of Blackstone's Commentaries," *Buff. L. Rev.* 28 (1979): 205.
7. Although Walt Whitman was pithier: "Whoever walks a furlong without sympathy walks to his funeral, drest in his shroud." (Preface, *Leaves of Grass,* 1855). And from "Song of Myself:" "Dazzling and tremendous how quick the sunrise would kill me,/If I could not now always send sunrise out of me."
8. Carl Auerbach, The Communish Control Act of 1954, *U. Chi. L. Rev.* 23 (1956): 173, 188–89.
9. See Herbert Marcuse, "Repressive Tolerance," in Robert Paul Wolff, Barrington Moore, Jr. and Herbert Marcuse, *A Critique of Pure Tolerance* (Boston,: Beacon Press, 1965), p. 81.
10. See Roberto Unger, "The Critical Legal Studies Movement," *Harv. L. Rev.* 96 (1983): 561.
11. Allan Hutchinson and Patrick Monahan, "Law, Politics, and the Critical Legal Scholars: The Unfolding Drama of American Legal Thought," *Stan. L. Rev.* 36 (1984): 199, 233.
12. See Robert Gordon, "Critical Legal Histories," *Stan. L. Rev.* 36 (1984): 57, 114, quoted at p. 119, *infra.* The "public-private distinction" has been a major target of recent critical legal scholarship. See, e.g., "Symposium: The Public-Private Distinction," *U. Pa. Rev.* 130 (1982): 1289–1609.
13. Kennedy, "Structure of Blackstone's Commentary," p. 213.
14. This phrase is Herbert Wechsler's in his famous Holmes Lecture

on legalist justification, "Toward Neutral Principles of Constitutional Law," *Harv. L. Rev.* 73 (1959): 1, 19.

15. See notes 3 and 4 above.

16. Moreover, the account is mysterious. We do not dispel the fogs from the temple of justice with idea that it's OK for judges to boss us around as long as they mean to do it only as oracles of some— it may be quite Delphic—body of principle, connected in some (often Delphic) way to some authoritative (if Delphic) legal source.

17. See, e.g., Martin Shapiro, *Law and Politics in the Supreme Court: New Approaches to Political Jurisprudence* (London: The Free Press of Glencoe, 1964); Jan Deutsch, "Neutrality, Legitimacy, and the Supreme Court: Some Intersections Between Law and Political Science," *Stan L. Rev.* 20 (1968): 169.

18. John R. Searle, "The Word Turned Upside Down," *New York Review of Books,* vol. 30, no. 16, Oct. 27, 1983, pp. 74–79, at 78.

19. see p. 12, *supra*

20. Gordon, "Critical Legal Histories."

21. See, e.g., Owen Fiss, "Objectivity and Interpretation," *Stan L. Rev.* 34 (1982): 739. For a defense against similar charges of the broader philosophical project of "deconstruction," to which Duncan Kennedy's work is plainly related, see Terry Eagleton, *Literary Theory: An Introduction* (Minneapolis: University of Minnesota Press, 1983), p. 148.

22. See Richard Rorty, *Consequences of Pragmatism* (Minneapolis: University at Minnesota Press, 1982), p. 164.

23. Thus I think Bruce Ackerman seriously overstates the hostility of CLS and its Legal Realist forebears to adjudicative use of systemic vision. Compare B. Ackerman, *Reconstructing American Law* (1984), pp. 42–43 and n. 13 with Duncan Kennedy, "Distributive and Paternalist Motives in Contract and Tort Law," *Md. L. Rev.* 41 (1982): 563.

24. Or anywhere within Duncan Kennedy. See Peter Gabel and Duncan Kennedy, "Roll Over Beethoven," *Stan. L. Rev.* 36 (1984): 1, 23. This article is a dialogue between the two authors, often disagreeing. Further references to it will make clear which author is being cited.

25. See David Trubek, "Where the Action Is: Critical Legal Studies and Empiricism," *Stan. L. Rev.* 36 (1984): 575, 591–98.

26. Compare Felix Cohen, "The Ethical Basis of Legal Criticism," *Yale L. J.* 41 (1933): 201, 214–17: ". . . Decisions are fluid until they are given 'morals.' It is often important to conserve with new obeisance the morals [he means the maxims, precepts] which lawyers and laymen have read into past decisions and in reliance upon

which they have acted. We do not deny that importance when we recognize that with equal logical justification lawyers and laymen might have attached other morals to the old cases had their habits of legal classification or their general social premises been different."

27. The notion of legal "stock stories" is developed in Gerald Lopez, "The Internal Structure of Lawyering: Lay Lawyering," *U.C.L.A. L. Rev.* 32 (1984): 1.

28. Robert Cover, "Foreword: Nomos and Narrative," *Harv. L. Rev.* 97 (1983): 4, 39.

29. Rorty, *Consequences of Pragmatism*, pp. 164–65. Rorty is not the only contemporary philosopher in whose work legal theorists may seek support for the needed conception of rationality not dependent on truth timeless and universal. See, e.g., Hilary Putnam, *Reason, Truth and History* (Cambridge: Cambridge University Press, 1981).

30. Cohen, "Ethical Basis of Legal Criticism."

31. Immanuel Kant, *Groundwork of the Metaphysics of Morals*, trans. H. Paton (New York: Harper & Row, 1964).

32. John Rawls, *A Theory of Justice* (Cambridge: Harvard University Press, 1971).

33. Ronald Dworkin, *Taking Rights Seriously* (Cambridge: Harvard University Press, 1977).

34. See, e.g., Ronald Dworkin, "Why Liberals Should Believe in Equality," *N.Y. Rev. of Books*, Feb. 3, 1983.

35. Joseph Singer, "The Legal Rights Debate in Analytical Jurisprudence from Bentham to Hohfeld," *Wis. L. Rev.* 1982: 975, 1059. For a later statement showing convergence between Singer's view and my own, see Singer, "The Player and the Cards: Nihilism and Legal Theory," Yale L. J. 94 (1984): 1.

36. See note 44, below.

37. Michael Sandel, *Liberalism and the Limits of Justice* (Cambridge: Cambridge University Press, 1982).

38. Compare Cover, "Foreword: Nomos and Narrative," p. 44: "Even those who deny the possibility of interpretation must constantly engage in the interpretive act."

39. Compare Gabel and Kennedy, "Roll Over Beethoven," p. 8 (Peter Gabel asserting the value of "people . . . not being transparent to themselves to understand in words with each other . . . to theorize or imagine with each other the meaning of what it was that just happened.").

40. The tie between the existence of rights and the intelligibility of law is a chief theme in Ronald Dworkin's work. See, e.g., *Taking Rights Seriously*.

41. C. B. Macpherson, *The Political Theory of Possessive Individualism: Hobbes to Locke* (Oxford: Oxford University Press, 1962).

42. Karl Klare, "Labor Law as Ideology: Toward a New Historiography of Collective Bargaining Law" *Ind. Rel. L.J.* 4 (1981): 450, 469, 478–79.

43. Peter Gabel and Paul Harris, "Building Power and Breaking Images: Critical Legal Theory and the Practice of Law," *N.Y.U. Rev. of Law & Social Change* 11 (1982–83): 369, 375–76. Compare Gabel and Kennedy, "Roll Over Beethoven," p. 26 (Peter Gabel speaking).

44. See Gabel and Harris, "Building Power and Breaking Images," p. 373, n. 10: " 'Reification' is the attribution of a thing-like or fixed character to socially constructed phenomena. This process . . . lead[s] people to accept existing social orders as the inevitable 'facts of life.' "

45. Peter Gabel and Duncan Kennedy have recently disagreed over how far this is valid criticism of Gabel's prior position. See Gabel and Kennedy, "Roll Over Beethoven," pp. 29–44.

46. The stronger view, that rights ultimately presuppose not just association but community, needs elaboration and defense—a hoary project to which, e.g., Thomas Hill Green, *Lectures on the Principles of Political Obligation* (London: Longman's Green, 1927) and M. Sandel (see note 37 above) have made contributions, and to which I hope to make some.

47. See pp. 110–114, *supra.*

48. See the powerful discussions of "the hegemonic function of the law" in E. Genovese, *Roll Jordan Roll: The World the Slaves Made* (New York: Random House, 1976) pp. 25–49, and of legal-positivistic compulsiveness in R. Cover, *Justice Accused: Antislavery and the Judicial Process* (New Haven: Yale University Press, 1975), pp. 159–74.

49. See generally, R. Unger, *Knowledge and Politics* (New York: The Free Press, 1975).

50. See Gabel and Kennedy, "Roll Over Beethoven," pp. 33–37: "Precisely what people don't need is their *rights.* . . . [T]he actual capturing of what it means to be human, and in relation to other people, is falsified by the image of people of rights-bearing citizens. It's a falsification of human sociability." That certainly poses the issue.

51. Duncan Kennedy, "Critical Labor Law Theory: A Comment," *Indus. Rel. L. J.* 4 (1981): 503, 506.

52. Peter Gabel is explicit that it is the "frozen" and "falsified"—not the abstract—character of rights discourse that he finds objectionable. See Gabel and Kennedy, "Roll Over Beethoven," pp. 3–6.

53. See pp. 102–115, *supra*.
54. Duncan Kennedy, "Structure of Blackstone's Commentaries."
55. See Roscoe Pound, "Mechanical Jurisprudence," *Colum. L. Rev.* 8 (1908): 605, 622.
56. See Roberto Unger, "Critical Legal Studies Movement."
57. Gabel and Kennedy see the danger that the contradiction idea may work as a demotivating "reified abstraction." See Gabel and Kennedy, "Roll Over Beethoven," pp. 15–16. They do not mention that among the wasted possibilities might be the pursuit of rights.
58. For a prior statement of mine to like effect, see "Comment: Universal Resident Suffrage: A Liberal Defense," *U. Pa. L. Rev.* 130 (1982): 1581, 1587–88.

6

LIBERALISM AND THE OBJECTIVE POINT OF VIEW: A COMMENT ON FISHKIN

CHRISTOPHER H. SCHROEDER

1. UNSUPPORTABLE CLAIMS OF OBJECTIVITY

Professor James S. Fishkin says modern liberal political theory faces a crisis because people expect it to be "objective" in ways that it cannot be, and I think he is correct.[1] Ordinary moral reasoners, he claims, believe that in order for liberal theory (or any other theory, for that matter) to qualify as a non-subjective, non-arbitrary set of claims about how society should be organized and how individuals in society should be constrained, it must be a theory that is, in his terminology, either "absolutist"

This comment was written in December 1983 for presentation at the December 27–28 meeting of the American Society for Political and Legal Philosophy. It was revised slightly in the summer of 1984. I have not attempted to acknowledge or incorporate references to recently published articles that bear on the topic raised here. There is a growing commentary literature on the Conferences of Cirtical Legal Studies, including an entire symposium, "Critical Legal Studies Symposium," *Stan. L. Rev. 34* (1984): 1–674. See also Shiffrin, "Liberalism, Radicalism, and Legal Scholarship," *UCLA L. Rev.* 30 (1983): 1103, arguing for an eclecticism of substantive liberal values that are non-absolute, and also analyzing the CLS. James Gordley's "Legal Reasoning: An Introduction," *Calif. L. Rev.* 72 (1984):183, is an excellent exposition of how legal decision-making can be non-absolute and also non-arbitrary. It might be consulted to supplement part 2C of this chapter.

or "rigorous".[2] However, because of certain constraints, self-imposed and otherwise, on the kinds of arguments that modern liberal theory can employ to defend its views on social organization and individual liberties, it can be neither.

At first glance, these constraints seem to consign modern liberal theory to the status of a "subjective" and "arbitrary" value system, having no special claim to legitimacy. However, Professor Fishkin argues that there is a species of objectivity, what he calls "minimal objectivism," to which modern liberal theories can lay claim. To retrieve liberal theory from the ignominy of subjectivity and arbitrariness one must focus on the kind of objectivity claim that liberalism can deliver. In a manner fitting for the political times, we must lower our expectations about what liberalism can be: it can be something different from merely another subjective and arbitrary claimant, but it cannot be absolutist or rigorous.

Furthermore, Fishkin's arguments imply an admonition that the impetus for realigning the "widely shared [expectations] of our common moral culture"[3] with what liberal theory can deliver must to a large degree come from within liberal theory, because liberal theory itself has contributed significantly to the crisis by avowing that it could be absolutist or rigorous. There is thus in his paper something of a sermon to liberalism's friends, in the nature of John Plamenatz's concern about democracy, when he wrote: "The friends of democracy too often speak loosely and carelessly in its favor, seeming to make impossible claims for it. If these claims are taken literally, what democracy is in fact falls so far short of what it is in theory supposed to be that it looks like a fraud."[4]

As I say, I believe Professor Fishkin's analysis is essentially correct. More than this, it illuminates an old debate within the liberal theory of law that has recently been revitalized by the Conference of Critical Legal Studies (CLS).[5] This debate goes to the heart of what counts as justification within liberalism's theory of law, and the recent CLS attacks have made it of current moment. Accordingly, I shall deploy and extend Fishkin's insights to review one recurring CLS criticism of the liberal theory of law, a criticism that bears striking structural similarity to the conflict between Fishkin's moral reasoners and the potentialities of liberal theory. To do this intelligibly, I am compelled to spend a little space summarizing part of his thesis and elaborating a bit on it, particularly on the status of minimal objectivism.[6]

To understand why modern liberalism cannot defend absolutism or rigorism, it is necessary to state what those positions are. The crucial ingredient in absolutism is the view that principles possess "an inviolable character [that] is rationally unquestionable."[7] Rigorism on the other hand admits that it is possible in reason to question principles, but asserts that those principles are ones that "it would be objectively wrong ever to violate (permit exceptions to)."[8] Rigorism claims that principles are not prima facie grounds for action, waiting to be overruled by some supervening consideration. Nor can they themselves conflict without some other principle in the theory providing a determinate or objective way of reconciling them. They are, rather, complete determinants of correct decisions. John Rawls's lexical priority of liberty over other primary goods aspires to rigor by denying a conflict between the system of liberties and the value those liberties have to individuals. Utilitarianism aspires to rigor by purporting to solve all public choice problems via the utilitarian calculus.

The crucial distinction between absolutism and rigorism consists in the claim of the former to being rationally unquestionable, a claim that would require further elaboration before being clearly understood. However, the critical division for present purposes lies between these two theories on the one hand (both of which I shall refer to as "absolutism") and the position of minimal objectivism on the other, so I can avoid a detour to consider the meaning of "rationally unquestionable."

Modern liberalism, Fishkin argues, cannot plausibly defend absolutism. The difficulty it faces is partially the difficulty of a certain species of modern moral philosophy generally, and is to that extent familiar. Much normative, modern moral philosophy has adopted the technique of building moral systems on some set of weak and plausible initial conditions, conditions that (it is hoped) many people can be brought to accept, more or less on inspection. Characteristically, this technique entails (1) describing, and arguing for, these initial conditions, usually in the form of some perspective and/or choice situation that is taken to be the appropriate starting point from which moral judgments are to be made, and (2) extracting normative principles or rules from that situation or perspective. Thomas Nagel has defined the relevant sense in which this kind of strategy can claim to be objective: objectivity, he claims, is a method of understanding in which "we step back from our view of [the world] and form a new conception which has that view and its relation to the world as its object."[9]

Some variants of the general technique just described may adopt the objective point of view by examining problems of moral choice from a vantage point removed from any observer's immediate viewpoint, then formulating rules of conduct meant to apply to people who do occupy those viewpoints. Rawls's original position is the best-known example. Alternatively, other variants may take the observer in his immediate position and impose conditions upon arguments he can employ, conditions that function to require the observer to step back from his purely personal views, as in Bruce Ackerman's neutral dialogue. In either case, the technique employed can be characterized as the objective point of view. Objectivity is the point of view; the norms that emerge from exercises in extracting principles from that vantage point are objective in a derivative sense.

Fishkin discusses a number of recent and well-known liberal political theories that employ what I have labeled the objective point of view, including those of Rawls, Peter Singer, Ackerman and Ronald Dworkin. All of these, he concludes, can at most support claims in the class of minimal objectivism. To encapsulate the argument in extremely crude form, they cannot claim to be absolute (true beyond rational questioning) just because there are far too many relatively appealing versions, each starting at a certain level of generality with highly plausible initial conditions, leading to some strongly divergent conclusions. (E.g., change one's conclusion about the risk-aversion of the people in Rawls's Original Position, and the procedure seems to generate a form of utility maximization rather than maximin.)[10] They cannot be rigorous (subject to reasonable questioning, but once adopted, true without exception) because one can construct damning counterexamples to each of them.[11] These counterexamples are themselves arguments against rigorism, because they urge exceptions to be made to the initial principles. They also reinforce a general claim that, lacking perfect

foreseeability, we should not adopt any kind of inviolable conclusions from theories that start with weak, albeit plausible initial conditions.[12] We cannot adequately anticipate conflicts of
values and circumstances that may compel admitting exceptions or alterations of principles once thought to be inviolate.

Notice that this analysis, while it is presented within the context of a consideration of the kinds of arguments liberal objectivism can legitimately make against subjective positions, is not
an argument addressed to subjectivists at all. Indeed, at several
points Fishkin draws attention to the inconclusiveness of any of
the arguments *between* rival objective positions as *against* the
subjectivists, and he really never presents reasons against subjectivism in favor of objectivism—that seems to be one of the
projects of his *Beyond Subjective Morality*.[13] What we are presented with we might denominate Fishkin's hypothetical imperative: *if* modern liberalism is going to claim to present an objective theory of value, it had better assert only minimal
objectivism, because on liberalism's own premises defending any
higher claim will fail. So put, it is an argument internal to that
community of liberal thinkers who want to hold out the hope
for an objective content to liberal theory, designed to dissuade
them from arguments that aspire to absolutism.

2. Liberalism as Minimal Objectivism

A. *The Critical Legal Studies Critique*

If liberalism cannot presently support absolutism, and if the
belief of moral culture that any non-absolute system of values
must be just subjective and arbitrary erroneously undermines
liberalism's appeal, the cure proposed by Fishkin seems to be
the only way of improving the situation. Work should be begun
on lowering the expectations of "widely shared elements of our
common moral culture," presumably by making the case that
theories of minimal objectivism have a legitimacy superior to that
of any form of subjectivism.

1. The trap of self-contradiction. It may be, however, that pursuing this cure is itself a trap for modern liberal theory. It would
be a trap, for instance, if it could be shown that the fundamental premises of liberalism themselves *require* absolutism in order
that the theory be internally consistent. Should the questions that

liberalism has set out to answer, questions about political organization, social order, and the sources of legitimate use of state force against individuals, somehow require absolute answers, embracing Fishkin's diagnosis would imply that no cure was available. The patient is either dying or dead, because its own demands for answers to political questions cannot be met within the framework of justifications to which liberalism has necessarily become limited.

Within contemporary scholarship on legal theory and jurisprudence, CLS has just this kind of attack against liberal theory on its main agenda. Arguments over the justifications that liberal theory can legitimately offer lead easily to a discussion of legal theory, because courts must decide conflicts between citizens, as well as conflicts between citizens and the state, and must do so within the liberal state on the basis of criteria considered to be just and justified by a theory of adjudication consistent with the political theory of the state that the courts represent. Hence it should not be surprising that one can find in debates over legal theory a controversy that largely replicates the problems Fishkin describes. A short exegesis of the relation between liberal political theory and the legal system that derives from it will bring out the similarities.

2. Liberalism, the problem of justice, and legal theory. Any brief definition of liberalism is bound to omit something important, and it is doubtful that a single, comprehensive definition could be produced. I must be content with identifying a central problem of liberalism. It is a problem that a wide range of CLS scholarship has taken to require a specific kind of answer.

Liberal theory presupposes first, the existence of scarce resources from which to satisfy the desires of individuals; second, a conflict between those individual desires that makes conflict over the resources inevitable; and third, the ability of individuals to increase the potential for satisfying those desires through common, or social, organization.[14] Together these circumstances create the *problem of justice*, which arises "for people who are engaged in a cooperative enterprise for mutual benefit, [namely] the problem of how the benefits of their cooperation are to be shared."[15] Not only do these circumstances create the problem of justly distributing the proceeds of mutual cooperation, they create a potentially deeper problem of justice, the problem of forestalling the total domination of the individual by the community established in the interests of mutual gain. The opportunity for mutual benefit induces the individual to join the community, while the existence of that community threatens the integrity and freedom of that individual. Because liberalism insists on treating the individual as the unit of analysis, these aspects of the problem of justice emerge as central problems of the theory.

For proponents of the theory who reject the Hobbesian solution to the problem of justice, the legal system operates to mediate between the call of cooperation and the risk of domination. That system can be considered to contain two kinds of principles or norms: substantive principles governing the resolution of disputes between individuals, complex and expressed at various levels of generality, and norms of application describing the methods by which those principles will be applied to specific cases. Within a constitutional system such as the United States, these principles must include a constitutional theory defining the constitutional restrictions upon the potential oppression of the minority by the majority as well as statutory and common law theories, defining how courts are to apply valid legislative instructions on the one hand, and how they are to elaborate or apply principles embeded in prior judicial decisions on the other.

These subtheories all face a similar difficulty: they must somehow ensure that the workings of the legal system do not themselves provide an opportunity for judicial tyranny, whether it be in the form of self-conscious application of the judges' own values to cases or in the form, perhaps less self-conscious, of the application of principles peculiar to their own background, social class or power structure that themselves have no claim to legitimacy. According to the CLS, avoiding judicial tyranny compels liberal legal theory to embrace special kinds of subtheories. At the constitutional level, it requires a method that finds the restraints the Constitution places on the legislature to be clear and determinate. It might include an interpretivist method that attempts to grasp the "real intentions" of the framers toward the dispute brought to the court. Liberal interpretivist method would require "both definite answers (because it is part of a legal system in which judgment is awarded to one side or the other) and clear answers (because it seeks to constrain and thereby to avoid judicial tyranny)."[16] It might include a theory of neutral principles, which claims that "a requirement of consistency [in the meaning and application of legal principles], the core of the ideal of the rule of law, places sufficient bounds on judges to reduce the risk of arbitrariness to an acceptable level."[17]

In all subparts of the legal system, the avoidance of judicial tyranny would seem to necessitate recognition of the principle of the rule of law, or the idea that legal principles and norms are to be uniformly applied to all and are to be knowable in advance by all. The requirement of uniform application, in return, implies a certain technique or rule of application:

> This technique must rely on the powers that reason possesses because it is a machine for analysis and combination: the capacity to deduce conclusions from premises and the ability to choose efficient means to accepted ends. Consequently, the major liberal theories of adjudication view the task of applying law either as one of making deductions from the rules or as one of choosing the best means to advance the ends the rules themselves are designed to foster.[18]

Because of its concern that solutions to the problems of justice do not themselves create the opportunity for judicial domination, liberalism seems to require a legal theory that contains both clear and determinate substantive principles and norms and an equally well-defined and determinate technique for applying those principles to particular cases.

A prime candidate for this critique is the style of reasoning that it most obviously describes—analytical jurisprudence, or formalism, the tradition of Christopher Langdell, Joseph Beale and others that flourished around the turn of the century. Formalism maintained that legal judgments can be made through a process of reasoning deductively from certain basic and indisputable principles to determinate applications in concrete cases. Yet other legal theories can be subjected to this critique. For instance, a rival view to formalism has been functionalism. It views the law as a method for best attaining certain basic and indisputable objectives of the social system through rational analysis of the consequences of rival rules of decision, thus also aspiring to determinate conclusions in concrete cases. In fact, maintains the CLS critique, *all* forms of liberal legal theory "assert that there is a proper place for collectivism, and that that place can be determined by the rational analysis of the content of legal rules."[19] Liberal legal theory thus supposedly reflects the basic liberal problem of justice, recognizing the conflict between community and the individual, and embodies its resolution, through the articulation of the boundary separating the two with a system of judgments that produces unequivocally correct solutions to all problems of boundary definition brought before it.

Saying that liberal legal theory just be capable of generating clear and determinate solutions to legal disputes is but another way of saying that the only methods of legal reasoning which will satisfy the liberal program are those that are absolutist, because only these classes of justificatory claims assert that judgments represent or reflect the clear application of principles that have no exceptions. But these classes of theory are those that we have assumed by hypothesis to be unavailable to liberal theory. Liberalism thus seems trapped in a self-contradiction.

This analysis can be reformulated in Fishkin's terminology. Liberalism's premises require, claim CLS, an absolutist liberal theory of law—only such a theory can supply clear and determinate answers that prevent judicial tyranny. Absolutism, however, is unavailable to liberalism. Liberal theory thus involves a self-contradiction.

Without here denying that specific CLS articles and projects have stimulated worthwhile debate and deserved skepticism, I shall argue that the CLS case just outlined is mistaken. The self-contradiction is a crisis of CLS's own making, and not in any sense inherent in the liberal program itself. In the course of the discussion, the value of Fishkin's analysis and terminology should be evident.

I shall make three points. First, if this self-contradiction were real, one would expect that at least some of the skilled practitioners who became aware that their intellectual craft contradicted itself would acknowledge this and perhaps become paralyzed by the awful recognition. Quite to the contrary, much traditional liberal legal scholarship is aware of the absence of absolutism within the available theories of liberal legal theory, but this has seldom been a source of paralysis. At least, CLS bears some burden of demonstrating that this considerable body of scholarship, which assumes the continuing vitality of the liberal program but avoids absolutism, and hence is not touched by the critique of self-contradiction, is self-delusional. Second, the principle of the rule of law performs an important role in limiting judicial tyranny that has legitimacy independently of the existence of clear and determinate answers. Insofar as liberalism posits that the rule of law mediates the tension between community and individual and thus reduces, rather than eliminates, the possibility of tyranny, the radical critique does not reach it. Third, the basic error in the argument that absolute values are indispensable to liberalism lies in maintaining that the problem of justice somehow requires a certain kind of answer, that is to say, an absolute answer. The truth is that liberalism simply *poses* the *problem of justice;* it does not insist that an answer to that problem assume some canonical form. Indeed, the posing of the problem does not insist that an "answer" in some determinate, absolute sense be available at all. Once the problem of justice is uncoupled from an unsustainable epistemology of values, the program of liberalism can move forward in a world without absolutism.

B. *Self-Awareness, Not Self-Contradiction*

An article by George Christie in the 1969 volume of the *Yale Law Journal,* entitled "Objectivity in the Law," took to task several different theories of legal reasoning for their inability to live up to the expectations of objectivity. In our terms, the basic argument of the piece was that those theories could not produce answers to legal disputes that met the standards of absolutism. They were indeterminate and sometimes even incoherent. Theories that have assumed law to be a system of rules or principles articulable in complete form in advance of particular disputes, of which formalism is an example, fail because they are incoherent when held up against the way legal reasoning is practiced. It is simply "counter-intuitive to contend that so-called rules of law can be completely stated and . . . still more implausible to maintain that the statement of a rule can completely indicate the situations to which it is applicable."[20] Such theories rely upon deductive logic for the application of rules to particular disputes, but almost by inspection one can see that legal reasoning as done by courts and lawyers has little to do with deductive reasoning. Consider the problem of whether a statute requiring "motor vehicles" to pay a road tax is applicable to go-carts. Without a statutory definition that includes go-carts, in which case the problem is amenable to deduction but is also trivial, the decision cannot be deduced until one decides whether a go-cart is a motor vehicle for purposes of the statute, and *that* initial step is not amenable to deductive reasoning.[21]

Other theories, such as Edward Levi's and Herbert Wechsler's, that rely largely upon generating an articulate principle or rule from the requirement of reasoned consistency from case decision to case decision, fall prey to indeterminacy. "In point of fact . . . there are logically any number of rules of law to be derived from any case or series of cases."[22] Reasoned consistency, in other words, cannot guarantee a well-defined set of outcomes across cases or across judges.

These criticisms as well as others in the article adumbrate arguments made recently by Mark Tushnet, one of the most prolific members of CLS, in an article in the *Harvard Law Review*.[23] Christie, however, is not a member of CLS, and the thesis of his article, despite sharing some ground with the later CLS critique, is not that orthodox legal thought is self-contradictory. Rather, it urges a reinterpretation of the requirement of objectivity. The question becomes whether legal reasoning can adequately respond to a hypothetical disappointed litigant who "claims that the court's statements about his arguments [for his position] are only window-dressing[,] that his participation in the process was merely a charade."[24] The objectivity necessary to respond to such an individual was not one that generates clear, determinate, and unique answers in all cases, since "it is impossible in many instances to establish objectively that there is only one correct decision to a case. The model to be presented will claim, however, that it is possible to establish objectively whether a decision was *incorrectly* decided. . . ."[25]

One more example must suffice. William Van Alstyne, another non-CLSer, has recently criticized a large number of "special" theories of constitutional law, including that of Tushnet, urging a renewed appreciation for the idea of Justice Owen Roberts that

> [w]hen an act of Congress is appropriately challenged in the courts as not conforming to the constitutional mandate, the judicial branch of the Government has only one duty—to lay the article of the Constitution which is invoked beside the statute which is challenged and to decide whether the latter squares with the former.[26]

This view of Mr. Justice Roberts' has frequently been considered a prime example of an unacceptable formalism. Van Alstyne's thesis might scarcely be thought worthy of "trashing," as CLS affectionately terms efforts to show that *all* liberal theories of law are indeterminant and contradictory:[27] one can simply trash it by referring to all the previous work done in demolishing formalism.

That thought, as I read Van Alstyne's work, would be off the mark. Elsewhere, after performing a graceful exposition of a number of different judicial theories of the free speech clause of the Constitution, "Congress shall make no law abridging the freedom of speech," he concludes:

> We have now traced nearly a dozen quite different pictures of the free speech clause. None was at odds with the language of the amendment. Few are foreclosed by any fair assessment of its history or its past judicial exposition. Each, moreover, is fraught with its own problems, and virtually all confide an unavoidable margin of textually uncertain discretion in our courts.[28]

Clearly, Van Alstyne does not expect his version of Justice Roberts's method to produce determinate, absolute, or inviolable answers. This conclusion may elicit a degree of existential despair, a longing for a state of affairs in which principles as simply worded as the First Amendment could also have equally simple, and clear, and universally recognized, meanings and applications, but it in no wise counsels resignation to arbitrariness or subjectivity. The words of the document remain as something more than empty vessels to be filled up according to the unrestrained favorite theories of the pourer.[29]

Examples could be multiplied within the legal literature and extended to judicial opinions[30] to show the widespread presence of an intellectual atmosphere that denies absolutism, yet continues to aspire to a theory of choice that is not simply arbitrary or subjective, and yet does not degenerate on account of these two ideas in to disenchantment with its own self-contradiction. Far from recognizing self-contradiction, these efforts seem engaged in constructive investigations of important problems, whether or not one agrees with the specific solutions any of them offers.

However, enough has been said on a point that can only be suggestive, never dispositive. It is always open to the proponents of the trap of self-contradiction to claim that these scholars and judges suffer from some kind of false consciousness, that their liberal vision is befogged in a way that prevents their appreciation of the true contradictions of their position.[31] But this reply requires a more penetrating defense than the bare observation that much of liberal thought and writing assumes there are absolute values, for the truth of the matter is that much of liberal scholarship is not expressed this way at all.

C. The Rule of Law Reconsidered

The concept that purportedly captures liberal legal theory's demand for absolute principles is the idea of the rule of law, and it is time to focus more closely on that concept. Many formulations of the rule of law ideal can be found in legal scholarship. A. Dicey, for instance, saw it as consisting of two fundamental requirements. First, it requires "the absolute supremacy or predominance of regular law as opposed to the influence of arbitrary power, and excludes the existence of arbitrariness, of prerogative, or even of wide discretionary authority on the part of government." Second, it requires "the equal subjection of all classes to the ordinary law of the land administered by the ordinary law courts [and] excludes the idea of any exemption of officials or others from the duty of obedience to the law which governs other citizens or from the jurisdiction of the ordinary tribunals."[32] In addition to identifying limits on the value judgments a legal system can make, this formulation illuminates the crucial role of the judge in the realization of the ideal. It is only through the equal subjugation of all by "ordinary law courts" to the regular law that the rule of law can be put into effect. As a consequence, ensuring the absence of judicial tyranny, which might now be defined as the deviation of individual judges from the implementation of the regular law, assumes central importance in the liberal theory of law. Surely the CLS critique is correct in focussing upon judicial tyranny as an important problem for liberal theory.

It remains to examine of what "deviation" from the regular law necessarily consists. F.A. Hayek amplifies further: "Government in all its actions is bound by rules fixed and announced before hand—rules which make it possible to foresee with fair certainty how the authority will use its coercive powers in given circumstances. Within the known rules of the game the individual is free to pursue his personal ends and desires, certain that the powers of government will not be used deliberately to frustrate his efforts."[33] There is an interesting change of emphasis here. Whereas the Dicey formulation stresses the absence of "arbitrariness, of prerogative," and thus focuses on what the application of the regular law may *not* involve, Hayek gives us a contention about what that idea affirmatively means: rules fixed and announced beforehand that allow individuals accurately to anticipate how legal disputes in which those rules are applied will be determined. The Hayek constraint thus seems to state that to be justifiable (that is, abiding by the rule of law) judicial decision must be reducible to a form of absolutism: clear and determinate outcomes based on rules or principles knowable in advance. Yet this is just what we have been assuming liberal legal theory cannot invariably deliver.

In their fine treatment of deviational discretion, Mortimer and Sanford Kadish have remarked that the Hayek and Dicey formulations express "similar" themes.[34] However, while the two formulations have an analytical relation, it is not one of identity. The absence of arbitrary power and the existence of absolute judgments are not analytically two sides of the same coin. Minimal objectivism, the objectivity that is defined by the perspective or point of view the evaluator assumes, remains as a non-absolute alternative to arbitrariness. The existence of this alternative raises a question: Which of these formulations expresses the necessary content of a liberal rule of law ideal, the absence of arbitrariness or the existence of certainty (absolute values)?

I cannot exhaustively examine this question here, but there are sound arguments denying that the rule of law ideal within a liberal theory of law requires absolutism within the legal system itself. While undoubtedly the advance knowledge of relatively stable laws is among the chief virtues of a legal system,[35] there is no a priori reason to believe that this is such a paramount virtue of a liberal polity that all other virtues must be sacrificed in its service. In particular, *if* it is the case that the best modern liberal theory can offer is minimal objectivism, this will imply that from time to time the formulas and principles through which antagonistic interests of individuals are mediated by the positive law may change, for example as various competing interpretations of the objective point of view become enacted into law. In addition, any particular instantiation of the objective point of view may formally recognize, by making it an operative part of the system of laws the society respects, that principles must admit of exceptions not knowable in advance.[36] Either circumstance might produce decisions in particular cases that were not fairly ascertainable in advance, because the operative legal principle had changed in a way that merited a different result than predicted, even taking into account the costs to individual planning and autonomy, or because the principles applicable to that case themselves embodied the possibility of exceptions. To state the matter differently, one should not expect judges in the system to have a grasp on more absolute principles than the system can in theory generate.

Some moral or political theories must be rejected once the rule of law ideal is even minimally accepted. For instance, thoroughly intuitionistic theories are disqualified if they totally deny the propriety of generalizing or classifying relevant characteristics in advance of their occurring, for the refusal to anticipate the outcome of all but cases completely identical to previously decided ones would entirely rule out any degree of predictability. To be an acceptable liberal theory, one's theory of decision-making would have to acknowledge an appreciable degree of formalizability and generalizability on the basis of principles fairly ascertainable in advance. However, generalizability is compatible with many political theories that do not aspire to absolutism.[37]

Rejecting absolutism as the necessary content of the rule of law ideal does not render that ideal meaningless: lack of arbitrariness can be achieved by a theory adopting the objective point of view, even if it is not an absolutist theory. In fact, many American judicial decisions on the qualifications of judges identify absence of arbitrariness, and not an absolutist jurisprudence, as the touchstone. Although the principles regulating disqualification of decisionmakers are hardly well organized, they exhibit a clear refrain that a judge must continually strive to remove himself and his personal preferences and desires from the judicial decision process. Judges and administrators charged with reaching adjudicatory judgments are enjoined "to be men of conscience and intellectual discipline, capable of judging a particular controversy fairly on the basis of its own circumstances."[38] What disqualifies a decider is personal knowledge of the facts, personal attachment to one of the parties, or any other attribute that tends to increase the difficulty of stepping back from the dispute and treating it not as one involved in it, but as one observing it and attempting to resolve the conflict. Such rules of disqualification are part of the arsenal of protection against judicial tyranny, and they are quite consistent with the idea that absence of arbitrariness is something distinct from the presence of absolute values. The idea, in short, appears to be the judicial analogue of minimal objectivism achieved in part by taking the objective point of view.[39]

I do not mean to understate here the complex problems involved in giving the objective point of view a clear definition, nor the real limitations faced by anyone aspiring to it—nor, indeed, the impossibility of even conceiving of what it would mean *totally* to remove oneself from a situation. The general conception, however, seems both intelligible and instructive in the context of judicial disqualification, just as Nagel and others are attempting to make it an intelligible idea in moral philosophy. Understanding the criterion of objectivity as attached to a perspective or vantage point, rather than directly to substantive principles, frees the search for non-tyrannous judges from an unachievable absolutism in a manner consistent with at least one construction of the rule of law ideal.

D. *Liberal Questions Without Absolute Answers*

Suppose, as we have been, that one became convinced (absolutely convinced?) that absolute systems of values were not available to modern liberal theory. How would this concession affect the liberal problem of justice? It would have no effect on the assumptions of scarce resources and conflicting values, for these were not dependent upon some presupposition of absolute truths in the first place. Nor would the empirical judgment that community organization and mutual cooperation provide the opportunity to improve individual conditions be challenged, for that is a speculation about the advantages of shared enterprise, not the existence of inviolable truths. The problem of justice, in short, stands undiminished by the concession that absolute values cannot resolve it. The directions in which one searches for solutions to that problem most assuredly change if absolutism is rejected, but the removal of a fog of pretended absolutism from liberal eyes does not change the nature of the dilemma that motivated the quest for those solutions in the first place.

In a non-absolute world, expectations for solutions would have to be scaled down, as Fishkin argues. Liberal theories of law could not be made proof against judicial tyranny through the methods of analytical jurisprudence or any of its relatives. The process of reaching determinate judgments in specific cases would have to be understood as implicating judgments unknowable in advance and contestable after the fact, at least in some cases. Judges could not claim absolutist imprimatur for their results, and hence would be forced to concede that under plausible alternative assumptions or judgments, themselves well within the pale of liberal theory, the case would have come out differently. In sum, the outcome of some disputes would in some respects turn on the particular judge deciding the case.

However, liberalism does not collapse under the weight of that confession. Believing it does requires elevating the total elimination of judge-dependency to the status of an absolute objective, failure to achieve which condemns the entire enterprise.

No license exists for so viewing the problem of justice, however. This problem is better conceived as demanding the best available accommodation of the conflicting demands of individual and community. The recognition and implementation of absolute truths promised the complete elimination of judicial tyranny and hence the complete control of community force so as to protect individual autonomy. But if absolute truths do not exist, the problem of justice remains and one must search for alternative devices. One of these might well be a legal system that controls judicial domination less absolutely, through restraints that include insisting on judges' striving always to decide cases from an objective point of view. The boundary between individual and community becomes more indistinct in such a system, but no conclusion can be drawn from that observation until one inquires whether more distinct boundaries can be secured without incurring greater losses of other values important to liberalism, such as a certain kind of neutrality toward individual values, or without excessively limiting the efficacy of community enterprise and thereby sacrificing the individual gains that presumptively flow from such enterprise.[40]

The claim of liberal legal theory in a non-absolute world must therefore be that a social order incorporating the ideal of an objective point of view accommodates the conflict between community and individual in an acceptable way *given the alternatives.* Part of the defense of that claim will likely require demonstrating how such a system avoids the charge that it does no more than empower certain privileged members of society (e.g., judges) to impose their own subjective values on the rest. This commentary has not attempted that defense. It has only built on Fishkin's analysis to show that elements of a non-absolutist liberalism, one that does not collapse into subjectivity, can already be found within mainstream scholarship.

The CLS critique misses this possibility altogether. It continually supposes that the only non-subjective values are absolutist ones. In such a world view, if judicial tyranny cannot be avoided absolutely, liberal legal theory can only be subjective. Fishkin's taxonomy helps us see how this world view is mistaken. Armed with that understanding, the pursuit of liberal solutions to the problems of justice does not terminate with the acknowledgement that non-absolute solutions are the only kind we have.

3. CONCLUSION

Liberal theory is currently struggling anew with its perennial problem—the felt conflict between the individual as an entity separate from community and the advantages that joining in and recognizing the significance of community can bring to the individual. No single, stable accommodation of these opposing aspects of human existence has emerged from that struggle, and none seems foreseeable. Only a predisposition to view absolute solutions to such conflicts as the only satisfactory solutions would find in this single fact sufficient justification to abandon the struggle. Reflecting just such a view, Tushnet has suggested that "[i]f a large number of people have gone round in circles and have not come up with a theory that can gain acceptance over time, there is reason to think that the problems derive, not from deficiencies in the particular theories scholars propound, but from the enterprise itself."[41] "Acceptance" for Tushnet and others seems to require the complete domination of the liberal field by some fixed, determinate and absolute solution to the problem of justice, rather than continuing partial steps that acknowledge their non-absolute character.

More apt for the liberal problem of justice are the observations and actions of Erik Erikson, who once wrote that "[i]n every field there are a few very simple questions which are highly embarrassing because the debate which forever arises around them leads only to perpetual failure and seems consistently to make fools of the most expert."[42] Erikson made that remark at the beginning of a book-length treatment of one such question, the nature and cause of neurotic disturbance. In the end, the book offered not a solution, but only "a way of looking at things."[43] The consistency between the opening remark and the analysis that followed must lie in a recognition that some of those very simple questions do not have determinate and complete answers. Rather they invoke a way of looking at things, together with a certain humility in the knowledge that any single vision can only be partial. The problem of justice is such a question, and the objective point of view a promising vantage point from which to study it.

NOTES

1. James S. Fishkin, "Liberal Theory and the Problem of Justification," in this volume.
2. Fishkin, "Liberal Theory," p. 212.
3. Fishkin, "Liberal Theory," p. 226.
4. John Plamenatz, *On Alien Rule and Self-Government* (London: Longmans, 1960) p. 74.
5. The Conference on Critical Legal Studies was organized in 1977. Members of the group are self-avowedly committed to radical politics, many Marxist or neo-Marxist, and, while methodology and specific views differ substantially within the membership, part of their "program" can be fairly characterized as carrying on an agenda developed by the Legal Realists. This comment is not at all about CLS politics, and it leaves much of the CLS program out of account. For fuller explanations of the movement see Note, "Round and Round the Bramble Bush: From Legal Realism to Critical Legal Scholarship," *Harv.L.Rev.* 94 (1982):1669; Robert Gordon, "New Developments in Legal Theory," in *The Politics of Law: A Progressive Critique*, ed. D.Kairys (New York: Pantheon, 1982), p. 28.
6. "Minimal objectivism . . . permit[s] exceptions and [its principles] are not beyond reasonable question." Fishkin, "Liberal Theory." For the sense in which minimal objectivism is "objective" see pp. 3–4 below.
7. Fishkin, "Liberal Theory," p. 208.
8. Fishkin, "Liberal Theory," p. 210.
9. Thomas Nagel, "The Limits of Objectivity," in I *The Tanner Lectures on Human Values*, (Salt Lake City: Univ. of Utah Press, 1980), pp. 77, 77. vol. I.
10. See, e.g., Richard Schmalbeck, "The Justice of Economics: An Analysis of Wealth Maximization as a Normative Goal," *Colum.L. Rev.* 83 (1983): 488, 513.
11. Constructing such counterexamples occupies much of James S. Fishkin, *Tyranny and Legitimacy: A Critique of Political Theories* (Baltimore: Johns Hopkins University Press, 1979).
12. Fishkin, "Liberal Theory," pp. 221–22.
13. James S. Fishkin, *Beyond Subjective Morality: Ethical Reasoning and Political Philosophy* (New Haven: Yale University Press, 1984).
14. "As things are, different groups have to compete for the relatively scarce quantity of goods that are or can be made available. If this competition were unrestrained, no man could ever count on 'peaceful enjoyment of what he may acquire by his fortune and

industry.' To avoid such a calamity men have found it in their interest to subscribe to a set of conventions which establish rights to property. . . . "A.J. Ayer, *Hume* (New York: Oxford University Press, 1980), pp. 89–90.

"One can say, in brief, that the circumstances of justice obtain whenever mutually disinterested persons put forward conflicting claims to the division of social advantages under conditions of moderate scarcity." John Rawls, *A Theory of Justice* (Cambridge: Belknap Press, 1971), p. 128.

"The circumstances of justice . . . are the conditions that prevail in human societies and make human co-operation both possible and necessary. Society is seen as a co-operative venture for mutual advantage, which means that it is typically marked by a conflict as well as an identity of interests—an identity of interests in that all stand to gain from mutual co-operation, a conflict in that, given their divergent interests and ends, people differ over how the fruits of their co-operation are to be distributed." Michael Sandel, *Liberalism and the Limits of Justice* (New York: Cambridge University Press, 1982), p. 28.

15. Thomas Scanlon, "Rawls' Theory of Justice," *U.Pa.L.Rev.* 121 (1973): 1020, 1066 (emphasis omitted).

16. Mark Tushnet, "Following the Rules Laid Down: A Critique of Interpretation and Neutral Principles," *Harv. L. Rev.* 96 (1983): 781, 793.

17. Tushnet, "Following the Rules," p. 805.

18. Roberto Unger, *Knowledge and Politics* (New York: The Free Press, 1975), pp. 74–75. See also Kennedy, "Form and Substance in Private Law Adjudication," *Harv.L.Rev.* 89 (1976): 1685, 1708: "A very deep-seated idea of the judicial function is that judges apply rules . . . The object is to draw on the popular lay notion that 'discretion' and 'value judgments' are the province of the legislature, juries and private parties, while judges are concerned with techniques of legal reasoning that are neutral and ineluctable, however incomprehensible."

19. Duncan Kennedy, "The Structure of Blackstone's Commentaries," *Buff.L.Rev.* 18 (1979): 209, 214.

20. George Christie, "Objectivity in the Law," *Yale L.J.* 78 (1969): 1311, 1314.

21. Christie, "Objectivity in the Law," p. 1315.

22. Christie, "Objectivity in the Law," p. 1320.

23. Tushnet, "Following the Rules."

24. Christie, "Objectivity in the Law," p. 1333.

25. Christie, "Objectivity in the Law," p. 1334. I am not here claiming

that Christie's thesis is a kind of minimal objectivism, only that it is consistent with it and that it shares with minimal objectivism the idea that a theory can be coherently objective without being absolute.

26. William Van Alstyne, "Interpreting This Constitution: The Unhelpful Contributions of Special Theories of Judicial Review," *U.Fla.L.Rev.* 35 (1983): 209, 225.

27. See Note, "Round and Round the Bramble Bush," pp. 1669, 1684, trashing aims at "the constant demonstration of indeterminacy, incoherence and contradiction."

28. Van Alstyne, "A Graphic View of the Free Speech Clause," *Calif.L.Rev.* 70 (1982): 107, 148–49.

29. Van Alstyne, "Interpreting the Constitution," pp. 232–235.

30. Frequently one must do more than read the bare language of judicial opinions to discern the absence of absolute principles, since much "opinion writing proceeds on the principle that the judge simply finds the law and that the conclusions reached are its inelectable result." Mortimer Kadish and Sanford Kadish, *Discretion To Disobey.* (Stanford: Stanford University Press, 1973), p. 88. (This is an example of liberal theory creating its own problems by responding to the cultural urge of absolutism as if liberal theory could satisfy it.) Even so, many undeniable examples exist.

Consider, for example, current Supreme Court doctrine with respect to the mandates of the due process clause as applied to alleged deprivations by the state of a person's liberty or property. *Mathews v. Eldridge* expressed the doctrine in a form relied upon numerous times since. In determining the sufficiency of procedural protections,

> our prior decisions indicate that identification of the specific dictates of due process generally requires consideration of three distinct factors: First, the private interest that will be affected by the official action; second, the risk of an erroneous deprivation of such interest through the procedures used, and the probable value, if any, of additional or substitute procedural safeguards; and finally, the Government's interest, including the function involved and the fiscal and administrative burdens that the additional or substitute procedural requirement would entail . . . (424 U.S. 319, 334–35 [1976].

This formulation has been roundly scored for what is thought its excessively utilitarian cast, ignoring important individual interests in autonomy and dignity that bear on the due process question independently of the three-factor weighing process embraced in *Mathews*. This criticism just provides an additional example of the kind of dispute over principles and meanings that can take place within the liberal community itself. Assuming arguendo that the *Mathews* expression represents *the* correct liberal interpretation of the due process clause, this "test" patently fails to provide clear and unique decisions in particular instances. Applying the test enjoins a judge to consider three factors. While the implication plainly present is that these factors are somehow countervailing and hence to be weighed against one another in some fashion, the test is totally silent on what that fashion might be. *Mathews* provides neither an algorithm for balancing the off-setting variables nor coefficients to apply to each variable in doing so.

The indeterminacy of *Mathews* seems self-evident. It beggars belief that judges applying the test perceive what they are doing as any less undetermined. While the cast of a particular decision may have a certain hue of inevitability, the substantive doctrine being announced to support the decisions scarcely can.

31. False consciousness is, of course, one of the concepts within Critical Theory generally. For an introduction to European Critical Theory, see R. Geuss, *The Idea of a Critical Theory: Habermas and the Frankfurt School* (1981). One of the programs of Critical Theory is to dissipate false consciousness: "The aim of the project is to demonstrate to [the agents in society who are deluded about themselves] *that* they are so deluded." Geuss, p. 12 (emphasis in original). So far, the CLS critique of liberal theory has not demonstrated to liberal scholars in any significant numbers that they are deluded.

32. A. Dicey, *Introduction to the Study of the Law of the Constitution*, 10th ed. (New York, 1961), pp. 202–203.

33. F. Hayek, *The Road to Serfdom* (Chicago: University of Chicago Press, 1944), pp. 72–73.

34. M. Kadish and S. Kadish, *Discretion to Disobey*, p. 41.

35. See Joseph Raz, *The Authority of Law* (New York: Oxford University Press, 1979), pp. 225–26: "The rule of law is the specific excellence of the law . . . [and] is among the few virtues of law which are the special responsibility of the courts and the legal profession."

36. See Fishkin, "Liberal Theory."

37. Fishkin, "Liberal Theory."

38. *United States v. Morgan*, 313 U.S. 409, 421 (1941). See also Benjamin Cardozo, *The Nature of the Judicial Process* (New Haven: Yale University Press, 1921), p. 129: "[The] power . . . to shape the

law in conformity with the customary morality is something far removed from the destruction of all rules and the substitution of the individual sense of justice, the *arbitrium boni vivi.* . . . " This perhaps suggests a constraint on judicial decisionmaking beyond that of the objective point of view: decisions made from that vantage point must conform in addition to customary morality. The judge, in other words, cannot engage in thought experiments removed from an appreciation of existing social norms. The role of customary morality as a further constraint is well beyond the scope of this essay. Even assuming conformity to an objectively viewed version of customary morality were paramount, ample room for reasonable disagreements about what that customary morality is would remain. But see Ronald Dworkin, *Taking Rights Seriously* (Cambridge: Harvard University Press, 1978), pp. 81–130, introducing Judge Hercules.

39. *See* above, section on "Unsupportable Claims of Objectivity."

40. Compare J. Raz, *Authority of Law,* p. 228: "Since the rule of law is just one of the virtues the law should possess, it is to be expected that it possesses no more than prima facie force. It has always to be balanced against competing claims of other values . . . Conflict between the rule of law and other values is just what is to be expected. Conformity to the rule of law is a matter of degree . . . [and] a lesser degree of conformity is often to be preferred precisely because it helps realization of other goals."

41. Mark Tushnet, "Truth, Justice and the American Way: An Interpretation of Public Law Scholarship in the Seventies," *Tex.L.Rev.* 57 (1979): 1307, 1322.

42. Erik Erickson, *Childhood and Society,* 2d ed. (New York: Norton, 1963), p. 23.

43. Erikson, *Childhood and Society,* p. 403.

7

A NOTE ON DISCOVERY AND JUSTIFICATION IN SCIENCE AND LAW

MARTIN P. GOLDING

The purpose of this chapter is to examine the applicability of the distinction between the context of discovery (invention) and the context of justification (appraisal), a distinction that has been almost orthodox doctrine in the philosophy of science, to the issue of the "objectivity" of judicial decisionmaking.[1] Its use in this connection, as far as I know, was first suggested by Richard Wasserstrom as a response to the attack on objectivity in law espoused by such legal realists as Jerome Frank.[2] Frank sought to demythologize the judicial process, and I suspect that his attack still has adherents today.

I propose to treat this distinction in more detail than Wasserstrom and explore a few of the apparent similarities and differences that hold between discovery and justification in science and law. One implication commonly drawn from the distinction is that there is no "logic of discovery" in science. This implication, however, is rejected by some writers. A more radical view rejects the distinction itself. I therefore also want to consider the bearing of these positions on the question of judicial objectivity. A full discussion of the issue is not undertaken in this chapter, though a suggestion about it is offered at the end.

THE CONTEXTS OF DISCOVERY AND JUSTIFICATION

The distinction between the context of discovery and the context of justification appears easy to make and in fact has seemed virtually self-evident to some philosophers of science. It is frequently introduced by a standard example: the chemist Kekulé's account of how the idea of representing the molecular structure of benzene by a hexagonal ring came to him while dozing in front of his fireplace and seeing the flames dancing about in snake-like arrays. Although this biographical fact is plainly relevant to explaining how the particular hypothesis came to be proposed, it is hardly relevant to whether the idea of the benzene ring is true or scientifically acceptable. Questions of the latter sort turn, not on facts about creation, genesis, or invention, but rather on reasons and evidence. Questions about truth, acceptability, verification, confirmation, etc., belong to the context of justification.

It appears that if the notion of objectivity in science is to be preserved some such distinction has to be made. But in itself this is not enough. An "objective" account of the logical structure and force of the arguments that establish conclusions in science and of the nature of the reasons that enter into them is also needed. The logical positivists, for whose epistemology of science the distinction between discovery and justification was canonical, undertook the task of supplying such an account, i.e., a logic of justification. They held that no logical or conceptual analysis of the process of discovery or invention of laws and theories in science could be given, although they allowed that considerations drawn from the context of justification may have an influence on discovery. Discovery, however, is the province of the psychologist, historian, or sociologist; and it is in any case irrelevant to justification, of which a logical analysis can be given, albeit in idealized terms (a "rational reconstruction," as Hans Reichenbach called it).

FRANK'S DEMYTHOLOGIZATION OF OBJECTIVITY IN LAW

Since Frank's realist attack on objectivity in judicial decision runs parallel to the illustration of the genesis of the idea of the benzene ring, it is useful to turn to it before considering more complicated matters. Until now, I have used the word "objectivity" quite freely; by examining this attack we can begin to get some sense of what objectivity in law meant to realist writers who impugned it. The attack involves a description of the process of judicial decisionmaking that has a classic source, the often-

cited 1929 article by Judge Joseph C. Hutcheson, with the title
"The Judgment Intuitive: The Function of the Hunch in Judicial Decision." A judge, says Hutcheson,

> really decides by feeling and not by judgment, by hunch-
> ing and not by ratiocination, such ratiocination appearing
> only in the opinion. The vital motivating impulse for the
> decision is an intuitive sense of what is right or wrong in
> the particular case; and the astute judge, having so de-
> cided, enlists his every faculty and belabors his laggard mind,
> not only to justify that intuition to himself, but to make it
> pass muster with his critics.[3]

The hunch is characterized by Hutcheson as "that intuitive flash
of understanding that makes the jump-spark connection between question and decision. . . . " This characterization, with
a qualification to be mentioned shortly, neatly describes Kekulé's experience in front of his fireplace.

It is not entirely clear to what aspect of judicial decision that
Hutcheson's remarks are addressed. Judges may be called upon
to decide at least three kinds of questions: (1) questions of law,
(2) questions of fact, and (3) questions involving the application
of legal rules or standards to complicated or unusual fact-situations. It is in relation to the last of these question-types that
Hutcheson's account is most plausible, that the "vital motivation
impulse for the decision is an intuitive sense of what is right or
wrong in the particular case."

Hutcheson's account, nevertheless, seems to have been
understood as applying also to questions of law. Jerome Frank,
who cites Hutcheson with approval in his book *Law and the
Modern Mind* (1930), speaks quite unrestrictedly of the "dominance of the conclusion" in judicial thinking, and he sets this
account within a broader philosophical context. Frank maintains that everyone's ideas and beliefs fall into two categories:
those based upon the direct observation of objective data and
those based upon subjective factors such as personal desires and
aims or, in a word, values. The latter condition the ideas and
beliefs of judges no less than ordinary people. Frank does not
explain what he means by "the direct observation of objective
data," but he is firm in claiming that judicial decisions are in-

fected by bias and that opinion-writing is an exercise in "rationalization." (It should be added, however, that in many places Frank so qualifies his position as to negate it.) The implication of this approach is that in order to explain a given judicial decision, even on a question of law, ineliminable subjective factors must be taken into account; the biography of the judge will be an essential part of the explanation.

That subjective factors play a role in judicial decision and are essential elements in the explanation of such decisions purportedly undermines the possibility of judicial objectivity. The "fully mature judge" is merely one who is aware of his biases, but that awareness makes him no more objective than the unaware judge. For in either case the "dominance of the conclusion" prevails, and the judge's ratiocination will be directed toward justifying a conclusion that is chosen, at least in part, because of personally held values. The (false) belief in the objectivity of judicial decisionmaking is explained by Frank along "Freudian" lines, with the image of the judge as father-figure playing a central role.

If we now ask what this "objectivity" is that Frank is impugning, the answer is plain: a decision could be said to be objective if and only if (1) the judge's opinion ("rationalization") contains no statement that is both (a) necessary to the judge's argument for the decision and (b) expresses a merely personal value, and (2) the opinion supplies an accurate picture of the process whereby the judge *arrived* at his decision on the question before him. On this model, which allows for the possibility that a decision may be objective without being correct, the premises of a judge's argument are givens that presumably are present to his mind at the beginning of deliberation, and it is the judge's task merely to infer a conclusion that both follows from the givens and decides the issue (whether that issue is a question of law or involves the application of law to a determined set of facts).

It seems to be Frank's view that it is impossible to meet both of the two conditions of objectivity: an opinion that did not contain a statement expressing a personal value would not be a full account of how the decision was reached, and a full account necessarily would contain a statement that expresses a personal value. But opinions are "rationalizations" that conceal the role of personal values. (Even the rare, fully mature judge is unlikely to put forward any such statement *as* a merely personal value judgment.) Judges' opinions, therefore, give a false picture of how they arrive at their decisions.

THE RESPONSE TO FRANK

The response to Frank proceeds by rejecting the proposition that judicial decisions need to be objective in the way marked out above. In particular it denies condition (2), that an opinion has to supply a picture of how a judge arrived at his decision, any more than Kekulé had to include the biographical fact of his dozing before the fire in the account of why the benzene ring hypothesis is true or scientifically acceptable. What is misleading in Hutcheson's statement about the hunch, as applied to Kekulé, is the suggestion that the "intuitive flash of understanding" determined his decision to accept the hypothesis as *true*. The genesis of the hypothesis is not relevant to its truth— and neither is the hunching of the judge relevant to the acceptability of his decision. The distinction between the context of discovery and the context of justification should be drawn in law as it is in science.

This response supposes an analogy between decisionmaking in law and science. The objectivity of science resides in the context of justification, for the criteria of truth or acceptability (experimental testing, consistency, fertility, simplicity, scope, and so on) are independent of a scientist's personal predilections and values. Similarly, the response to Frank's demythologization locates the objectivity of judicial decision in the context of judicial justification, that is, in the "rationalizations" that judges give in support of their conclusions. The crucial question is whether the given reasons are adequate to establish the conclusions, and not whether they were the products of hunch, bias, or personal value-predisposition. Judicial decision need not adhere to the model described above. The model is in fact silly.

This response, I think, serves to blunt Frank's attack on judicial objectivity. But does it lay it to rest? Suppose Frank and his realist allies were to concede that a distinction should be made between justification and discovery, so that it is not necessary to objectivity that an opinion give a picture of how the judge arrived at a decision (condition (2) above). Still, as was mentioned earlier regarding the case of science, it is not enough to draw a distinction between the two contexts; an account of the structure and force of justification in so-called objective terms is also required, for otherwise there is not much point to the distinction. And while Frank seems to grant that such an account is possible for science, he could still deny it for the law. For won't it (often, at least) be the case that a judge's argument for a decision will have to contain a premise that expresses a value judgment, specifically the judge's personal value judgment, even though it might not be presented as such? If so, condition (1) would be violated.

The notion that judicial justification of decisions on (many) questions of law requires a value judgment of *some* kind appears, in the United States, to go back to an 1879 article "Common Carriers and the Common Law" by Justice O.W. Holmes, Jr. (Holmes was the exemplar of the "Fully mature judge" for Frank.) The growth of the law, Holmes argues, is legislative and rests upon judges' views of public policy, which consists of "considerations of what is expedient for the community."[4] This theme is returned to again in his seminal 1897 article "The Path of the Law" where he maintains that the legislative, policy grounds on which judges make decisions are concealed by the "logical form" into which judicial opinions are cast. "Behind the logical form," says Holmes, "lies a judgment as to the relative worth of competing legislative grounds, often an inarticulate and unconscious judgment, it is true, and yet the very root and nerve of the whole proceeding."[5] A full statement of the justifying reasons for decisions on (many) questions of law, therefore, would include value judgments.

If this proposition be accepted, the nature and epistemological status of these value judgments are crucial to the problem of the objectivity of judicial decision. Although the legal realists undoubtedly were influenced by Holmes, it is far from certain that they had the same thing in mind when speaking of judges' value judgments. I shall return to the status of value judgments at the end of this chapter. For the moment, let us continue our examination of the applicability to the law of the discovery–justification distinction.

The Structure of Justifications

I now want briefly to consider some possible comparisons between the structure of justifications in law and science as that structure was conceived by philosophers of science who emphasized the discovery–justification distinction and whose approach was dominant until the decline of logical positivism in recent years.[6] R.B. Braithwaite's statement is fairly representative: "A scientific system consists of a set of hypotheses which form a deductive system . . . arranged in such a way that from some of the hypotheses as premises all the other hypotheses logically follow . . . the establishment of a system as a set of true propositions depends upon the establishment of its lowest level hypotheses. . . . "[7] The method of science, therefore, is *hypothetico-deductive* (H-D). Briefly put, justification has the following structure:

(1) Suggestion of a hypothesis H, whose origin is indifferent,

(2) Deduction from H of observation statements O, which turn out to be true,

(3) Thus establishing hypothesis H.

An established hypothesis is said to explain the observation statements that support it.[8]

If the Frank-Hutcheson view of the "dominance of the conclusion" is grafted on to the discovery–justification distinction, it seems apparent that the H-D model fails as a description of judicial justification of decisions on questions of law. For here the structure (R-L) would be:

(A_1) Suggestion of a result R, whose origin is indifferent,

(A_2) Statement of propositions of law L (and perhaps also of fact F), which are correct or true,

(A_3) Inference of R from L (or L and F),

(A_4) Thus establishing R.

In light of the previous discussion, it may be necessary to add:

(A_2') Statement of propositions of value V, which are correct or true,

and revise (A_3) to read:

(A_3') Inference of R from L and V (or L, F, and V).

It seems clear that the H-D and R-L models are disanalogous. For while the (true) observation statements O function as reasons for accepting H, the legal propositions L (or L, F, and V) function as reasons for accepting R. And if L (or L, F, and V) can be said to explain R, this explanation in a sense is quite different from that in which H explains O. The warrantedness, however, of R-L structured arguments is not necessarily impugned thereby.

On the other hand, there appears to be a structural analogy between H-D and R-L when the models are used *negatively*. In the case of science:

(B_1) Suggestion of H, whose origin is indifferent,

(B_2) Deduction of O, which turns out to be false,

(B_3) Thus disconfirming H.

In the judicial case (somewhat simplified), a possible analog would be:

(C_1) Suggestion of a putative proposition of law L,

(C_2) Inference of R, which is strongly felt to be incorrect,

(C_3) Thus establishing the incorrectness of L.

Judges sometimes argue in this reductio ad absurdum way when they have to decide questions of law, i.e., decide between L and not-L.[9] Such arguments work when the inference of R from L

is deductive and there are no countervailing considerations in a case. These conditions, however, do not always obtain. In any case, a problem remains regarding R. (C_2) has been formulated so as to conform with the Frank-Hutcheson approach. But, obviously, to defend the objectivity of judicial decision more may be required here than a strong feeling of R's incorrectness; the actual incorrectness of R may be requred. (And what do "correct" and "incorrect" mean anyway? I shall have a bit to say about this large jurisprudential issue later on.)

A "Logic" of Discovery

We have been comparing judicial justification with the H-D model because the model was canonical for leading exponents of the discovery–justification distinction. It must now be mentioned that many of these philosophers admitted that the model has some difficulties. First of all, the model seems to suffer the embarrassment of committing the fallacy of affirming the consequent: it is fallacious to infer the truth of H from the conjunction of O and H implies O. To avoid this embarrassment various writers sought to develop a "logic of confirmation" or to embed the H-D model within some theory of probability. A further limitation of the model is that other factors seem relevant to the *acceptance* of scientific theories than are suggested by this simple account of the context of justification: factors such as simplicity, fertility, connectedness, etc. This does not mean that the model was abandoned; the model does emphasize the ultimate necessity of observational testing. Nor does it at all mean that the distinction between the two contexts was abandoned.

In fact, an important consequence was drawn from the distinction, namely, that no "logic of discovery is possible." No manual of procedure (such as, for instance, Mill's Methods) *guarantees* the discovery of truths.

Nevertheless, some writers still hold that there is something *like* a logic of discovery in science. Thus, Norwood Russell Hanson maintains that the process by which hypotheses are generated is amenable to a conceptual analysis.[10] And Herbert Simon argues that methodological principles for the discovery of patterns in a body of data can be formulated, and this need not await a solution to the problem of induction.[11] Although both writers admit the need for observational testing to validate hypotheses, they deny that the process of discovery is necessarily arrational. Hanson and Simon wish to go farther than those theorists who were willing to allow that considerations that are relevant to the context of justification may also have a psychological influence on the process of discovery. Hanson and Simon want to revive C.S. Peirce's view that, in addition to inductive and deductive patterns of reasoning, there is also an *abductive* pattern, in which one reasons from a problematic phenomenon to a hypothesis that explains it.[12]

These views may strengthen the response to the realist attack on the objectivity of judicial decisionmaking. For while the discovery–justification distinction itself blunts this attack, it might also be possible to claim that the process by which decisions are "hunched" is guided by analyzable, rational considerations. Analogously to the case of science, a judge reasons to a decision on the legal issue (problematic phenomenon) before him. Our discussion will concentrate on Hanson's approach.

It may strike one as interesting that both Hanson and Jerome Frank begin, in a way, at the same place. Hanson argues that philosophers of science have been too much enamored by the "Logic of the Finished Research Report," just as Frank holds that legal theorists have been too much enamored by judges' opinions. But they diverge from this point. For while Frank holds that the result is "hunched," Hanson maintains that the focus on the Finished Research Report has led philosophers to overlook the fact that scientists usually have reasons for proposing a hypothesis, for thinking that a given hypothesis is plausible and deserving of being subjected to testing. His basic contention is that it often will be reasonable to anticipate that a hypothesis will be of a certain *type*, and this supposition is not dependent on hunches, as examples from the history of science show. But the traditional H-D analysis, which sharply distinguishes the contexts of discovery and justification, is mistaken in holding that the origination of hypotheses is to be treated as a matter of indifference to the scientific enterprise. Inquiry into the grounds of plausibility, Hanson insists, is a conceptual, not a psychological inquiry. His main argument for this proposition is that, in reasoning to plausible hypotheses and in eliminating hypotheses of the wrong type, scientists draw heavily on analogies between their own problematic situation and laws or theories that have already been established. (Whether all this amounts to a logic of discovery is of no moment to us.)

The Hanson-like response to the Hutcheson-Frank notion of judicial hunching would be that judges reason to plausible decisions on questions of law and that this process is amenable to logical or conceptual analysis. (The "testing" of a proposed decision, so to speak, occurs in the "rationalization" given in the opinion, that is, in the argument that shows that the decision can be inferred from correct propositions of law.) Except, perhaps, in cases of first impression, high-level constitutional decisionmaking, and unusual fact-situations, legal issues come before a judge in a highly structured fashion, maybe more so than in science, and many of these issues are decided on the basis of analogies. Clearly, reasoning by analogy of precedent plays an important role in judicial justification and there are good grounds for supposing that analogies play a role in reasoning toward initially plausible results.

This response to the realist can in fact be strengthened. Hanson's own understanding of the reasons that establish plausibility is that they are different in *kind* from the reasons that render a hypothesis true or acceptable.[13] Now, to the extent that plausibility is established only by analogies, this may be correct; analogies do not appear to be sufficient to establish truth or acceptability in science. In the parallel judicial case, however, the reasons that establish the plausibility of a decision on a question of law are not different in kind from those that establish its acceptability. Moreover, arguments by analogy are often taken as establishing the correctness of such decisions.[14]

It seems to me that these considerations further serve to blunt Frank's demythologization of the judicial process: there is something like a "logic of discovery" in the law. If Frank's position is to stand, he will have to retreat to the contention that the problem with objectivity in the law resides in the context of judicial justification, that somewhere in the judge's argument, explicitly or implicitly, lurks a value premise. And, he would argue, these value premises express the subjective, personally held values of the judge.

The Radical Rejection of the Discovery–Justification Distinction

If Hanson and Simon reject a consequence of the discovery–justification distinction, Thomas Kuhn rejects the distinction itself. Since his position and Frank's argument against the objectivity of judicial decision are somewhat similar, a very brief discussion will be worth our while. As against the logical positivists, Kuhn denies that there can be a study of the standards for accepting or rejecting scientific theories that is completely independent from the psychological, social, or cultural factors that contribute to such acceptance or rejection. He does not deny that a good theory must have certain characteristics (accuracy, consistency, scope, simplicity, fruitfulness), but claims that they often will be insufficient to account for theory choice.[15] Thus, the abandonment of one theory in favor of another "cannot be resolved by proof."[16] The mechanism of theory choice requires talk about techniques of persuasion or about argument and counter-argument in a situation in which proof is impossible.[17] Kuhn therefore holds that the discovery–justification distinction fails to constitute even a plausible or useful idealization of the method of science.

The similarity between Frank and Kuhn is fairly obvious. Like Frank, Kuhn maintains that subjective factors, value-predispositions, are ineliminable elements of decisions to adopt a scientific theory. One can explain why particular men made particular choices at particular times, but for that, says Kuhn, one must go beyond the list of shared criteria of a good theory to "characteristics of the individuals who made the choices."[18] It seems to me that Kuhn's doubts over the discovery–justification distinction extend beyond so-called revolutionary science to normal science as well. He argues that textbooks (the "context of pedagogy") oversimplify the choices scientists make; the distinction, however, makes these choices seem unproblematic, while in fact there often are good reasons for each possible choice.

Now I am not concerned, here, to evaluate Kuhn's position, but merely to emphasize its similarity to Frank's critique of judicial objectivity.[19] I think that Frank, too, would reject the discovery–justification distinction. And the arguments of both these writers turn on the centrality of value judgments in decisionmaking, judicial and scientific. What is not entirely clear is how far Frank could admit that there may be good reasons on each side in answers to questions of law without considerably undermining his own position. For he would then be maintaining, as Kuhn claims in respect to science (appearances to the contrary), that judicial objectivity is limited, not that it is nonexistent. To me, at any rate, it seems difficult to hold this more limited thesis, in law or science, without acknowledging a distinction between the contexts of discovery and justification, though it would be a distinction of degree.

Frank and Kuhn exhibit another similarity: both hold that biography is an essential part of the explanation of decisions. It appears to me that in a sense this claim is true of the law. Since a decision, or choice of a result, is in one sense an event in a particular judge's biography, the explanation of that event will contain details of that biography, including the judge's values. To put the matter a bit differently, we might want to know the "reason why" a judge decided a question of law in a certain way, just as we may want to know why a given event—say, the collapse of a bridge—occurred. Reasons in this sense are *explanatory reasons*. A full statement of the explanatory reasons, furthermore, will have to contain much more than details of biography, for social and cultural factors (which Frank actually underplays) will be required in order to explain why the question of law came up when it did. But we may also want to know what a judge's *justifying reasons* for a decision were. If we call these an explanation of the judge's decision, they clearly constitute an explanation in a different sense of the term; and an explanation in this sense typically will not include a judge's personally held values *as* personally held values.

OBJECTIVITY, VALUES, AND SOCIAL JUSTIFICATION

Although our discussion has shown, I think, that it is possible to analyze judicial decisionmaking without necessarily postulating an "irrational" element, it is clear that the dispute with Frank turns on the status of value judgments in judicial justification, assuming that such judgments are required in complete arguments for decisions on (many) questions of law. As a conclusion to this chapter I want to suggest why the dispute should be resolved against Frank.

As we saw, both Kuhn and Frank reject the discovery–justification distinction for substantially the same reason, namely, that decisions in science and law rest on (require) value judgments. And it is for this reason that Kuhn holds that choices between theories cannot be resolved by proof and that the mechanism of theory acceptance by the scientific community is dependent on persuasion and rhetoric, which presumably is not amenable to logical analysis. I suspect that Kuhn holds to a subjectivistic metaethical theory according to which value judgments cannot be said to be true or false. But even if (as I believe) such a theory is wrong, no difficulty is presented for Kuhn because value judgments, he could maintain, are in any case extra-scientific. Making the necessary changes, Frank holds comparable views with respect to the law, except that his position is not that judicial value judgments are extra-legal (as Holmes held); it is more explicitly subjectivistic. As has been repeatedly emphasized, according to Frank judicial value judgments, whether explicit or not, are expressions of personal values. This notion, however, is ambiguous, and that a value is personal does not mean that it is also not widely held by others. Assuming that value judgments are components of judicial opinions, this point has great importance because judicial justification is a form of social justification.[20]

I can best put my point by mentioning a criticism commonly made of Kuhn, namely, that Kuhn rejects the discovery–justification distinction because he confuses the context of justification with the "context of acceptance." That is, he confuses the justification, truth, or acceptability of a theory with what it takes to get the theory accepted by others; "true" does not mean "accepted." Whatever the validity of this criticism, I think that the soundness of judicial justifications of decisions on questions of law should not be sharply distinguished from what *socially* passes for acceptable legal arguments, and the correctness of propositions of law is, in part, determined by whether sound legal justifications can be given for them.

Earlier I referred to, but did not discuss, Herbert Simon's claim that there is something like a logic of discovery in science. The nub of his argument is useful here. Simon holds that norms of discovery can be derived from the goals of scientific activity. Whether or not this is right, I think it can be argued that norms of justification can be derived from the goals of the judicial process. One of these goals is the resolution of disputed questions by law by means of *reasoned* decisions on such questions. Conclusions of law, therefore, have to be supported by justifying reasons. But judicial justification is not justification in the abstract. Rather, it is a process in which the judge is attempting to justify his decision to the losing party, to other persons who may be affected by the result, and to the legal community at large. The reasons for the conclusion must therefore be acceptable to this group as legitimate grounds of decision. That judicial justification has a social component does not have the extreme relativistic consequences that it may have in other justification situations. (In law, of course, a justification is also relative to the system for which it is supposed to hold.) If values enter into a judicial justification, they do not do so as personal predilections.[21] The values must have some purchase on the community to which they are addressed. Although these considerations do not supply a way of demonstrating that a given justifying reason is a good legal reason, they suggest the lines along which the objectivity of judicial decision may be defended.

NOTES

1. The "discovery–justification" terminology goes back to Hans Reichenbach, *Experience and Prediction* (Chicago: University of Chicago Press, 1938). The term "discovery" is misleading and some recent writers use "invention–appraisal." See Wesley C. Salmon, "Carl G. Hempel on the Rationality of Science," *Journal of Philosophy* 80 (1983): 555. For a survey of the literature and a defense of the distinction, see Carl R. Kordig, "Discovery and Justification," *Philosophy of Science* 45 (1978): 110–117; Harvey Siegel, "Justification, Discovery and the Naturalization of Epistemology," *Philosophy of Science* 47 (1980): 297–321.

2. Jerome Frank, *Law and the Modern Mind* (Garden City, N.Y.: Anchor Books, 1963; original ed., 1930). Richard Wasserstrom, *The Judicial Decision* (Stanford: Stanford University Press, 1961), pp. 25–

31. I have followed Wasserstrom in Martin P. Golding, *Legal Reasoning* (New York: Knopf, 1984), pp. 2–10.

3. *Cornell Law Quarterly* 14 (1928–29): 278. A comparison with Ronald Dworkin's notion of "discretion as judgment" would be interesting but out of place here. See Dworkin, *Taking Rights Seriously,* rev. ed., (Cambridge: Harvard University Press, 1978), pp. 31–39.

4. *American Law Rev.* 13 (1879): 630.

5. *Harvard Law Rev.* 10 (1897): 466.

6. The discussion that follows in this section is a partial treatment of the subject. Many philosophers of science today lean toward a "coherence" account of justification. For a good treatment of coherence justifications in science and law, with emphasis on Ronald Dworkin's views, see Marsha Hanen, "Justification as Coherence," in *Law, Morality and Rights,* ed. M.A. Stewart (Dordrecht, Holland: D. Reidel, 1983), pp. 67–91.

7. *Scientific Explanation* (Cambridge: Cambridge University Press, 1955), pp. 12–13.

8. Various restrictions have to be placed on *H*. It must be relevant, testable, not ad hoc, etc. We cannot go into the subject here.

9. See, e.g., *Lubitz v. Wells,* 19 Conn. Supp. 322, 113 A.2d 147 (1955).

10. "Is there a Logic of Discovery?," in *Current Issues in the Philosophy of Science,* eds. H. Feigl and G. Maxwell (New York: Holt, Rinehart and Winston, 1961) pp. 20–34; and see Paul K. Feyerabend's comments on Hanson, ibid., pp. 35–39; and Hanson's rejoinder, ibid., pp. 40–42.

11. "Does Scientific Discovery Have a Logic?" *Philosophy of Science* 40 (1973): 471–80.

12. See the selection from Peirce's *Collected Papers* in *Pragmatic Philosophy,* ed. A. Rorty (Garden City, N.Y.: Anchor Books, 1966), pp. 90–100.

13. For a criticism of Hanson, see Kordig, "Discovery and Justification."

14. For an analysis and defense, see Golding, *Legal Reasonings.*

15. "Objectivity, Value Judgment, and Theory Choice," in the collection of his papers, *The Essential Tension* (Chicago: University of Chicago Press, 1977), p. 322.

16. *The Structure of Scientific Revolutions,* 2nd ed., (Chicago: University of Chicago Press, 1970), p. 148.

17. Kuhn, *Structure of Scientific Revolutions,* p. 151ff.

18. Kuhn, "Objectivity, Value Judgment, and Theory Choice," p. 324.

19. For a good discussion of Huhn, see Siegel, "Justification, Discovery and the Naturalization of Epistemology." The literature on Kuhn is enormous.

20. For the view that the whole issue of objectivity in moral and legal argument is "a kind of fake," see Ronald Dworkin's essay in *The Politics of Interpretation,* ed. W.J.T. Mitchell, (Chicago: University of Chicago Press, 1983), especially pp. 297–303.

21. Judges also decide cases against their personal value-predilections. Holmes is a good example. Writing to Sir Frederick Pollock in 1910, Holmes states: "Of course I enforce whatever constitutional laws Congress or anybody else sees fit to pass—and I do it in good faith to the best of my ability—but I don't disguise my belief that the Sherman Act is a humbug based upon economic ignorance and incompetence." In *Holmes–Pollock Letters* ed. M.D. Howe, 2nd ed. (Cambridge: Harvard University Press, 1961), vol. 1, p. 163.

8

RATIONALITY AND CONSTRAINTS ON DEMOCRATIC RULE

JEFFRIE G. MURPHY

INTRODUCTION

There are various reasons why one might prefer democratic rule over alternative institutions.[1] One might believe it is the most rational way to maximize preference satisfaction, or that it does the best job of giving persons the socially beneficial illusion that preference satisfaction is being maximized, or that it is the fairest way to make collective social decisions, or that it gives persons the socially beneficial illusion of being the fairest, or that it is—though highly defective on grounds of both utility and fairness—still less defective than any alternative mechanism, or that certain societies are simply used to it and any radical change would be disruptive, or some combination of all of these considerations.

Whatever one's grounds for advocating democracy as a political institution, one might well want to place some constraints on it—constraints that will make it difficult or sometimes even nearly impossible for the majority or its elected representatives to act in certain ways—no matter how strong or widely held the preferences for so doing. Such constraints will typically involve matters of both procedure and substance; and one might desire them for two different sorts of reason: (1) the belief that whatever one most expected from democracy (e.g., preference maximization) will be better realized in the long run by inhibiting what the majority can do in the short run or (2) the belief that certain values that deserve protection cannot be analyzed in terms of the values served by democracy (e.g., cannot be analyzed in terms of preference satisfaction) and thus must be defended on separate grounds.

Certain *rights* (especially some that have been designated by the United States Supreme Court as "fundamental") are often taken—e.g., by Ronald Dworkin—to be values of the latter sort.[2] Dworkin thinks of our basic constitutional rights as embodying a value so sacred that it must be protected against the dangers of democratic rule—the potential "tyranny of the majority" of which John Stuart Mill wrote. The basic value in Dworkin's account is the equal concern and respect owed to a person simply because he or she is a person; according to Dworkin, this respect is not insured simply by guaranteeing that each person is equally consulted (has an equal vote, or a fair contribution to the decision procedures of society) but also requires certain substantive protections—e.g., that a person not be disadvantaged simply because of contempt that the majority might feel for his or her race. Persons who are disadvantaged because of racial contempt still have a fundamental complaint against their society even if they had an equal opportunity to vote (and presumably voted against) the policy or law that puts them at this disadvantage. They would not have such a complaint, however, where fundamental rights were not involved, for there majority preference may legitimately be allowed to have its sway. An underlying assumption of this line of thought seems to be that citizens and legislators are incapable of engaging in sustained and motivating moral thought and discourse, but that courts can. This assumption must be one reason why Dworkin discusses principles only in the context of judicial decisionmaking, suggesting that legislators merely add up interests and preferences. One is reminded of Bickel's notion that judges are "teachers in a vital national seminar" on values.[3]

The topic that interests me is the following: To what degree, if at all, is it possible to give a rational, i.e., coherent, account of the concept of fundamental rights, in both moral and constitutional terms, and to what degree, if at all, might one rationally defend a political theory in which the protection of these rights is rated lexically prior to (serves as a side-constraint on) the realization of majoritarian preference? Some writers, e.g., Dworkin, Laurence Tribe and John Rawls,[4] claim that it is possible to articulate and defend a rational theory of fundamental rights, but other writers, e.g., Alasdair MacIntyre, John Hart Ely, and Paul Brest,[5] are highly skeptical, arguing that what is claimed to be a systematic theory is really an incoherent bundle of personal intuitions and bygone social conventions. The idea that philosophers can construct rational theories of anything, even science, is being increasingly held up to skeptical ridicule—e.g., note the influence of the work of Richard Rorty in metaphysics, Thomas Kuhn in the philosophy of science, and Alasdair MacIntrye in ethics[6]—and the philosophy of law is no longer insulated from this skepticism. Here I explore these doubts about fundamental rights as providing a rationally defensible moral and constitutional theory of democratic limitation. Is it indeed a genuine theory, or at least a start toward one, or does it, as Paul Brest argues, merely rationalize issues that are "essentially incoherent and unresolvable"?[7]

Fundamental rights analysis, though now sometimes applied to substantive matters (e.g., privacy and Eighth Amendment adjudication), got its start in procedural matters of due process and equal protection.[8] I shall thus begin with these matters.

Justifying Departures from Equal Treatment

The injunction that we should "treat like cases alike" is often put forth as a fundamental principle of justice and rationality. Procedural justice seems to require this treatment, at least in a great many cases, in order that institutionally encouraged expectations will not be thwarted, one possible reason behind the moral power of legal precedents. Retributive justice would seem to require this kind of treatment also, for how can a system of punishment give to each his or her just deserts if equally deserving persons are treated differently? So too for any other kind of justice where the idea of "equal protection of the laws" has application. Basic to the arguments from justice, however, may be an even deeper idea that it is simply *irrational* not to treat like cases alike. Leibniz's Principle of Sufficient Reason, very likely a part of any acceptable theory of rationality, may informally be put this way: Given two objects or persons or states of affairs

A and *B,* a rational being will not prefer *A* over *B* unless that being can find some relevant property or attribute possessed by *A* but not by *B* that justifies, is the sufficient reason for, the preference.

Once one gets beyond intuitions and slogans, however, the principle "treat like cases alike" is plagued with many problems. For example: (1) What makes two cases alike in relevant respects? We need, of course, a theory of relevance; and it may be very difficult to articulate one that does not beg the very questions we hoped to illuminate with the principle.[9] (2) When we realize that our previous decisions involved error, were even substantially unjust, are we bound, even prima facie, to continue in our pattern of error?[10] Of course there is now a difference, namely, that we have changed our moral, or legal, attitude. But this is not a difference *in* the cases—not a difference that makes *them* unlike. It is more a difference in *us*. (3) In some contexts, is it not sometimes both just (not unjust) and rational (not irrational) to prefer one object or person over a relevantly similar one? If it is correct that nobody has a right to be saved by me, that my saving someone is supererogatory on my part, then may I not permissibly save drowning Jones but not save equally drowning Smith simply because I *like* Jones better than Smith? If one says that my likings can themselves constitute a part of the relevant differences between the two situations, the door is open to real problems. How can the Principle of Sufficient Reason be a test of the rationality of my preference between *A* and *B* if my preference can itself count as a relevant difference?

In spite of these problems, let us suppose for a moment that there is a class of cases where we know reasonably well what the principle "treat like cases alike" means and where the principle is properly regarded as morally and legally binding. The question I wish briefly to explore is this: In the cases where the principle "treat like cases alike" clearly is prima facie binding, under what circumstances may it legitimately be overridden? Human social and legal practices are not precision instruments, and some of them will inevitably treat like cases differently. When is this outcome tolerable and when is it intolerable? Given space limitations, I cannot possibly develop an adequately detailed theory on this issue in the present context. I can at least, however, indicate the kinds of philosophical questions that ought to be asked and give some hint of how one might start to answer these questions. I will limit myself to a legal context and raise this question: Under what circumstances might a *state* action be permissible even if it results in like cases receiving different treatment?

The prevailing doctrine in U.S. constitutional law is that these outcomes are tolerable in the vast majority of cases. Consider Justice Stewart's remarks in the 1970 case of *Dandridge v. Williams:*

> In the area of economics and social welfare, a State does not violate the Equal Protection Clause merely because the classification made by its laws are imperfect, if the classification has some "reasonable basis." It does not offend the Constitution simply because the classification "is not made with mathematical nicety or because in practice it results in some inequality." The problems of government are practical ones and may justify, if they do not require, rough accommodation—"illogical, it may be, unscientific." A statutory discrimination will not be set aside if any state of facts reasonably may be conceived to justify it. (397 U.S. 471)

The standard here being articulated by Justice Stewart is often called the "rational basis test," though it would be better named the "not irrational basis test," and the level of judicial review involved is often called "minimal scrutiny." The standard, applied in the vast majority of cases where equal protection objections are raised, is this: State action, even if it results in inequality, will pass judicial review if it serves a purpose that could be regarded as rational. This is clearly a very weak test, since it should be possible to think of some plausible reason in defense of all but the most silly state actions.

If the principle "treat like cases alike" is really so basic to both justice and rationality, how can such a weak standard be used in defense of that principle—a standard that allows frequent departures from the principle? At least three kinds of consideration might be relevant here: (1) The inequality of treatment might result from a social practice, e.g., wide administrative or judicial discretion in certain areas of law, that is judged to be of greater social value than is strict equality of outcome. Juvenile sentencing often results in like cases being treated differently, but this is often defended by the argument (perhaps unsound) that the paternalistic function of juvenile courts would not properly be served unless judges in juvenile cases have wide discretion.[11] (2) Requiring agencies to develop standards or procedures that would guarantee the elimination of unequal outcomes might be more costly that it would be worth. This could place a crippling burden on the state. Economic efficiency often requires that some matters, e.g., the setting of automobile insurance rates, be done in actuarial terms, e.g., a function in part of such statistically significant factors as age and sex; this makes it certain that some persons who are actually safe drivers will pay a premium as high as careless drivers. Since care in driving seems to be the relevant attribute, the safe-driving young male will no doubt resent as unjust that he pays rates higher than a younger female or older male who is no more careful, perhaps even less, than he is. But if insurance companies were required to bear the high cost of investigating and individuating so to avoid this unequal outcome, the cost of automobile insurance for everyone would very likely be absurdly high. A great many state policies are necessarily and properly based upon actuarial calculation. (3) It may be judged that certain rights are worthy of protection even if their exercise will produce inequality. "Grandfather clauses" might be so defended. That I have been allowed to do something for a very long time, e.g., sell my wares on the city streets, may earn me the right to continue doing this even if no other persons will be allowed to do so.[12]

These arguments, at least the first two, might appear to be mere appeals to utility, but the story is actually a bit more complex. If it could be shown, as it probably could be in the insurance case, that even the persons paying the higher premium are better off than they would be under a practice that eliminated this inequality, then these persons are in no obvious sense being exploited for the general welfare. So it is by no means clear that they experience, at least ultimately, any injustice. They are winners too, and they might well have rationally willed this inequality-producing actuarial practice in something like a Rawlsian original position.

Let us suppose that it is justified to override the demand for equal treatment in cases like these. Why not allow an override in all cases? Why should courts ever use any standard other than minimal scrutiny and the rational basis test that this involves?

The hornbook answer is: The rational basis test is perfectly appropriate when matters of only "economics and social welfare" are involved. Sometimes, however, something of considerably greater importance is thought to be at stake, namely, the *fundamental rights* of citizens. Rights that have been identified by the courts as fundamental include enumerated rights such as freedom of speech, press and religion and such "penumbral" rights as privacy. When these rights are encumbered or when special burdens are placed on members of "suspect classifications," e.g., racial minorities, "strict judicial scrutiny" is triggered. This involves the "compelling state interest/least restrictive alternative" test: State action will pass constitutional review only if the encumbrance of the right is justified by a *compelling* or *overriding*, not merely rational or legitimate, state interest and if the encumbrance is actually necessary to promote that interest. This would seem to be a very tough test to pass, a test that in many ways seems to incorporate a liberal or libertarian view on rights, liberty, and state coercion. Expanded beyond equal protection analysis to do some work in "substantive due process," the test looks as though it could be a very powerful tool indeed to check government intrusions into the basic rights and liberties of citizens.[13]

But is it? One cannot answer this big question, of course, until one gets beyond the edifying slogans and answers two basic philosophical questions: (1) What does it mean to say and how does one support the claim that some rights are *fundamental* and others not? (Why do economic rights not currently enjoy this status? Is this just a matter of shifting opinion and ideology? If so, what is interestingly fundamental about rights so grounded?) (2) What does it mean and how does one support the claim that a particular state interest is *compelling* and not merely rational or legitimate or permissible? Here I can only attempt to raise the central issues and give some indication of how I think discussion ought to proceed.

FUNDAMENTAL RIGHTS ANALYSIS: INTUITION, CONVENTION, OR RATIONAL THEORY?

As I have argued elsewhere,[14] rights may be understood as having three different sorts of foundation: as serving social utility (happiness or preference maximization), as being instrumental to the healthy workings of political institutions that are justified on other grounds; or as based upon the respect each person is owed as a person. I have argued that the right of a policeman, but nobody else, to carry a concealed weapon is essentially a right of the first sort; that freedom of the press, where this involves more than freedom of speech, is essentially a right of the second sort; and that freedom of speech, freedom of religion, and privacy are essentially rights of the third sort. The same right can, of course, be defended on more than one of these grounds; my classification is simply an attempt to emphasize the support that I take to be dominant in each case.

The philosophically most interesting rights that may be regarded as fundamental are those of the third kind, i.e., respect-based rights. Rights based on mere social utility appear to lack any consitutional status. If rights are supposed to function to constrain majoritarian preference, how could they themselves be analyzed in terms of majoritarian preference? And rights defended as instrumental to the health of political institutions will seem important only to the degree that we know why the institutions are themselves important. One intuitively plausible answer to this question, of course, is simply this: Certain political and legal institutions are important because they enshrine and protect the value of respect for persons and the rights that grow out of respect. A similar point could also be made to show that the values of utility are derivative from respect for persons. For it seems plausible to argue that the happiness of persons matters only because persons matter—surely not the other way around. If people do not matter, why should satisfying their preferences matter?

This kind of rhetoric is inspiring and in our society has a venerable institutional history—approximately from Thomas Jefferson through Earl Warren. Those who describe Ronald Dworkin as doing a systematic philosophical reconstruction of the thinking of the Warren court strike me as not totally off base. The philosophical problem, of course, is: Is this talk just rhetoric or can it be turned into a coherent and rationally defensible theory of morality, the United States Consitution (at least part of the Bill of Rights), and the links between those two?

Some powerful considerations are initially inclined to make one skeptical about the possibility of developing a rational theory of fundamental rights. Most generally, we might first ask this question: What would a rational theory of values be and what would count for adequacy of such a theory?

Typically there are two ways of conceptualizing theory construction for ethics: (1) deductive-foundationalist models proceeding from axioms taken to be noncontroversial, e.g., Rawls's "original position," a social contract/hypothetical consent model, or (2) coherence models systematically connecting pretheoretical intuitions or judgments that are taken to be noncontroversial, e.g., Rawls's "reflective equilibrium."[15]

Each approach has serious problems. The deductive approach will suffer if it is impossible to find noncontroversial axioms or if the deductions from those axioms can be made to work only with the introduction of artificial devices. Both problems plauge Rawls. His starting points, e.g., the priority of liberty as a value, are controversial, as are some of the devices employed to make the argument go, e.g., the assumption that rational persons will necessarily adopt a maximin strategy. Indeed, some of the devices, e.g., the veil of ignorance, may seem quite ad hoc, serving mainly to guarantee the desired result, e.g., unanimity of decision or egalitarianism over elitism. Thus a deductive model seems highly unlikely to work.[16] Even if it did work in moral theory, however, there would still be the problem of explaining how it deserves priority in constitutional analysis, i.e., why assume that a moral theory judged to be rational or correct on deductive grounds is also to be found embedded in the Constitution? What a piece of incredible luck if that should turn out true. The more likely story is illustrated in a remark by Dean Harry Wellington: "The Fourteenth Amendment, as Holmes has said, does 'not enact Mr. Herbert Spencer's *Social Statics*.' Nor does it enact Mr. John Rawls's *A Theory of Justice*."[17]

What about reflective equilibrium or some analogous coherence test? This would at least have the virtue of making a connection between moral and constitutional theory more likely, because it might be expected that what "we" would find satisfying in pure moral analysis would overlap to a large degree what "we" would find satisfying as an interpretation of the moral content of the Constitution. (Both sets of intuitions have similar and overlapping causal histories.) Thus, not suprisingly, Ronald Dworkin, who wants to break down the legal positivist's sharp law/morality distinction, develops his own legal and moral theories in terms of a coherence model, arguing that judges should adopt the assignment of rights that is required by the most coherent theory of the body of law in question.

Coherence criteria of course, also face some serious problems. Consider, for example, the Rawlsian device of reflective equilibrium. It is likely that the deeply felt pretheoretical intuitions or convictions of even one person form a highly inconsistent set, having, as they do, radically different origins (biological, cultural, religious, idiosyncratic, or learned, as C. D. Broad said, at our mother's knee or some other joint). Moving from the individual to the level of a whole culture or society, particularly one as highly pluralistic as ours is often said to be, one might genuinely despair of ultimate coherence or agreement about values. Alasdair MacIntyre, criticizing Dworkin's reliance on coherence, writes as follows:

> Moral philosophy, as it is dominantly understood, reflects the debates and disagreements of the culture so faithfully that its controversies turn out to be unsettlable in just the way that the political and moral debates themselves are. . . . Important conclusions follow for constitutional theory. Liberal writers such as Ronald Dworkin invite us to see the Supreme Court's function as that of invoking a set of consistent principles, most and perhaps all of them of moral import, in the light of which particular laws and particular decisions are to be evaluated. [Dworkin suggests that we should view the *Bakke* case in this way, criticizes the court for the degree to which it politicized the decision rather than making it one of pure and consistent principle, and attempts to articulate the principles the court should have used.] But even to make such an attempt is to miss the point. The Supreme Court in *Bakke,* as on occasion in other cases,

played the role of a peacekeeping or trucekeeping body by negotiating its way through an impasse of conflict, not by invoking our shared moral first principles. For our society as a whole has none.[18]

MacIntyre does not, however, limit himself to criticism. He is also a man positively consumed with historical nostalgia who longs for his vision of the good old days (really old—Aristotle and the Middle Ages) when there was, so he claims, little value pluralism and thus a reasonably coherent evaluative outlook to which one could appeal. Reflective equilibrium really was possible. But nostalgia, in terms of a theory of rationality, is of course misplaced. Unless one has independent reasons for thinking that a society's shared intuitions are correct, then one is hardly going to be overly impressed by a theory that makes them systematic and coherent. Would the critic of Nazism be converted by learning that the ideology is coherent? Would the defender of a justice model for tort litigation be converted by being shown that this body of law could be organized around the concept of economic efficiency? Indeed, coherence of intuitions might make one worry that any fundamentally unsatisfactory features of the moral view involved would be overlooked. For where, internally, will the skeptical challenges to it come from? Aristotle, remember, felt in reflective equilibrium with a set of values that approved slavery and sexism. Reflective equilibrium analysis is in many ways a moral version of ordinary language philosophy and is open to some of the same objections, one of the major ones being: How do we, without begging any questions, identify the relevant linguistic sample from which to take polls on what "we" would ordinarily say, or intuitively prefer, on some matter? A coherence model of rationality is thus almost certain to incorporate certain biases—biases that will be present, but unnoticed, when everyone agrees, but will be dramatic when there is lack of agreement. Ely puts the point in this way: "The list of values the Court and the commentators have tended to enshrine as fundamental . . . [includes] expression, association, education, academic freedom, the privacy of the home, personal autonomy. . . . But watch most fundamental rights theorists start edging toward the door when someone mentions jobs, food, or housing: these are important, sure, but they aren't *fundamental*."[19]

Coherence alone is no test of rationality of a system of values; we also need to know that the values themselves are valid. We need something in morality and law comparable to the distinction between a coherent but still *fictional* story or paranoid delusion and a coherent and also *correct* account of the way things really are. But if we have some way of finding out what is correct on such evaluative matters independently of the coherence account, why bother with the coherence account at all? At most coherence can be a necessary condition for the adequacy of moral theory, not a sufficient condition. This worry also applies, as Nietzsche and Kant both noticed, to "transcendental" arguments in support of moral first principles, e.g., arguments that claim that we must accept some principle P because it is presupposed for the intelligibility of some accepted system of values S. Unless we have independent grounds for thinking S is a system worthy of acceptance, which we will not have if we think that S is simply sublimated resentment, bourgeois rationalization for class oppression, leftovers from our evolutionary history, and the like, then we will not find this a good reason for embracing P. Nor will P help in the rational justification of S.

Let me develop these worries in the context of judicial review. Suppose the court, in attempting to decide what constitutes "cruel and unusual punishment," protection against which is surely established by the Eighth Amendment as a fundamental right, wants coherence. Will it find it in the shared values of the society? If MacIntyre is correct, there are none. But suppose there are. What better way of finding them out than by looking to what legislators enact? But on what meaningful theory of constitutional review can it be the case that basic rights are to be interpreted in terms of majoritarian preference or legislative enactment? If any punishment approved by the legislator or reflecting majority preference ceases to be cruel and unusual for just that reason, in what sense does the Eighth Amendment constrain the majority? If not everyone's values are relevant to evaluative coherence, whose then are? Justices Warren and Marshall, opposing capital punishment, favored a consensus of the moral elite, the "morally mature," arguing that the clause must "draw its meaning from the evolving standards of decency that mark the progress of a mature society." But how does one tell who is the mature elite? Not those approving of capital punishment apparently, and thus the question is pretty obviously being begged. Adapting the discussion in Plato's *Euthyphro*, we might want to argue in this way: the good is not good because the elite love it, rather the elite love it because it is good. What is it about the good that makes the elite love it? If we know that we shall have the kind of insight that the elite has and will be one of them, and we will not have to care about consensus or coherence. Appeal to these considerations is either irrational or redundant.[20]

To summarize. We might initially be charmed by the following kind of attempt to justify fundamental rights analysis: Fundamental rights are those rights that would be identified as such in terms of the principles of a correct moral theory, where "correct moral theory" is understood to be a theory rationally justified in terms of either a deductive-fundationalist model or a coherence model. Given the problems raised for each model, however, the charms of fundamental rights analysis might now be seen as beginning to fade.

What Is a Compelling State Interest?

Let us suppose for a moment that we could develop a satisfactory analysis and defense of the concept of fundamental rights, rights to be overridden only if necessary, i.e., the least restrictive or intrusive means, for the realization of a compelling state interest. Problems would still remain, for we would still need rational theories on these matters as well: What makes one action more intrusive or restrictive than another? What makes one state interest rationally compelling and another only rationally permissible or legitimate? These questions will be difficult to answer in a nonarbitrary way for reasons analogous to those already noted above in the discussion of fundamental rights. For example: Is not an uncritical bias built into the common liberal assumption that incarceration is more intrusive or restrictive than a fine? Might this not really depend upon what you have more of—time or money?

And what makes a state interest compelling or overriding? When one considers the interests that have actually been identified as compelling by the Supreme Court, one might well wonder whether this is merely a laundry list or whether any coherent moral, political, and legal theory binds all these interests together in a rationally defensible way.[21] Without such a theory, of course, the compelling state interest test will hardly count as an important frame in which to structure our thinking about state intrusions into fundamental rights. Mere judicial intuition ("sure seems compelling to me!") will hardly do the job, for the doctrine needs to be a doctrine about what judges *should* value, not about what they do in fact value. Neither can the values or preferences of a democratic majority function to explicate the doctrine—i.e., a compelling state interest cannot be understood simply as a state of affairs deeply desired by a majority of citizens. A strict standard of judicial scrutiny is supposed to protect fundamental rights against majoritarian preference, a job it certainly cannot perform if it is itself interpreted in terms of majoritarian preference. Where then do we go for analysis of this concept?

One temptation is to analyze the concept of compelling state interest in terms of some of the traditional concepts of liberal social and political philosophy, the tradition that generated the whole idea of fundamental rights as a foundation for the legal and political order. Consider, for example, the idea of a social contract model for rational social choice. If a group of persons living in competitive proximity to each other did not have a state or government what good reasons might they have for *forming* one and accepting the resulting curtailments of liberty that this would entail, i.e., what reasons might they find "compelling" in reluctantly making this choice? Using Robert Nozick's metaphor, we might also consider the matter in this way: If we think of the state as an agency that we might *hire*, at a cost in both money and liberty, to do a certain job, how would we write the job description?[22] What would be worth the price? These questions suggest one possible theoretical answer to the question of how the concept of a compelling state interest might be analyzed: A state interest is to be viewed as compelling if and only if it is one of the interests or goals that one can properly imagine rational persons forming a government to achieve.

The difficulties with this, of course, are obvious, precisely the ones previously raised against the Rawlsian machinery of the original position. One with a libertarian bias will surely define "rational person" in such a way that these persons will tolerate government only to prevent force, theft, and fraud. These, mandating limited national defense and police power, will be the only compelling interests. This person might also see certain economic liberties to be just as fundamental as, perhaps even more fundamental than, such liberal favorites as sexual privacy, and thus will not view *Lochner v. New York* to be quite the abomination that most others take it to be.[23] Welfare-state liberals will add such matters as poverty relief, health, and education to their list of compelling interests. Marxists will have an even longer list. Disagreement by itself, of course, proves nothing. But it does leave a troubling question: Is there any rational way to resolve such disagreement that does not presuppose the very result it would seek to justify? If you impose a thick and carefully designed veil of ignorance, then you can, of course, get whatever hypothetical agreement you want. But, for reasons already noted, these agreements are doubtful models of rational choice. Why is it now rational for me to act contrary to what I now know simply because I might have agreed to act in that way before I knew? The only way to answer this question is to make sure that the grounds for imposing the ignorance in the model beg no questions. I might, in constructing my theory, accept ignorance of any fact that is "morally arbitrary." But how can I have a rational belief about what is morally arbitrary prior to the theory?

Our original question—Fundamental Rights Analysis: Intuition, Convention, or Rational Theory?—now looks as though it might merit this answer: yes, yes, no. How disquieting would this answer be?

If Fundamental Rights Analysis Fails, What Are the Consequences for Judicial Review?

One might think that if fundamental rights analysis fails, nothing is left for judges to do except constrain democracy solely by the literal meaning or what is actually written in the Constitution. Raoul Berger argues that, because of linguistic vagueness, this literal reading approach often will not work, but that something equally restrictive of judicial review is available in such cases, namely, a knowledge of what the framers *strictly intended* by the language, a knowledge of how the framers would have decided a case arising under the enactment at the time of enactment.[24] But Berger's approach will not work either because, as Paul Brest has pointed out, it confuses the framer's "intentions with their mere personal *views.*"[25] Perhaps they sought to protect some value but, because of factual ignorance or prejudice, failed to see how that value might be compromised in certain situations. What is worthy of allegiance—their values or their factual ignorance? Strict intentionalism would seem to suggest the latter. Also, it is possible that the framers themselves had interpretive intentions. And perhaps these intentions were inconsistent with Berger's own strict intentionalist theory, for perhaps they wanted their provisions read in terms of of some rather general and open-ended set of purposes and values. And how could we really tell anyway? Strict intentionalism "pretends to constrain constitutional decisionmaking while inviting, if not demanding, arbitrary manipulation of sources and outcomes."[26]

Thus some kind of meaningful interpretive activity on the part of the judiciary is clearly going to be necessary; and, if fundamental rights analysis fails, in what will this activity reasonably consist?

One might, of course, attempt to salvage some notion of fundamental rights from the previous criticisms by severing the connection between legal rights and moral rights so favored by Dworkin and other natural law theorists. Fundamental *moral* rights are rights that are defensible in terms of a true moral theory; and so to the degree we doubt that there can be a correct moral theory, then to that same degree will we doubt fundamental moral rights and will see their constitutional enforcement as simply the judicial legislation of personal prejudice. But consider fundamental *political* rights defined in this way: rights presupposed for the working of our particular political system, for the working of what the Court has called "our system of ordered liberty." This kind of theory, found in the writings of Alexander Meiklejohn, John Hart Ely, and others, does not involve an attempt to establish the moral preferability of our political system or the rights it establishes, but rather argues in this way: We have, as a matter of fact, a certain kind of political system, e.g., a representative system that seeks to afford everyone participation, and the job of the judiciary is to make sure that individuals are accorded the rights that insure the participation and the maintenance of the system.[27] For example: If there is a "penumbral" right to privacy, this will be a right to the kind of privacy presupposed by the political system that seeks, in furtherance of political association and discussion, to protect personal papers and meetings in homes and thus prohibits "unreasonable searches and seizures." This kind of view would be silent on things like abortion as a privacy right, however, for that kind of right would have to grow out of a controversial moral theory, privacy and control of one's body being understood as a part of one's self-respect, and would lack a significant political dimension.

Will this limited fundamental political rights analysis work? Since it makes fewer controversial moral commitments than fundamental moral rights analysis, and since it is relativized to a particular institutional context, it may have some promise. However, it is not totally free from some of the same kinds of worries that haunted fundamental rights analysis of a moral nature. For just what is "our" political system (the theory of our system that puts "us" in reflective equilibrium?), and what is the meaning of concepts like "political" and "participation?" Can these concepts really be analyzed in full independence of controversial moral concepts? I doubt it. Consider political participation: Suppose, adapting an example from John Simmons,[28] the state says to its citizens: "Anyone dissenting from this proposal will signify dissent by chopping off his left arm." Has my participation in the process been secured by this proposal? We are inclined to answer no, of course, because we tend to read "participation" as "fair participation." But fairness is a moral concept requiring moral analysis and justification. Thus judges cannot really secure the rights that help to keep our political system going unless they have a theory, including a moral theory, of the nature of our system and why it is worthwhile that it be kept going. And if they get to speculate on these matters, they must be allowed, perhaps even required, to speculate on such matters as fundamental moral rights. The political-rights

approach may constrain moral speculation more than the re-
spect-rights approach, e.g., abortion might not get in, but it will
by no means eliminate moral speculation entirely.

One further model might be used to conceptualize judicial
review, one based not in intent, not in political rights, and not
in moral rights. Following MacIntrye, one might say that in hard
cases such as *Bakke* [29] the court should accept an overtly political
role, functioning as a "peacekeeper" among rival evaluative factions. (On this view, the Court's decision in the *Roe v. Wade* [30]
abortion case would be a masterpiece: every ideology gets its own
trimester.) There is something to be said for this approach. As
Thomas Hobbes argued, in cases lacking any "right reason" we
need an authoritative umpire to keep the peace by ending controversy with a final decision. But why suppose that the *courts*
are the proper agency to be umpire? Might not the legislature
or exective be more appropriate for this function?

It begins to look as though the abandonment of fundamental
rights analysis will not be without serious consequences for judicial review. One might, of course, either welcome or lament
this outcome. Brest tends to welcome it. He believes that schol-
arly thinking about legal principles has for too long been "court-
centered" and that attention should be turned to political problems of legislation. Brest condemns the elitism that mistrusts the
capacity of citizens and legislators to enter into helpful debate
about values—an elitism that, in his view, blinds them to the
dangers of an imperial judiciary making authoritative pro-
nouncements on the basis of crackpot moral theories.

Brest is on to something here, but he overstates the case. Legal philosophers have been too court-centered. Indeed, "legal
philosophy" in these Dworkinian days almost means "the philosophy of judicial decision." The philosophy of legislation is out
of fashion, a situation Bentham would have found abominable,
and Brest may have discovered part of the reason. My own
generation's vision of democracy tends to be one of George
Wallace and Orval Faubus barring the door of schools to black
children, a vision that includes the Supreme Court as the only
agency that has a chance of keeping rampant redneckism in
check. This vision is, of course, too limited, and the court ado-
ration it inspired too uncritical. We should be open to Brest's
admonition: do not give up on the capacity of legislators to think

and talk about values, get involved in politics, do not expect the Supreme Court to save all things valuable without your having to dirty your own hands, and work to establish a real community of participation.

Good rhetoric, however, is not necessarily good philosophy. And what Brest seems not to realize is that the problems he has raised for fundamental rights analysis will plague his own participatory-community view. If he has a faith in the capacity of Mr. and Mrs. Front Porch to reason about values in citizen or legislative groups, he must think there is such a thing as reasoning about values. And, if so, he must accept some kind of distinction between reasoning well and reasoning badly. He must also accept that such reasoning will involve *general* views—views that connect various reasons and value judgments in a systematic way. But this is rather like having a theory of these matters. Will he not then want to distinguish between a good theory and a bad one? And will this not be very like distinguishing between a rational account and an irrational account? But is it not the case that, on his official view, these accounts are "incoherent and unresolvable?" Brest had better think about all of this some more, for unless he can meet his own worries, his participation-legislative communities will be little more than large encounter groups. They cannot even be considered consciousness-raising groups, for to judge that a consciousness has been raised rather than lowered is to make a value judgment.

MacIntyre is in similar trouble. He ridicules the theories and methods of rationalistic moral philosophy, but he frequently uses those methods to attempt to persuade his reader. He denies any evaluative consensus or coherence in contemporary pluralistic society, but he talks to a large audience and seeks to persuade them. How could he intelligibly do this if he and his audience are not intellectually and evaluatively linked in some fundamental way, a way that presupposes, if not agreement on all particular value judgments, at least agreement on what Ian Hacking has called a certain "style of reasoning" or some common notion of what is relevant?[31] And what about his fondness for the virtue-centered and community-based ethics he sees in bygone ages? If this is supposed to be more than the autobiography of his own preferences (in which case, who cares?), he must think that there are good reasons in support of his nostalgia, reasons he can share with us (otherwise why write a book?). As Socrates noted long ago, radical skeptics tend to be self-destructive.

Where are we? Brest, MacIntyre, Ely and others are surely on to something when they raise doubts about the comprehensive rationalistic theories of moral rights that are propounded by such philosophers as Rawls and Dworkin. But their doubts cannot be so pervasive that they undermine all reasoning about values. Otherwise their own evaluative recommendations would be incoherent. These writers must be presupposing some conception, perhaps a very modest one, of rational discourse and argument about moral values. But, if such a conception exists, perhaps it can be placed into the service, not merely of nostalgia, community, and participation, but of some limited concept of fundamental rights as well. Those who saw in Wallace and Faubus grounds to distrust majorities and legislatures may have overreacted, but the grounds they saw were really there. A concern about democratic excess and some role for the courts in constraining that excess seems reasonable. We should not bury too quickly the idea that our legal system functions in part to protect fundamental moral rights.

To summarize. These who would salvage some form of fundamental rights analysis must aim at something considerably less ambitious than what we get from such writers as Dworkin and Rawls. For all is not well in the domain of rationalistic moral philosophy. Granted it is true that MacIntyre and Brest use value skepticism to mount an attack on fundamental rights analysis while tacitly making value judgments that are inconsistent with their own skepticism. This, however, does not show that fundamental rights analysis is acceptable. It might simply show that all moralizing, whether based on fundamental rights or the virtues of a bygone age, is suspect. A similar point can be made against those who take quick comfort in the fact that post-Kuhnian philosophy of science is prepared to admit a high degree of cultural and historical relativity into its account of science. One could say that this shows that morality now has a clean bill of health because it is in no worse shape than science. One could also, of course, begin to sign the death certificate on the pretensions of science by arguing that it is in no better shape than morality. Bentham maintained that the doctrine of natural moral rights is simply "nonsense on stilts"—i.e., nonsense based on such metaphysically controversial claims as the existence of immortal souls given special value by God. (Would that necessarily involve moral value even if the picture were true?) The metaphysical stilts are perhaps now gone from the doctrine, but they may have been replaced by stilts of another kind: controversial and question-begging models of rational choice. And some of the nonsense may still remain.

In spite of all of these problems, it is my hope that it may still be possible to make a rational case in defense of certain fundamental moral rights, and I hope to develop it. Of two things about this project, however, I am fairly confident: (1) The view of what constitutes rationality will be something considerably more piecemeal and relativized to institutional and historical context than the models of rational choice that we think of as theories of rationality.[32] (2) The list of fundamental rights will be shorter and less ambitious than many fundamental rights proponents would like.

NOTES

1. I am currently working on a book entitled *Moral Theory, Constitutionalism, and Judicial Review.* This chapter is a preliminary and tentative study for that book. My main purpose is to raise some important questions about moral theory and fundamental constitutional rights. In the book I hope to answer some of these questions or—if that fails—at least to provide explanations of why the questions are unanswerable. I also want to explain how certain answers (or certain theories about unanswerability) have important implications for judicial review.

   The second part of the chapter has previously appeared in a slightly different form as "Justifying Departures from Equal Treatment" in *Journal of Philosophy,* vol. 71, no. 10, (October 1984): 587–593. Versions of the entire chapter were presented at a Liberty Fund conference on rationality in October 1984 and at a philosophy of law symposium at the Eastern Division meetings of the American Philosophical Association in December 1984. Many persons made valuable comments and criticisms on those occasions. I can promise those persons that what they do not see dealt with here will be dealt with in the book.

2. Ronald Dworkin, *Taking Rights Seriously* (Cambridge: Harvard University Press, 1978).

3. Alexander Bickel, *The Least Dangerous Branch* (Indianapolis: Bobbs Merrill, 1962), p. 26, quoting Rostow, "The Democratic Character of Judicial Review," *Harvard Law Review* 66 (1952): 193, 208.

4. Dworkin, *Taking Rights Seriously,* Laurence Tribe, *American Constitutional Law* (Mineola, N.Y.: Foundation Press, 1978); John Rawls, *A Theory of Justice* (Cambridge: Harvard University Press, 1971).

5. Alasdair MacIntyre, *After Virtue* (Notre Dame: University of Notre Dame Press, 1981); John Hart Ely, *Democracy and Distrust: A Theory of Judicial Review* (Cambridge: Harvard University Press, 1980); Paul Brest, "The Fundamental Rights Controversy: The Essential Contradictions of Normative Constitutional Scholarship," *Yale Law Journal* 90 (1981): 1063.

6. MacIntyre, *After Virtue,* Richard Rorty, *Philosophy and the Mirror of Nature* (Princeton: Princeton University Press, 1979); Thomas Kuhn, *The Structure of Scientific Revolution* (Chicago: University of Chicago Press, 1962).

7. Brest, "Fundamental Rights Controversy," 1063.

8. Fourteenth Amendment adjudication, and the doctrine of "substantive due process" that it produced, has had a fascinating history. In the famous (or notorious) case of *Lochner v. New York* (198 U.S. 45 [1905]), the court held invalid—on grounds that it encumbered the fundamental right to contract—a New York law that limited the number of working hours in a week. This same philosophy later inclined the court to hold invalid much of FDR's legislation designed to promote economic recovery—a fact that prompted FDR to attempt to "pack" the court, thereby scaring the court away from further substantive due process decisions of this nature. As substantive due process reemerged, its focus shifted away from economic liberties as fundamental rights to such personal rights as privacy. For a good general survey of these matters, see John E. Nowak et al., *Constitutional Law,* 2nd ed. (St. Paul: West Publishing Co, 1983), pp. 425 ff.

9. One way of interpreting Kant's Categorical Imperative is an instantiation of the Principle of Sufficient Reason: claim no liberty for yourself that you could not, as a rational being, extend to relevantly similar persons in relevantly similar circumstances. This appears to make good on Kant's promise to derive the ultimate principle of morality from the concept of rationality. A problem with this, however, is that the concept of relevant similarity will no doubt have to be explicated in moral terms—a circularity that will

prevent the Categorical Imperative from being the ultimate principle of morality.

10. See David Lyons, "Formal Justice, Moral Commitment, and Judicial Precedent," *Journal of Philosophy,* vol. 81, no. 10 (October 1984), pp. 580–587.

11. See Ellen Canacakos, "Indeterminate Juvenile Sentencing: A Denial of Equal Protection?" *Arizona Law Review* 22 (1980): 141.

12. *New Orleans v. Duke,* 427 U.S. 297 (1976).

13. I have recently attempted to apply the criterion of compelling state interest in evaluating state aims for the practice of punishment. See my "Retributivism, Moral Education, and the Liberal State" forthcoming in 1985 in *Criminal Justice Ethics.* For a good general discussion of the various levels of judicial scrutiny (including the emerging "intermediate" standard of review), see Nowak, *Constitutional Law,* pp. 590 ff.

14. Jeffrie G. Murphy and Jules L. Coleman, *The Philosophy of Law: An Introduction to Jurisprudence,* (Totowa, N.J.: Rowman and Allanheld, 1984), chapter 2 (by Murphy).

15. This is, of course, a gross oversimplification of Rawls's theoretical machinery. My forthcoming book will contain a detailed examination of his views.

16. It might be possible to generate some constraints on democratic rule from a model of pure rational self-interest—e.g., that adopted by James Buchanan and Gordon Tullock in *Calculus of Consent* (Ann Arbor: University of Michigan Press, 1967). It is an interesting question, of course, whether the constraints or rights so derived would count as morally fundamental in any interesting sense or if they would map in any interesting way on existing constitutional rights. This is an issue also to be explored in my book.

17. "Common Law Rules and Constitutional Double Standards: Some Notes on Adjudication," *Yale Law Journal* 83 (1973): 221, 285.

18. MacIntyre, *After Virtue,* p. 235.

19. Ely, *Democracy and Distrust,* p. 59.

20. This argument is condensed from "Cruel and Unusual Punishments" in my *Retribution, Justice and Therapy: Essays in the Philosophy of Law* (Dordrecht, Holland: D. Reidel, 1979), pp. 223–249.

21. Some interests that seem to have been identified by the court as compelling are the following: national security and public safety (*Korematsu v. U.S.* 323 U.S. 214 [1944]); maternal health (*Roe v. Wade,* 410 U.S. 113 [1973]); and future life as represented in a human fetus *(Roe v. Wade).* The courts also seem to recognize as a compelling interest the protection of those rights that have been identified as fundamental.

22. Robert Nozick, *Anarchy, State and Utopia* (New York: Basic Books, 1974).

23. *Lochner v. New York*, 198 U.S. 45 (1905).

24. Raoul Berger, *Government by Judiciary* (Cambridge: Harvard University Press, 1977).

25. Brest, "Fundamental Rights Controversy," p. 1090.

26. Ibid.

27. Meiklejohn's theory of the First Amendment was that constitutionally protected speech is essentially *political* speech—speech that has some important role in the political processes of our democracy. Only the exercise of speech of this nature could be said to involve a fundamental right. See his *Free Speech and Its Relation to Self-Government* (New York: Harper and Row, 1948).

28. A. John Simmons, *Moral Principles and Political Obligations* (Princeton: Princeton University Press, 1979), p. 81.

29. *University of California v. Bakke*, 438 U.S. 265 (1978).

30. *Roe v. Wade*, 410 U.S. 113 (1973).

31. Ian Hacking, "Language, Truth and Reason," in *Rationality and Relativism,* ed. Martin Hollis and Steven Lukes (Cambridge: MIT Press, 1982), pp. 48–66.

32. In his 1980 Dewey Lectures, Rawls acknowledges that his model of rational moral choice is relativized to a particular culture and history. He argues that this is not a shortcoming, however, so long as one realizes that the point of his theory is to articulate the moral principles that form the basis of that culture and history and "not . . . to find a conception of justice suitable for all societies regardless of their particular social or historical circumstances." I am not sure if this represents a scaling down of the ambitions Rawls originally held for his theory of justice as fairness or if this relativity was a part of the theory all along. (If the latter, then my earlier identification of the original position model as "foundationalist" was mistaken.) In any event, the path now being suggested by Rawls seems very promising (if less Kantian) and merits detailed study and consideration. See John Rawls, "Kantian Constructivism in Moral Theory: The Dewey Lectures 1980," *The Journal of Philosophy,* Volume LXXVII, Number 9, September, 1980 (the entire issue). Let me again emphasize how keenly I am aware that Rawls's theory deserves a much more careful treatment than I am able to accord it in this essay.

9

THE RULE OF RIGHTS OR
THE RIGHT TO RULE?

AMY GUTMANN

Can we justify the adjudicatory power of judges in our society? In presenting the argument of Critical Legal Studies in its most favorable and lucid light, Frank Michelman persuasively argues that we cannot if we rely on the legalist justifications of positivism or natural law. Should we search for a new liberal form of legalist justification which, like positivism and natural law, relies upon some categorical prescriptive idea ("the law" or "rights"), or should we look for something substantially different from legalist justification? Michelman's constructive suggestions point in both directions. He is "interested in the defense of positions . . . partaking both of legalism and liberalism," but he also recognizes that "our safeguards against judicial tyranny . . . lie not only in institutional practices other than judicial self-justification . . . but in forms of judicial explanatory or argumentative discourse other than the quasi-syllogistic form of legalism."[1] There are reasons for believing that the more promising approach to justifying judicial decisionmaking is to develop something substantially different from a legalist, even a liberal legalist, justification of adjudication. Instead of looking for a certain type of reasoning that we can identify as distinctly legal (rather than political or ethical) justification, we should try to

I wish to thank Walter Murphy and Roland Pennock for helpful comments on an earlier draft of this chapter.

165

justify certain kinds of decisions, those made by judges in courts (rather than politicians in legislatures or citizens in their private lives).[2]

In section I below, I offer some reasons for doubting that there is a kind of legalist justification, based on either the law or rights, that is peculiar to judges and courts. In place of the prevailing view that there is and ought to be a division of moral labor between judges who take rights seriously and legislators who do not, I propose what one might call a "unity of moral labor" among legislators and judges. Once we doubt the dominant wisdom that judges are peculiarly responsible for defending rights, legislators for making policy, we also must rethink the case for justifying the power of courts in a liberal democracy. In section II below, I suggest some reasons for trying to develop a contextualist case for justifying judicial decisionmaking. Such a case would be immune from the attack levelled by the Critical Legal theorists against legalist justifications and consistent with the unity of moral labor.

I

Those who view the courts as bastions of a special kind of justification point either to the courts' defense of the law or rights as a basis for judicial authority.[3] As a basis for judicial authority, the law is sorely insufficient. In hard cases, of which there are many, law speaks in favor of both sides to the dispute, or neither. So while any acceptable theory of adjudication must admit that judges are bounded by the law, it must also recognize that they often cannot find in the law a conclusive verdict. The recognition of judicial discretion per se does not undermine the positivistic case for judicial authority. But the positivist theory of adjudication fails to provide a further argument as to why we should respect the discretion of judges in hard cases rather than (say) the discretion of legislators, who are at least democratically accountable for their discretionary decisions. If it is true that judges have morally *and* democratically unbridled discretion in such cases, then it is hard to see how the positivists' case for judicial authority can be both internally consistent and compatible with liberal democratic values.

Theories of adjudication based on rights provide a more

plausible defense of judicial authority in hard cases. Even when the law is silent or inconclusive, judges can and must rest their decisions on a consideration of rights. By contrast, legislative decisionmaking is and should be aimed at achieving collective goals. (In Ronald Dworkin's language, adjudication is "rights-based," while legislation is "goal-based.")[4]

Since rights routinely ought to trump goals (otherwise they would not be rights), judges should have authority in all cases where rights are at stake because such cases must be decided on the basis of rights-based principle, not goal-based policy. That judges generally disagree over hard cases and often apply the wrong principles (or wrongly apply the right principles) is not in itself evidence against justifying judicial authority, any more than that politicians routinely disagree and often make the wrong policies (on utilitarian grounds) is evidence against justifying legislative authority. If the moral labor of defending rights and making policy is properly divided between courts and legislatures, then we have a good reason to justify judicial power where rights are at stake: judges at least *try* to defend rights and sometimes succeed, whereas legislators do not even try and therefore succeed, if at all, only by accident. I take this line of reasoning to be the strongest defense of judicial power implicit within rights-based theories of adjudication.

Were it true that courts defend rights while legislatures make policy, rights-based theories could provide a sufficient justification of judicial authority. But we ought to doubt this comparison taken as either a description of, or a prescription for, judicial and legislative behavior. The best reason for doubt can be found within the most sophisticated rights-based theory of adjudication. Consider Hercules, Ronald Dworkin's model of the wisest judge. His responsibility is to interpret and apply the political morality that is presupposed by the laws and institutions of his community.[5] Before deciding hard cases, the question Hercules must answer is not "What is the best political theory and the ideal legal system?" but rather "What is the best justification that can be provided for the actual legal system we have?"[6] His decisions therefore are dependent on the body of laws that are legislatively established. Although he must override legislative policy when it conflicts with a clear constitutional right, his theory of legislative supremacy demands that he uphold the specific authority of most laws, even those that he treats as mistakes.[7]

Hercules' theory makes sense only if legislators in his society accept responsibility for making laws that create a set of rights that are worth taking seriously. Otherwise Hercules would face the choice of violating his own technique of adjudication by attempting to formulate an acceptable political morality out of a body of laws that violate liberal democratic principles more often than they uphold them, or else of giving up liberal democratic principles as inappropriate to the specific political conditions of his society. The practical and moral force of Hercules' own technique of adjudication, assuming (as Dworkin does) that it respects legislative supremacy, therefore depends on legislators taking rights at least as seriously as judges.

A plausible case can be made (I shall only suggest its outlines) that legislators must take rights even more seriously than judges. In making new laws, they are responsible not only for respecting rights that already are clearly articulated in the Constitution or legal doctrine, but also for recognizing new concrete rights. As I use the term, concrete rights specify the claims that individuals have against the state or other individuals either by converting abstract political ideals into specific claims (for example, the ideal of treating persons as equals as entailing a right to a minimum income) or by resolving the conflict between two abstract rights in specific circumstances (for example, holding that a right against racial discrimination trumps that of free association in the case of tax-exempt institutions).[8] In recognizing new concrete rights, legislators make it possible for judges to play their role in furthering the abstract rights of liberal democracy without usurping democratic sovereignty.

Of course, judges sometimes recognize new concrete rights. That is what the Court did in *Brown vs. Board* when it decided that black children had a constitutional right to attend schools that were equal by virtue of not being separate.[9] One can support the Court's decision in *Brown* and still consistently believe that we would have been morally and practically better off as a liberal democratic society had legislators recognized that right before the Court had to act. We *were* better off after Congress passed the Civil Rights Act of 1964, and we would have been better off still had Congress acted ten years earlier. We can applaud the Warren Court for its "activism" and still argue that in a liberal democracy legislators should take primary responsibility for creating new concrete rights. For when they do not, judges are put in the morally and practically uncomfortable position of legislating—recognizing *new* concrete rights—against or beyond the will of the democratically elected representatives of the people.

Because many of us now tend to take for granted the results of *Brown,* we may doubt the appropriateness of the Court's discomfort at the time. But consider instead two concrete rights that would (rightly) strike most Americans as new today: the right to a minimum income and the right to equal access to (necessary) health care. In an earlier essay, Michelman makes a very powerful case for believing that liberal justice requires us to recognize such welfare rights.[10] But should the Supreme Court therefore require Congress to provide all citizens with a minimum income and adequate health care even if Congress has passed no law indicating its support of either right?

It is one thing to conclude that a constitutional democracy that fails to uphold welfare rights is unjust, quite another that judges are justified in enforcing justice whenever rights are at stake. In theory, authorizing judges to enforce all rights entails reinterpreting liberal democracy to mean that legislatures have the right to rule only when they rule justly. If Congress fails to guarantee to every citizen a right of equal access to health care and the best interpretation of our Constitution supports that right, then the courts should enforce it. In practice, the theory of judicial supremacy entails sanctioning the imposition of the judicial sense of justice (right or wrong) on the rest of us. There is no feasible means of authorizing egalitarian judges to enforce a right to equal access to health care without authorizing libertarian judges to enforce a right to resist taxation for redistributive purposes. So even in most cases where abstract rights conflict and correct answers exist, we cannot assume either that judges have authority to impose the correct answer on democratically elected legislatures or that they are more likely than legislators to arrive at the correct answers. The most compelling rights-based theories of adjudication do not adequately meet either of these challenges to judicial authority. They therefore leave unresolved the crucial issue of whether and when courts or legislators (or both) are responsible for recognizing concrete rights.

If we take democracy seriously, our theory of adjudication will rest *primary* responsibility for recognizing most new rights with legislators rather than judges. But I cannot settle the meaning and value of democracy and legislative supremacy here.[11] All I hope to have established, at least provisionally, is that (1) rights-based theories of adjudication depend for their force on the assumption that legislators have at least as much responsibility for recognizing and upholding rights as judges; and (2) it therefore follows that the fact that judges do and should take rights seriously is not a sufficient condition for justifying their authority, at least on any democratic theory.

Although a rights-based theory provides a more compelling explanation and justification of specific judicial decisions than positivism, it similarly provides an incomplete answer to the question of why judges rather than legislators are justified in deciding hard cases. Many legal theorists suggest an obvious way of completing the answer: they claim, often in passing, that judges are more willing and able to reason about rights than any other group, and in particular than legislators. The greater willingness and capacity of judges to reason about rights would supply at least a presumption in favor of justifying judicial rather than legislative authority.

Dworkin considers the possibility that "since judges are fallible they should submit questions of institutional rights raised by hard cases to someone else." He then asks: "But to whom? There is no reason to credit any other particular group with better facilities of moral argument; or, if there is, then it is the process of selecting judges, not the techniques of judging . . . that must be changed."[12] But Dworkin may move too quickly here. Even if legislators do not have better facilities of moral argument, they are more accountable to more people than most judges. And *in some categories of hard cases* (for example, where the conflict is between market freedoms and material welfare), this fact may be a weightier qualification for decisionmaking authority than quality of mind. In other categories of cases (for example, where freedom of political speech is at issue), greater accountability to the majority may be a serious moral handicap rather than a qualification. It therefore remains an open question whether all rights are better secured by judges who take rights seriously but are more insulated from democratic accountability than legislators. Even if we could devise a process by which we could select judges with better moral faculties than legislators, the question would still be open, assuming that we take democracy as well as rights seriously.

Despite his doubts about the possibility of finding right answers in hard cases, Michelman also suggests a defense of judicial over legislative authority on grounds that "arbitration by someone chosen for practical wisdom, and institutionally guaranteed to be free of personal partiality, is fairer, or decenter, or safer, than constant recourse to the contest of raw power, whether between the parties directly or their legislative champions."[13] An argument along these lines may be sufficient to counter the extreme view that denies courts *any* authority. But it is misleading to characterize the legislative process as a "contest of raw power," just as it would be to characterize the judicial process as a triumph of syllogistic reasoning. Legislators like judges respect, and commonly fall short of meeting, the demands of practical wisdom, or judgment in the Kantian sense. Satisfying popular preferences may be a weightier component of legislative than of judicial judgment, but it is by no means the only major component of practical judgment for legislators nor a totally irrelevant consideration for judges. Despite their many differences, John Rawls and Brian Barry agree that on issues of "general public morality," abolition of the death penalty for example, legislators should place greater weight on principles than on the preferences of their constituents.[14] While there may be times when, as John Stuart Mill argued, a legislator should set aside his own principled judgment and defer to the fundamental convictions of his constituents, so may there be times when judges should defer to popular conviction in order to command authority on other issues.[15]

The demands of practical judgment on legislators and judges may differ by virtue of their distinct institutional roles, but not in the simple way suggested by the rule that legislators make policy and judges enforce rights.[16] If rights trump policy, then both legislators and judges had better put considerations of rights before those of policy when the two conflict, as they often do. Once we recognize that a liberal democracy demands a unity of moral labor in creating and upholding rights, we must find a basis in addition to the rights-consciousness of judges for defending judicial as distinct from legislative authority.

II

What might that basis be? If theories that ascribe a certain form of reasoning to judges are bound to be either incorrect or insufficient justifications of judicial authority, then we might consider what role courts should play within a society that is committed to upholding liberal democratic principles of justice. I take this argument to be in the spirit of Michelman's search for "justifiability" rather than "justification" of adjudication, although I would redescribe the distinction as between the legitimacy of a judicial decision and its rightness. A contextualist theory of adjudication would justify judicial decisionmaking on the basis of the legitimacy of judicial authority in deciding certain categories of cases rather than the rightness of its decisions or its special decisionmaking technique. The general principle guiding a contextualist justification of judicial authority might be the following: courts should be authorized to make decisions in those categories of cases where they are likely to contribute more than any other institution to upholding the liberal democratic constitution of our society.

A common stock of unsystematized contextualist understandings of judicial authority come quickly to American minds. Federal courts are constitutionally empowered to overturn violations of constitutional rights by lower levels of government. To deny courts this power without amending the Constitution would be undemocratic. We also have some good reasons to support the constitutional basis of judicial authority over the coordinate branches of the federal government as well. The federal courts serve as an essential part of the balance of political powers in protecting us from legislative, executive and bureaucratic tyranny. In addition to these reasons for supporting our judicial institutions quite generally, there are contextualist reasons for empowering the courts to decide certain kinds of issues, especially those where the rights of minorities are at stake and where democratically accountable institutions are likely to be more deferential to prejudiced popular opinion. A good case can be made that judges are more trustworthy than democratically accountable legislators in defending freedom of speech, for example. These are hardly original or surprising suggestions. Neither do they amount to what we need: a systematic contextualist theory of the extent and limits of judicial authority in a large-scale, liberal democracy.

John Hart Ely's *Democracy and Distrust* comes the closest of any existing theory to incorporating contextualist understandings into a justification of adjudication in American society.[17] The problem with Ely's theory is that he gets the context wrong. He mistakenly assumes that most of our constitutional values are purely democratic or procedural, and his theory therefore limits courts to safeguarding the process of democratic decisionmaking.[18] According to Ely, judges must not base their opinions on "fundamental values," which are incompatible with democratic ones. But if (as I would argue) our basic constitutional values are liberal as well as democratic, *or* if (as Ely's argument implies) the value of democracy itself depends on the safeguarding of many "fundamental values" (religious freedom, personal security, freedom of speech, racial and sexual nondiscrimination, and so on), then a contextualist justification of adjudication must not limit itself to considering only procedural justifications of judicial authority. What we need is a contextualist theory that begins with a less truncated account of the substantive values that are basic to *liberal* democracy (the democracy we value), and therefore considers a broader range of roles that courts can justifiably play in contributing to the fulfillment of those values.

I am not equipped to develop such a theory here, or elsewhere for that matter. All I can do is to suggest some advantages that a contextualist theory would have over legalist theories of judicial justification, and hope that legal theorists like Michelman might be persuaded to turn their energies in the direction of developing such a theory.

The first virtue of a contextualist justification of judicial authority is that it would not require us to settle the question of what courts should decide in particular cases. We need not know what the right decision is, or even what the precise chances of courts arriving at it are, in order to support judicial authority in certain categories of cases. If we do not know what the right decision is (even if we know one exists), our most sensible and effective demand is that the authoritative decisionmaker use the best process of reasoning available to arrive at an answer. All we need to know therefore is whether the courts are more likely to base their decisions on the correct process of reasoning, or a better process than are legislatures.[19]

A second and related virtue of contextualist justification is that we need not settle the question of whether hard cases have right answers. Perhaps judges are not bound by moral logic to unique decisions in all cases in which rights are at stake. Perhaps they are. We know that judges along with other groups of morally serious people disagree over the right answers in hard cases. We also know that people disagree even when right answers exist. The available evidence leaves the answer to whether there are right answers indeterminate. Yet even if it is impossible to settle this question, it may be possible to proceed with justifying adjudication. Either way, judges should decide cases by enlisting their greatest capacities for practical moral reasoning.

But practical reasoning is not limited to the application of an ideal political theory or even an existing body of laws to particular cases. It also requires judges to consider the implications for judicial authority of the fact that they as well as legislators will make significant moral mistakes, not just because they are less intellectually gifted than Hercules, but also because (again, like legislators) they are more sympathetic to certain interests and values than to others. Practical reasoning might lead wise judges to entertain serious doubts about not only their ability to find right answers but also their authority to decide certain kinds of cases, where they are no more likely to take rights seriously and less likely (by virtue of their institutional roles) to take democracy seriously than legislators.

We might therefore consider a new (and perhaps more useful) model of Hercules as a moral guide to judges in our society. Hercules II resembles Socrates in understanding how little he knows, how few right answers he is capable of providing in hard cases. But unlike Socrates, Hercules II values democracy. He therefore recognizes that, by virtue of his role, he is responsible not only for taking rights seriously but also for asking to what extent his imperfect knowledge and partiality should limit his authority.

A third virtue of a contextualist theory is that it would thereby attend to the distinctions among various categories of hard cases. Rather than trying to establish or refute the claim that judges should decide hard cases, it would inquire into the types of cases that judges, rather than legislators or bureaucrats, are most capable of deciding well, by virtue either of their legal training or their institutional insulation from certain kinds of partisan political pressures. Michelman rightly observes that even the most vehement critics of legalist justification "have not advocated abolition of the courts or even of their power to set aside statutes as unconstitutional."[20] Once we put aside the unacceptable extremes of advocating the abolition of judicial review on the one hand and elevating judges into our political sovereigns on the other, we are left with the hard work of determining when courts should rule over rights and when they should leave the ruling to others. A contextualist theory of judicial authority must pose this question directly and treat it as an essential element in arriving at an adequate justification of judicial authority.

Where, then, would a contextualist theory of judicial justification stand in relation to existing theories? It would be compatible with the insight of Critical Legal Studies that legalist theories cannot provide an adequate justification of judicial power, but incompatible with the view that judicial power is therefore unjustifiable. A contextualist theory would allow us to appreciate Dworkin's impressive contribution to our understanding of the technique judges should use in reasoning through hard cases. But it would require judges (along with the rest of us) first to figure out which hard cases they have legitimate authority to decide. I would be among the last to suggest that anyone short of Hercules II could succeed in developing a complete contextualist justification of judicial authority. But as long as we aspire to such a lofty goal as justifying adjudication, we might as well set our sights on the complete target.

NOTES

1. Frank Michelman, "Justification (and Justifiability) of Law in a Contradictory World," in this volume.
2. We still may want to argue that certain methods of reasoning are necessary for judicial decisions to be justified. My point is not that

judicial justification is independent of judicial reasoning but rather that such reasoning is neither (1) peculiar to judges nor (2) sufficient to justify judicial decisionmaking.

3. There are also those who view courts as having other special capacities: maintaining continuity of legal development, creating a coherent body of law, being insulated from temporary waves of public opinion, and/or imparting authority to unpopular policies. None of these capacities entails the claim that judges engage in a process of reasoning unique to judicial institutions. Such views are therefore not subject to my critique of legalist justification, but rather potentially part of the contextualist perspective that I wish to defend.

4. See Ronald Dworkin, *Taking Rights Seriously* (Cambridge: Harvard University Press, 1978), pp. 90–94. Virginia Held has suggested a similar distinction and argued for a division of moral labor between courts and legislatures in *Rights and Goods: Justifying Social Action* (New York: The Free Press, 1984), pp. 105–65.

5. Dworkin, *Taking Rights Seriously,* p. 126.

6. "A Reply by Dworkin," in *Ronald Dworkin and Contemporary Jurisprudence,* ed. Marshall Cohen, (Totowa, N.J.: Rowman and Allanheld, 1983), p. 254.

7. Dworkin, *Taking Rights Seriously,* p. 121.

8. Cf. *Taking Rights Seriously,* pp. 92–94 for Dworkin's use of the term.

9. 347 U.S. 483 (1954).

10. Frank Michelman, "In Pursuit of Constitutional Welfare Rights: One View of Rawls's Theory of Justice," *University of Pennsylvania Law Review* 121:962–1019.

11. I say more (although still not enough) about this issue in "How Liberal Is Democracy?" in *Liberalism Reconsidered,* eds. Douglas MacLean and Claudia Mills, (Totowa, N.J.: Rowman and Allanheld, 1983), pp. 25–50.

12. Dworkin, *Taking Rights Seriously,* p. 130.

13. Michelman, "Justification (and Justifiability)."

14. See John Rawls, *A Theory of Justice* (Cambridge.: Harvard University Press, 1971), p. 361; and Brian Barry, *The Liberal Theory of Justice* (London: Oxford University Press, 1973), p. 150. But Barry disagrees with Rawls's more general argument that the "rational legislator is to vote his opinion as to which laws and policies best conform to the principles of justice. No special weight is or should be given to opinions that are held with greater confidence, or to the votes of those who let it be known that their being in the minority will cause them great displeasure."

15. John Stuart Mill, *Considerations on Representative Government,* in *Col-*

lected Works, vol. XIX, ed. J.M. Robson (Toronto: University of Toronto Press, 1977), ch. 12, p. 510; Martin Shapiro, *Law and Politics in the Supreme Court: New Approaches to Political Jurisprudence* (New York: The Free Press, 1964).

16. The problem is not just that there are exceptions to the general rule, but that the rule is seriously misleading. Cf. Held, *Rights and Goods,* pp. 157–58. Although Held argues that the legal system should be concerned with rights and the political system with policy, she goes on to say that a legislature "occupies a position in the overlap between the political and legal systems" and therefore "must concern itself with the domain of rights." But if my previous suggestions are correct, even this concession to the unity of moral labor does not sufficiently capture the degree to which liberal democracy depends on legislators for creating and upholding rights.

17. John Hart Ely, *Democracy and Distrust: A Theory of Judicial Review* (Cambridge: Harvard University Press, 1980).

18. For incisive critiques of Ely's proceduralism, see Lawrence H. Tribe, "The Puzzling Persistence of Process-Based Constitutional Theories," *Yale Law Journal* 89 (May 1980):1063–79; and Walter F. Murphy, "Constitutional Interpretation: Text, Values, and Processes," *Reviews in American History* (March 1981):7–14.

19. "All that we need to know" is quite enough to commit us to a challenging moral and intellectual task: determining the best process of reasoning. Judges who heeded the call for a contextualist theory would be freed not from hard work, only from the need to claim knowledge of the right answer in order to justify their decisions.

20. Michelman, "Justification (and Justifiability)."

10

LAW, RIGHTS, COMMUNITY, AND THE STRUCTURE OF LIBERAL LEGAL JUSTIFICATION

JEFFREY H. REIMAN

Legal officials generally come in three varieties: legislators to make the law, police officers to enforce it, and, in between, judges to decide what the law requires in particular cases. In their official capacity, all three make decisions that are normally backed up by force. As such, they exercise legal power in need of moral justification.[1] I understand "legal justification" as the attempt to meet this need, and I contend that "liberal legal justification" can succeed in this attempt. Rather than try to prove this for all three types of legal official, I shall try to formulate and defend the liberal legal justification of judges' power. To do this, I shall sketch out the shape of liberal theory, but no more than enough to show generally how it works and what its critics are missing. Though I focus on judges' power, I think that it will be clear how the argument could be extended to the other types of legal official.

1. LIBERAL LEGAL JUSTIFICATION AND ITS CRITICS

Liberalism is libertarianism's compromise with Leviathan: the attempt to obtain the benefits of coercive governance without losing liberty, to eat the cake of freedom and have it too. Libertarianism is the doctrine that force may not be used against any adult person except to prevent him from physical aggression against others (including their property).[2] On this view, forcing people for any other purpose amounts to making them slaves to the ends of others. Consequently, libertarianism forbids the nonpreventive uses of force by the state normally thought acceptable in modern liberal societies. For example, taxing people for the purpose of building schools or libraries, or hospitals or highways, amounts to threatening to use force against those who don't wish to pay even though their not paying is no aggression against others. We may think of a liberal, then, as a libertarian who has come to believe that some of the things that states can accomplish with the use of force (beyond prevention of aggression) are so essential to civilized life, or at least so enriching of it, that a blanket prohibition of its use is irrational. I think that this, or something like this judgment underlies liberalism and is true, but I shall just assume that it is and not try to defend it. Clearly, it places our liberal in a tight spot. Part of him sees the rationality of establishing governing institutions that can exercise nonpreventive force, and the other part, the libertarian in him, sees this as the creation of Leviathan, a monster that forces innocent people to be slaves to the ends of others. Thus, a compromise must be made between libertarianism and Leviathan.

Roughly, the compromise works by delimiting a zone of social issues subject to nonpreventive force, and a zone of basic individual freedoms, enshrined as "rights," and protected from such force. The justification of the compromise is the judgment stated in the last paragraph combined with the belief that, as long as the basic rights are protected, people still stand to one another in free relations, and thus they are not enslaved if force is used in other areas for the general good. This belief, too, I shall assume to be true. Moreover, the use of force for the general good can at least be tamed by making it representative, and majoritarian. Not because popular majority rule is more likely to do the good than minority, but rather because, while no *less* likely than minority rule to do the good, majority rule is the only form of rule that gives each citizen an equal say in the outcome. Requiring less *or more* than a simple majority gives a minority the power to block the wishes of the majority and thus gives members of the minority relatively more say than members of the majority. Majority rule is in short, as Winston Churchill said of democracy, the worst form of government except for all the rest. Thus emerges the characteristic shape of modern liberalism: a broad area of social issues subject to popular majority rule backed by force, and an area of basic individual rights thought so fundamental to the maintenance of free relations between individuals as to be off limits to majority rule.[3]

Such a system needs judges since the laws made by the people's representatives cannot by themselves announce what they require in particular disputes, and thus, without judges to decide this, there would be no clear rule for all. Moreover, liberalism hands judges a two-sided responsibility: They must determine what the law requires in particular situations *and* protect individuals' rights against the law. Judges' power is morally justified according to liberalism, then, to the degree to which it is necessary and conducive to the realization of these two aims. And it is the capacity of these two aims to justify judicial power that is called into question in the two critiques of liberal legal justification discussed in Professor Frank I. Michelman's "Justification (and Justifiability) of Law in a Contradictory World." I call the first critique the "fundamental contradiction" thesis, and the second the "rights-vs.-community" thesis.

The "fundamental contradiction" thesis is a critique of "legalism," the notion that the judge's exercise of power is justified as long as he decides *according to law,* or equivalently, as long as he brings the instant case under the appropriate legal rule or rules and renders the decision *required by law.* Legalism aims to quiet our suspicions about judicial power by portraying judges as "more the organs than the originators of decision." Against legalism, the "fundamental contradiction" thesis argues that we are constituted by opposing impulses toward others—desires for their company and assistance as well as fear that they will dominate or hurt us—and thus any general rule must favor one side of this opposition at the expense of the other. Bringing a case under one general rule rather than another, then, requires choosing between the opposing impulses. Consequently, legalism amounts to pretending that judges are applying rules when in fact they are making choices, thus bestowing a mask of legitimacy on what are essentially uncontrolled acts of power.

The "rights-vs.-community" thesis is a moral critique of the doctrine of individual rights. The thesis holds that appeal to individual rights in some way slights our communal natures. Here the argument generally seems to be this: Rights normally either limit what others may do to us or require that they must do something for us like it or not (my right to free speech prohibits you from shutting me up and it may require you to give me time to speak on your television station). Consequently, rights imply that people will stand to each other in antagonistic relations, either intruding when they are not wanted or failing to cooperate when they are. Moreover, rights are generally (and literally) open-ended. They protect people's ability to act for their ends whatever they may be (my right of freedom of movement is my right to go where I wish, not my right to go to some predetermined destination). Consequently, appeal to rights seems to imply that individuals are the final arbiters of their own ends and thus there are no common ends that all members of the group can be required to pursue. Though the rights-vs.-community thesis is a critique of individual rights generally, I shall consider it as a critique of those basic individual rights that are necessary to make the liberal compromise with Leviathan work—the sorts of rights that are exemplified in the Bill of Rights. Thus I take the rights-vs.-community thesis as rejecting the claim that the judge's power is morally justified (wholly or in part) because (or as long as) he or she protects our *basic liberal rights*.

In my view, both theses are fundamentally wrongheaded, as I shall try to prove in what follows. Along the way, I shall have occasion to speculate on what divides legal positivists from natural law theorists, and to comment on the views of Michael Sandel, who has recently offered a sophisticated, but I think mistaken, defense of the rights-vs.-community thesis. Before taking up these theses, it will be helpful to consider liberal legal justification in light of the general project of legal justification.

2. Two Kinds of Legal Justification

Many confusions about legal justification can be avoided by recognizing from the outset that the law—at least this thing we recognize as "law"—is a hybrid.

On one side, it is a set of assertions (not necessarily true, of course) about what people are morally required to do (or refrain from doing). This is necessary if the law is to be distinguished from rule by the stronger and have its characteristic claim to obligatoriness. Some commentators have held that for this a legal system need only be accepted by its subjects as legitimate, and that such acceptance is not necessarily based on moral beliefs.[4] But the law characteristically claims supremacy for its requirements over others, and since moral requirements are widely agreed to be supreme, the law's claim to supremacy must in effect be a *moral* claim if it is a claim to legitimate supremacy, and not just to superior force.[5] Insofar as the law asserts that some course of action is rightly required of its subjects, then it asserts that that action is morally required.

Note, however, that when legal institutions—legislators or judges—determine what the law is or what it requires, they do not simply assert what is morally right, but what is morally required *in light of the law*. The decisions of legal institutions are not simply those that they would make in a given case taken in isolation; they are those that are required in light not only of the case but of the project of guiding behavior by law. Legal institutions are not arrangements for determining in every instance what the best moral outcome is. They seek what is morally required subject to the constraints of being legal institutions, themselves governed by law, exercising delegated power, required to give due regard to precedent so that people can take guidance from the law and confidently plan in terms of it, and so on. Thus, when legislators decide what the law is to be on a given issue, they do not simply assert their view of what is morally right in that matter, but what is morally right for them to require in light of the legal limits on their power and jurisdiction, which are also of moral value. Likewise, a court may regard a given case as one in which the best moral outcome for the parties in the case would be one thing, but the clear meaning of legislation, the decisions of higher courts, the weight of legal precedent, and so on, require another. Insofar as the court issues this other decision, it is not choosing some alternative to what is morally required. It is acknowledging the moral constraints unique to resolving disputes within a legal system. That is, it is deciding what is morally required in the instant case, in light of the law's stated requirements, of the moral value of laws that bind both citizens and courts whether or not they agree with them, of the values of respecting structured legal authority, maintaining consistency of judicial interpretation between courts, and so on, as well as the facts of the particular case.[6] This is what I mean in saying that law as we know it is a set of assertions about what people are morally required to do, and legal institutions assert what people are morally required to do in light of the law. It seems to me that this is necessary if the law—as legislation and as legal decision—is to have the claim to obligatoriness that distinguishes it from rule by the stronger.

On the other side, the law is an institutional arrangement that compels compliance (not necessarily complete, of course) with certain assertions about what people are required to do (or refrain from doing) by attaching a discouragingly high price to noncompliance. And it seems that law must be this as well, since if it were only a set of assertions about what people are morally required to do, without an institutional apparatus for compelling compliance with those assertions, the law would be just another voice in disputes rather than the means to bring them to a close.

In sum, to establish the supremacy of its rules while claiming that they are obligatory and not just commands backed by force, the law must be assertions about what its subjects are morally required to do. And to be a mechanism for the settling of disputes, it must be an institutional arrangement for compelling compliance. This is the hybrid nature of law. It is both moral theory and coercive practice, appeal to right and to might—and could not be law without either.

Given the narrow horizons of the "fact–value" distinction, philosophers have naturally thought that the law must be one or the other. Consequently, some (the positivists) have affirmed that the law *really* is the institutional apparatus for compelling compliance with assertions about how to behave (law is command + sanction," or "predictions of what judges will decide"), and that the appeal to morality is either hype (moral sheep's clothes to cover naked wolves) or gravy (the lucky fact that our wolves really are expected to act not too much like wolves on pain of loss of office). And others (the natural law theorists) have affirmed that the law *really* is the assertions as to what people are morally required to do. From this angle, the law itself seems to invite moral assessment of its assertions as the test of its va-

lidity ("an unjust law is not a law"), and the institutional apparatus for compelling compliance with those assertions seems
either neutral instrument or necessary evil. If I am right and
the law must necessarily be both, then the positivists and the
natural lawyers are like the blind men and the elephant—accurately reporting the part they've got their hands on and mistakenly assuming that the rest is just more of the same.[7]

The judge's role partakes of the law's hybrid nature. Judges
make binding decisions about what the law requires in particular cases of conflict between members of a society. Let's call
these binding decisions "judgments." What I have said above
about law in general applies with particular force to judgments:
Each judgment is a move in two "games." It is a move in the
game of reasoning about what is morally required in light of
the law; and it is a move in the game of social control. (I use
the term game here in the extended sense common in philosophy these days to suggest a rule-governed practice of some sort,
but not to suggest that it is a competitive contest or that it is
merely a game, or that it is not rightly subject to standards beyond itself.) In the first game, the judgment occurs as the *conclusion* of an argument. In the second game, the (same) judgment occurs as the *trigger* of a social process by means of which
noncompliance is rendered prohibitively costly.

In the first game, the judgment is a *proposition* about which
reasonable people can continue to raise doubts. In the second
game, the judgment is a *social fact* which confronts people with
a kind of intractability and finality indifferent to their doubts.
I do not mean to suggest that it is always reasonable to doubt
the validity of a judgment. Some, perhaps even most, of the cases
that judges decide are open-and-shut, or at least clear enough
to render further doubt gratuitous. But judges must also decide cases which do not come unambiguously under a given law,
or in which the law itself is ambiguous, such that an argument
about the meaning of the law, the case, the weight of prior decisions, and so on, must be made in defense of the judgment.
Since it is judgments in cases such as these that raise the largest
obstacles to justifying what judges do, I shall proceed as if such
cases were the standard fare in our courts. I do not mean to
suggest, even in these cases, that there is no right answer that
once reached obviates all further rational doubting—only that,

in the real world, conflicts must be decided before it is clear that we have reached this answer.[8]

What is important here is that, since the judgment plays roles in two games, it requires two distinct (though not unrelated) types of justification. As a conclusion of an argument, it requires justification in the form of grounds for believing that it is the *correct* decision. As the trigger of a coercive social process, it requires justification in the form of grounds for believing that it is a *legitimate* exercise of social power. The question about the correctness of the judgment (as a conclusion) is a question about the judge's reasons (those he gave or those he could have given).[9] But the question about the legitimacy of the judgment (as a social fact) is a question about the institutional framework within which it occurs and that bestows upon it its social power. This is a question of the design of institutions, not of arguments. A complication comes in because one of the key questions we want to ask about institutions, in assessing their legitimacy, is whether they are designed so that playing by their rules is reasonably likely to issue in correct decisions. But this is not the same as requiring the decisions to *be* correct in order to be legitimate.

Since human institutions are staffed by human decisionmakers, we can rest assured that some outcomes will be incorrect though no one knows it. If the legitimacy of decisions rested on their being correct, then (except for the easy cases) we could never know when they were legitimate. Indeed, with the difficult cases, decisions would lack clear legitimacy in the very degree in which they needed it. It follows that, if the decisions made in human institutions can be known to be legitimate, then they must be legitimate even when some are incorrect.[10] This doesn't require that we ignore correctness entirely; rather, it requires that we pose the question about correctness in the form appropriate to institutions: Are they designed in such a way that correct decisions will be their likely outcome, though they will sometimes fail? The fact is that many institutions are designed in a way that, playing by their rules, a correct outcome is considerably more likely than the reverse: Trials, markets, the scientific community, the free press, subcommittees (sometimes), committees (rarely), are some examples.

Consider the question of the legitimacy of the verdict reached in a criminal trial. It is impossible to design a trial system so that it will never convict an innocent person or acquit a guilty one. This doesn't mean that correctness is irrelevant to the legitimacy of trial outcomes; it means that it enters in a different way than it does in the consideration of the outcomes of arguments. It enters when we look at the institutional arrangements that define trials and ask whether they are likely to issue in correct outcomes. Then, assuming that the criminal law itself is legitimate, the fact that the trial is public, that both sides get to make their cases, that rational rules of evidence obtain and only objective methods of proof are allowed, and so on, are what establish the legitimacy of the outcomes of trials because of their contribution to the likelihood of correct outcomes, even though some outcomes will be incorrect. Moreover, since some incorrect outcomes are worse than others, we can design institutions to favor some incorrect outcomes over others. Thus, we traditionally ask of our courts, not that they never convict an innocent person, but that they be ten times less likely to do this than to acquit a guilty one.

Let's call grounds for the *correctness* of a judgment its "intellectual" justification, and grounds for the *legitimacy* of the judge's power in making the judgment its "institutional" justification. Intellectual justification is what the judge himself must offer in presenting the judgment. But his judgment will be binding on us whether or not we are satisfied with the intellectual justification. The judge's distinctive power is his capacity to determine that his intellectual justification is enough, and that we shall be bound by the judgment, agree or not.[11] And since this power is derived from the institutional setting which enables judges to trigger social processes with their decisions, this power requires institutional justification.

While both intellectual and institutional justifications are moral justifications, and seem to overlap, they are nonetheless distinct. They seem to overlap because part of the institutional justification of the judgment lies in the fact that the judge must present intellectual justification for it that can be challenged in appeals to higher courts. But the institutional justification requires that the intellectual justification be *presented* to higher courts who may overturn the decision if they do not find the intellectual justification satisfactory, not that it *be* satisfactory. Though the institutional justification makes reference to the intellectual, it does it in an institutional way. Thus, though the test of legitimacy makes reference to the test of correctness, the two are nonetheless distinct. To be legitimate, the decision must be *ruled* correct by the appropriate institutional officers; it need not *be* correct. We cannot design institutions so that they will only rule correct those decisions which are correct. What we can do, however, is design institutions so that they are more likely to do this.

To bring the discussion around to liberal legal justification, we must specify the standards of justification as those of liberal moral theory, and then consider both liberal *intellectual* justification and liberal *institutional* justification. The first amounts to grounds for believing that a given judgment is *correct* according to liberal theory: The judgment expresses the intention of the lawmakers (including what is arguably implicit in the intention to promote the common good by means of making laws, such as due regard for precedent, predictability, intelligibility, fair sharing of social burdens, and the like),[12] while not violating the basic rights that must be respected if people are to remain free with a coercive government in their midst. I shall not try to elaborate this last requirement further, except to say that I think of it as more or less what Ronald Dworkin takes judges to be doing in *Taking Rights Seriously*.[13]

Liberal institutional justification amounts to grounds for believing that the judge's exercise of power in making his or her judgment is *legitimate* according to liberal theory: The judge has acted within and in accord with an institutional framework which—by insulating judges from political pressures while requiring them to give liberal intellectual justifications for their judgments, to align their judgments with those of other judges and the written law itself, to act publicly, to withstand challenges of partiality and conflict of interest, to be subject to review, appeal, overturn, public outcry and even legislative remedy—tends to favor decisions that do in fact satisfy the requirements of liberal intellectual justification.

This, of course, is only part of the story. Judges' power is necessary for laws to function because laws cannot themselves announce what they require in (at least the difficult) particular cases. The institutional justification (and thus legitimacy) of judges' exercises of power, therefore, rests on the institutional justification (and thus legitimacy) of lawmakers' exercises of power, on whether the lawmakers have acted within and in accord with an institutional framework that tends to favor decisions that represent the majority's views about how to promote the common good, without violating individuals' basic rights. If both judges and lawmakers have satisfied the requirements of liberal institutional justification, then the laws made and judgments rendered are *morally justified and legitimate according to liberal theory*. And if the beliefs that support the liberal compromise with Leviathan are true, then such laws and judgments are truly morally justified and legitimate. On this view legitimacy is not an either-or thing. It admits of degrees depending on how well the institutions are designed, how likely the correct outcomes are, and so on.

3. THE FUNDAMENTAL CONTRADICTION THESIS AND THE CRITIQUE OF LEGALISM

Recall that *legalism* is the view that the judgment is justified if it is *according to law,* or *required by law.* It might seem that this is too simpleminded to justify what judges do, since they are most necessary when what the law requires is least clear. But the legalist need not think all that judges do is apply the law mechanically to open-and-shut cases. He might think that standards are implicit in the lawmaking project, or in the moral fundaments that support the legitimacy of this project, to which the judge should appeal in deciding difficult cases. And since such standards might be thought built into the law (in some larger sense than being written into particular laws), a decision made by interpreting existing laws in light of such standards could still count as "according to" or "required by law." Moreover, such standards could themselves be formulated as general rules ("accord due weight to precedent," "promote the general good," and so on), and these taken as, if not laws, then *legal* rules. Thus, we can take legalism as the doctrine that judgments are justified if made according to the appropriate legal rules, and then, depending on how strict a constructionist our legalist is, these legal rules will include at least the existing laws and possibly other general rules as well as long as they can be defended as implicit in the lawmaking project or its fundaments.[14] Though I shall not try to defend any form of legalism in particular, it is important to note that versions of legalism may vary in what they mean by "according to" or "required by law."

Michelman states the "fundamental contradiction" thesis as follows:

> Suppose you think that people's attitudes toward their social situations, their relations with others, are comprised, always and necessarily, of a duality of strictly opposed impulses—like separation versus union, or freedom versus order. . . . The opposition of impulses . . . does not prevent you, in particular concrete circumstances, from deciding what is in your interest, or what you want. . . . It does prevent you from living and acting for very long, without fear of self-betrayal, by maxim or precept of even modest generality. . . .
>
> So to think is to think, as well, that strong pretension to a legal order of decision according to highly general rule must issue in miscarriage and betrayal of one or another kind . . . : either the illusion of ruledness cloaking arbitrary power, or wrongheaded decision according to inapt rule. . . .
>
> That, in summary, is the situation portrayed by some contemporary critics of legalism.[15]

There are, in my view, three flaws in this argument. The first is that it is a non sequitur. It just does not follow from the fact that we have opposing impulses, that it is impossible to act on general rules without fear of self-betrayal or other miscarriage. One might just as well think that because we both desire to move our arms freely and fear others using their arms to hurt us, we cannot act on a rule against assault and battery without self-betrayal; or that, because we both want traffic to move quickly (so that we reach our destinations soon) and not too quickly (so that we reach our destinations safely), we cannot establish nonarbitrary speed limits; or that, because we both want to be warm enough (not to freeze) and cool enough (not to faint) that we cannot determine an optimal thermostat setting and live with it without miscarriage of some kind.

The mistake here is the exaggeration of opposition into contradiction, which is the inevitable reward of those who take contradiction out of its native home in the relations between propositions, and attribute it to facts in the world. For the fundamental contradiction thesis to work, opposing impulses must be such that the satisfaction of one is strictly incompatible with the satisfaction of the other. For this, however, mere opposition is not enough. Opposing impulses are, I take it, impulses for opposite satisfactions, heat and cold, sweet and sour, freedom and order. But opposing satisfactions do not exclude one another from the world in the way that contradictory propositions exclude one another from truth. Opposing satisfactions exclude one another rather the way physical objects exclude one another, that is, to put it somewhat crudely, by leaving no room (in the satisfaction receptors) for the other. Thus that impulses are opposing is not enough to tell us that their mutual satisfaction is impossible, unless we also know that the impulses desire their satisfactions *in such a large degree that there is no room left for satisfying the other.* In short, unless the impulse for freedom insists on total freedom and the impulse for order insists on total order, that these impulses are opposed to one another does not preclude the possibility that people can have enough freedom and enough order to satisfy both. And general rules that succeeded in protecting enough freedom and establishing enough order (or enough separation and enough union) could be acted on without fear of self-betrayal. This is what the examples in the previous paragraph show.

The second flaw in the fundamental contradiction thesis is that it is *not,* in the first instance, a critique of what judges do. It is an attack on general rules and thus, in the first instance, a critique of what lawmakers do. If the attack on general rules is defeated with respect to lawmakers, then, the power of judges is automatically vindicated, since the laws themselves cannot announce what they require in every particular case. On the other hand, if the attack is sustained then it will undermine legal institutions at a point logically prior to the judicial role. Moreover, this particular critique of general rules must turn round on itself and come out defending general rules! This is because its criticism of general rules is that they cover uncontrolled exercises of power, which are presumably objectionable. But the alternative to general rules is either ad hoc governance or anarchy. And, since the former would add to the power of the judge that of the dictator over all, and the latter would render each individual judge and dictator for himself, both alternatives would lead to even greater uncontrolled power than the system of general rules. Consequently, the critic must ultimately recognize (as Plato did long ago in *The Statesman*) that general rules, though second best in an ideal world, are the best we can do in reality—which of course is where we are.

The third flaw in the fundamental contradiction thesis is that its target, legalism, is a straw man. It is wrong to seek the justification of the judge's *power* in the notion that he or she is putting individual cases under the appropriate legal rules, whether these are interpreted narrowly to include only the written law or broadly to include other legal standards as well. This is to seek the justification of the judge's power to render a judgment which is a *social fact* in the adequacy of the grounds for the judgment as the concluding *proposition* of an argument. Legalism takes the grounds that the judge must offer to justify his or her particular decision as the grounds that justify his or her power to make decisions that are binding on others. But this confuses games. It treats institutions as if they were arguments. It confuses the question of the *correctness* of the judge's decisions about what is right to do with the question of the *legitimacy* of his or her power to make socially binding decisions about what must be done.

What's more, failure to distinguish the question of legitimacy from that of correctness makes the judge's power appear unjustifiable! A device fashioned to justify decisions intellectually will run out of "justifying power" when it is harnessed to the task of justifying decisions institutionally. As a social fact, the judgment is "something more" than the judge's argument for it as a proposition can support. This is because the judge's argument is (if not always, often enough) open to counterargument, and thus the rendering of the judgment as a social fact is a kind of stopping short of argument that the judge's argument itself cannot support. Thus the rendering of the judgment as a social fact seems to be just that feature of the judge's power that is not justified by the argument he or she makes for it. And then the argument appears to be a cover for uncontrolled power, rather than its justification. In short, failure to see that the judgment plays roles in two games makes the judge's power look the way it looks to upholders of the fundamental contradiction thesis.

The three arguments I have made in response to the three flaws in the fundamental contradiction thesis do not prove the capacity of liberalism to justify legal decisions, but they do strongly support it. The first argument shows that the fact that the needs to which liberalism responds are opposed represents no insuperable obstacle to the liberal project. The second argument shows that some problems thought congenital to liberalism are really problems with the tools of governance available to it, namely, general rules. Since any alternative to governance by general rules poses greater threats of uncontrolled invasions of freedom than it does, that general rules require us to be satisfied with only approximations of the best that can be done in particular cases is an unavoidable cost of nontyrannical governance. Rather than bankrupting liberalism, liberalism provides the theoretical funds for paying this cost. The third argument shows that looking for the legitimacy of legal decisions in their correctness "according to law" will make such decisions appear to be uncontrolled exercises of power even when they can be adequately controlled by the institutional framework within which they are made. And, though I have made these arguments with judge's power in view, I think enough has been said to show how they could be extended to all three varieties of official legal power.

4. THE RIGHTS-VS.-COMMUNITY THESIS

Among the things that judges in liberal societies must do in presenting their decisions is to show that they are compatible with the rights of the affected parties. This too is a move in two games. Appeal to rights is an important way of showing that a judgment is correct according to liberal moral theory, while the requirement of presenting and supporting judgments in terms of rights is an important way in which the institutional framework that bestows power on the judge increases the likelihood that his decisions will be correct according to liberal theory. However, for this to help in *morally* justifying judgments, the appeal to rights must itself be a good thing, and this is called into question by those who take rights to be somehow in conflict with the establishment of community among human beings. Michelman is less susceptible to this argument than to the fundamental contradiction thesis, and he even goes so far as to assert that a right is "a claim grounded in community." I shall go further still and argue that community is grounded on justice and thus upon rights, rather than vice versa. Bear in mind that it is *basic liberal rights* that I take to be at issue here.

The critics that Michelman cites hold "the very idea of rights to be morally corrosive in that it reinforces a distortedly one-sided, asocial vision of human nature," envisioning freedom as "escape from community," implying "the necessity of social antagonism," and excluding "the possibility of conceiving human freedom as self-expression and growth in and through community." Presumably, this all stems from the fact that rights are asserted by individuals as limits or requirements on the actions of others. Consequently, they protect the individual from the contrary wishes of others, giving him a legal weapon to stop them from interfering when they wish to or to get them to cooperate when they wish not to. As such, it seems that appeal to rights assumes that freedom is *freedom from* others, and that people will find themselves in need of legal weapons to get others to do things (or stop) against their wishes.

Moreover, rights protect people's freedom to pursue their ends whatever they are, rather than some particular end. By "end," here, is understood any object of anyone's desire or preference. Thus it includes people's ideals or conceptions of the good. Since rights protect people's capacity to pursue their ends against interference by others, they limit the degree to which others can impose their ends on them. Consequently, liberal rights are thought to imply that there are no communally shared ends (or ideals or conceptions of the good) that all can be required to pursue, and that in fact, freedom consists in not being forced to pursue the ends of other individuals or of the group as a whole. Since community seems a good thing, this thesis calls into question whether appeal to rights by judges will in fact improve the moral quality of their decisions.

There is a short way and long way with the rights-vs.-community thesis, both of which grant the moral goodness of community. The short way is this: The community that is put forth as a moral value in competition with liberal rights must be real community. Real community exists among people in some interpersonal relationship, when each desires, not only his own satisfaction, but that of the others as well—and the satisfaction of the others must be desired as good in itself, not just as a means to one's own satisfaction, as say a slave might desire that his master be happy so that his own life be less miserable. For the parties to some relationship to desire each other's satisfaction as good in itself, the relationship itself must not be forced on some by others. A forced relationship is no more communal than forced laughter is happy or forced religious observance faithful. But only individuals can either voluntarily accept a relationship or have it imposed on them by force, and rights limit the ways in which others can do the latter. Rights, therefore, provide the "social space" in which individuals can voluntarily embrace a relationship with others. Thus real community exists only among people who share their relationship from within the very space that it is the job of rights to keep clear of force, that is, only among people who—intentionally or because it would never occur to them to do otherwise—refrain from infringing on one another's basic liberal rights. Community implicitly promises respect for rights as communication implicitly promises respect for truth. Far from rights slighting community, or even being grounded in community, respect for individuals' rights is the precondition of community.

It might be thought that, whatever their relations of priority, rights or justice could not exist without community. But this seems to me false. It seems that we can respect (or fail to respect) the rights of future generations, without sharing community with them; that warring nations can treat each other justly (say, be respecting some limits on the treatment of noncombatants or prisoners), without anything resembling community existing between them; and (though it's not clear how long this will last) that we are currently acting justly to, and not violating the rights of, all the intelligent creatures on other planets in the universe, with whom we are surely not in community. Thus, while there can be justice and respect for rights without community, if my argument above is granted, there can be no real community without justice and respect for rights, only sham community resting on the false belief that conditions are shared voluntarily when they are not.

Also, it might be maintained that the *sense of justice,* or the inclination to respect the rights of others, develops only among members of a community. There is some truth to this claim, but I think the examples in the previous paragraph suggest that it is exaggerated—if warring nations can treat each other justly, then a sense of justice might arise among people who perceive their common vulnerabilities without necessarily sharing one another's fates. Nonetheless, as any other-directed concern, the sense of justice is most likely to develop among people who care for each other, and thus we can say that the sense of justice or the inclination to respect the rights of others will more likely, or more fully, develop within community. If this is what Michelman means by calling the assertion of rights "a claim grounded in community," then I don't disagree. However, it does not contradict my claim that community itself presupposes that people's relationships be in fact just and in accord with their rights. The claim about the conditions for the development of the sense of justice is a claim about the conditions under which a certain kind of awareness or inclination develops. My claim is about the preconditions for something really being community. There is no contradiction in the fact that the sense of justice might arise in community, while the latter already had to correspond to the requirements of justice in order really to be community. That awareness of grammar or an inclination to apply grammatical rules develops only among language-speakers does not contradict the fact that language presupposes that people's words are uttered according to some grammatical structure.

The long way with the rights-vs.-community thesis requires that we plumb its depths a bit further. And this I shall do by taking up a recent and very sophisticated version of the attack on liberal rights, Michael Sandel's critique of the "primacy of justice." The primacy of justice is equivalent to the notion that societies should be organized to protect individuals' rights to pursue their ends (or ideals or conceptions of the good) freely rather than organized to promote some particular set of ends over others. Basic liberal rights are the coins in which justice is doled out. Thus the primacy of justice that is Sandel's target is the same emphasis on basic liberal rights at which Michelman's critics are aiming, and we can, without doing violence to Sandel's project, take them as equivalent doctrines. Indeed, Sandel takes the primacy of justice to flow from "deontological liberalism," the sort of moral theory that harks back to Kant, but which has most recently been defended by John Rawls. Sandel writes: " 'Deontological liberalism' is above all a theory about . . . the primacy of justice among moral . . . ideals. Its core thesis can be stated as follows: society, being composed of a plurality of persons, each with his own aims, interests, and conceptions of the good, is best arranged when it is governed by principles that do not *themselves* presuppose any particular conception of the good."[16]

Against the primacy of justice, Sandel raises several objections, the most important of which for our purposes follows from the fact that justice is appropriate only in the *circumstances of justice:* moderate scarcity, persons with conflicting aims, limited altruism, and so on (the very conditions of antagonism that make communitarian critics worry about rights). Sandel maintains that if these circumstances were replaced by what might be called the *circumstances of benevolence,* in which (with or without scarcity) people were moved by common ends or benevolent feelings for one another, justice would be irrelevant, as courage would be in the absence of danger. Primacy of justice, then, presupposes universality of the circumstances of justice, and thus a view of society in which resolution of conflicting claims is always the highest priority.[17] Since Sandel holds that the circumstances of benevolence do exist often enough (say, in the family or other communal organizations), and that they are attractive enough so that we may be morally bound to try to establish them, the primacy of justice is neither absolute nor morally neutral. It relates only to those situations in which the circumstances of justice prevail, and accepting it inclines us toward establishing the sorts of social arrangements in which the circumstances of justice rather than those of benevolence *do* prevail. Consequently, the primacy of justice and, with it, the basic liberal rights presuppose the intractability of social antagonism and contribute to it. Ergo, rights are the enemy of community.

I believe that Sandel's critique of the primacy of justice—and thus of liberal rights—is wrong. The primacy of justice can be established by reference to crucial features of the human condition that continue to exist in the circumstances of benevolence. Even then justice is primary, and liberal rights fundamental.

The primacy of justice rests on two facts: the physical separateness of human beings, and our inability to prove that any end (or ideal or conception of the good) is obligatory for all human beings. By our physical separateness, I mean no more than that our brains and nervous systems are encased in the physical envelopes of our skins. As a result, each person's desires and experiences, no matter how like those of others, are *that* person's desires and experiences, much as when a hundred people watch the same film, a hundred separate experiences occur, no matter how identical or sympathetic they are in feeling or content. From this a kind of "individualism" arises, not as a moral ideal, but as an ontological fact about where moral ideals of any sort can occur or their realization matter.[18]

Since the realization of ends matters to separate individuals, the realization of one person's ends will matter (positively) to another, if that other has the same ends or is benevolent toward the first person. To the extent that either of these is the case, then conflicts between the two persons will not arise and they will cooperate voluntarily toward the realization of the ends in question. If, however, their ends differ and they are not moved benevolently to support each in the pursuit of his own ends, it is always possible that one's pursuit of his ends will conflict with the other's realization of his. These conflicts may be resolved voluntarily because people are moved by fellow-feeling to compromise. But it is *always possible* that such conflicts will not be resolved voluntarily, and that a resolution will have to be forced on someone. And without being able to establish any end as binding on all, such force is always suspect as no more than subjugating some to the ends of others. The only way to refute this suspicion is by showing that the force has been exercised according to principles that are neutral with respect to people's different ends. These are the principles of justice, and, since they limit how far people can impose their ends or ideals on others, they have primacy over people's ends or other ideals. Thus the characteristic (though not the only) rules of justice are those of criminal justice that do not so much impose one end over others as place limits on the use of force by one person on another, irrespective of their ends.

The primacy of justice, then, does not represent some dubious preference for one sort of moral ideal over others, as Sandel suggests. It represents acknowledgment of the limits to which physically separate people can rightly be forced to serve ideals that they are not moved voluntarily to pursue, when no ideal can be proven binding on all. In the circumstances of benevolence, when people are moved to serve one another's ideals, either because they have the same ideals or are moved by benevolence to embrace those of others, then they act voluntarily. If they do not act voluntarily, then it is false to call these the circumstances of benevolence. But if they do act voluntarily, then they act *within* the limits on force set by justice, and thus within what justice permits, not according to some alternative to justice.

Justice and the rights it defines surround the circumstances of benevolence, much as the criminal law and the rights it protects surround peaceful loving families. And, much as peaceful families are not acting according to some alternative to criminal law but within the limits of what the criminal law permits, so in the circumstances of benevolence people do not act according to some alternative to justice. Rather they act within the limits permitted by everyone's rights. That people don't experience those limits when benevolence moves them to act voluntarily within them leads to the mistake of thinking that community transcends the limits of rights. The truth, however, is just the other way round: Since community is transformed into its opposite, subjugation, when those limits are transgressed, they are the preconditions of community. To the extent, then, that judges succeed in protecting people's basic liberal rights, rather than the enemies of community, they are the guardians of its outer perimeter.

NOTES

1. "It is naive to think that judicial decisions can be justified simply by invoking established rules. The rules themselves or their invo-

cation also require justification." David Lyons, "Justification and Judicial Responsibility," *California Law Review* 72, no. 2: 179.

2. See, for example, Robert Nozick, *Anarchy, State, and Utopia* (New York: Basic Books, 1974), p. 33, inter alia. The phrase in parentheses is the Achilles' heel of libertarianism: Libertarianism claims as the fundamental moral principle a prohibition on aggression against individuals including their property, but determination of what is "their property" requires a moral argument, and thus is more fundamental still. When libertarians try to develop their theory of property on the basis of their prohibition on aggression, their position becomes viciously circular. I have shown this at least with regard to Nozick's version of the theory, in "The Fallacy of Libertarian Capitalism," *Ethics* 92 (October 1981): 85–95. To be sure, liberalism is also prone to this weakness. However, since it is less categorical than libertarianism in prohibiting force, it has resources available to it that the latter lacks. Moreover, I believe that liberalism can be formulated in way that leaves the question of property distribution open to independent considerations of justice. I have argued for a solution to the problem of property distribution, compatible with the liberalism I defend here, in "The Labor Theory of the Difference Principle," *Philosophy & Public Affairs* 12, no. 2 (Spring 1983): 133–59.

3. This way of characterizing the genesis of the theory of the modern liberal state is meant to indicate the considerations essential to it, not to describe its actual historical development. Nevertheless, as history, this much can be said for it: The social contract theory is one (if not the) source of the theory of the modern liberal state. The contractarian theorists were very much concerned with a characteristically libertarian problem, namely, how a free person could come to be obligated not just to obey the laws of a state per se, but particularly to obey the laws of a state decided upon by a majority, when they were members of the dissenting minority. In the hands of contractarians like John Locke, the tacit contract from which the liberal state emerges was in part a device to solve this problem, and so it is not unreasonable to think of the solution as libertarianism's compromise with Leviathan. See J.W. Gough, *The Social Contract*, 2nd ed. (Oxford: Clarendon, 1957), pp. 75 and 140, inter alia.

4. See, for example H.L.A. Hart, *The Concept of Law* (Oxford: Clarendon, 1961), pp. 198–99.

5. "The law provides the general framework within which social life takes place. It is a system for guiding behaviour and for settling disputes which claims supreme authority to interfere with any kind

of activity. It also regularly either supports or restricts the creation and practice of other norms in the society." Joseph Raz, *The Authority of Law* (Oxford: Clarendon, 1979), pp. 120–21. Even in systems that acknowledge that some moral claims rightly override the law, the law is asserted as having some moral weight, and in fact considerable moral weight. It is never merely asserted as a fact to be coped with or a threat to be accommodated. Needless to say, in speaking of the law as asserting that its requirements are moral requirements, I say nothing about whether the law's assertions are true. See notes 7 and 11 below.

6. An "important consequence of the difference between law and a system of absolute discretion . . . is that legal systems contain, indeed consist of, laws which the courts are bound to apply and are not at liberty to desregard whenever they find their application undesirable, all things considered" (Raz, *Authority of Law*, p. 113). Legal systems, it might be said, represent the judgment that what is lost by tying legal officials' hands with pre-established rules is made up for by the gains in predictability, and the like, that such rules promote. But this judgment is itself a moral judgment, and thus legal officials limited by rules can still be said to be making a decision about what is morally required *in light of this judgment* in addition to the facts of the case.

7. Joseph Raz is a legal positivist who is willing to grant natural lawyers just about anything they want, even, for example, the possibility that the law "has of necessity a moral character." What he rejects is the notion that "the identification of law involves . . . moral argument" (*Authority of Law*, pp. 38–9). According to Raz, the legal theorist can recognize (in a "detached" way) that the "law presents itself as justified" (ibid., pp. 158–9), but he need not ask whether it truly is justified to determine if it is law. This seems to me correct. What the natural lawyer sees is that the law presents itself as justified and thus implicitly invites moral assessment as its test of validity. What the natural lawyer fails to see is that the same system that makes this invitation is also an institutional arrangement for determining which law will be held to pass the test, and if it wasn't it wouldn't be law. The positivist is a wallflower content to pass up the law's invitation and merely describe it; the natural lawyer just can't resist accepting it.

8. For a defense of the view that (at least in legal systems like ours) there is always a right answer, see Ronald Dworkin, "No Right Answer?" in P. Hacker and J. Raz, eds., *Law, Morality and Society* (Oxford: Clarendon, 1977), pp. 58–84.

9. The decision can be correct even though the judge has not given

good reasons for it, if there are good reasons that the judge could have given for it. When previous decisions are examined to determine if they hold in a present case, it is not uncommon for a judge to find that a previous decision was correct but for reasons other than those the deciding judge gave.

10. "The fact that a court may make a binding decision does not mean that it cannot err. It means that its decision is binding even if it is mistaken. . . . To be a binding application of a norm means to be binding even if wrong, even it if is in fact a misapplication of the norm. This seemingly paradoxical formulation illuminates the nature and function of primary norm-applying organs." Raz, *Authority of Law*, p. 108.

11. Raz takes the acceptance of authority to involve "giving up one's right to act on one's [own] judgement on the balance of reasons" (*Authority of Law*, p. 26). Interestingly, he takes the question of whether there is an obligation to obey the law as equivalent to the question of whether the law has the (legitimate) authority it claims to have, and goes on to argue that there is "no obligation to obey the law . . . , not even a prima facie obligation to obey it" (ibid., pp. 233 ff). Presumably, then, for Raz, the law always claims legitimate authority and the claim is always false. It seems to me that Raz has recently modified his view on this, and in a direction compatible with the analysis of legitimacy defended here. See his "Authority and Justification," *Philosophy & Public Affairs* 14, no. 1 (Winter 1985): 3-29. There he argues for something like the view that authority is legitimate to the extent that, by complying with it, people are more likely to end up acting for the right reasons than they would if they were to act on their own judgments on the balance of reasons.

12. I do not want to enter the thorny debate about how far judges can accurately interpret legislators' intentions, or even whether doing so always makes the best law. I contend only that liberal theory demands that public power represent the free choices of the citizenry. This means that lawmakers must in some sense be interpreters of the intentions of the citizens, and that judges must in some sense be interpreters of the intentions of the lawmakers subject to whatever other intentions the citizens may have toward the judges directly. Thus, I take it that the judge may interpret the intentions of lawmakers subject to considerations not voiced by the lawmakers, such as those arguably implicit in the citizens' intention to have the common good promoted by law, or their intention (implicit in the way the judicial office is insulated from various interests) to achieve fairness, and the like. Though "intention"

can be interpreted quite widely, I don't think it can be taken as a general invitation to the judges to promote the common good however they think best since this would render nugatory the intention to promote the common good *by law*. Within these fairly broad limits, then, for liberalism, any consideration a judge appeals to beyond the plain reading of the law itself, must be arguably something intended by the citizens in the establishment of legal institutions, or arguably something intended by the lawmakers.

13. Ronald Dworkin, *Taking Rights Seriously* (Cambridge: Harvard, 1978). That judges make moral arguments in determining what the law requires does not entail that a legal theorist must make a moral argument to determine what the law is. He may, of course, have to consider a moral argument in order to determine what the judge will rule, and thus to predict what the law will be. Thus, I don't think that Dworkin's description of what judges do entails a natural law theory of the sort rejected by Raz (see note 7 above). I suspect that Dworkin thinks otherwise.

14. Cf. note 12 above. David Lyons goes so far as to say that any theory for deciding "hard cases" that identifies "standards [such as economic efficiency, that] courts must invoke when the resources of the law have been exhausted" must hold that a decision made according to *any* of these standards is "made according to law," indeed, "*required* by law" (Lyons, "Justification and Judicial Responsibility," p. 189). It doesn't seem that anything but confusion between the resources of the law and other resources is gained from going this far. Lyons's argument for it is that law characteristically requires courts to look at the facts of particular cases and, though the facts are not given by the law, judging in light of them is part of rendering the judgment required by law. From this he generalizes to the conclusion that decisions are required by law as long as they appeal to considerations without which they cannot soundly be made, and thus a theory that identifies other such considerations only extends the content of what is required by law. This argument is faulty because, while the facts of particular cases are not given in laws (laws against murder do not tell us who will be killing whom and how), the directive to look at the facts of particular cases is clearly implicit in the very project of making laws for particular cases (laws against murder do ask us to apply them to what the facts indicate is a case of murder). Consideration of facts is not just a consideration without which decisions in particular cases cannot be soundly made, it is a consideration without which decisions about particular cases cannot be made at all. To treat considerations such as economic efficiency as if they related to the law

the way the facts of cases do is to take an unwarranted jump across a vast divide.

15. Michelman attributes this argument to Duncan Kennedy's "The Structure of Blackstone's Commentaries," *Buffalo Law Review* 28 (1979): 209–382. As far as I can see, the quote from Michelman adequately sums up Kennedy's theoretical argument. Kennedy adds the claim that rights are essentially a means to deny our painful inner contradiction, since they seem to suggest that a reasonable means to satisfying both sides of our dual natures exists, when applying or defining rights requires yet again the choice for one side and betrayal of the other (see pp. 258–61). Most of his argument for this hinges on the fact that defenders of rights have themselves taken conflicting positions of their definition and source, etc. Needless to say, this does not imply that the problem is with rights—it may be with the defenders. In any event, since legal rights are a type of general rule, if I can show that the argument as quoted from Michelman doesn't work, I shall take this as refuting Kennedy's accusations about rights as well. None of this should be taken as detracting from the rich and insightful tour of Blackstone's *Commentaries* that occupies most of Kennedy's article.

16. Michael Sandel, *Liberalism and the Limits of Justice* (New York: Cambridge University Press, 1982), p. 1. There is some overlap between the criticisms that Sandel urges against the ideal of justice, and those put forth by some Marxists. I have taken up Marxist critiques, specifically, in "The Possibility of a Marxian Theory of Justice," *Canadian Journal of Philosophy,* supplemental volume VII: *Marx and Morality* (1981): 307–22.

17. Sandel, *Liberalism and the Limits of Justice,* p. 30.

18. The realization of an end need not be *felt* to matter, but it must at least satisfy the desire for its realization. A person's desires can be satisfied posthumously, say, by following the terms of his will, and thus when *feeling* is no longer possible. Since only individuals have desires, it remains the case that realization of ends only happens for individuals.

PART III

JUSTIFICATION IN POLITICS

11

LIBERAL THEORY AND THE PROBLEM OF JUSTIFICATION

JAMES S. FISHKIN

What strategies of argument are available to a liberal state attempting to justify itself—attempting to support claims to its own moral legitimacy? In what sense should we expect a liberal state (or liberal theories applying to it) to establish principles appropriate for its own moral evaluation?

I will approach these questions in three parts. First, I present a scheme of classification for the range of possible metaethical positions. Second, I argue that liberal theory faces distinctive limitations: it can, at best, aspire only to certain of the positions in the scheme. Third, these limitations of liberal theory provide the ingredients for a legitimacy crisis. Our culture contains widespread expectations about what a morality must be like in order to be objective. The inability of liberalism to satisfy those expectations leads it to undermine its own legitimacy—in the eyes of those who share those expectations and who draw the required inferences about the apparently inadequate foundations of liberalism. This legitimacy crisis is avoidable, but only through a revision in moral culture, through revision in the shared

Portions of this essay are borrowed from my book, *Beyond Subjective Morality: Ethical Reasoning and Political Philosophy* (New Haven: Yale University Press, 1984), where these issues are explored in greater detail. I would like to thank the John Simon Guggenheim Memorial Foundation for its support of my work with a fellowship.

ground rules on what might constitute an adequate basis for
moral judgments.

This chapter summarizes my attempt to bring together work
in three disparate fields: metaethics in part 1; the limited strategies available to liberal theory and the liberal state in part 2;
and the empirical study of moral reasoning in part 3. Here I
draw on recent empirical work exploring the logic of subjectivism in the forms it commonly takes among ordinary reasoners
in our culture.

1. Seven Ethical Positions

Chart 1 depicts a scheme of classification. I believe that the
seven positions defined by the total scheme combine to capture
the full range of consistent positions on the issues they classify.
While further subdivisions are, of course, possible, any consistent position on the issues classified by the scheme must fit one,
and only one, of the proposed seven possibilities. In this sense
the scheme captures the full range of possible ethical positions.

The strongest claim commonly made on behalf of a moral
position is:

(1) That one's judgments are *absolute,* i.e., that their inviolable character is rationally unquestionable.

By "inviolable" judgments I mean those formulated in terms
of principles that it would always be wrong[1] to violate. One is
never morally justified in overriding such absolute principles.
An absolute judgment is also "rationally unquestionable." By this
I mean that it is not open to reasonable disagreement. Perhaps
it is a necessary truth, if such a thing is possible in ethical matters. Or if not, it has a kind of apodictic basis that renders skepticism inappropriate. Of course, any particular position that laid
claim to this would have to include an account of the meaning
of "rational" or "reasonable" and also of the basis for the principle's immunity from reasonable questioning. But these details
of particular positions need not concern us at the moment.

A second, less demanding claim would weaken the absolutist
character of one's judgments. This is:

Chart 1. Seven Ethical Positions

	I Absolutism	II Rigorism	III Minimal Objectivism	IV Subjective Universalism	V Relativism	VI Personalism	VII Amoralism
1. The Absolutist Claim	+	–	–	–	–	–	–
2. The Inviolability Claim	+	+	–	–	–	–	–
3. The Objective Validity Claim	+	+	+	–	–	–	–
4. The Universalizability Claim	+	+	+	+	–	–	–
5. The Interpersonal Judgment Claim	+	+	+	+	+	–	–
6. The Judgment of Self-Claim	+	+	+	+	+	+	–

(2) That one's judgments are *inviolable,* i.e., that it would be objectively wrong ever to permit exceptions to them.

This proposition, while retaining the inviolability claim, drops the absolutist claim to being rationally unquestionable.

A third, even less demanding claim may be identified as:

(3) That one's judgments are *objectively valid,* i.e., that their consistent application to everyone is supported by considerations that anyone should accept, were the issue viewed from what is deemed to be the appropriate moral persepective.

This claim no longer includes the inviolability requirement. These judgments may be formulated as weak, prima facie or ceteris paribus principles that may, with logical consistency, be overriden in cases of conflict with other principles. Furthermore, unlike the absolute and inviolable judgments they need not take the form of general principles at all; they may be merely particular judgments in specific cases.

But such judgments, even though not inviolable, make a minimal claim of objective validity (as do principles conforming to claim 2 above). The proponent of such a moral judgment asserts that from the appropriate moral perspective, one which he believes should have jurisdiction over anyone's choice of values (one that, in other words, he believes to be valid for anyone), his position has sufficient support.[2] This notion of the "appropriate moral perspective" may be formalized in a decision procedure such as Rawls's "original position" or the perfectly sympathetic spectator of the classical utilitarians. Or it may be simply the informal appeal to impartiality familiar from the Golden Rule or from appeals that one should look at a situation from the perspective of the others affected. As Thomas Nagel puts it, "the general form of moral reasoning is to put yourself in other people's shoes."[3] However formal or informal, these conceptions of the moral point of view provide the basis for a claim that a given moral position has objective validity. Of course, proponents of different positions may have quite different notions of the appropriate moral perspective, but that is only another way of saying that the objective validity claim (3 above) is far weaker than the absolutist claim (1 above). It is weaker in that there is no claim that the basis for the judgment is beyond reasonable question. Unlike claim 1, no immunity from rational disagreement is advanced for the crucial assumptions, the "appropriate moral persepective" from which the judgment can be supported.[4]

A fourth, still weaker claim is:

> (4) That one's judgments apply *universalizably,* i.e., that they apply consistently to everyone, so that relevantly similar cases are treated similarly.

If a moral judgment is formulated as a general principle such as "All avoidable killing of human beings is forbidden" then the meaning of its universalizable application is evident from the formula. However, if a judgment is formulated merely for a particular case, such as "X should not have murdered Y on September 22" then so long as the applicability of similar judgments to relevantly similar cases is granted, the universability claim is satisfied.[5]

A fifth, even weaker claim is:

> (5) That one's judgments apply *interpersonally,* i.e., to others as well as to one's self.

This claim is weaker than universalizability because one may apply moral judgments interpersonally without applying them universally, that is, consistently to everyone. For example, a relativist may attempt to deal with moral disagreements by applying X's values to X and Y's values to Y. This relativist still makes judgments of others, but he refrains from applying the values involved universally—X's values, for example, are not applied to relevantly similar cases involving Y and vice versa.

Lastly, the weakest of the six claims is:

> (6) That one's judgments apply to one's self.

Some proponents of subjectivism deal with moral disagreement by asserting this claim but none of the others, not even the weak claim of interpersonal judgment. However, in avoiding even interpersonal judgment and universalizability they face questions about the sense in which their values can retain the characteristic structure of moral values and not imply at least some moral judgments of others for some possible cases.

The properties mentioned in these six claims stand in certain logical relations to each other. An "absolute" judgment (in the sense of claim 1) must also be "inviolable" (in the sense of claim 2); it must be "objectively valid" (as in claim 3); it must hold with universalizable consistency (claim 4); and, obviously, it must satisfy interpersonal judgment (claim 5) and judgment of self (claim 6). These claims are defined in such away that a moral position satisfying a given claim must, logically, satisfy all of those *following* it in the order presented. That is why I presented the strongest claim first; those following it were, progressively, weaker.

On the other hand, if a position fails to satisfy a given claim, then it must also fail to satisfy those which *precede* it, but not those following it. For example, if a judgment is not objectively valid (claim 3), then it cannot be either inviolable (claim 2) or absolute (claim 1) according to our definitions. Satisfaction of a claim requires satisfaction of those following it and rejection of a claim requires rejection of those preceding it—if the resulting positions are to be consistent.

Either of these two logical patterns would be sufficient to reduce the consistent possibilities for combining these claims to the seven positions depicted in chart 1.

Accepting all six claims produces a position commonly called "Absolutism" (position I)—an assertion of rationally unquestionable principles that hold inviolably, with objective validity, with universalizability and, of course, that apply to others as well as to one's self. Kant's ethics offers an influential example of this position. In postulating the necessity of moral imperatives that are "categorical" he endowed them with an "unconditional" and "apodictic" character; in consequence, they hold "let the consequences by what they may." Like all a priori judgments, they hold "with strict universality, that is, in such a manner that no exception is allowed as possible."[6]

Rejecting the absolutist claim, one may consistently embrace the five that follow, producing a position I have labelled "Rigorism" (position II) because it applies objective principles "rigorously," without any exceptions.[7] Utilitarianism, on the one hand, and Rawls's theory of justice on the other, both provide examples.[8]

If we reject both claims 1 and 2 but accept those remaining, we find ourselves in position III, which I have labelled "Minimal Objectivism." This position is the least stringent of the three objectivist positions. Moral principles at this position may permit exceptions and they are not beyond reasonable question. In fact, judgments need not be formulated in terms of general moral principles at all; they may be restricted merely to particular prescriptions for particular cases. The doctrine Rawls is most concerned to argue against, "intuitionism," offers a good example. Lacking some single inviolable principle (or group of inviolable principles in lexical order), we may, nevertheless, lay claim to objective principles that are weak or prima facie, that hold only ceteris paribus and hence are capable of being overridden or traded-off. This position is often termed intuitionism because it requires a careful weighing of moral factors in each particular case.[9] Isaiah Berlin's advocacy of a "plurality" of irreconcilably conflicting ultimate principles offers a good recent example.[10]

If one were to reject the first three claims but accept those remaining, one would arrive at position IV, which I call "Subjective Universalism." Because this position rejects objective validity, the choice among alternative judgments is admitted to be arbitrary and hence subjective; yet those subjective values are applied with universalizable consistency, to others as well as to one's self. While all three of the objective claims are rejected, universalizability, interpersonal judgment and judgment of self are accepted. A good example of this position is offered by the early existentialist Jean-Paul Sartre in the period exemplifed by his essay "Existentialism Is a Humanism." There it is clear that the arbitrariness of moral choice is asserted as the ultimate meaning of human freedom. Since "man is condemned to be free" his choices are without "any means of justification or excuse."[11] Yet this subjectivity does not undermine universality. On the bare thesis of universalizability, he agrees with Kant: "although the content of morality is variable, a certain form of this morality is universal." In this sense, one is "to invent the law for himself."[12]

A more extreme variety of subjectivism follows from rejecting claim 4, universalizability, in addition to the preceding three. I have reserved the term "Relativism" (position V) for this position, since it relativises the application of values to the persons or groups who subscribe to them. Sometimes this position is formulated in terms of conflicting individual positions and sometimes, in terms of conflicting societal positions or cultures. An example of the former can be found in Edward Westermarck's classic *Ethical Relativity*,[13] while the cultural relativists, William Graham Sumner and Ruth Benedict, exemplify the latter.[14] In both versions, the crucial point is that despite the denial of universalizability, moral judgments are applied interpersonally, but according to the respective values held by those judged.

Thus far, we have considered rejecting claims 1 through 4. Now imagine the even more extreme position that would result from rejection of claim 5, interpersonal judgment, as well as all those preceding it. In his critique of the universalizability thesis, Alasdair MacIntyre mentions this possibility as a "private morality:" "The fact that a man might on moral grounds refuse to legislate for anyone other than himself (perhaps on the grounds that to do so would be moral arrogance) would by itself be enough to show that not all moral valuation is universalizable . . . In other words, a man might conduct his moral life without the concept of 'duty' and substitute for it the concept of 'my duty'. But such a private morality would still be a morality."[15]

I will appropriate the term "Personalism" (position VI) for such a private morality, for it restricts the range of moral judgment to one's self.[16] This position avoids the distinctive issues of nonuniversalizable interpersonal judgment faced by the Relativist. It also avoids the problem faced by the subjective universalist, that of imposing admittedly "arbitrary" subjective judgments upon others. But it avoids these two difficulties at the cost of restricting the application of values, sui generis merely to one's self. While MacIntyre defends the possibility of such a "private morality," others might argue that once restricted in this way, values begin to lose the character of being recognizably "moral" values at all.

The most extreme position, the "Amoralism" of position VII, results from rejection of all six claims. The "nihilism" discussed by Nietzsche as a "transitional" phase to the "revaluation of all values" can be thought of as belonging to this position.[17]

2. The Limits of Liberal Theory

Let us distinguish, broadly, between arguments for a moral position that are *internal* to the characterization of morality or the moral point of view, and those that are *external*, in that they depend on propositions that are not part of the characterization of morality or the moral point of view, but depend on other propositions—for example, about God or the structure of the universe or human destiny.

My central line of argument here will be (a) that external strategies are insufficiently neutral between controversial religious and metaphysical assumptions to be compatible with liberalism and (b) that internal strategies are inevitably inconclusive. This inconclusiveness does not rule out miminal claims to objective validity such as those made by position III in our scheme. However, if more is demanded the inevitable limitations of liberal theory can be troublesome. As I have found in an extensive empirical study of moral reasoning, there are expectations in our culture that, short of achieving absolutism (position I), or rigorism (position II), value judgments are inevitably arbitrary and subjective (they must conform to positions IV, V, VI or VII). If these expectations are accepted, then (c) the inevitable inconclusiveness of liberal theory becomes self-undermining. Once its limitations are realized, liberalism self-destructs as a coherent moral ideology in a culture embued with absolutist expectations. The remedy is to disabuse people of their absolutist expectations. Unless we learn to expect less, liberalism must, on any realistic appraisal, undermine its own moral legitimacy.

Let us begin with internal strategies. The key strategy of recent liberal theory has been the definition of an appropriate moral perspective or decision procedure for the selection of principles that are to have priority in a liberal state, at least under ideal conditions. Rawls's "original position,"[18] Ackerman's "neutral dialogue,"[19] Dworkin's "equal concern and respect,"[20] the perfectly sympathetic spectator of the classical utilitarians (an argument recently reformulated by Peter Singer)[21] all have this structure. They define a perspective of *impartiality* for the equal consideration of relevent claims or interests, and this perspective is offered as the foundation for social choice in a just society. Some of these decision procedures also extend to individual choice, but these extensions have sometimes proved controversial.[22]

There are two essential elements in any such decision procedure: (1) the account of impartiality or equal consideration and (2) the account of the interests or other relevant claims that are given equal consideration. Even slight modifications in 1 or 2 can produce enormous variations in the resulting principle. The disparity between Rawlsian maximin justice and average utility, for example, finds its parallel, at the level of decision procedures, in a construction of the original position in which probabilistic calculations are ruled out (leading to Rawls's solution) and one in which they are accepted as rational (leading to average utility). If Ackerman's argument were reformulated with utility as the stuff for distribution—note that his perfect technology of justice is presumed to deal successfully with problems of interpersonal comparison—it would have entirely different implications than would the same neutral dialogue applied to income, genetics or education.[23]

Any of these proposals and others waiting to be invented, would grant equal consideration, in some plausible sense, to everyone's relevant claims and interests, again in some plausible sense. *Which* senses of either 1 or 2 are most plausible is not, itself, an issue that can be settled by invoking any of these procedures. It is a prior issue, some solution to which must be assumed or arrived at, before the application of any moral decision procedure can be unproblematic.

Let us imagine how a proponent of one of our subjectivist positions could maintain his position in the face of arguments that might reasonably be made on behalf of an objective decision procedure. First, notice that proponents of these procedures grant explicitly that an 'egoist" or an "amoralist" who refrained from making any moral claims at all, could consistently avoid commiting himself to any procedure. The claim for these decision procedures is a weak one that I will call *comparative supremacy:* those who affirm validity for rival moral principles should, in some sense to be specified, come to see the appropriateness of the proposed procedure as the basis for choice.[24] However, this construction of the central claim—even if it were true—would leave room for maneuver to our subjectivists that was more than sufficient for them to deny validity to the procedure. Subjectivists need not offer rival moral principles to which they attribute validity. Since they view their own values as arbitrary tastes or preferences, they are not committed to entering the competition that these moral decision procedures purport to resolve. If the amoralist and the egoist who avoid making any substantive moral claims can avoid committing themselves to any moral decision procedures, then so can proponents of any of our other subjectivist positions.

Of course, there is considerable looseness and controversy about the sense in which any of these decision procedures plausibly fulfills even this weakened ambition, the claim to *comparative* supremacy. I mention it only because it is the most sympathetic possible interpretation of what they purport to have accomplished. And this interpretation leaves more than enough room for maneuver for our subjectivists to deny any validity or appropriateness to the procedure.

A more basic difficulty is that there is no basis for adjudicating among alternative claims to comparative supremacy. Proponents of a particular principle—who would justify it by reference to a particular procedure for which comparative supremacy is claimed—can always be challenged by rivals who offer precisely symmetrical claims for their own principles based on their own procedures. Proponents of a particular solution can always be challenged at the point of commitment to the proposed procedure; they can be challenged on the grounds that the construction of the procedure is *biased* in its account of impartiality or of relevant claims or interests so as to favor a given principle. The result is always open to reasonable disagreement because good faith disputes over substantive principles can always find their parallel in good faith disputes over decision procedures, i.e., over the appropriate reasonable basis for resolving disputes. The issue of which procedure to adopt cannot be settled by the procedure itself. And given the variety of procedures, each one supporting a different substantive outcome, the mere invocation of a decision procedure supporting one particular proposal is not enough to settle a moral disagreement.[25]

Just as different arbitration panels can be expected to produce different results in, say, a labor management dispute, different moral decision procedures clearly yield different principles of justice. But in a labor management dispute, the jurisdiction problem can be solved either by mutual consent of the parties involved or by recourse to the mutually acknowledged authority of a court order. But our moral decision procedures have no basis for actual consent, and no mutually acknowledged source of authority tying us to one particular decision procedure rather than another. There are only further moral arguments about what we ought to agree to, or about what our actual notions of morality would commit us to, if we thought about them as the theorist advocates.

This room for reasonable disagreement about the jurisdiction of rival procedures, like the room for maneuver available to our subjectivists to deny the appropriateness of any procedure, undermines the possibility that any decision procedure could hold beyond reasonable doubt.

Hence the attempts to resolve moral disagreements by reference to a decision procedure are inevitably inconclusive. This inconclusiveness arises from the fact that decision procedures are always open to jurisdictional challenge—through invocation of a rival procedure or through challenge to any procedure. This kind of inconclusiveness means only that the results of any given procedure are not rationally unquestionable in the sense required for Absolutism—precisely because the availability of rival procedures is, in itself, a specification of alternative senses of moral reasonableness, of alternative notions of the impartial consideration of relevant claims, that yield rational grounds for disagreeing with any particular results.

These decision procedures represent rigorous examples of what we referred to earlier as the internal strategy. It should be obvious that one might argue from some characterization of the moral point of view without formalizing it in a procedure. Familiar invocations of the Golden Rule, where many crucial steps are left to common sense, have this character. Clearly, everything we have said about the inconclusiveness of the rigorous and formalized versions of the strategy must also apply to looser and more informal versions. Not only are they subject to jurisdictional challenge by competing procedures, but if they are sufficiently informal, they may be invoked by rival claimants each in support of his own position.[26]

The general point is that internal strategies of argument for a particular moral position are inevitably open to reasonable disagreement in that they are open to challenge by rival positions that can also invoke a comparable internal strategy sufficiently different in its particulars as to yield competing conclusions. They are open to reasonable disagreement in the fundamental sense that rival positions can all invoke alternative conceptions of moral reasonableness (as specified by their use of the internal strategy) to support their positions.

A further difficulty arises for internal strategies from the inherent *unforeseeability* of the full range of difficult cases to which any position will apply. Imagine a panel of *perfect* moral judges capable of judging *any* particular cases presented before them. We might imagine a panel of judges operating with complete consensus, or we might imaging ourselves endowed with such capacities as members of the panel. In any case, let us assume for purposes of argument that there are never any reasonable grounds for disputing the resolutions of particular cases dictated by these perfect moral judges. Of course, this is an heroically optimistic and counterfactual assumption. It is meant, however, to dramatize that even such an idealized panel of perfect judges could not provide us with a moral position that would avoid the foreseeability problem. Our inference from any finite sequence of decisions to a general moral position is an inductive one. It carries with it implications for an open-ended class of possible cases in addition to the sequence from which it has been inferred. Even if all the cases thus far decided were resolved by perfect moral judges endowed with superhuman powers, such powers would not produce for us a general moral position we could credibly offer as holding proof against further exceptions.

The difficulty is that such a general moral position, even if it were based on a sequence of perfect resolutions of particular cases, would have to consist in more than the event-specific descriptions of those cases already resolved. If it were to be a general moral position, applying to an open-ended class of possible cases, it would have to specify certain descriptive dimensions employed for singling out the preferred states of affairs or courses of conduct prescribed for future cases as they present themselves. However, these descriptive dimensions employed for singling out the prescribed choices will, inevitably, amount to *incomplete descriptions* of the preferred alternatives—incomplete descriptions of the states of affairs or courses of conduct prescribed.

This necessary incompleteness opens the resulting general position to a crucial source of vulnerability. It is always possible that *other* aspects of the partially described states of affairs or courses of conduct will be of sufficient importance—to any credible moral position—that they require a different resolution. The element of moral complexity that clinches the difficulty is that these moral issues of possibly overriding importance are inherently unforeseeable. If we could, in some way, enumerate them, or know that we had anticipated *all* of them, then we could build into our general moral positions provisions for the solution of those difficult cases. But there is no basis for our presuming that we have ever fully anticipated such cases. Barring some unforeseen breakthrough in moral methodology, our positions must be constructed without the benefit of any such complete enumeration or anticipation of possibly overriding factors. Without complete enumeration, we can expect any general moral position—even one constructed from the decisions of prefect moral judges in particular cases—to yield exceptions and indeterminacies in new cases as they arise. Unanticipated factors of moral relevance can be expected to crop up as new cases present themselves (1) so as to require exceptions to the prescriptions required by any general moral position, as already constructed, and (2) so as to support new prescriptions for issues about which the moral position, as already constructed, says nothing. As new factors present themselves with new cases, the proponent of any given general moral position must make the revisions required for particular cases, or he must relinquish the claim to credibility for the position, as already constructed.

The difficulty is reminiscent of the tale of the monkey's paw. An English couple acquire a magic talisman, a monkey's paw, that will grant them three wishes. Their wish for money, £200, is answered by a messenger offering it to them in condolence for their son's death in an accident at work. Their second wish, to have their son back, is answered by the appearance of an agonized apparition. They then got their third wish, that this apparition go away.[27]

The couple's three wishes, like the prescriptions in any general moral position, pick out certain dimensions of the desired alternatives, dimensions that must incompletely describe the states of affairs or courses of conduct prescribed. Just as the couple had each of its wishes fulfilled but with accompanying factors so terrible that they were fulfilled to their extreme regret, so may any general moral position be adhered to, but with accompanying factors so terrible that its proponents would view its fulfillment with extreme regret in particular cases.

Consider the vulnerability of some typical political principles commonly advanced in serious debate. Given certain circumstances: classical utilitarianism will justify slavery;[28] Rawlsian maximin justice will violate both equality and utilitarianism at the same time distributing less in total, less equally;[29] equality will make everyone, including those at the bottom, worse off;[30] and any procedural principle of democracy will legitimate tyrannous outcomes inflicted on some portion of the population.[31] In each case, we might reformulate our initial version of the principle so as to include provisions for the particular objectionable cases. But this process is continually open to repetition; the flood of counterexamples, many of them unexpected, directed at Rawls,[32] Nozick,[33] and utilitarianism[34] in recent debates, shows how the process of finding counterexamples fully compatible with any extant position as defined, may continue.

In another work, I have explored counterexamples that can be deployed against most of the principles prominent in contemporary political theory—procedural principles such as majority rule and unanimity, structural principles such as equality, maximin justice and utilitarianism, and absolute rights principles such as Nozick's side-constraint theory. These counterexamples display the hand of the monkey's paw. Each is compatible with complete fulfillment of the states of affairs or courses of conduct specified by the principles under discussion. Yet in each case, *other* elements of the incompletely described situation or policy are so terrible that reasonable proponents of these positions would surely wish the prescribed result to be avoided.[35]

We could only be reasonably confident that our position was invulnerable to such further attacks if we had some strategy for completely specifying, in advance, the full range of crucial factors that might present themselves—the full range of overriding claims, of new moral issues and of possible dilemmas that might require that the principle be reformulated.

None of us, I presume, can plausibly claim to be a "perfect" moral judge. If we substituted ourselves for the perfect moral judges in resolving some finite sequence of particular cases, we would find some cases both controversial and debatable. Hence there is all the more reason to doubt that we can arrive at a general moral position that will be adequate to the complexity of all the new issues that may present themselves.

One target of this argument is what might be called the *inductive* variant of the internal strategy of moral justification. The versions of the internal strategy discussed earlier are employed in an essentially *deductive* manner. We are asked to assume the applicability of a decision procedure (or some other, more informal account of the moral point of view) and then to accept the implications that follow from it (or that are, at least compatible with it, as in Ackerman's case).[36] In any case, the decision procedure is fundamental and the principles are derived from it. But if we accept certain particular judgments as fixed points, as necessary conditions for an acceptable position, then we have incorporated those judgments in our interpretation of morality or the moral point of view. Hence such inductive generalizations from particular cases can also be considered variations of an internal strategy of argument since they are based on assumptions internal to the characterization of morality itself.

Of course, if we follow Rawls's method of "reflective equilibrium," we attempt to combine deductive and inductive strategies. Our considered judgment of particular cases provides an independent basis, one which, Rawls hopes, can be employed so as to work back to the decision procedure and to the general principles derivable from it. The portion of Rawls's method that would have us work from the decision procedure to the resulting principles is essentially deductive.

Note that the foreseeability problem is not confined to this inductive strategy. So long as our considered judgments of particular cases as they arise affect the determination of what is a credible moral position, the difficulties just sketched have to be faced, even if our strategy of justification is essentially deductive. If we assume the applicability of a given decision procedure and find its implications provisionally acceptable for the cases we can think of, we still have to face the unforeseeable range of future cases that may require exceptions or reformulations. So long as we lack a method of enumerating or anticipating the new moral issues that will arise with particular cases, we have no basis for concluding that our positions, as formulated, will hold proof against further exceptions and reformulations.

Now consider external strategies. The credibility of an external strategy depends, of course, on the particular assumptions (external to the characterization of morality itself) that are invoked. Depending on the rest of a person's belief system, some external strategies may appear more convincing than others. However, for our purposes, the first point to emphasize is that the implications of an external strategy of justification can always be evaded with consistency by at least *some* construction of any of our subjectivist positions, Each of those positions has been defined so that its commitments are completely open on any questions external to the characterization of morality and the moral point of view. So while it may be the case that a particular subjectivist believes in some assumption that provides the basis for an external strategy of justification (a belief in God, for example), it is always possible for the subjectivist position in question to be formulated—and consistently defended—without any commitment to that assumption. Hence a defender of any given subjectivist position can always neutralize the relevance or jurisdictional claim of an externalist strategy of argument—since he can always maintain his metaethical position while denying whatever assumptions (external to the characterization of morality itself) provide the basis for the argument. Because it is always possible for a subjectivist to defeat an external strategy of argument in this way, such strategies cannot be expected to fulfill the absolutist expectation for principles beyond reasonable question. While an account of moral reasonableness might be developed so that it was part of the *definition* of "reasonable" that a given external assumption be accepted, this strategy would obviously require a controversial definition of the "morally reasonable"—controversial precisely in the sense that rival external strategies (rival religions, for example) could employ the same definitional move for *their* respective crucial external assumptions. Hence the development of an external strategy that would provide a position beyond reasonable question faces decisive impediments.

However, the most important point to emphasize is that external strategies are ultimately unsuitable for liberal theory as we now understand it. They are unsuitable because they are insufficiently neutral between the controversial religious and metaphysical beliefs of particular groups.

At earlier stages in the development of liberalism, religious and metaphysical consensus may have been sufficient to support external strategies of argument with enough conclusiveness to satisfy (or appear to satisfy) absolutist expectations. As John Dunn has shown, the religious assumptions crucial to Locke's *Two Treatise* were "rigidly conventional" and widely shared; they were a "common backcloth" available in the culture providing a shared foundation for argument.[37] The same goes for the God-given natural rights, the "self-evident" truths appealed to by the American founding fathers.[38]

However, this kind of religious and metaphysical consensus is not available to contemporary liberal theorists. Science has undermined crucial religious and metaphysical claims.[39] Furthermore, the ethnic and cultural diversity of modern pluralistic societies brings disagreement about religious and metaphysical assumptions into sharper relief.

Most importantly, were a state to base itself, today, on the controversial religious or metaphysical assumptions of any particular group, that would, in itself, seem illiberal: it would lack the minimal degree of *neutrality* required by a liberal state on these matters. Particularly in the United States where the separation of church and state has given rise to an elaborate doctrine of state neutrality,[40] the state could not enshrine the ultimate convictions of any particular group by public commitments and avoid the charge that it was biasing the marketplace of ideas by giving certain religious and metaphysical claims, certain ultimate convictions, the stamp of state authority and legitimacy.

If this account of the minimum degree of neutrality necessary for liberal theory is correct, then external strategies of justification are not available to contemporary liberalism. But the alternative general category of *internal* strategies (whether deductive or inductive) will, as we have already seen from our analysis of the jurisdiction problem, produce only inconclusive results. The distinctive difficulties applying to the various liberal strategies of justification are summarized in chart 2.

Here and elsewhere,[41] I have tried to argue that the inevitable inconclusiveness of liberal theory need not be fatal to objective claims for liberalism. One could reject position I and even position II without having to adopt any of the subjective positions in the scheme (IV, V, VI, or VII) because position III still remains as an objective possibility. Liberal theory is not necessarily trapped in subjectivism. However, whether or not I am correct in this interpretation of the metaethical possibilities, this inevitable inconclusiveness to liberal theory does pose a crucial *cultural* problem for the viability of liberalism as a coherent moral ideology.

3. Liberalism's Legitimacy Crisis

I have recently completed a detailed study of the arguments employed by ordinary reasoners for the various subjectivist positions distinguished in our scheme.[42] One striking fact about these arguments is that they are based on absolutist expecta-

Chart 2. Liberal Strategies of Justification

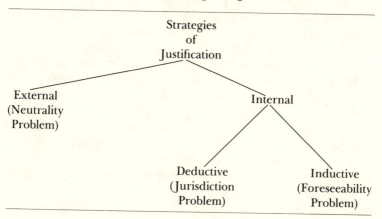

tions about the necessary conditions for an objective moral position. These expectations include the assumption that if a position is not beyond reasonable question (as in position I) or if it does not hold rigorously without exception (as in position II) then it must be "arbitrary" and "subjective," a matter of mere personal taste (as in positions IV through VII). These expectations form the basis for arguments by ordinary reasoners and they constitute widely shared elements of our moral culture. The difficulty is that once such absolutist expectations are combined with the inherent limitations of liberalism, the ingredients are created for a legitimacy crisis, for the self-destruction of liberalism as a coherent moral ideology.

The problem is that external strategies of justification are unavailable to liberalism. But internal strategies cannot support either positions I or II. Position III, however, will not be regarded as adequate in a culture embued with absolutist expectations. In such a culture, a moral position that is not beyond reasonable question and that is not invulnerable to exceptions will seem to be nothing more than arbitrary, a matter of mere personal taste, of purely personal subjectivity. It will seem to be nothing more than an ideology in the pejorative sense.

Some familiar attacks on liberalism fit this pattern. Leo Strauss, attacked Isaiah Berlin's affirmation of conflicting ultimate principles as "a characteristic document in the crisis of liberalism—of a crisis due to the fact that liberalism has abandoned its absolutist basis and is trying to become entirely relativistic."[43] Similarly, Roberto Mangabeira Unger's polemic against liberalism depends on the assertion that liberalism cannot avoid commitment to the "subjectivity of values" and hence, that its claims to legitimacy must be self-undermining.[44] These attacks are not unique. They constitute the "irony of liberal reason," as Thomas Spragens has argued in a recent historical study—a recurring pattern according to which liberal claims to objective justification have been self-undermining.[45]

My purpose here is not to retrace the history of such attacks. Rather, it is to make an analytical point about the strategies available to liberal theory. Any version of liberal theory we might plausibly envisage cannot employ an external strategy so as to satisfy absolutist expectations. It cannot do so because that would make the resulting state illiberal in its bias toward the controversial ultimate convictions of a portion of its citizens. Alternatively, internal strategies cannot be expected to satisfy absolutist expectations. If the groundrules for an objective moral ideology are to be set by these expectations, then liberalism cannot be expected to satisfy them. Given those groundrules, those who probe the foundations of liberalism will find only subjectivism. But a moral ideology that is not objective—one that supports claims to its own subjectivity or arbitrariness—strips itself of legitimacy and authority.[46] In that sense, liberalism self-destructs as a coherent moral ideology in a culture embued with such expectations.

The solution is a revision in moral culture, a revision in our common expectations about what would constitute an adequate basis for a moral position. Only if we learn to expect less can liberalism maintain its viability and coherence. Otherwise, it must undermine its own legitimacy in the eyes of those who share absolutist expectations and who draw the requisite inferences. This chapter is the beginning of a proposal for such a revision, but it is a revision that challenges assumptions that are deeply rooted and widely shared.

NOTES

1. Such a principle is "strong" rather than "weak" or "prima facie." For further discussion of this distinction and related issues see my *Limits of Obligation* (New Haven: Yale University Press, 1982), chapter 6. Violating such a strong principle, even when it conflicts with another, is morally prohibited. Conflicts among principles of this kind are often dramatized in tragic situations. See Bernard Williams, *Problems of the Self* (Cambridge: Cambridge University Press, 1977), pp. 172–4.

2. The same notion of "objective" moral judgments applies to the second and third positions. The difference between the two is in the permissibility of exceptions or overridings. They are compatible with claim 3 but not with claim 2.

3. Thomas Nagel, *Mortal Questions* (Cambridge: Cambridge University Press, 1979), p. 126.

4. See the discussion of reflective equilibrium below. The first three claims in this scheme are briefly discussed in chapter 5 of my *Justice, Equal Opportunity, and the Family* (New Haven: Yale University Press, 1983).

5. I take this notion of "universalizability" from Hare's famous discussion. See R.M. Hare, *Freedom and Reason* (Oxford: Oxford University Press, 1963). For some crucial ambiguities in Hare's discussion see J.L. Mackie, *Ethics: Inventing Right and Wrong* (New York: Penguin, 1977), chapter 4.

6. The quotation is from Immanuel Kant, *Critique of Pure Reason* trans. Norman Kemp Smith (London: Macmillan, 1929) p. 44. See also the *Groundwork of the Metaphysics of Morals,* trans. H.J. Paton (New York: Harper and Row, 1964). Kant's reluctance to permit exceptions is notorious. For the case of lies, see his "On a Supposed Right to Tell Lies From Benevolent Motives," in *Kant's Theory of Ethics,* trans. T.K. Abbot (London: Longman's, 1909).

7. I take the term "rigorism" from Marcus George Singer, who employs it for the notion that "certain moral values hold absolutely or in all circumstances." Marcus George Singer, *Generalization in Ethics* (New York: Atheneum, 1971), p. 228.

8. For a recent attempt to refine a rigorous version of utilitarianism, see Peter Singer, *Practical Ethics* (Cambridge: Cambridge University Press, 1979). Rawls is classified at this position because he proposes his theory as a solution to the "priority problem" for ideal theory. See John Rawls, *A Theory of Justice* (Cambridge: Harvard University Press, 1971), pp. 40–5, 302–3.

9. See Rawls, *Theory of Justice,* pp. 34–9. For an influential recent statement, see Brian Barry *Political Argument* (London: Routledge and Kegan Paul, 1965), chapter I. For an application to public policy, see Arthur Okun, *Equality and Efficiency: The Big Trade-Off* (Washington: The Brookings Institution, 1975).

10. Isaiah Berlin, *Four Essays on Liberty* (Oxford: Oxford University Press, 1969). See especially pp. 167–72.

11. Jean-Paul Sartre, "Existentialism Is a Humanism," in Walter Kaufman, ed., *Existentialism: From Dostoevsky to Sartre* (New York: Meridian Books, 1956), p. 295.

12. Ibid., pp. 306–8. As Hare notes in discussing this essay, "Sartre himself is as much a universalist as I am." R.M. Hare, *Freedom and Reason,* p. 38.

13. Edward Westermarck, *Ethical Relativity* (London: Kegan Paul, Trench and Traubner, 1932; reprint ed., Westport, Conn.: Greenwood Press, 1970). See, for example, page 145: "My view that the same act can be both good and bad, according as it is approved of by one individual and disapproved of by another."

14. William Graham Sumner, *Folkways* (Boston: Ginnard Co., 1906), and Ruth Benedict, *Patterns of Culture* (New York: Penguin Books, 1934).

15. Alasdair MacIntyre, "What Morality Is Not," in G. Wallace and A.D.M. Walker, eds., *The Definition of Morality* (London: Methuen, 1970), p. 30.

16. The term "personalism" has also been employed for a quite different position. See Emanuel Mounier, *Personalism* (London: Routledge and Kegan Paul 1952).

17. For the claim that Nietzsche was himself a nihilist, see Arthur C. Danto, *Nietzsche as Philosopher* (New York: Columbia University Press, 1965). For a sharply contrasting interpretation, see Richard Schacht, "Nietzsche and Nihilism," in Robert C. Solomon, ed., *Nietzsche: A Collection of Critical Essays* (New York: Anchor 1973).

18. Rawls, *Theory of Justice*, pp. 17–22.

19. Bruce Ackerman, *Social Justice in the Liberal State*, (New Haven: Yale University Press, 1980). p. 11.

20. Ronald Dworkin, *Taking Rights Seriously* (Cambridge, Mass.: Harvard University Press, 1978), pp. 234–8, 275–8. For an illuminating discussion of Dworkin's general strategy, see H.L.A. Hart, "Between Utility and Rights," in Alan Ryan, ed., *The Idea of Freedom* (Oxford: Oxford University Press, 1979), pp. 77–98.

21. The classic discussion of the perfectly sympathetic spectator can be found in Adam Smith, *The Theory of Moral Sentiments* (Indianapolis: Liberty Classics, 1969) pp. 22, 31, 33, 35–8, 41, 71, 161–2, 271, 247–9. For recent discussion see Rawls, *Theory of Justice*, pp. 183–92 and Peter Singer, *Practical Ethics*, chapter 1.

22. See my *Limits of Obligation*, parts I and III, for a critique of such efforts.

23. I consider some of these alternatives applied to Ackerman's theory in "Can There Be a Neutral Theory of Justice?" *Ethics* (January 1983).

24. Rawls, for example, treats egoism "not as an alternative conception of right but as a challenge to any such conception." *A Theory of Justice*, p. 136.

25. In this section, I elaborate an argument made more briefly in chapter 5 of my *Justice, Equal Opportunity, and the Family*.

26. Alan Gewirth, "The Golden Rule Rationalized," *Midwest Studies in Philosophy*, III (1978) offers a useful discussion of the looseness in many common inferences from the Golden Rule.

27. Laurence H. Tribe, "Policy Science: Analysis or Ideology," *Philosophy and Public Affairs*, vol. 2, no. 1 (Fall 1972): pp. 102–3. See also W.W. Jacobs *The Monkey's Paw*, a story in three scenes by W.W. Jacobs; dramatized by Louis N. Parker (New York: S. French, 1910).

28. Rawls, *Theory of Justice*, pp. 158–9. This objection holds for direct rather than indirect utilitarianism and provided that very strong

assumptions are made about the slaveholders' capacities for satisfaction.

29. Douglas Rae, "A Principle of Simple Justice." in Peter Laslett and James Fishkin (eds) *Philosophy, Politics and Society, Fifth Series* (New Haven: Yale University Press, 1979).

30. Rawls, *Theory of Justice,* p. 144.

31. See my *Tyranny and Legitimacy,* (Baltimore: Johns Hopkins University Press, 1979). chapter 8.

32. For a representative collection, see Norman Daniels, ed., *Reading Rawls: Critical Studies of A Theory of Justice* (New York: Basic Books, 1975).

33. For a representative collection, see Jeffrey Paul, ed., *Reading Nozick: Essays on Anarchy, State and Utopia* (Totowa, N.J.: Rowman and Littlefield, 1981). See also my *Tyranny and Legitimacy,* chapter 9.

34. For a good summary of the emerging anti-utilitarian consensus in recent liberal political theory see Hart, "Between Utility and Rights."

35. I have made this more general argument in *Tyranny and Legitimacy,* part two.

36. Ackerman's strategy is basically deductive. His principles are derived from the neutrality, rationality and consistency constraints and from whatever other assumptions can be introduced into the argument without violating those constraints.

37. John Dunn, *The Political Thought of John Locke: An Historical Account of the Argument of the "Two Treatises of Government"* (Cambridge: Cambridge University Press, 1969), p. 88.

38. Morton White, *The Philosophy of the American Revolution* (New York: Oxford University Press, 1978), chapter 4.

39. For a brief account of some of these conflicts, both apparent and real, see Paul Roubiczek, *Ethical Values in the Age of Science* (Cambridge: Cambridge University Press, 1969), part 1.

40. For an influential statement, see Philip B. Kurland, *Religion and the Law: Of Church and State and the Supreme Court* (Chicago: Aldine, 1962).

41. *Beyond Subjective Morality: Ethical Reasoning and Political Philosophy* (New Haven: Yale University Press, 1984).

42. *Beyond Subjective Morality.*

43. Leo Strauss, "Relativism," in Helmut Schoek and James W. Wiggins, eds., *Relativism and the Study of Man* (Princeton: Van Nostrand, 1961), p. 140.

44. Roberto Mangabeira Unger, *Knowledge and Politics* (New York: The Free Press, 1976), especially pp. 85–7.

45. Thomas A. Spragens, Jr., *The Irony of Liberal Reason* (Chicago: University of Chicago Press, 1981).

46. By this I mean *moral* legitimacy and authority. The Marxist strategy of basing claims to a kind of legitimacy on historical inevitability remains a possibility. It is, however, based on controversial assumptions and is not available to liberalism in the same way that it is available to Marxism, For a sympathetic account, see G.A. Cohen, *Karl Marx's Theory of History: A Defense* (Princeton: Princeton University Press, 1978).

12

IS THERE A PROBLEM OF JUSTIFICATION? A REPLY TO FISHKIN

BARBARA BAUM LEVENBOOK

According to Fishkin, the legitimacy crisis that faces the liberal state is that whatever arguments the state uses to justify its form of government, the conclusion for which it argues will *appear* to be nothing more than an arbitrary opinion to those people who have two characteristics: they take the time to examine the proffered justification but they cling to what Fishkin claims is a widespread belief about the status of moral judgments. That is what I think Fishkin is arguing for, even though he overstates the case when he says that under the above conditions "liberal theory becomes self-undermining" and that "liberalism self-destructs as a coherent moral ideology."

This overstatement is, however, only a minor defect. So is his false claim that anyone's metaethical position must fit exactly one of the positions he sets out. His first metaethical claim, the absolute claim, does not imply the inviolability claim 2, nor the objective validity claim 3; the inviolability claim 2 does not imply the objective validity claim 3; nor do claims 1, 2 or 3 imply the fourth claim about universalizability. It follows that one might believe, for example, that moral judgments are rationally unquestionable but do not apply interpersonally or with objective validity, thus failing to be an Absolutist or anything else in Fishkin's taxonomy. Likewise, one may believe that moral judgments are rationally unquestionable but only prima facie, thus failing to be an Absolutist, a Rigorist or anything else in Fishkin's taxonomy. These are minor quibbles, however, because to my knowledge no one in the history of moral philosophy has taken any of the positions I have suggested. Perhaps they are initially implausible and would not be adopted by any defender of liberalism.

1.

My major objection to Fishkin's essay concerns his two attacks on the (apparent) adequacy of internal justifications of a liberal state. They are his "jurisdiction" argument and his "unforeseeability" argument. I will consider the "jurisdiction" argument first. This argument is also meant, I think, to apply with appropriate changes to arguments that use no particular decision procedure and rely solely on normative claims to justify the liberal state. Fishkin's argument may be stated as follows:

(1) Someone might always in good faith offer a moral decision procedure different than the one used in an internal justification of a liberal state, and that decision procedure may yield moral principles different than the ones used in the internal justification.

(2) The issue of which procedure to adopt cannot be settled by appealing to any procedure.

(3) Therefore, there is always "room for reasonable disagreement about the jurisdiction of rival procedures. . . ."

(4) "Hence the attempts to resolve moral disagreements by reference to a decision procedure are inevitably inconclusive," that is, they are "not rationally unquestionable in the sense required for Absolutism."

This argument, on which Fishkin relies so heavily, is invalid. It depends on an equivocation in premise 3. Moreover, in assuming the sense of premise 3 that is necessary to support the conclusion, Fishkin is shirking his burden of proof. Let us take each of these points in turn.

Good-faith attempts to offer rival decision procedures, or rival moral principles, are perfectly consistent with the good-faith efforts being objectively mistaken. That is, they are consistent with it nonetheless being true that only one decision procedure (the one, say, offered in the internal justification of a liberal state) is correct and only one set of moral principles (the one, say, relied on in that justification) is correct. So from premise 1 it does not follow that no one decision procedure (or set of moral principles) can be correct. Nor does it follow that there is no way, even in principle, to demonstrate which decision procedure (or set of moral principles) is correct.

Neither do these claims follow from premise 2. Premise 2 is perfectly consistent with there being another way to settle the issue of which decision procedure is correct. Perhaps Fishkin cannot imagine what it may be, but I can. It might, say, be an argument by analogy from justification in science, or perhaps an argument from the analysis of the concept of justification.

For reasons similar to those given above, the conjunction of premises 1 and 2 will not yield the conclusion that the issue of which decision procedure is correct cannot be settled at all. So if premise 3 is interpreted as meaning that there is no rational basis for regarding one decision procedure (or set of moral principles) as correct (or more correct than the others), the move from premises 1 and 2 to the conclusion in premise 3 is invalid.

It may not appear to be invalid because 3 is ambiguous. Premise 3 might mean that there is no rational basis for regarding one decision procedure as correct, or more correct than others. It has to mean this to support his conclusion 4, that "attempts to resolve moral disagreements by reference to a decision procedure are inevitably inconclusive." However, we have just seen that Fishkin has failed to provide a reason to believe that there is no such rational basis. So interpreted in this sense, premise 3 is an unsupported assertion.

There is a sense of premise 3 that is supported by premises 1 and 2. It is, however, useless for Fishkin's purposes, for it does not yield the conclusion that arguments using decision procedures are bound to be inconclusive. There is, in one sense, "room for reasonable disagreement" whenever reasonable men disagree about some claim. They will do this whenever contrary claims are equally initially plausible. In this sense, there is room for reasonable disagreement over what causes cancer, as there are several equally initially plausible claims about it. Likewise, there is room for reasonable disagreement about the correct moral decision procedure or the correct set of moral principles, as there are several equally initially plausible claims about these matters. However, we have seen that such "room" is compatible with only one such claim being correct, and so, with the possibility of conclusive moral arguments.

The invalidity of Fishkin's argument is hidden by a parallel ambiguity in part of his conclusion 4, which is also present in his definition of Absolutism. This is an ambiguity in the phrases "rationally unquestionable" and "not rationally questionable." Their ambiguity parallels the ambiguity of "room for reasonable disagreement," as one might expect. There are two senses in which a claim may be rationally unquestionable. In the first sense, it is self-evident upon very little reflection. In this sense, the truth of the claim that all actresses are women is rationally unquestionable—to anyone, that is, who understands English. However, in this sense, most true empirical claims fail to be rationally unquestionable. It is true, for example, that the heavenly object that we call the Morning Star is the same object that we call the Evening Star and that cholera is caused by a microorganism found in contaminated food and water. However, the truth of these claims is hardly rationally unquestionable. Some of them (particularly the causal claim) have, no doubt, been questioned by reasonable people who were thinking clearly. The questioning of them may have led to the process by which they were discovered to be true.

In the second sense, a claim is rationally unquestionable if it is true and its truth can be established. Claims that are rationally unquestionable in this sense may seem false, and may lead many serious thinkers to question them and to propose contrary claims in which they believe. Indeed, the contraries may seem initially as plausible or more plausible than the rationally unquestionable ones.[1]

Now we come to the crucial empirical question: In which sense of "rationally unquestionable" does the ordinary person assume that a moral claim must be rationally unquestionable in order not to be merely a matter of opinion? My contention is that it is the second sense. For even an ordinary thinker understands that science discovers the truth of claims that are not rationally unquestionable in the first sense, and such a thinker never supposes that these claims are merely matters of opinion. Some writers in the history of philosophy have, of course, claimed that true normative moral claims are rationally unquestionable in the first sense—that is, self-evident to the careful thinker. However, the definition of Absolutism is useful for Fishkin's purpose, which is to make a claim about what must be done to persuade the ordinary thinker of the justification of the liberal state, only if he means to define Absolutism using the second sense of "rationally unquestionable." Using this sense, his "jurisdiction" argument fails.

It might be objected that by insisting that the ordinary person thinks enough not to expect moral claims to be rationally unquestionable in the first sense, I am requiring too much reflection of him (or her). What Fishkin is reporting, he might maintain, is an unreflective belief. However, Fishkin requires a great deal of reflection from his ordinary citizen in order for the "legitimacy crisis" to arise. The citizen must reason in a rather sophisticated way, along the lines of Fishkin's arguments, or he will not conclude that a particular moral claim to legitimacy is doubtfully founded.

2.

As I have pointed out, Fishkin has failed in the "jurisdiction" argument to present a reason to believe that the truth of some claim about right and wrong or about the correct moral decision procedure *cannot* be established. He may think he has presented one by claiming that there is no rational basis for regarding one decision procedure as correct, or more correct than others. (This was, it will be recalled, one interpretation of the ambiguous premise 3). Yet that claim is hardly self-evident and requires support, and this, I have pointed out, Fishkin's "jurisdiction" argument fails to supply. That failure is especially serious, since with a skeptical claim the burden of proof is on the skeptic to present reasons in its defense.

3.

Fishkin's "unforeseeability argument" likewise fails to present a reason to suppose that moral claims cannot be established (and so, that moral claims cannot be rationally unquestionable in the second sense). The error here is subtler than the errors in his "jurisdiction" argument. It will be helpful to begin by reconstructing the argument, which can be stated as follows:

(1) Considered judgments of particular cases may lead a reasonable person to reject a moral decision procedure whose results do not match (or to reject a set of moral principles that, when applied, has contrary results).

(2) We "lack a method of enumerating or anticipating the new moral issues that will arise with particular cases. . . ."

(3) Therefore, possible counterexamples to any moral decision procedure (or set of moral principles) are "inherently unforeseeable."

(4) Hence, we cannot be "reasonably confident" (and, he says, "we have no basis" for believing) that any decision procedure (or set of moral principles) is invulnerable to counterexamples that will "present themselves" in the future.

There is also an unstated grand conclusion:

(5) Hence, any argument for the conclusion that a state is justified which uses a moral decision procedure (or a moral principle) fails to establish that conclusion as true.

This argument, like its predecessor, is invalid. The mistake Fishkin makes is the skeptic's mistake of demanding too much in order for one to be justified in believing something. To see its invalidity, consider a parallel argument about empirical generalizations:

(1) Careful observations of particular cases may lead a reasonable person to reject an empirical generalization that, when applied, has contrary results.

(2) We lack a method of enumerating or anticipating the new observations that will arise.

(3) Therefore, possible counterexamples to any general empirical proposition are "inherently unforeseeable."

(4) Hence, we cannot be "reasonably confident" that any general empirical proposition that is believed is invulnerable to counterexamples that will "present themselves" in the future.

(5) Hence, any argument for an empirical conclusion which uses a general empirical proposition fails to establish that conclusion as true.

Unless one wants to commit oneself to a sweeping form of skepticism, this argument must be rejected as invalid. Premises 1 and 2 are true. I will ignore premise 3 because it is multiply ambiguous. Conclusions 4 and 5 can be accepted at true only at the price of committing oneself to the view that no one is justified in being reasonably confident in beliefs like the following:

(a) The sun will rise tomorrow.

(b) A penny will fall if it is released in a gravitational field.

(c) Cholera is caused by microorganisms.

(d) Clouds are masses of water droplets or other particles in suspension.

(e) An ordinary person in our culture believes that if moral claims are not rationally unquestionable, they are subjective like preferences of taste.

Worse, one commits oneself to the view that no one ever has *any* reason to believe these propositions.

Such views are counterintuitive, and I strongly doubt that Fishkin wishes to embrace them. (He certainly assumes that he is justified in being reasonably confident about belief e.) If he does wish to embrace these views, a discussion about general skepticism is in order, but that is beyond the scope of this essay. It will, perhaps, suffice here to point out that epistemologists have recently developed various accounts of the ways in which our perceptual and scientific beliefs are justified, some of them fully. It is alleged that these will be full justifications even though we lack a method of enumerating or anticipating all the new observations that will arise and that would justify us in revising some of these beliefs.

To sum up: That counterexamples to any general statement might arise, and that we cannot anticipate them all, does not support the conclusion that we cannot be justified in believing a general statement and in using it to draw further, particular, conclusions. This holds for empirical generalizations and for general moral claims as well. Hence, the "unforeseeability" argument fails to show that internal justifications of a liberal state are bound to be inconclusive.

4.

Fishkin may assume there is something fishy about general moral claims, so that they cannot be well-grounded, as can general empirical claims. If so, the burden is on him to provide some reason for believing so. Moral philosophers have recently suggested that the justification of moral claims is analogous to the justification of scientific claims. It should be added that in neither case do they believe the justification to be largely grounded on a long line of particular cases, or, for that matter, to be inductively grounded at all. A discussion of moral justification, however, must await another forum.

It is up to the skeptic to provide a reason for his position. This Fishkin has failed to do. He has failed to provide a reason to believe that an internal justification of a liberal state is bound to be faulty or inconclusive. Whether or not it is bound to *ap-*

pear faulty to the ordinary citizen (who is, perhaps, bound to make some of Fishkin's errors) is another question, It is an empirical question and I am, unfortunately, not qualified to answer it. If it were true, however, it would generate a far less interesting "legitimacy crisis" for liberal theory than the one Fishkin claims to have discovered.

NOTES

1. In neither of these senses, nor in any sense of the term, does consensus make a moral claim rationally unquestionable, as Fishkin assumes. At the most, consensus can make a claim unquestioned.

13

SUBJECTIVE VALUE AND JUSTIFICATORY POLITICAL THEORY

GERALD F. GAUS

1. Subjectivism, Relativism And Liberalism

One of the most controversial issues regarding justification in normative ethics and political theory is how, if at all, varieties of metaethical relativism or subjectivism can have substantive moral or political implications. Social scientists, and particularly anthropoligists, have tended to stress the extent to which such metaethical commitments do indeed have practical implications. Most typically, social scientists have argued, along the lines of Edward Westermarck, that recognition of the essentially subjective nature of ethical judgments quite properly leads to an increased tolerance of the different judgments and values of others.[1] Indeed, at one point, an American Anthropological Association executive committee concluded that the absence of any scientific method for "qualitatively evaluating cultures" validates an attitude of "respect for the differences between cultures."[2] Perhaps more importantly, however, James Fishkin has recently argued that an individualized variant of this position is not unknown among "ordinary moral reasoners." Using interview data, Fishkin examines a variety of "subjective" moral reasoners, including those who insist that, since all values are ultimately a matter of personal taste, all values have equal standing.

And from this, such "ordinary reasoners" conclude, one should respect the values of others.[3] These reasoners thus attempt to justify what is perhaps the central principle of the liberal state— respect for, or tolerance of, those with different notions of what is valuable in life[4]—by insisting on the essentially subjective or arbitrary nature of all values, including their own.

Despite its longstanding appeal, this argument has not been treated kindly by philosophers. Richard Brandt, for instance, points out that since the "relativist" holds all values to be "equally valid", "the value of intolerance is as justified (or unjustified) as that of tolerance."[5] So why should he advocate tolerance rather than intolerance? Of course Brandt and other critics acknowledge that those upholding the essentially arbitrary nature of all values may opt for tolerance as one of their own subjective values; nevertheless, it is widely accepted that their metaethical position does not itself entail a commitment to tolerance, respect, etc.[6] William Galston appears to go even further in his criticism: "Relativism, taken by itself," he says, "does not entail tolerance. . . . Full skepticism about the good leads not to tolerance, not to liberal neutrality, but to an unconstrained struggle among different ways of life. . . . "[7] Apparently he thinks that this sort of metaethic actually inclines toward *in*tolerance. Fishkin criticizes the subjectivists from yet another direction. So far from justifying the central principles of the liberal state, Fishkin maintains that the subjectivist view actually tends to destroy liberalism as a "coherent moral ideology." Subjectivism, he charges, makes nonsense of the idea of moral disagreement and, so, of moral discourse. "If I say 'X is right,' and you say 'X is wrong,' we think we are disagreeing about something. But . . . these statements are logically compatible once they are interpreted as 'From my perspective X is right' and 'From your perspective X is wrong.'"[8]

In sum, then we can find support for the following positions:

(1) A commitment to ethical or value subjectivism/relativism provides a justification of the central liberal principles of respect, neutrality, tolerance, etc. (e.g., Fishkin's subjectivists).

(2) A commitment to ethical or value subjectivism/relativism does not provide any justification of tolerance, respect, neutrality, etc. (e.g., Brandt).

(3) A commitment to this sort of metaethic actually inclines toward intolerance (e.g., Galston).

(4) A commitment to ethical or value subjectivism/relativism makes nonsense of ethical/value discourse (e.g., Fishkin).

I shall argue two theses in this chapter:

(5) Any "subjectivist-relativist" who engages in public justification is committed to liberal-like arguments.

(6) Thesis 4 cannot be supported, at least in relation to one plausible theory of *subjective value.*

My main thesis 5 is not inconsistent with Brandt's position 2; he is quite right that a commitment to relativism (or subjectivism) alone cannot justify liberal tolerance, neutrality, etc. However, I shall argue that *if* the "subjectivist-relativist" does engage in sort of interpersonal justification that I call "public justification," he finds that the range of possible arguments is circumscribed; what remains can be called "liberal-like" arguments. Thesis 5 thus provides some support for the line of reasoning suggested by thesis 1, although the connection between subjectivism and liberalism is less direct than liberal subjectivists are apt to think. Thesis 5 is, however, hypothetical: it merely maintains that *if* the subjectivist engages in public justification, he is committed to liberal-like arguments. I shall also point, though, to several good reasons for subjectivists to engage in such justification; these reasons cast doubt on the plausibility of thesis 3, as I will suggest that the weighing of reasons is likely to incline the subjectivist against intolerance. However, demonstrating my main thesis 5 would not do much to help the subjectivist's case if thesis 4 is valid—i.e., if subjectivism really does undermine liberalism by making nonsense of moral or value discourse. I thus also argue thesis 6, that significant moral and value-based discourse remains under a subjective theory of value.

This chapter has three main parts. The next section examines a plausible notion of subjective value and presents the main argument showing that thesis 4 is unsound. Section 3 then considers the relation between this *subjective* theory of value and *relativism;* relativism, I hold, seems to be the logical outcome of this sort of subjectivism. Finally, section 4 examines (1) the concept of a "public justification" and (2) in what sense subjective-relativist publicly justificatory polical theory must be liberal.

2. Subjective Value

1. The Taste Model of Value

Commenting on his interview data, Fishkin draws a sharp distinction between what he calls a "minimal objectivist," whose "values are 'beliefs'" which can be rationally supported, and a subjectivist, who maintains that values are simply "private tastes."[9] And indeed the notion that values are somehow tastes is mentioned often in the interviews. Brian, for example, sees no difference between moral values and a taste for asparagus since "They both come from the same place—which is somewhere in the middle of my stomach."[10] Sam also draws on the taste analogy in accounting for his values: "I prefer a T-bone steak to a sirloin because we used to have T-bones instead of sirloins. In the same sense, I grew up and developed a taste for honesty. That's as far as I can take it."[11] And Harvey, who professes to be an amoralist, tells us that values, and indeed ethics, are "a matter of personal taste."[12]

This general conception of value is by no means novel; it is certainly not restricted to ordinary reasoners. Quite to the contrary: a taste or subjective reaction account is a dominant model in modern value theory.[13] C.I. Lewis, for example, used the "good and bad taste" of a bite of an apple as an example of the basic value experience;[14] to say that the apple tasted good implies that one experienced some sort of gratification, satisfaction, pleasure, joy, etc., while to say that it tasted bad implies discomfort, nauseousness, disagreeableness, offensiveness, etc. On this analysis, then, to assert that something tastes good is not simply to take up a pro-attitude toward it or to desire it; it is also to say that one has an experience which we might refer to by terms such as joy, satisfaction or pleasure.[15] Stated thus, it is clear that the taste model of value is not new. Indeed, we find what is perhaps its clearest statement in Locke:

> The Mind has a different relish, as well as the Palate; and you will as fruitlessly endeavour to delight all Men with Riches or Glory, (which yet some Men place their Happiness in,) as you would to satisfy all Men's Hunger with Cheese or Lobsters; which, though very agreeable and delicious fare to some, are to others extremely nauseous and offensive: And many People would with Reason preferr [sic] the griping of an hungry Belly, to those Dishes, which are a Feast to others. Hence it was, I think, that the Philosophers of old did in vain enquire, whether *Summun bonum* consisted in Riches, or bodily Delights, or Virtue, or Contemplation: And they might have as reasonably disputed, whether the best Relish were to be found in Apples, Plumbs or Nuts; and have divided themselves into Sects upon it. For . . . pleasant Tastes depend not on the things themselves, but their agreeableness to this or that particular Palate, wherin there is great variety. . . .[16]

According to the taste model of value, then, all ascriptions of value and disvalue are ultimately founded upon what might be called taste experiences, whether they be the positive experiences of joy/satisfaction/etc. or the negative ones of disagreeableness/offensiveness/etc. (I shall leave aside the question as to whether "satisfaction" or "pleasure" are attributes of more basic experiences such as sweetness or whether they are generic terms for classes of experiences.)[17] To understand a subjective theory of value it is thus necessary to grasp the relations between this fundamental sort of experience and (1) intrinsic and non-intrinsic value and (2) value judgments.

2. *Intrinsic Value*

Perhaps the most obvious relation between these fundamental experiences and ascriptions of intrinsic value is one of identity. Lewis points toward this relation when insisting that only the agreeable, satisfying, pleasurable, etc. is "valuable *for its own sake.*"[18] Hedonistic utilitarianism also tends toward this view, generally insisting that all pleasure and only pleasure has positive intrinsic value (although, as did J.S. Mill, the hedonistic utilitarian may amend this to include the absence of pain as also being intrinsically valuable).[19] Now, Lewis believed, if only experience could be intrinsically valuable, the value of objects must be *extrinsic*, of which there are two sorts. *Inherent* extrinsic value is ascribed to objects that are somehow capable of directly giving rise to intrinsic value (e.g., esthetic objects), while objects are *instrumentally* estrinsically valuable if they are "an instrumentality to some other [valuable] object."[20] Roughly, Lewis's (and, I think, Mill's) aim is to distinguish those things that we value because they directly give rise to intrinsic value (e.g., a tree as an object of contemplation and appreciation) from those that are valued because they are a means to other valued things (e.g., lumber as a resource). This difference, then, is essentially that between agreeable and useful things.[21]

Oddly enough, however, this obvious sort of analysis does not really cohere well with the taste model. If to value a thing (intrinsically) is to have in some sense a taste for it, or is parallel to having a taste for it, it is hard to see what sense can be made of saying that enjoyment or pleasure is intrinsically valuable; one is not usually said to have a taste for pleasure or enjoyment, but for, say, things or activities with which one is acquainted and which are known normally to give one enjoyment, satisfaction, etc.,[22] e.g., in Sam's case, T-bones and honesty. This line of reasoning suggests an account in which *objects and activities* have *intrinsic*, rather than simply inherent, value if they give rise to, or are characterized by, pleasure, enjoyment, satisfaction, joy, etc. Although Ralph Barton Perry grounded his general theory of value on interest in an object rather than satisfaction, on this point he agrees with the taste model, arguing, for example, that "the primrose *as enjoyed* is intrinsically good."[23] In contrast to accounts such as Lewis's, then, this sort of analysis stresses that ascriptions of value, while grounded in experience, essentially indicate one's relations to objects, activities, persons, etc. In this sense all ascriptions of value are outward looking.

3. Value Judgments

My aim in the foregoing was not to defend either view of subjective intrinsic value, but to show that plausible variants of the taste model can make a distinction between judging whether an experience is agreeable or disagreeable, and judging whether some object or activity gives rise to, or is characterized by, that experience. Now this permits us to see the limits of Fishkin's claim that a subjectivist or taste model of value undermines the possibility of significant value disagreement. Only in respect to Lewis's type of account of intrinsic value is Fishkin's claim even plausible. Lewis, like others before him, certainly did believe that each person is a definitive judge as to whether his present experience is agreeable or disagreeable. "If I bite an apple," Lewis wrote, "I cannot be in error about the good or bad taste of the present bite." And, hence, "Value as immediately found is subject to no critique."[24] Fishkin's criticism is sound if directed at such an analysis; if intrinsic value judgments are subject to no critique, little room exists for significant disagreement. But even if we grant that each is a definitive judge of whether his present experience is agreeable or disagreeable, significant areas of possible disagreement remain.

On Lewis's general account, disputes about inherent and instrumental value are still sensible while, on Perry's sort of analysis, all attributions of value remain open to real disagreement. Any valuation of any object is subject to error. "All attributions of value to objects . . . ," Lewis argued, "express beliefs which are verifiable or falsifiable."[25] Brian might be the definitive judge as to whether his present experience is agreeable, but it by no means follows that he is in a similar position vis-à-vis his judgment that it was asparagus which gave rise to that experience, and therefore he has a taste for asparagus. These judgments may be wrong in a variety of ways; perhaps he is eating some other vegetable, perhaps it is the spices and not the asparagus he finds agreeable, or perhaps it is the two bottles of wine he drank with dinner that he really found agreeable. And in more complex judgments, regarding, say, a person, an occupation or a painting, the possibility of such errors becomes much more serious. A related case is where one's taste for something can be undermined by further analyzing it or by demonstrating new facts about it.[26] One technique of journalism—as, for instance, regarding apartheid—is to undermine someone's positive valuation of something by bringing to light aspects of it which are (to understate the case) unpalatable. By demonstrating the true nature of the thing, one seeks to show the valuer that his liking it is based on a mistaken conception of it, just as one may undermine someone's liking of a "house" by showing that it is actually a movie prop with no sides or back.[27]

The taste model of value is thus *not* subjective in the sense that all value judgments (or valuations) are simply expressions of emotions. Indeed, if we accept Perry's view, no valuations are simply expressions of emotions or attitudes. Consequently, the taste model does not do away with the possibility that someone may make mistaken value judgments. But this would certainly not be enough to satisfy Fishkin. Whatever one may think of a taste model as an account of general value, Fishkin might say, it cannot serve as a model of *moral* values, for one of characteristics of moral values is that we believe others too have reason to embrace them, something we do not necessarily believe about our taste for asparagus.[28] But even assuming (for now) that Fishkin is right that moral values necessarily entail a claim about universal acceptance, it does not follow that they cannot be accommodated within a subjective account such as I have sketched. Universality need not require objectivity. Consider Hobbes's subjective theory of value.[29] Although Hobbes clearly believed that good and evil are, at least originally,[30] relative to what each person happens to desire or hate, Hobbes also believed that every man happens to have (1) a strong aversion to his own sudden and violent death and (2) a powerful desire for his own preservation and commodious living. And it is these universal subjective values and disvalues that inform what Hobbes calls the "Laws of Nature," "upon which men may be drawn to agreement."[31] Hobbes thus insists that every man has a self-interested reason to observe the Laws of Nature because each has a desire for his own perservation. At least in principle, then, a subjective theory of value can accommodate universal values qua universal instrumental values that advance the interests of each. Thus, for Hobbes, everyone does have a strong reason to promote peace because it is in the interest of each and every person to do so.

3. RELATIVISM: VALUES AND REASONS

1. The Objective Point of View

One of the most important revelations arising from Fishkin's interviews with his subjective reasoners is the extent to which the taste model of value is the result of what may quite rightly be called a commitment to an objective point of view. As Fishkin puts it, the typical subjectivist strives after a position of "cosmic neutrality"—"a neutral position between his own assumptions and those of anyone else he might be judging."[32] According to Brian, for example, "I realize that my reasons are exactly symmetrical with the other guy who [sic] I'm condemning, but somehow he's wrong and I'm right?"[33] And Doug insists that "I am not an external observer; I am an internal observer and it is not fair for me to judge. My criteria are not fundamental. They are relative to *my position* in the problem."[34] As are many individual relativists, Doug is inspired by the cultural relavitism of many anthropologists (although, of course, the two varieties of relativism are inconsistent).[35] Thus, just as anthropologists such as Ruth Benedict believe that the study of the diversity of cultures endorses a "cultural relativity," with its assertion of a mutiplicity of "equally valid patterns of life,"[36] Fishkin's relativists believe that the an impartial or objective study of individual valuations leads to the conclusion that in some sense all are equally valid.

This attempt by Fishkin's subjective reasoners to overcome what they see as the partiality of their own perspective and achieve a neutral viewpoint is what Thomas Nagel has described as the pursuit of an objective point of view. "The first stage of objectification of the mental," Nagel writes, "is for each of us to be able to grasp the idea of all human perspectives, including his own, without depriving them of their character as perspectives. It is the analogue for minds of a centerless conception of space for physical objects, in which no point has a privileged position."[37] Fishkin's subjective reasoners are, in the main, seeking to do just that: confronted by the diversity of subjective viewpoints—including their own—they seek to construct a centerless account of the moral universe in which no particular perspective is in a privileged position. Any other account, they clearly believe, is merely the assertion of a particular subjective perspective. And that, one respondent tells us, is "rationally unsupportable."[38] However, the subjective reasoners radically differ from Nagel regarding the consequences of this mental experiment: whereas Nagel believes that the objective perspective reveals "what is of value in itself, rather than *for* anyone,"[39] our subjectivists insist that to be objective is simply to grasp the multiplicity of valuers, each with "equally valid" tastes and grounds for action based upon them. As they see it, the only values are those that are values *for* someone.

This difference between Nagel and the subjectivists stems, I think, from a more fundamental disagreement as to how much one can abstract from one's particular point of view. To our subjectivists, the most that can be achieved is a position of neutrality. One sees that one's particularistic point of view is just one of a multitude of points of view; objectivity consists in recognizing that one's own tastes are no more firmly grounded than those of others. And, thus, from the objective point of view, no perspective is intrinsically superior to any other. Nagel, however, ultimately endeavors to achieve a higher level of abstraction from particularistic perspectives. For him, it would seem, to be objective is to see things entirely abstracted from particular viewpoints: one discovers what is valuable in itself, not what is valuable from some viewpoint.

Bernard Williams has criticized this attempt by subjectivists to seek a "midair place." According to Williams, when the subjectivist asks (as we saw Brian does) "Who am I to say that they [i.e., others] are wrong?" he is asking from a position that is ". . . not within his own subjective compound, but in midair above his own and other people's; it tries to stand outside all moral positions (including the thinker's own) and yet still be a moral thought."[40] In a way Williams is right; the idea of an objective metaethical perspective is indeed an attempt to stand outside one's own point of view. Like Nagel, the subjectivists seek a centerless moral universe. But thus far I have not claimed (although some of Fishkin's subjectivists tend to) that the objective perspective is itself a moral or even a valuational position; it is, rather, a metaethical thesis that all basic value experiences are in some sense similar. Each individual, occupying a particular perspective, still makes particular value judgments and has reasons to act on them. What I hope to show in the remainder of the chapter is that this objective metaethical perspective, while not a moral or valuational perspective, does have implications concerning what reasons others have and, consequently, implications as to what constitutes a good argument to them.

2. *Universal and Personal Reasons*

The taste model of value informing the responses of Fishkin's subjectivists clearly assumes that to say that something is valuable is to imply that one has a reason to act to secure it, promote it or, at a minimum, to choose its existence rather than its nonexistence.[41] Although this assumption is not entirely uncontroversial, it seems plausible enough. Since according to our subjectivists all value ultimately rests on having a taste for something—and that in turn implies some agreeable experience—to say that the recognition of value implies a reason to act is to hold (roughly) that recognizing that an experience is agreeable (or that something gives rise to, or is instrumental in bringing about, such experience) is always a reason to act to secure it or at least choose it. Note that this is a fairly modest claim. "*A* reason" is not the same as "a *conclusive* reason:" other, more important, reasons may dictate that one's tastes not be indulged. Nevertheless, some, such as John McDowell, dispute even this modest claim: as he sees it, for a "temperate person" a prospective enjoyment may count as no reason whatsoever to secure or choose it.[42]

Much more contentious is the second claim made by a subgroup of Fishkin's subjectivists—the "relativists." According to these relativists, your correct value judgments (I shall call these "well-grounded values") do not necessarily provide others with reasons to act, nor do the well-grounded values of others necessarily provide you with any reasons to act. Not all of Fishkin's subjectivists adopt this position: what he calls the "subjective universalist" agrees that values are a matter of taste, but still insists that others conform to his (i.e., the subjective universalist's) tastes.[43] (This latter position, though I think it puzzling, is not unusual; Geoffrey Harrison, for instance, is just one among many who argue that a "relativist metaethic" is entirely consistent with espousing a universalistic normative ethic such as utilitarianism.)[44] Here I think Fishkin is quite right: if one really does think that values are simply tastes, then it seems arbitrary to insist that others have reason to promote your values.[45] As I said, it is plausible to contend that recognition that one has a taste for something always provides one with a reason to secure it, choose it, etc.; but to contend that others necessarily have a reason to promote your tastes seems entirely unsupported by the analysis from the objective point of view. Of course, the universalist may not think that others do have any reason to promote his tastes, but nevertheless insist that they do so anyway. To the extent such a position is intelligible, it can be described as acting without justification, something we shall examine in section 4.

Much more troubling to our relativists is Nagel's argument that a thoroughgoingly agent-relative position such as theirs is "crazy." Consider, says Nagel, the position of the relativist if ". . . he and some other people have been admitted to a hospital with severe burns after being rescued from a fire. 'I understand how *my* pain provides *me* with a reason to take an analgesic,' he says, 'and I understand how my groaning neighbor's pain gives *him* a reason to take an analgesic; but how does *his* pain give *me* any reason to want to give him an analgesic? How can *his* pain give *me* or anyone else looking at it from outside a reason?' "[46]

"This question," Nagel concludes, "is crazy. As an expression of puzzlement, it has that characteristic philosophical craziness which indicates that something very fundamental has gone wrong. This shows up in the fact that the *answer* to the question is *obvious*, so obvious that to ask the question is obviously a philosophical act. The answer is that pain is *awful*. The pain of the man groaning in the next bed is just as awful as yours. That's your reason to want him to have an analgesic."[47]

Nagel suggests, then, that it is only philosophers who get themselves into difficulty here, by asking for justification where it isn't called for. Perhaps, in a sense, he is right. It may well be that many would agree with Nagel that the question is odd since the answer is obvious. To some extent, then, our relativists are probably calling into question something that seems obvious to many people, and that may rightly be called a philosophic attitude. But while perhaps infected with a philosophic attitude, Fishkin's relativists are interesting just because they are not professional philosophers trying to make a point, but ordinary enough (if by no means typical) practical reasoners who have come to question some "obvious" assumptions. The issue, then, is whether in any strict sense they would be crazy, i.e., irrational, to ask the question Nagel discusses. We must be very clear here that the issue is not whether we think the question immoral or shockingly insensitive, but whether we think it crazy, irrational or insane. Now Nagel's charge of actual craziness would be sound if the reasoning in this case was something like the following: (1) pain is itself bad, and so there is a reason for everyone to alleviate it; hence (2a) my pain is bad, and so there is a reason for me to alleviate it and (2b) my neighbor's pain is bad, and so there is a reason for him to alleviate it; but (3) my neighbor's pain is bad, yet there is no reason for me to alleviate it. Nagel's thesis—step 1—is that the objective perspective shows that pain itself is bad, and so everyone has a reason to alleviate it, wherever it may occur. Step 3 is thus inconsistent with 1: if you accept 1, then it really would be irrational to assert that you have no reason to alleviate your neighbor's pain. But our subjectivists deny that the objective perspective shows that pain in itself is bad. All it shows, they argue, is that each person has a reason to avoid what he finds distasteful; and assuming everyone finds his own pain distasteful, everyone has a reason to alleviate his own pain. If someone admitted that he found his own pain terribly distasteful, but nevertheless failed to see how this provides him with any reason at all to do anything about it, the question of irrationality would not, I think, be out of place. Basic to our concept of practical rationality is a close tie between prudential beliefs and reasons for action, and the relativist's model of value reasoning remains very close to prudential reasoning.[48] However, to ask how another's pain provides me with a reason to do anything about it seems intelligible enough; people who ask that question are terribly insensitive and uncaring, but not, I think, necessarily crazy or irrational. Because the subjectivists reject Nagel's first step—i.e., that recognition that anyone is experiencing pain necessarily provides anyone (who is able to do something about it) with a reason to act—it is both consistent and sane for them to insist that their neighbor's pain does not necessarily provide reasons for them to act. As Philippa Foot concludes, "if it means nothing to speak of an 'objectively valuable end,' then there are no reasons such as Nagel describes and I may say that another has reason to aim at his own good without implying that I too have reason to promote this end."[49]

An argument in many ways similar to Nagel's was put forward by utilitarians such as Hastings Rashdall and Henry Sidg-

wick. Both acknowledged that as long as an egoist simply asserted that he was only interested in his own pleasure or well-
being, he could not be argued out of his position. But, it was
contended, his egoism becomes internally inconsistent if he introduces the notion of goodness or value. As Rashdall put it,
"The egoistic Hedonist who says not merely 'I like pleasure and
therefore I intend to pursue it,' but 'the wise man is he who
pursues pleasure,' shows that he has this ultimate and unana-
lysable idea of good or value in his mind as much as the ideal-
izing moralist who says 'Virtue is the true end of human pursuit.' "[50] But, the argument runs, if the egoist admits that the
pleasure of each has value, then it is arbitrary for him to insist
that only his own pleasure—a small part of total value—provides a reason for him to act. Hence, Rashdall concluded, "it is
rational for him to pursue his neighbor's pleasure as well as his
own, and to prefer the larger amount of pleasure to the smaller,
even though the larger pleasure be the pleasure of others, and
the smaller his own."[51]

It would seem that our relativists, though not committed to
egoism,[52] are open to a parallel objection. Since the taste model
relates all value back to some agreeable experience, it appears
that anyone who accepts the model also accepts that such experience is either itself intrinsically valuable or the ground of
all intrinsic value. But if so, then the relativist appears to be li-
able to Rashdall's charge that he is ignoring a great deal of what
is valuable by focusing his reasons for action entirely on his own
experiences. This argument appears convincing, I think, only
if one confuses (1) a theory of what is valuable to all with (2) a
theory about what is valuable to each. Many value theorists who
base their accounts on individual responses to objects do indeed present theories of the first type. For example, Perry appeared to believe that if any person is interested in an object,
that object is valuable and, so, *everyone* potentially has a reason
to act.[53] But, as I already pointed out, our relativists deny that
one sees anything as intrinsically valuable for which one does
not have a taste. They thus present a theory of the second type,
a theory about what is valuable to each. And according to this
theory, it is *not* the case that I necessarily see any value in my
agreeable experiences. Consequently, in not seeing your agreeable experiences as reasons for action I am not ignoring any-

thing of value, since, according to the relativist, I explicitly deny that, from my perspective, your agreeable experiences are necessarily valuable. And, mutatis mutandis, the same holds true regarding disvalue.

4. SUBJECTIVE VALUE AND PUBLIC JUSTIFICATION

1. Public Justification

I have been arguing that the relativist is not necessarily committed to acknowledging that what others nonerroneously value, he too must value. Nevertheless, the subjectivist-relativist's metaethical position does ascribe some status to the values of others: given his thesis as to the essential symmetry between the reasons of subjective valuers, he acknowledges that from a position of "cosmic neutrality," "the other guy has a perfectly [sic], as sound a ground as I do for acting."[54] This thesis, I want to argue, does have an important implication for political theory: namely, the subjectivist must acknowledge that a range of traditional political theories cannot be *publicly justified*. Let me explain.

In order to qualify as a public justification for a political arrangement, a proffered justificatory argument must provide everybody who is to be subject to the arrangement with sufficient reasons for submitting to the arrangement. Or, put somewhat differently, the justification must convince any member of the public who is not rationally defective that he should submit to the proposed arrangement. This notion of a public justification captures, I think, the twofold nature of justification, as both (1) a primarily interpersonal practical activity and (2) a form of reasoning. As Rawls says, ". . . justification is argument addressed to those who disagree with us, or to ourselves when we are of two minds. It presumes a clash of views between persons or within one person, and seeks to convince others, or ourselves, of the reasonableness of the principles upon which our claims and judgments are founded."[55] Now it seems reasonable to take the interpersonal sense as primary. Rawls's description of the purely personal case—being "of two minds"—itself is a metaphor borrowed from the interpersonal case. Moreover if, as Rawls says, in the personal case we are trying to convince ourselves, we are assuming both the roles of advocate and judge—he who is doing the convincing and he who is to be convinced—again assimilating the case to the interpersonal model. But justification does not seek simply to persuade or convince others, but to do so by providing good reasons.[56] As Rawls says, it is argument; it is thus to be distinguished from nonrational persuasive techniques. One way to combine both of these facets is to understand justificatory arguments as seeking to convince those who are moved if and only if they are presented with good reasons. Consequently, if the justificatory argument is not to be abandoned, when someone is not convinced the justifier must be able to maintain that the rejector is not being moved by good reasons, and in that sense is rationally defective.[57] To be sure, the argument need not end here; further argument can center on what constitutes a good reason. But for my present purposes the crucial point is that *if the would-be justifier admits that he has not provided good reasons, he is committed to acknowledging that the justificatory argument fails.*

The sense in which the justificatory argument is public, then, is that it seeks to provide good reasons for submitting to everyone who is to be subject to the proposed political arrangement. However, it does not require publicness in the stronger sense that the reasons offered to justify the arrangement must be based on beliefs actually shared by all, for some of the potential public may not entertain beliefs they have good reason for accepting. (Aristotle's natural slaves would seem to be such people.) So a public justificatory argument need not seek the consent of all, for it has succeeded if it has provided good reasons to submit even if actual consent is withheld. This sheds light on the justificatory force of social contract theories. It is often remarked that, while contract theories appear to rely on consent, this consent is ultimately bogus; the choice conditions are typically so constructed that everyone must consent to the arrangement and, consequently, withholding consent is not a real option. At best, it is said, consent (e.g., in theories such as Kant's or Locke's) is otiose, since the theory provides sufficient reasons justifying the arrangement: the "consent" adds nothing. But we can now see that a consent argument—even if it is a "rationally mandatory consent"—does play an important role: it stresses that the justificatory argument is public in that it provides good reasons to *everyone* to submit to the arrangement. The important point is not that all are free to consent or withhold consent, but that *everyone* is provided with good reasons why he *must* consent. This is true even of social contract theories such as Rawls's, in which imaginary parties consent to the principles of justice behind the "veil of ignorance." For the justificatory force of Rawls' argument is not simply that these imaginary parties happen to agree to the principles; the justification stems from the claim that their hypothetical agreement provides good reasons for all actual persons (e.g., Rawls's readers) to submit to liberal arrangements.[58]

This is not to say that only social contract theories present public justificatory arguments. Although their form stresses the publicness condition, nearly all arguments in the history of political theory have sought to be public in this way. To refrain from presenting an argument that (is at least claimed to be) publicly justificatory one must acknowledge that some person or group of people to whom the arrangement will apply are not even in principle the proper subjects of a justification. It is difficult to find instances of this position in the history of political theory. On some readings, Marx seems to offer such a position. It has been argued recently, for instance, that Marx accepted that "In the course of history, normal people have had deep moral differences that were not due to unreason or ignorance. Similarly, in the present day, there are conflicting conceptions of the good that cannot be resolved through rational persuasion."[59] Nevertheless, it is said that Marx did not let this belief interfere with his commitment to advancing socialism, even though, in my terms, it could not be publicly justified. But I think that Nietzsche is a clearer case. In his parable of the lambs and the birds of prey, the views of the birds on the subject of lamb-eating are, understandably enough, unacceptable to the lambs. But apparently the birds do not think that the lambs are in any way rationally defective because of this. The lambs could not be expected to accept the birds' views on lamb-eating, but that is not to say that the lambs are ignoring good reasons, but only that they are lambs. Thus the birds don't think the lambs flawed or evil: "*We* don't dislike them at all, these good little lambs; we even love them: nothing is more tasty than a tender lamb."[60] Nietzsche thought that the great mistake of birds of prey was to engage in any attempt to justify their actions to lambs at all; as much as anything, Nietzsche's parable is aimed at demonstrating the dangers (to birds of prey) of all justificatory arguments. In essence, Nietzsche is saying that it is inappropriate to present some people with reasons why they should accept a political or social arrangement. And it is not merely that, as Aristotle presumably thought regarding slaves, they are incapable of accepting good arguments for their subordinate position; it is the much more radical position that, in relation to some humans, good arguments, or indeed any arguments, are simply out of place. To be sure, Nietzsche's birds may still argue among themselves about what to do with the lambs; but that is precisely parallel to the sort of argument which takes place among citizens about what they should do with resources. No possibility of justification exists between the groups.

2. Subjective Value and Liberalism

A relativist, I have argued, accepts that from an objective point of view, the values of others are as "valid" as his own, and this leads him to maintain that their value-based reasons for action are as firmly grounded as are his own. He also accepts that just as another person's well-grounded values do not themselves necessarily generate reasons for him to act, his well-grounded values do not necessarily provide others with any reason to act. Moreover, and this is an important point, he acknowledges that others are not rationally defective for not seeing his well-grounded values as necessarily generating reasons for them to act. Given all this, then, it seems impossible for any subjectivist to give a public justificatory argument for political arrangements that promote his values over those of others because of their intrinsic superiority. Although his well-grounded values provide sufficient reasons for him to act, they cannot *in themselves* provide the basis of a publicly oriented argument: others are not necessarily committed to accepting that his well-grounded values provide them with any reasons for doing anything, and he must also accept that others are not rationally defective because of this.

It seems very difficult indeed for our subjectivist-relativists to reject this conclusion. The most radical maneuver aimed at avoiding the conclusion would be for a subjectivist, while admitting that from the objective perspective all tastes are equally valid, to simply insist that, after all, he does not have a taste for objectivity, so he will persist in justifying his preferred arrangements on the basis of his own values. But this won't do. Whatever his tastes, if nondefective others have no reason to accept his values as reasons for them, those values cannot provide the basis of a public justificatory argument. To be sure, such a subjectivist may then reply that he is not interested in justification; like Nietzsche's birds of prey, he intends to do what he has his own reasons for doing without worrying about justifying himself to others. Now, as I said at the outset, my thesis 5 concerns what sort of justifications a subjectivist-relativist can offer; a subjectivist's metaethical commitments, I want to stress, do indeed have significant consequences for any attempt to develop a publicly justificatory political theory. My main aim, then, is not to demonstrate that a subjectivist is inescapably rationally committed to engaging in justification. Nevertheless, we can point to at least three lines of argument which indicate that subjectivists typically have good reason to justify themselves.

(1) The most straightforward argument is the sort of prudential case presented by Hobbes and which more recently has been defended by Kurt Baier. The Hobbesian analysis, including its modern game theoretic formulations, provides reasons to believe that it may well be self-defeating for a subjectivist to abandon justificatory practices (e.g., morality) in order to pursue his own values. If, as Baier argues, "Moralities are systems of principles whose acceptance by everyone as overruling the dictates of self-interest is in the interest of everyone alike . . . ,"[61] the subjectivist has reason to be moral. (2) Doubts as to whether a subjectivist or relativist has any reason to engage in justification (or whether people have any reason to be moral) almost always fail to give due regard to the natural fact that humans are social beings with social sentiments. Although it is not a logical necessity, it is a natural fact that we value friendship, the good of our fellows and indeed experience some sympathy with many with whom we are not directly acquainted.[62] Subjectivist-relativists who have such "tastes"—and it most likely is a fact that normal humans are so constituted as to have them— have reason to engage in justificatory argument. For to act without justification—especially in the construction of rules governing social institutions—would seem to undermine these social sentiments.[63] (3) Lastly, recent analysis of the moral emo-

tions demonstrates that abandonment of justification would require a radical revision of our conception of other humans.
Following Nagel, David A.J. Richards and S.I. Benn, we can see
that it would be incoherent to feel resentment or indignation
toward those excluded from the justification if they oppose the
arrangement, violated its rules or subverted it.[64] Resentment and
indignation presuppose beliefs about the responsibility of the
transgressor; they are only appropriate when someone has
transgressed rules, principles or norms when, as we say, he
should have know better. They are thus not appropriate, for
instance, toward babies or those who could not have possibly
known about the rule. Nor are they appropriate emotions if one
acknowledges that the transgressor had no good reason for accepting the rule and was not in any way defective for not having such a reason. Now if it is incoherent to blame such trans-
gressors or to feel resentment or indignation, one is committed
at least in this respect to treating them as simply natural or social factors. As with Marx's capitalists they might be obstacles
which induce anger or, like Nietzsche's lambs, they may simply
be regarded as resources; they can, like pets or babies, even be
treated as objects of concern. But the typical attitudes which assume some sort of moral personality are undermined by abandoning public justification. We may plausibly say, then, that
public justification is a minimum condition for respecting moral
personality; to act without public justification is, quite literally,
to treat some as objects.

None of these arguments is conclusive in the sense that it is
impossible to imagine a sufficiently Nietzschean subjectivist whose
tastes still incline him to abandon justificatory arguments. But
they seem quite sufficient to undermine the claim (i.e., claim 3)
that somehow subjective-relativism leads to intolerance. The
weight of these considerations seem to present a strong case for
public justification. Now according to my main thesis, the subjectivist-relativist cannot consistently[65] offer a public justificatory argument that rests on the claim that some values are intrinsically valid for all and so necessarily provide reasons for all
to act. Given this constraint, it is very difficult indeed to envisage subjectivist-relativist public justifications of political arrangements premised on, for example, perfectionism, altruistic
utilitarianism or most theories centered on the idea of the hu-

man good. All such theories are typically based on the claim that a certain value (e.g., developed personalities of a certain sort, the happiness of sentient creatures, human welfare) provide reasons for action for everyone regardless of his tastes. As John Finnis, a proponent of such a theory, puts it, "It is one thing to have little capacity and even no 'taste' for scholarship, or friendship, or physical heroism, or sanctity; it is quite another thing, and stupid and arbitrary, to think or speak or act as if these were not real forms of good."[66] And from that, Finnis concludes, we all have reason to respect and affirm these goods; which, in turn, provides the foundation of his common good theory. This sort of justificatory argument, and a host of others like it, are closed to a subjectivist publicly justificatory political theory. Unless each person has the relevant value experience, values such as perfection, the greatest happiness, scholarship or whatever, cannot provide the basis of a public justificatory argument.

The argument thus points in the general direction of Bruce A. Ackerman's neutrality principle, according to which "No reason is a good reason if it requires the power holder to assert: (a) that his conception of the good is better than that asserted by his fellow citizens, *or* (b) that, regardless of his conception of the good, he is intrinsically superior to one or more of his fellow citizens."[67] But while Ackerman's principle captures the spirit of a subjectivist public justificatory argument, and so provides strong support for the idea that subjectivism is closely allied with liberalism, we ought to be cautious about this liberal link. Not only key arguments of Ackerman, Alan Gewirth and Michael Oakeshott, but theories as diverse as Hobbes's and those of individualist anarchists seem open to the subjectivist.[68] For Hobbes argues that by appealing to the values of each, each can be provided with reasons to submit to the will of one, while the individualist anarchist is apt to insist that by appealing to the values of each, each can be provided with reasons to submit to the will of no one. But perhaps this need not be too unsettling for the subjectivist liberal. Individualist anarchists almost imperceptibly merge into libertarian liberals[69] and Hobbes, despite his obvious illiberalism, is apt to be included as an honorary, if wayward, member of the liberal tradition. Most significantly, Hobbes is typically accorded this honorary membership just because his method of justification, demonstrating that the values of each provide each with a reason to submit to the Leviathan, is a characteristically (if by no means intrinsically) liberal mode of argument. And it is just this sort of "liberal-like" argument to which our subjectivist-relativists seem committed.

More troubling perhaps for the liberal connection is the problem of paternalism. Although Ackerman sees his neutrality principle as tapping "the liberal's opposition to paternalism,"[70] paternalist public justifications are certainly open to a subjectivist political theory. A political arrangement can be justified if it shows that it promotes the values of each, even though many fail to see this, or are mistaken as to what they value, etc. As we have already seen (section 2, part 3), value *judgments* can be in error; there also can be mistakes as to whether an action is consistent with the reasons generated by one's own *correct* value judgments. Much more problematic, indeed too problematic to resolve here, is whether one's refusal to become acquainted with something for which one would develop a taste constitutes a defect (a defect, that is, in the sense relevant to the criterion of public justification, namely that it undermines the force of one's refusal to accept the justification). On the one hand, it seems that the fact that one would develop the relevant taste may be a reason for acting, and to ignore a reason for acting seems a defect of rationality; yet, on the other hand, if one does not as yet have the taste, there is no value, and so far it has only been argued that one's values provide one with reasons to act. The reason-generating power of potential values seem somewhat murky. In any event, it should be manifest that a subjectivist-relativist metaethic by no means commits one to nonpaternalist justifications; whether this possibility is necessarily hostile to a liberal political theory is something I shall not pursue here.[71]

5. Conclusion

My aim in this chapter has been twofold. First, I have tried to show that a theory of subjective value need not undermine liberal theory by making nonsense of value-based discourse (thesis 6). Indeed, once it is recognized that a subjective theory of value does not imply that value judgments are somehow private and irrefutable, a good deal of the attraction of theories claiming a somewhat deeper, if not altogether clear, objectivity evaporates. We thus need not embrace a theory of objective value simply in order to retain value discourse. Secondly, I have sought to show that at least one variety of subjectivism does indeed have commitments regarding political justification (thesis 5). I have not tried to demonstrate here, however, either (1) that such subjectivists always have an absolutely conclusive reason to engage in justification (though I think they have strong reasons to) or (2) that such subjectivists actually can succeed in justifying a liberal order, or indeed any order. In this sense my main thesis is modest: namely, if our subjectivists do proffer a publicly justificatory political theory, they find themselves significantly constrained at the outset regarding the range of possible arguments. Subjectivism by no means logically commits one to liberal political arrangements; it does, however, require public justificatory political theories to demonstrate that proposed political arrangements advance the well-grounded values of each and every citizen, whatever they may be. It is in this sense that subjectivists are committed to liberal-like or characteristically liberal modes of argument. And it is this commitment that underlies the longstanding link between subjectivism and liberalism.

NOTES

1. Edward Westermarck, *Ethical Relativity* (London: Kegan Paul, 1932), pp. 59–60.
2. Quoted in Richard B. Brandt, *Ethical Theory* (Englewood Cliffs, N.J.: Prentice-Hall, 1959), p. 288.
3. James S. Fishkin, *Beyond Subjective Morality* (New Haven: Yale University Press, 1984), pp. 1, 37–41. Fishkin's respondents were students and recent graduates of Yale and Cambridge. Ibid., p. 25. See also Fishkin's "Relativism, Liberalism and Moral Development," in Richard Wilson and Gordon J. Schochet, eds., *Moral Development and Politics* (New York: Praeger, 1980), pp. 85–106.
4. I am not claiming that respect or tolerance (or neutrality, see below) all amount to the same thing; I do, though, think they are closely related notions. For analyses of these principles and their

relation to liberalism, see: John Rawls, *A Theory of Justice* (Cambridge: Harvard University Press, Belknap Press, 1971), esp. pp. 541ff; Bruce A. Ackerman, *Social Justice in the Liberal State* (New Haven: Yale University Press, 1980), pp. 10ff; Ronald Dworkin, "Liberalism" in Stuart Hampshire, ed., *Public and Private Morality* (Cambridge: Cambridge University Press, 1978), pp. 113–43; pp. 127ff; Michael Oakeshott, *On Human Conduct* (Oxford: Oxford University Press, 1975), part II; Alan Gewirth, *Reason and Morality* (Chicago: University of Chicago Press, 1978), p. 242.

5. Brandt, *Ethical Theory*, p. 289. Brandt admits, however, that "there may be something about the relativist doctrine that tends to *incline the attitudes* of its advocates toward tolerance."

6. In addition to Brandt, see: Geoffrey Harrison, "Relativism and Tolerance" in Peter Laslett and James Fishkin, eds., *Philosophy, Politics and Society*, 5th series (Oxford: Basil Blackwell, 1979), pp. 273–90; Neil Cooper, *The Diversity of Moral Thinking* (Oxford: Clarendon Press, 1981), p. 152; Bernard Williams, *Morality* (New York: Harper and Row, 1972), pp. 20ff. I am indebted here to Robert Kocis.

7. William Galston, "Defending Liberalism," *American Political Science Review* 76 (1982); 621–29, 625.

8. Fishkin, *Subjective Morality*, pp. 145, 2. Critics of liberalism tend to focus on the alleged pernicious consequences of this sort of subjectivism, which they see as characteristic of liberalism. See: Roberto Mangabeira Unger, *Knowledge and Politics* (New York: The Free Press, 1975), ch. 2; Alasdair MacIntyre, *After Virtue* (Notre Dame: Notre Dame University Press, 1981).

9. Fishkin, *Subjective Morality*, pp. 32–35.

10. Ibid., p. 35.

11. Ibid., p. 38.

12. Ibid., pp. 44–45.

13. On the history of modern value theory, see W.H. Werkmeister, *Historical Spectrum of Value Theories* (Lincoln, Neb.: Johnson, 1970).

14. C.I. Lewis, *An Analysis of Knowledge and Valuation* (LaSalle, Ill.: Open Court, 1946), p. 410.

15. See W.H. Werkmeister, *Man and His Values* (Lincoln: University of Nebraska Press, 1967), ch. IV.

16. John Locke, *An Essay Concerning Human Understanding*, ed. Peter H. Nidditch (Oxford: Clarendon Press, 1975), p. 269 (bk. II, ch. xxi, section 55). See John Laird, *The Idea of Value* (Cambridge: Cambridge University Press, 1931), pp. 118ff. For a discussion of an objection to the taste model, see Willis Moore, "The Language

of Values" in Ray Lepley, ed., *The Language of Value* (New York: Columbia University Press, 1957), pp. 9–28, 13.

17. I am assuming what Brandt calls a "quality of experience" theory of the enjoyable, agreeable, etc. rather than his preferred view, a "motivational theoretical-construct" theory. See Richard B. Brandt, *A Theory of the Right and the Good* (Oxford: Clarendon Press, 1979), pp. 35–42.

18. Lewis, *Analysis of Knowledge and Valuation*, pp. 383ff, 389ff.

19. See John Stuart Mill, *Utilitarianism* (Indianapolis: Bobbs Merrill, 1957), pp. 10–11 (ch. II, para. 2). Mill is discussing what is intrinsically desirable here. For a discussion of Bentham's value theory, see Werkmeister, *Value Theories*, vol. I, pp. 1–8.

20. Lewis, *Analysis of Knowledge and Valuation*, p. 391; cf. Mill, *Utilitarianism*, pp. 10–11 (ch. II, para. 2).

21. See Howard O. Eaton, *The Austrian Philosophy of Values* (Norman: University of Oklahoma Press, 1930), p. 94. Lewis, however, defined "utility" in a wider sense; see *Analysis of Knowledge and Valuation*, p. 385.

22. This raises difficult issues concerning the conditions under which enjoyment is to be expected, the likelihood it will be had, etc. See Lewis, *Analysis of Knowledge and Valuation*, ch. XVII.

23. Ralph Barton Perry, *General Theory of Value* (New York: Longman's, Green and Co., 1926), p. 133. This view is criticized by DeWitt Parker in his *Philosophy of Value* (Ann Arbor: University of Michigan Press, 1957), ch. 1.

24. Lewis, *Analysis of Knowledge and Valuation*, pp. 410, 485. Compare Locke, *Essay Concerning Human Understanding*, p. 272 (bk. II, ch. xxi, p. 58).

25. Lewis, *Analysis of Knowledge and Valuation*, p. 410. See also Locke, *Essay Concerning Human Understanding*, pp. 276ff (bk. II, ch. xxi, pp. 64ff); Perry, *General Theory*, pp. 362ff.

26. Cf. J.S. Mill's comments concerning the ability of "the power of analysis" to break down the artificial association of things with pleasure and pain. *Autobiography* (New York: Columbia University Press, 1924), pp. 96–97.

27. For a related discussion concerning Meinong's theory, see Eaton, *Austrian Philosophy of Values*, pp. 212ff.

28. Fishkin, *Subjective Morality*, pp. 50, 140. A very similar point is made by Richard Werner, "Ethical Realism," *Ethics* 93 (1983); 653–79, 676–77.

29. Hobbes's theory, while subjective, centers on conation rather than affective experience. See *Leviathan*, ed. Michael Oakeshott (New

York: Collier, 1962), pp. 48–49 (ch. 6). See also Laird, *Idea of Value,* pp. 135ff.

30. Once in the civil condition, Hobbes holds that the sovereign is a definitive judge of good and evil. *Leviathan,* p. 49 (ch. 6).

31. Ibid., pp. 102ff (last para. of ch. 13, chs. 14, 15). See also Hobbes's essay "On Man," in *Man and Citizen,* ed. Bernard Gert (New York: Anchor Books, 1972), pp. 48–49 (ch. XI, section 6).

32. Fishkin, *Subjective Morality,* pp. 61, 69.

33. Ibid., p. 69.

34. Ibid., p. 66.

35. Ibid., p. 64. J. Kellenberger examines the distinction between individual and societal ethical relativism in "Ethical Relativism," *Journal of Value Inquiry* 13 (1979): 1–20. Note, however, that I am concerned here with value relativism, not ethical relativism.

36. Ruth Benedict, *Patterns of Culture* (London: George Routledge and Sons, 1935), pp. 200–201.

37. Thomas Nagel, "The Limits of Objectivity," in Sterling M. McMurrin, ed., *The Tanner Lectures on Human Values* (Cambridge: Cambridge University Press, 1980), vol. I, pp. 76–139, 85.

38. Fishkin, *Subjective Morality,* p. 70.

39. Thomas Nagel, "Subjective and Objective" in his *Moral Questions* (Cambridge: Cambridge University Press, 1979), pp. 196–213, 209. See also "The Limits of Objectivity." For an analysis of objectivity with more emphasis on the relativity of values, see A.W. Price, "Varieties of Objectivity and Values," *Proceedings of the Aristotelian Society* (1983): 103–119.

40. Williams, *Morality,* p. 29.

41. It is widely held that the recognition of values necessarily implies the recognition of reasons for action. See, for example, E.J. Bond, *Reason and Value* (Cambridge: Cambridge University Press, 1983), p. 95; Joseph Raz, *Practical Reason and Norms* (London: Hutchinson, 1975), pp. 25ff; S.I. Benn, "Persons and Values; Reasons in Conflict and Moral Disagreements," *Ethics* 95 (1984), 20–37. For an argument disputing this link, see Michael Slote, *Goods and Virtues* (Oxford: Clarendon Press, 1983), ch. 5.

42. John McDowell, "Are Moral Requirements Hypothetical Imperatives?" *Proceedings of the Aristotelian Society,* supplementary volume 52 (1978): 13–29; pp. 27ff.

43. Fishkin, *Subjective Morality,* pp. 35–37, 141ff.

44. See Harrison, "Relativism and Tolerance."

45. Fishkin, *Subjective Morality,* pp. 141ff.

46. Nagel, "The Limits of Objectivity," p. 109.

47. Ibid., p. 110. See also R.M. Hare, *Moral Thinking* (Oxford: Clarendon Press, 1981), ch. 5.

48. ". . . [W]hereas everybody has adequate reason to follow precepts following which favorably affects his life, not everybody has reason to follow precepts following which favorably affects other people's lives. . . . [F]or it would seem to be impossible for a normal person to be entirely unconcerned about himself, but possible for him to be unconcerned about many other persons. It seems that total indifference towards or unconcern about one's own fate is characteristic of psychotics. . . ." Kurt Baier, "The Practice of Justification," *The Journal of Value Inquiry* 9 (1975): 34–41, 40. See also Philippa Foot, *Virtues and Vices* (Berkeley and Los Angeles: University of California Press, 1978), chs. XI, XII. For an argument linking prudential reasoning to moral reasoning see Thomas Nagel, *The Possibility of Altruism* (Princeton: Princeton University Press, 1970).

49. Foot, *Virtues and Vices,* p. 154.

50. Hastings Rashdall, *The Theory of Good and Evil* (Oxford: Clarendon Press, 1907), vol. I, pp. 47–48. See also Henry Sidgwick, *The Methods of Ethics,* 7th ed. (Chicago: University of Chicago Press, 1962), pp. 420–21; J.L. Mackie, *Ethics* (Harmondsworth: Penguin, 1977), pp. 142–43.

51. Rashdall, *Good and Evil,* vol. I, p. 48.

52. Lawrence C. Becker argues that the relativists' position is indeed a form of egoism in *On Justifying Moral Judgments* (London: Routledge and Kegan Paul, 1973), pp. 56–57. But this is to confuse self-centered and selfish reasons for action; it thus appears more accurate to speak of the "ego-centric" characteristic of the theory. See Parker, *The Philosophy of Value,* p. 207; Eaton, *Austrian Philosophy of Values,* pp. 237–39.

53. See R.B. Perry, *Realms of Value* (Cambridge: Harvard University Press, 1954), pp. 2–3, 13. For a different view linking individual responses to objects with reasons for all, see Lewis, *Knowledge and Valuation,* ch. XVII.

54. Fishkin, *Subjective Morality,* p. 47.

55. Rawls, *A Theory of Justice,* p. 580.

56. Carl Wellman questions the link between justification and providing good reasons in his *Challenge and Response: Justification in Ethics* (Carbondale and Edwardsville: Southern Illinois University Press, 1971), ch. 5. For analyses closer to that presented here, see Baier, "Justification;" John Kleinig, *Punishment and Desert* (The Hague: Martinus Nijhoff, 1973), ch. 1.

57. According to David A.J. Richards, there are "examples of men of

warped moral character whose acceptances and rejections have no weight" in determining whether political and moral principles are justified. He thus appears to believe that moral, as well as strictly rational, defects can prevent someone from accepting a genuine justification. However, although Richards does not believe that such moral defects imply irrationality, he does maintain that they point to "unreasonableness." *A Theory of Reasons for Action* (Oxford: Clarendon Press, 1971), pp. 12, 75ff, 227ff.

58. See Rawls, *A Theory of Justice*, pp. 21–22. See also Fred D'Agostino, "The Method of Reflective Equilibrium," Philosophy Department Seminar, Research School of Social Sciences, Australian National University.

59. Richard W. Miller, "Marx and Morality" in J. Roland Pennock and John W. Chapman, eds., *NOMOS XXVI: Marxism* (New York: New York University Press, 1983), pp. 3–32, 31. See, however, Patrick Riley's and Frederick G. Whelan's comments on Miller's interpretation in the following two chapters of the volume.

60. Frederick Nietzsche, *On the Genealogy of Morals,* trans. Walter Kaufmann and R.J. Hollingwood (New York: Vintage Books, 1967), p. 45 (first essay, section 13).

61. Kurt Baier, *The Moral Point of View* (Ithaca: Cornell University Press, 1958), p. 314.

62. For a discussion of social sentiments and their limits in liberalism, see my *Modern Liberal Theory of Man* (London and New York: Croom-Helm and St. Martin's Press, 1983), chs. II, III.

63. See Rawls's discussion, "The Morality of Association," in *A Theory of Justice,* section 71.

64. See Nagel, *Possibility of Altruism,* pp. 82ff; Richards, *Theory of Reasons for Action,* pp. 250ff; S.I. Benn, "Freedom, Autonomy, and the Concept of a Person," *Proceedings of the Aristotelian Society* (1976): 109–30.

65. Again, a subjectivist may argue—as some of Fishkin's do—that consistency too is just a matter of taste; and if one does not have a taste for it, my argument certainly fails. But, then again, if consistency is not a reason to accept an argument, all possibility of rational discourse and justificatory argument is undermined. Alan Gewirth, I think, is quite right that reasons of consistency are of a more fundamental nature than other commitments; indeed, it is doubtful that they are value-based at all. *Reason and Morality,* pp. 22ff. See Fishkin, *Subjective Morality,* p. 37.

66. John Finnis, *Natural Law and Natural Rights* (Oxford: Clarendon Press, 1980), p. 105.

67. Ackerman, *Social Justice,* p. 11.

68. On the distinction between communal and individualist anar-
    chists, see John P. Clark, "What is Anarchism?" in J. Roland Pen-
    nock and John W. Chapman, eds., *NOMOS XIX: Anarchism* (New
    York: New York University Press, 1978), pp. 3–28, 21–23.
69. This is obvious in James M. Buchanan, "A Contractarian Perspec-
    tive on Anarchy," in *NOMOS XIX: Anarchism,* pp. 29–42.
70. Ackerman, *Social Justice,* p. 10.
71. John Kleinig shows the extent to which paternalism can be justi-
    fied within the liberal framework. *Paternalism* (Totowa, N.J.: Row-
    man and Allanheld, 1984).

I would like to express my gratitude to Stanley Benn for his
criticism and constructive comments regarding both my analysis and its presentation. I also benefited from discussions with
Peter Forrest and Philip Pettit. Written comments by Fred
D'Agostino and John Kleinig were particularly useful; my
thanks to both.

14

POLITICS AND THE
PURSUIT OF AUTONOMY

RICHARD DAGGER

There are two ways, broadly speaking, to conceive of politics. According to the first, politics is an activity, one among many, in which men and women compete for power and advantage. For those who conceive of politics in this way—for Thrasymachus in the *Republic,* for instance, and for those today who regard politics as a matter of who gets what, when, how—justification in politics proceeds as straightforwardly as it does in any competitive game. In a tennis match, say, or Monopoly or chess, a player provides a satisfactory justification for a course of action simply by showing how it could be construed as a reasonable way of winning. In much the same fashion, on this view, political actors can justify their actions and policies by demonstrating how the action or policy in question advances their interests, usually at their opponents' expense. As in any competitive activity, then, justification in politics is an essentially strategic business.

There is some truth to this conception of politics, as politicians themselves remind us when they accuse one another of "playing politics" or of acting from "purely political" motives. When they do this, however, they also remind us that this is not

I am indebted to the editors for their comments on an earlier draft of this essay. An even earlier version was presented at the Midwest Political Science Association's 1982 convention as "Rights, Justice, and Public Policy."

the whole truth, for if it were they could not sensibly *accuse* one another of "playing politics." To accuse someone of "playing politics" or of acting from "purely political" motives is to charge him with impropriety, and this would be absurd if politics were nothing more than a contest for power and advantage—as absurd as accusing John McEnroe or Martina Navratilova of "playing tennis."

If the charge does not strike us as absurd, it is because we commonly conceive of politics in the second way. According to this view, politics is a fundamentally ethical enterprise. Strategy plays a part, to be sure, but it is subordinate to the requirement that the men and women who engage in political activity place the interests of their community, whatever they may be, ahead of their personal interests. Those who fail to do this—those who act as if politics were nothing more than a contest for power and advantage—will usually be charged with abusing their office, even if it is only the office of citizen. Politics is an ethical enterprise, moreover, because the questions we face and the decisions we reach in politics force us, either directly or indirectly, to consider how we are to order our lives in and our life as a community. For in politics we are ultimately concerned with an *ethos,* a way of life, and our deeds and decisions determine what this ethos happens to be.

This ethical conception of politics is richer than its rival, but its richness carries a price. For if politics is fundamentally ethical, we will not be able to justify our conduct in politics by straightforward appeals to strategic considerations. These considerations may be all we need to undertake when the end or objective of an activity is reasonably clear, as it is in tennis, carpentry, or the practice of medicine. But they will not be sufficient when the end or purpose of the activity is not definite or, as in politics, when an essential part of the activity is to determine what ends we ought to pursue. In these circumstances, attempts to justify conduct will have to refer, at least implicitly, to ethical standards. Political justification, in short, is a form of ethical justification, and this implies that an adequate justification in politics will have to rely on a compelling theory of ethics.

In Anglo-American political philosophy, this has usually meant that arguments over justification in politics have turned on the dispute between utilitarians and deontologists. For quite some time the utilitarians seemed to have the better case, and public policy in the West often took its bearings from the Benthamite notion that "The business of government is to promote the happiness of society, by punishing and rewarding."[1] In the last decade, however, philosophical opinion appears to have shifted. Different as they are in other respects, the books that commanded the attention of political philosophers in the 1970s—including John Rawls's *A Theory of Justice*, Robert Nozick's *Anarchy, State, and Utopia*, and Ronald Dworkin's *Taking Rights Seriously*[2]—almost all share the conviction that utilitarianism, whatever its form, is deficient.[3] On this point, at least, they seem to have won the agreement of most of their readers. Utilitarianism may still be a force in political philosophy, but it is no longer the dominant force.

If the utilitarian foundation for political action and public policy is faulty, then the task is to replace it with an ethical theory that does not suffer from its defects—and the obvious candidates are theories based on rights rather than consequences. My purpose here is to present the leading features of such a theory. In particular, I shall sketch a rights-based theory that meets two of the objections often raised against theories of this sort: (1) that they lead to the radical individualism espoused by Nozick and the Libertarians, a view many find narrow, insensitive, and blind to the social nature of human beings; and (2) that they correct the utilitarian's neglect of rights only by committing the equally damaging error of neglecting consequences.[4]

1.

Although utilitarianism takes a variety of forms, many devised to meet criticisms, the core of the utilitarian position is its emphasis on the consequences of actions. The moral person, according to utilitarians, is the one who strives to promote the greatest happiness of the greatest number, to maximize aggregate welfare, or to produce the highest sum of individual satisfaction. The difficulty with this principle, as critics have long complained, is that it is purely aggregative. It tells us to maximize happiness (or welfare or utility), that is, without regard to how that happiness is distributed. Since the utility some people gain from a course of action may outweigh the disutility inflicted on others, the principle of utility may even require us to sacrifice the interests of some individuals in order to produce the highest overall sum of utility. As a consequence, conscientious utilitarians may find themselves in the morally awkward position of condoning the enslavement, torture, or "punishment" of innocent people whenever they believe that they can maximize aggregate utility by doing so. In these and less dramatic cases, utility seems to be purchased at the expense of justice.

Nor is the sacrifice of interests all that is at issue. Another common complaint is that utilitarianism, which grants equal consideration to the interests of everyone affected by an action, fails to recognize that individuals have *rights*—claims to the respect and forbearance of others that are independent of considerations of utility.[5] For the utilitarian, rights are nothing more than presumptions of utility, mere rules of thumb that enable us to maximize utility in ordinary circumstances without engaging in tiresome calculations. To say, for instance, that individuals have the right to express themselves freely is to say only that in most cases, or as a rule, allowing individuals to express themselves freely will maximize utility, welfare, or happiness. Such a (mis)conception does not capture the point of rights, however, for a right is meant to stand as a moral bulwark against social pressure or aggregative considerations. For this reason, anyone who takes rights seriously will find utilitarianism unacceptable.

Underlying both these difficulties is a more fundamental problem, which is simply that utilitarians regard all preferences as continuous, as subject to trade-offs.[6] Preferences are continuous, or substitutable, when they may all be measured on a common scale, such as utility, or when they may be exchanged for one another. I may attach more value to attending professional conferences than professional basketball games, for example, but it is nonetheless possible for me to draw an indifference curve, albeit a crude one, establishing a trade-off rate between conferences and basketball games. The same may be said for other valued goods and activities: so much pushpin exchanged for so much poetry, x amount of guns for y amount of butter, this much efficiency for that much equality, and so on.

But this is too crude a way of treating what may actually be complex sets of preferences. Our preferences may be discontinuous or lexical, and we may want to insist that some things we value—clean air and water, perhaps, or rights we think fundamental—are not open to trading off or compensation. We may find that no amount of increased efficiency can compensate for loss of certain kinds of equality, and we may therefore choose to establish a lexical ordering of preferences that requires us to meet some of the claims of equality before we even consider efficiency. But a lexical ordering is foreign to utilitarianism, for the utilitarian "conflates all persons into one . . . and all goods into the production of a single good—individual satisfaction—whose maximization over the sum of all persons becomes the sole end of rational policy."[7]

These are not the only difficulties that beset utilitarianism—interpersonal comparisons of utility is another—but these should serve to display its major flaws. Now it is time to turn to the construction of a more satisfactory alternative—a foundation for justification in politics free from the defects of utilitarianism. The cornerstone of this alternative is the fundamental right of autonomy.

2.

It may seem redundant to speak of the right of autonomy, for "autonomy" is sometimes taken to mean the *right* of self-government.[8] This is what we mean, I take it, when we say that a nation-state is autonomous. But there is also a stronger sense of the word, one that better fits our use of "autonomy" to characterize individual men and women. In this sense, autonomy is the ability or capacity to govern oneself—an ability or capacity which someone who is free (from external restrictions) to govern himself may not always enjoy. Insane people may be "at liberty" without being autonomous, for instance, for it is not the *right* to rule their lives they lack, but the *capacity* to do so.[9] On the stronger sense of autonomy, then, it is not redundant to maintain that men and women have a right, understood as a claim against others, of autonomy. And to say that every person has a right of autonomy is, on this view, to say that every person is entitled to live as he or she sees fit.

This does not mean that the right of autonomy is nothing more than the right to be left alone or nothing less than the right to do whatever one may wish. Like other abilities, autonomy is not something we either have or do not have; it is something we may have to a greater or lesser extent, just as the ability to play chess varies considerably among chess players. Like other abilities, too, autonomy may be cultivated, neglected, or impaired. Its cultivation demands some effort on the part of the individual, but it also requires the aid of parents, friends, teachers, and others, perhaps even therapists of one kind or another. Autonomy is not a form of rigid self-mastery we impose on ourselves by denying our appetites and inclinations, that is. It is, instead, the ability to control our lives through reasoned choice, an ability that grows out of knowledge of our needs and desires, our talents and limitations.

If this seems to stray from the usual understanding of autonomy as self-legislation, then one ought to consider what self-legislation entails. A person is self-legislating, autonomous rather than heteronomous, insofar as he chooses the principles by which he lives. But if he truly *chooses* the principles that guide his conduct, the autonomous person must *know* something about the alternatives from which he can choose. He must also know that he is capable of choosing, which means that he must be able to think of himself as something more than an object at the mercy of outside forces, like a leaf tossed about in the wind. Yet we cannot acquire the knowledge necessary to choice, and necessary therefore to the ability to legislate for ourselves, without the assistance of others. Because it establishes a claim to this assistance, the right of autonomy is more than merely the right to be left alone: it is the right to the protection and promotion of the ability to lead a self-governed life.

It is also less than the right to do whatever one may wish. Since it is a human right, the right of autonomy is a right every person shares with every other person, and this limits what we may do as *a matter of right*. Jones may have the right to live as she chooses, but this does not entitle her to violate others' rights to live as *they* choose. This follows from the correlativity of rights and duties, for if Jones has a right to something, then at least one person must have a duty to assist her, or at least not to interfere with her, when she sets out to do it. When the right in question is one every person has, furthermore, rights and duties are then completely reciprocal, by which I mean that every person has both a *right against* and a *duty to* every other person. Thus Jones's right of autonomy implies that everyone else has a duty to respect her choices, but everyone else's right of autonomy implies a correlative duty on Jones's part. Given this complete reciprocity, it is clear that the right of autonomy is no warrant to do whatever we may wish.

In what sense, then, is the right of autonomy the fundamental right? In the sense that all other, more specific rights follow from it. Recognizing this right requires us to respect the dignity of the person; to treat others not as playthings or objects or resources we may use for our own pleasure and purposes, but as individuals who are capable, at least potentially, of forming plans, entering into relationships, pursuing projects, and living in accordance with an ideal of the worthwhile life. Everyone possesses this right simply because he or she is a person, moreover, so the right of autonomy is also a right everyone shares equally. This is not a right to equal treatment, but a right, as Dworkin suggests, to be treated *as an equal:* "the right, not to receive the same distribution of some burden or benefit, but to be treated with the same respect and concern as everyone else."[10]

At this point I can imagine two objections that might well be raised. The first concerns the justification, or the absence of a justification, of the right of autonomy, a right I have so far only asserted. Do human beings indeed have a right of autonomy? I shall try to answer this question in the next section. Then, in section 4, I shall take up the second objection, which is that the right of autonomy, as I have described it, is too vague to serve as a justifying principle in politics.

3.

Of the many arguments devised to justify the claim to human rights, the most persuasive, to my mind, is H.L.A. Hart's argument in "Are There Any Natural Rights?"[11] If we have any moral rights at all, Hart contends, we must then have at least one natural right; otherwise, the rights we acquire from promises, contracts, and laws would have no ground or foundation. These are all *special rights,* to use Hart's terms, because they arise out of special relationships between specific individuals—relationships in which one person, Jones, may confer upon another, Smith, the right to limit Jones's liberty in one way or another. Jones may promise to take Smith to the big game, for example, and this promise gives Smith the right to regulate Jones's conduct on the day of the game. But Smith acquires this right only because Jones grants it to him, and it is hers to grant only because she, Jones, is a free agent, a person entitled to live free from the unwarranted interference of others. If we have any moral rights at all, therefore, we must also have what Hart calls an equal right to be free.

This argument is strictly conditional, of course, and some may regard this as a weakness. Yet in two respects the conditional nature of Hart's argument actually lends it power. The first is that Hart's analysis of special rights helps to explain how we can confer rights on one another, as we do when we make promises. What, after all, gives us the right to give rights to others? Hart's answer is that we can do this only because we have a fundamental right to govern our own conduct, which is to say that special rights presuppose a natural or human right to liberty. We must *have* a right, in short, in order to *grant* a right.

The conditional nature of Hart's argument also reveals what is at stake in disputes about the existences of human rights: not only Human Rights, abstract, metaphysical, and overblown as the claims of their proponents may sometimes makes them seem, but *all* moral rights, even the petty rights we assign one another in the course of our daily lives. If Hart is correct, the price of denying that there is at least one human right, the equal right to liberty, is greater than most people will want to pay. Those who think themselves willing to pay it should try to conceive of a society without rights—one in which promises, vows, pledges, and grants of authority have no place.[12] To do this requires a radical transformation of the moral landscape, a transformation few philosophers have been willing to undertake because of the violence it would do to widely shared conceptions of morality.

In both these respects, the conditional nature of Hart's argument seems to contribute greatly to its strength. This may be granted, though, without granting that Hart's reasoning is completely persuasive. A critic, noting that Hart's "natural right" is an *equal* right to liberty, might go on to question whether this is indeed a right everyone possesses equally, or whether some people possess it at all. Perhaps, the critic might say, some people have a right to liberty—masters, let us call them—while others, whom we shall call slaves, have only those special rights that the masters choose to confer upon them. This move would allow the critic to acknowledge that special rights do exist and that they do presuppose a fundamental right to be free; but this fundamental right, from the critic's point of view, would belong only to the masters. On this interpretation, the right to be free is not a *human* right at all, for it is the right only of some persons, not all.

Whatever else the merits of this objection may be, it does serve to reveal the importance to Hart's argument, and mutatis mutandis of any effort at justifying human rights, of the belief that in some morally relevant sense all human beings are equal. Anyone who denies this, as my hypothetical critic does, will also deny that mere humanity, or personhood, is the foundation for rights of any sort. If we are to make a case for human rights, therefore, we must also make a case for human equality, understood as the view that every person is entitled to equal concern and respect *as a person*.

So far as I can see, there is no way to *prove* that we are all equal in this sense, but neither is there any way to *prove* that we are not. Human beings are unequal in many ways, certainly, but none of these bears on the question of whether we are all entitled, as human beings, to equal concern and respect. Gregory Vlastos puts this point neatly when he notes that those who argue against human equality tend to conflate two distinct concepts: human worth and human merit.[13] Merit is a grading concept, and even the staunchest egalitarian can readily admit that there are degrees and differences of merit among human beings. But we cannot grade people according to their worth, Vlastos points out, because human worth is something that must inhere in each individual as a person without regard to his or her merits. Thus the indisputable fact that some people are superior in some way, or even a number of ways, to others cannot count against the claim that all human beings are entitled, by virtue of their equal worth, to be treated as equals. By conflating merit with worth, those who argue from unequal merit to unequal rights simply miss the point.

Important as Vlastos's distinction is, however, it is not sufficient to establish the case for equality, for it remains possible for someone to deny flatly that there is such a thing as human worth. Human beings exist, according to this objection, but human worth does not. If one accepts this view, there then seem to be only two ways to proceed. One is to take a position similar to that attributed to Thrasymachus and to maintain that what we think of as good or bad, right or wrong, just or unjust, are really nothing more than matters of interest, advantage, and power. If this seems too extreme and too narrow, then one may argue that, in the absence of any proof of the existence of human worth, some other human property must provide the foundation for rights—some property not found in equal measure in all men, women, and children.

Although it is less extreme, this second way of proceeding is no more persuasive than the first. In this case the problem is settling on the property or capacity in terms of which merit leads to rights. Is it intelligence or rationality? Race or nationality? Gender? Strength? Intuition or insight of some sort? Whatever one chooses, one will have to demonstrate that this is *the property* that confers the fundamental right of liberty on those who possess it—a daunting task, surely. Perhaps such a property may some day be identified, but the history of attempts to do so, from Aristotle onward, seems to warrant our skepticism. Indeed, the very attempt to find a property or capacity of this sort, and to trump up "evidence" to prove that some people or peoples lack it, testifies to the strength of the conviction that every person is in some sense equally worthy of respect and concern.

In the absence of any conclusive negative arguments, I believe that we are entitled to retain this conviction. There is a case for human equality, that is, and this means that there is also a case for Hart's *equal* right to be free. This leaves one final matter to be resolved before I turn to the second of the objections I mentioned earlier, a matter which concerns a possible discrepancy between Hart's position and mine. I have tried to show that Hart's argument in "Are There Any Natural Rights?"

provides a justification for a human right of autonomy; but Hart refers to an equal right to be free, not a right of autonomy. The question, then, is whether Hart's argument supports the right of autonomy as well as it supports the right to liberty or freedom.

"Liberty," "freedom," and "autonomy" are closely related words, but they are not interchangeable. The difference between "liberty" and "freedom," on the one hand, and "autonomy," on the other, is especially pronounced. "Autonomy" carries a connotation of consciousness, of the capacity to make choices upon reflection, that is absent in ordinary uses of "liberty" and "freedom." We occasionally speak of a lion that is "born free," for instance, or of a stallion which gains his liberty when he escapes from a corral, but the only animal we commonly characterize as autonomous is homo sapiens. Yet this difference is of no significance in the present case. Hart may use "liberty" and "freedom" rather than "autonomy," but his arguments transfer with no problem from an equal right to liberty to an equal right of autonomy. Indeed, the way Hart ties special rights to a fundamental right to govern our own conduct suggests a degree of consciousness or reflectivity more in accord with "autonomy" than with "liberty" or "freedom." Hence I see no difficulty in using Hart's argument to provide the justification for a human right of autonomy.

4.

If the preceding analysis is correct, we have good reason to believe that every person has a right of autonomy. But this still leaves the second objection I mentioned earlier: that this right is too vague to serve as a justifying principle in politics. There is, of course, a certain vagueness to any right or principle that provides a foundation or ground for other, more specific rights or principles, and the right of autonomy is no exception. To meet this second objection, then, I shall have to add some detail to my sketch of this fundamental right by providing an account of some of the more specific rights that emerge from, or stand as instances of, the right of autonomy.

From the standpoint of politics, the most important of these derivative rights is the right of citizenship. This is the political analogue of the right of autonomy, for it requires the men and women who share the benefits of a political order to treat each other with special concern and respect. More precisely, the right of citizenship is the right *of* those men and women whose cooperation, particularly their obedience to the law, produces these benefits, and it is a right *to* the reciprocal cooperation of those who accept the benefits. Fairness demands that we bear our share of the burdens of the common enterprise, other things being equal, so it also confers a right to our obedience on those who, by bearing their share, enable us to enjoy the benefits of the enterprise.[14] All other legal or political rights, whether the right to free speech or the right to medical care at public expense, are instances of this right to civic reciprocity, which is itself an instance of the right of autonomy.

In this fashion the right of citizenship forms the link between an ethical theory founded on the right of autonomy, on the one hand, and political action and public policy, on the other. But what practical guidance can we extract from this theory? To this point I have said only that every person has a right to the development and exercise of his or her ability to lead a self-governed life. When united with the right of citizenship, this suggests the following principle for political action: Pursue policies that protect and promote the autonomy of all members of the body politic.

This principle seems straightforward enough, but it carries many implications, too many to sort out here. We can begin to see some of these implications, however, and to clarify the principle as well, if we apply it to some areas of public concern.

What, for instance, should we say about crime and punishment if we hold to the principle of autonomy? We should say that the criminal law exists to protect the autonomy of the members of a body politic, for one cannot lead a self-governed life when he or she is at the mercy of thugs or scoundrels. Thugs and scoundrels might reply that the criminal law diminishes their autonomy, as indeed it does when it narrows their range of choice to activities within the law. This is not to say that the law-breaker is denied the rights of autonomy and citizenship, however, or that he is not being treated with equal concern and respect. Indeed, what justifies the punishment of the criminal—what serves as a necessary condition for punishment, at least[15]—

is his failure to respect the rights of others. The thief wants others to respect his right to his property, but he is unwilling to respect theirs. When we punish him, consequently, we actually affirm his right of autonomy by treating him as a person capable of sharing both the benefits and burdens of political order—unwilling, perhaps, but capable nonetheless.

From this we may draw three further implications about crime, citizenship and autonomy. If we follow the principle of autonomy, first, we must presume that criminals are responsible persons who deserve to be punished, not hapless psychopaths or sociopaths who must be subjected to therapy. This presumption may be overridden, of course, but overridden only when therapy promises to establish or restore the conditions for autonomy in the offender, or when the offender is so hopelessly psychopathic that neither punishment nor therapy will avail.[16] The second implication is that our methods of punishment must be consistent with the principle of autonomy. Rather than treat criminals as mere brutes, that is, we should look for methods of punishment that enhance their capacity to lead self-governed, and law-abiding, lives. In this regard, punitive schemes that force the offender to make restitution to his victim(s) are attractive, for making restitution may lead the offender to recognize that he has wronged another person, someone with plans and desires of his own.[17] And the third implication is that the political order must itself be reasonably just in its distribution of benefits and burdens if it is to punish some for violating the rights of others. In T.H. Green's words, society must give everyone at least "a fair chance of not being a criminal."[18] Where this condition does not obtain, punishment may be nothing more than a euphemism for exploitation of the weak by the strong.

This suggests that the principle of autonomy has both negative and positive aspects. It warrants governments to protect the rights of their citizens against invasion, and in this sense the principle is negative or passive; but it also commands governments to take positive steps to promote the autonomy of their citizens. Since autonomy is the ability to lead a self-governed life, it follows that anything which extends the range of choice open to a person promises to extend his or her autonomy, and this implies that there are many ways in which governments may act to promote autonomy as well as to protect it. Some of these ways are more fundamental than others, however, and these should be the first concern of governments.

. Two clear examples are education and health care. In both cases the connection with autonomy is both obvious and fundamental. A healthy person has a wider range of choice than someone who is in poor health, so it seems reasonable to say, other things being equal, that the healthy person enjoys greater control over his or her life, and therefore greater autonomy, than the sickly person. In much the same way an educated person usually commands a wider range of choice, and therefore greater autonomy, than an uneducated one. Now if the justifying aim of political action is to protect and *promote* the autonomy of the citizenry, we may conclude that education and health care are in some sense public responsibilities and governments should do whatever they can to foster the health, both physical and mental, of their citizens. This includes, among other things, programs warning people of health hazards, attempts to eradicate some of those hazards, special training and facilities for disabled citizens, and medical care for all who need it.

How far will this concern for the promotion of autonomy take public policy? It is impossible to be precise on this point, largely because the requirements will vary from one set of circumstances to another. In an affluent society, the principle of autonomy will insist on more strenuous efforts than it would demand in less affluent or desperately impoverished societies.[19] We may charge the governments of advanced industrial nations with a lack of concern and respect for some of their citizens if they do not provide, say, hearing aids, eyeglasses, and wheelchairs at public expense for those who cannot afford them; but we could not reasonably bring this charge against the government of a country like Bangladesh. In this respect, the principles of autonomy makes different demands in different circumstances. But in another respect, the demand is always the same: that governments do what they can to promote the citizen's ability to lead a self-governed life.

This already suggests that the rights-based theory I am advancing includes no inviolable right to property. As with all other rights, the right to property must eventually be derived from, and therefore justified in terms of, the fundamental right of autonomy. If autonomy is best protected and promoted when property is in private hands, then that is where property should be. But if public control, or some mixture of public and private ownership, promises best to secure and further autonomy, then policy ought to follow one of these directions. Efficiency is an important consideration here, as it is in the utilitarian model, for the most efficient system of property control is, ceteris paribus, the most desirable. In this case, though, the most efficient system is the one that protects and promotes autonomy, not utility, at the least cost.

This means, once again, that the principle of autonomy will call for different strategies with regard to property in different situations. With this in mind, I should like to hazard the following general considerations that seem to apply reasonably well in most circumstances. The first is that there appears to be some connection between affluence and autonomy. The connection is neither immediate nor exact, but affluence often provides increased leisure and opportunity, and these lead in turn to greater autonomy. For if autonomy is the ability to control and direct one's life, then those of us living in the advanced industrial nations are likely to enjoy greater autonomy than the peasant in Latin America. We usually have a choice of occupations, for instance, even if the choices are not as attractive as we might wish, while the peasant may have no choice but to eke out his subsistence on the land. We may also pursue a wide range of activities—teach in the morning, write in the afternoon, and criticize poetry after dinner, for example—while he may be forced to work the land for almost all his waking hours. Affluence does not guarantee autonomy, to be sure, but it comes much closer than poverty to doing so. Those who make public policy should therefore presume, but not take it for granted, that programs promoting affluence will probably promote autonomy as well.[20]

The second consideration is that private ownership seems to further autonomy in some cases, if not in all. The ability to control the use of something, whether it be a bicycle, a house, a farm, or a business, surely contributes to one's autonomy. The farmer who owns the land he works may choose what to plant, when to plant, and where to plant it, and this ability to make decisions of fundamental importance to his life seems to be one of the principal attractions of farming. Much the same can be said of the men and women who are willing to run the risks of the small entrepreneur in order to be, as they say, "my own boss." This relationship between private property and autonomy has its limits, certainly, limits which the modern corporation far exceeds. Yet within these limits there is reason to presume that private ownership is likely to advance the cause of autonomy.

This brings us to the third consideration, which may seem to run counter to the first two. Although I suggested, with qualifications, that affluence and private property are conditions that secure and advance autonomy, I must also note that the distribution of this affluence and property is crucial. For when wealth and property are concentrated in the hands of a relatively small number of men and women, these men and women will be in a position to direct not only their own lives, but the lives of those who depend upon them as well.[21] This situation is all too common in both agricultural societies, where a few powerful families may have title to most of the land, and in their industrial counterparts, where those who control the mines, mills, and factories may hold the fate of whole cities in their hands, or on their ledgers. When wealth and property are unequally distributed, in short, we may expect that the same will be true of autonomy.

How, then, would the principle of autonomy have us distribute property and wealth within a society? My judgment is that policymakers who wish to protect and promote autonomy should probably follow a rule that resembles Rawls's "difference principle"—the rule that inequalities in wealth and property are justified only when they promote the autonomy of the least autonomous members of society.[22] This will often prove difficult to measure, for autonomy may be enhanced or impaired in a number of ways. Applying this rule with the connection between affluence and autonomy in mind, however, should lead to the relatively straightforward conclusion that an unequal distribution of wealth is justified only when it increases the wealth of the poorest members of society. If it fails to do this, then it is unwarranted.

Not all applications of this rule will be this straightforward, and even straightforward applications may be difficult, as the difficulty of assessing the "trickle down" effect of economic policies demonstrates. But these problems plague utilitarianism, too. Problems and difficulties notwithstanding, it should by now be

clear that a theory that takes the right of autonomy as its point
of departure does offer some guidance in matters of political
action and public concern. Much more remains to be said on
the issues I have only briefly discussed—crime and punishment, health care, education, the control and distribution of
property and wealth—but the foregoing discussion should show
that the right of autonomy is definitely not too vague to serve
as the basis for a justifying principle in politics.

                                   5.

If the preceding arguments and examples are as clear and
convincing as I meant them to be, I should now be able to dis-
patch the two complaints against rights-based theories noted in
the introduction. There is no reason to believe, first, that a rights-
based theory *must* lead to some variety of radical individualism.
For if our starting point is the right of autonomy, the result will
be a rights-based theory which, by emphasizing interdepen-
dence and reciprocity, fully recognizes the social nature of human beings.

Nor need we hold that rights-based theories correct the utilitarian's neglect of rights only to commit the equally damaging
error of neglecting consequences. Policy that takes the right of
autonomy as its ethical foundation must be concerned with
consequences, for the policymaker must always ask if the policy
will protect or promote the autonomy of all citizens of the polity. On the theory set out here, that is, rights and consequences
are complementary rather than antagonistic concerns.

Yet this is not say that a theory of political action founded on
the right of autonomy will be entirely free from problems. There
will be the usual problems of prediction and assessment, as I
have noted, problems besetting any theory that attempts to take
consequences into account. Even more serious are the problems that arise when one person's exercise of his or her autonomy comes into conflict with another's. What should we do when
the protection or promotion of one person's autonomy seems
to come at the expense of another's? What should we do when
we will have to diminish the range of choice for some people,
perhaps by taking away some of their money through taxation,

in order to extend the range of choice, through schooling, say, or health care, for others?

Conflicts of this sort are troublesome, but we do have at least two promising ways to resolve them. The first, suggested earlier, is to apply something like Rawls's difference principle with the intent of promoting the autonomy of the least autonomous, even if this comes at the expense of those who enjoy greater autonomy. Autonomy, like utility, is by no means easy to measure, so we may have to settle for rough calculations. Even so, the ideal is to insist that every citizen have as nearly equal a range of choice as possible *unless* there is reason to believe that an unequal distribution of opportunities will somehow extend the range of choice for the least autonomous beyond what they would be likely to enjoy with an equal distribution.

The second way of resolving these conflicts is to employ, on the model of a minimum standard of living, either a floor or a ceiling for autonomy. We might decide, that is, that a transfer of resources is just whenever it helps to bring one or more persons up to a certain standard of autonomy—up to a point where the range of choice is at least wide enough to begin to resemble true autonomy. Or, to take the ceiling approach, we might consider a transfer just when it does not drop those who must surrender resources below a certain level—a level that seems to be as high as we can reasonably go in the name of autonomy. To put this less abstractly, we might say that a man or woman who lives in poverty makes some choices; but these are so narrow and constrained that we do not consider him or her to be truly autonomous. Conversely, the person who must settle for a Mercedes-Benz because he can no longer afford a Rolls-Royce may suffer a diminished range of choice, but the diminution hardly represents a notable loss of autonomy. Autonomy admits of degree, in other words, but it also exhibits some of the features of diminishing marginal utility—enough to make the floor/ceiling method a promising way to resolve conflicting claims with respect to individual autonomy.

Whatever one thinks of these two suggestions for dealing with a troublesome problem, it should still be clear that a theory based on the right of autonomy is superior to utilitarianism in this regard. For the utilitarian either must concede, as Bentham does, that one man's pushpin is as good as another's poetry, or look, as Mill and Moore do, for some way of accommodating higher pleasures and truer interests within a theory that regards all preferences as continuous or substitutable. On the theory I have advanced, however, neither of these moves is necessary. For if we take the pursuit of autonomy as our aim in politics, we know that some things are more important than others, and these things—health, education, and liberty—must be our first concerns.

NOTES

1. Jeremy Bentham, *Introduction to the Principles of Morals and Legislation* (New York: Hafner, 1961), p. 70.
2. John Rawls, *A Theory of Justice* (Cambridge: Harvard University Press, 1971); Robert Nozick, *Anarchy, State, and Utopia* (New York: Basic Books, 1974); and Ronald Dworkin, *Taking Rights Seriously* (Cambridge: Harvard University Press, 1977).
3. For utilitarian exceptions to the deontological rule, see Rolf Sartorius, *Individual Conduct and Social Norms* (Belmont and Encino, Calif.: Dickenson, 1975), and Peter Singer, *Practical Ethics* (Cambridge: Cambridge University Press, 1979).
4. On this second point, see H.L.A. Hart, "Between Utility and Rights," in A. Ryan, ed., *The Idea of Freedom: Essays in Honour of Isaiah Berlin* (New York: Oxford University Press, 1979), pp. 77–98, and Amartya Sen, "Rights and Agency," *Philosophy and Public Affairs* 11 (Winter 1982): 3–39.
5. There is a sense in which the utilitarians who share Bentham's conviction that every one should count for one, no one for more than one, actually hold to a belief in a fundamental human right. For why should everyone count for one and no one for more? Surely utilitarian considerations cannot provide an answer to this question, for we cannot know how to proceed with a calculation of utilities until we know how much weight to attach to each individual's utility. An appeal to social or legal conventions will not justify utilitarian equality, of course. It seems that the utilitarian must believe that everyone is *entitled* to be counted as (and no more than) one; which is another way of saying that everyone has a right to be counted as an equal.
6. For an illuminating discussion of this problem, see Laurence Tribe, "Policy Science: Analysis or Ideology?" *Philosophy and Public Affairs* 2 (Fall 1972): 84–97. See also Jon Elster, *Ulysses and the Sirens: Studies*

in Rationality and Irrationality (Cambridge: Cambridge University Press, 1979), p. 126.

7. Tribe, "Policy Science: Analysis or Ideology?," p. 85, where he goes on to say, "Such a vision lies at the core of 'cost-benefit' analysis, with 'total net benefits' serving to replace the concept of total individual satisfaction."

8. This section draws upon my "Rights, Boundaries, and the Bonds of Community: A Qualified Defense of Moral Parochialism," *American Political Science Review* 79 (June 1985).

9. And we usually justify the deprivation of certain of their rights on the grounds that the insane lack the necessary capacity, at least temporarily, to exercise them.

10. Dworkin, *Taking Rights Seriously,* p. 227.

11. H.L.A. Hart, "Are There Any Natural Rights?" *Philosophical Review* 64 (1955); reprinted, among other places, in A.I. Melden, ed., *Human Rights* (Belmont, Calif.: Wadsworth Publishing, 1970), pp. 61–75.

12. Joel Feinberg employs this "thought experiment" quite effectively in "The Nature and Value of Rights," *The Journal of Value Inquiry* 4 (1970): 243–257; reprinted in Feinberg, *Rights, Justice, and the Bounds of Liberty* (Princeton: Princeton University Press, 1980).

13. Gregory Vlastos, "Justice and Equality," in R.B. Brandt, ed., *Social Justice* (Englewood Cliffs, N.J.: Prentice-Hall, 1962); reprinted, in part, in Melden, ed., *Human Rights,* pp. 76–95; see esp. pp. 86–95.

14. For a more extensive discussion of this point, see my "Rights, Boundaries, and the Bonds of Community."

15. The criminal's failure to respect the rights of others is a necessary condition for punishment, but not a sufficient one, because there may well be cases where one person's violation of another's rights is not serious enough to invoke the criminal sanction.

16. See the essays in part III of Jeffrie Murphy's *Retribution, Justice, and Therapy* (Dordrecht, Holland: D. Reidel, 1979), for a valuable discussion of these matters.

17. I argue the case for restitution more fully in "Restitution, Punishment, and Debts to Society," in J. Hudson and B. Galaway, eds., *Victims, Offenders, and Alternative Sanctions* (Lexington, Mass.: Lexington Books, 1980), pp. 3–14.

18. T.H. Green, *Lectures on the Principles of Political Obligation* (Ann Arbor: University of Michigan Press, 1967), p. 190. See also D.A.J. Richards, *The Moral Criticism of Law* (Encino and Belmont, Calif.: Dickenson Publishing Co., 1977), pp. 243–244, where the passage

from Green is cited, and Jeffrie Murphy, "Marxism and Retribution," in *Retribution, Justice, and Therapy*, pp. 93–115.

19. The principle of autonomy may also require that the citizens of an affluent polity contribute to the autonomy of those who live in less affluent countries. For related arguments to this effect, see Henry Shue, *Basic Rights: Subsistence, Affluence, and U.S. Foreign Policy* (Princeton: Princeton University Press, 1980), and my "Rights, Boundaries, and the Bonds of Community."

20. But when the pursuit of wealth becomes an end in itself, the leisure and opportunities wealth provides are likely to be consumed in the pursuit of more wealth. Economics was originally the art of managing the household, Hannah Arendt has reminded us, and its purpose was to sustain and refresh men so that they might better participate in the affairs of the *polis*. Now that economics seems to be a preoccupation rather than a mere means to more worthy ends, the leisure and opportunity that follow from affluence seem remote from autonomy. Arendt develops this argument in *The Human Condition* (Chicago: University of Chicago Press, 1958), passim, but esp. part II.

21. "There are two sorts of dependence: dependence on things, which is from nature; and dependence on men, which is from society. Dependence on things, since it has no morality, is in no way detrimental to freedom and engenders no vices. Dependence on men, since it is without order, engenders all the vices, and by it, master and slave are mutually corrupted." Jean-Jacques Rousseau, *Emile*, trans. Allan Bloom (New York: Basic Books, 1979), p. 85.

22. For Rawls's discussion of the "difference principle," see *A Theory of Justice*, esp. section 13.

15

JUSTIFICATION IN POLITICS

J. ROLAND PENNOCK

This chapter does not deal with "justification" as such. That may be left to the philosophers. The question to which these remarks will be addressed is how that process is used, or should be used in politics. How does one go about demonstrating the validity of things political? The political things in question might be the state itself (i.e., the use of coercion by government), or a particular form of government, or a particular government, or a particular act of government, whether it be a decision to build (or use) an MX missile or to appoint a dogcatcher. Clearly the first three of these examples relate to justification "in politics;" but the fourth is a less clear case. At least it might seem at first glance that a decision to hire a dogcatcher involves nothing peculiar to politics and therefore that its justification would be based on the same principles as the decision by an individual whether or not to own a dog. But an element is (or should be) involved in the decision by the local government to hire a dogcatcher that is not (or certainly need not be) involved in the individual's decision: the element of public good, or general welfare.

1. POLITICAL THEORY AND METAETHICS

How then do we go about justifying matters of this nature? Moral philosophers are broadly in agreement on many of these things. Those who support anarchism are exceedingly scarce. Some form of democracy also enjoys a wide degree of support,

as does the ban on slavery. Likewise the requirement that people who drive automobiles should observe rules calculated to
facilitate the movement of traffic and to protect the safety of
those using the highways. Yet if one ventures into the field of
metaethics it soon appears that agreement on principles of political ethics by no means implies agreement on the method for
arriving at, and substantiating those principles. At that point the
doctors are in sharp disagreement. Professor James Fishkin, in
this volume, finds this discord among the doctors disturbing. The
first step for one who would justify a form of government, he
believes, is to select the proper "moral decision procedure." Yet
this is the very matter on which disagreement is rife. It is not
just as a philosopher that this lack of agreement concerns him;
he fears the practical consequences. From his own empirical
studies he has concluded that the person-in-the-street believes
in moral absolutes. It follows, in Fishkin's view, that anything
that casts doubt upon those absolutes and all that is derived from
them tends to lose legitimacy, leading him to conclude that liberal democracy faces a "crisis of legitimacy."[1]

For several reasons Fishkin's argument is not persuasive. First,
the cognitive dissonance that he assumes would disturb the person-in-the-street and lead him or her to doubt the legitimacy of
democracy assumes a degree of philosophical knowledge and
sophistication that is quite unrealistic.[2] Most people, I believe,
are unaware of the differences, say, between consequentialists
and deontologists and would not be greatly concerned if they
were. Further, the argument, if it proves anything, proves too
much. It is a common phenomenon for philosophers to argue
that the metaethical theories of certain other philosophers are
invalid, while being in agreement with these philosophers on
many, often most, matters of practical ethics. That is to say, they
concur as to conclusions but not as to supporting arguments.
But why then are the commonly held moral concepts like truth-
telling, promise-keeping, and avoidance of harm to innocent
people not facing a similar crisis, for in these cases too philosophers, while concurring in the result, differ sharply regarding
their first principles? Fishkin's overkill is self-destructive.

More generally, are the political theories of philosophers determined by their metaethical theories? The evidence seems to
me to support a negative answer to this query. Probably the most

obvious example of common political conclusions (justifications) arrived at by theorists of differing ethical and metaethical persuasions is that of the justification of the coercive power of the state itself. Plato, Aristotle, Thrasymachus, Stoics, Epicureans, Church Fathers, St. Thomas, Hobbes, Locke, Rousseau, Bentham, Hegel—the roster of philosophers of widely diverging ethical theories all in agreement on justifying the coercive political power of the state goes on and on.[3]

When we turn from the justification of coercive government to that of particular forms of government much the same situation prevails. Thinkers as far removed from each other with respect to metaethical beliefs as Thomas Aquinas and Thomas Hobbes both support monarchy, while the utilitarian J.S. Mill and the neo-Hegelian T.H. Green find common ground in liberal democracy. The same is true of deontologists like John Rawls and Alan Gewirth, on the one hand, and utilitarians like Mill or R.M. Hare, on the other.

Incidentally, when it comes to questions of public policy, I do not claim that ethicists of all persuasions agree on such political issues as whether or not the state should permit women to have abortions at their discretion. What does seem to be true, however, is that they do not divide on this and other questions along the same lines that separate them with respect to ethical theory.

If, as I have been arguing, political philosophers' conclusions about political ethics are not dictated by their metaethical principles, what does determine them? Some would say that they are determined by their environment or their training; that, insofar as they reflect rational processes at all, they are simply rationalizations. We need not decide to what extent this is true; I am concerned with what determines their *rational* thought.[4] It is my belief that the kinds of disagreements among thinking people we are here concerned about, especially as they apply to the justification of forms of government, generally arise out of differences as to matters of fact—generally quite complicated matters of fact. For instance, the question may be whether a much more steeply graduated income tax will so retard investment that the incomes of members of the most disadvantaged class will be reduced.[5] Another, and perhaps more important, complicated matter of fact has to do with human nature. Does political participation have the self-improving tendency that Mill supposed? If people enjoy the franchise, do they *enjoy* it? If they are denied it, do they suffer psychologically? Do people behave in the voting booth in the same way, vis-à-vis their self-interest, as they do in the marketplace? If they do, is this destructive of civic virtue? And so on. (It is worth noting too that Fishkin's assumption, on which his conclusions depend, that the common man will be alienated by the discovery that philosophy does not give an unchallengeable justification for the form of government under which he is living, also rests upon a factual assumption, albeit one derived from survey data.)

Again, let us look at some particular political theorists. Consider, for instance, the question of why Plato advocated a quite different form of government in the *Laws* from that outlined in the *Republic*. It was not that his metaethics had changed. Rather it was that (either because of the differing purposes of the two works or because his own views of the facts had changed) he made different assumptions about human nature in the *Laws* from those he made in the *Republic*. In the discussion above about those who support coercive government no anarchists were named, but a glance at the basis of their position is highly instructive. Contrary to the others, they believe that human nature is such that men can live together, whether communally or in highly individualistic fashion, without being reduced to a war of all against all. It is this belief about a factual matter—what humans are like or can be made to be like—that accounts for, or at least provides their justification for, their belief in the feasibility and desirability of anarchy. Even the Church Fathers, departing from the communistic ideal of primitive Christianity, came to the conclusion that the Fall made reliance on political institutions a necessity to check selfishness and concupiscence.

On examination, then, it appears that disagreements on matters involving political justification generally arise from differing views of the facts or divergent calculations of probable consequences. (The generality of this statement exceeds what can be proved in the available space, but I believe its validity will be evident to the informed reader, on reflection. In any case, as will appear, my argument does not depend on its universality.) Even when, for instance, it appears that the argument is about the *meaning* of a key term, investigation generally reveals that it can be traced back to disagreement as to what will be the consequences of selecting this or that definition. Those who wish to define liberty narrowly, as absence of direct interference, tend to believe that, with a minimum of protection of life and property, the individual can do best for himself and for society by being left to his own devices; while those who would define this key concept in terms of enablements as well as protections doubt the validity of this factual proposition. Similarly, different concepts of equality, can generally be reduced to divergent views of the facts. Some believe that legal equality is all that is required because the large amount of liberty it allows will so greatly increase production that even the least advantaged will be better off than they would have been under another system. (This was Locke's belief, at least as far as concerned the move from primitive to more fully developed economies.) Others, unconvinced that this would be the case, believe that the relatively unchecked individual liberty will lead to gross inequalities of fortune that are themselves unjust and, because of the power they give to the rich, will result in exploitation of the weak.

The important point is that utilitarians can logically take either position; and the same is true of Rawlsian deontologists. Godwin's utilitarianism led him to a far different position than that of Jeremy Bentham. Hegel's followers divided sharply between the Right and the Left. Robert Paul Wolff, a Kantian deontologist, supports anarchism, in opposition to Kant himself as well as to most other deontologists. How much these differences owe to disagreements of a factual order and how much to varying ethical intuitions it is impossible to say, but each pair of contrasting political-theoretical conclusions grew out of the same type of metaethical theory. And if the same metaethical theory leads philosophers to opposing political-theoretical conclusions, and if the same political-theoretical conclusions are grounded by various philosophers on opposing methethical theories, how can it be argued that a political philosopher's conclusions are dictated by his metaethical beliefs?

Note that I say "dictated." Whether certain metaethical theories may *predispose* philosophers to accept one view of the facts of human nature rather than another is a different question from the one I have been discussing. It is *logical* connections with which I am concerned. Even regarding dispositions, however, it is worth noting that their common acceptance of radical individualism did not prevent Hobbes and Bentham from moving in opposite directions regarding the best form of government. Moreover, a holistic view of society in earlier periods seemed to favor non-democratic forms (e.g., Hegel), while in more recent times a similar outlook as to the nature of men and society inspires Marxian and many other collectivists.

Rather than add more supporting instances from the history of political theory, I shall attempt to provide an example of political justification that will illustrate the principles I would apply generally and also the *method* of political justification that I believe is usually (and properly) used by political philosophers.

2. The Justification of Democracy: An Illustration

My case will be the justification of liberal democracy as the ideally best form of government for humans as we know them. In saying "ideally" best I mean that it would be best under the appropriate conditions and that the existence of those conditions is to be desired. And when I say "humans as we know them," I am allowing for the possibility of educating, training, and conditioning, but I am also assuming the existence of certain broad limits (e.g., limited altruism) to what these processes can accomplish.[6] If genetic engineering removes those limits and is applied to making radical changes in human nature, all bets are off.

A. Definitions

What is this "liberal democracy" that I would justify? Is it a form of government and only that, or something more? First and foremost, it is a *form of government,* a set of procedures for making political decisions and putting them into practice. When the man-in-the-street is asked what he thinks about democracy, I daresay this is what comes to his mind. He (or at least I) has in mind a constitutional regime in which major policy decisions are made by officeholders selected by periodic popular elections, or by persons subject to the control of those so elected. (This discussion will be confined to *representative democracy.*) These elections must be open to participation by all adult citizens, with a few well-recognized exceptions. Further, each voter has one, and only one vote; votes count equally and the person or question receiving the most votes wins (except that for certain purposes a clear majority or even an extraordinary majority may be required). It will be noticed that this definition of democracy implies majority rule in the sense of no minority rule over a majority, with institutions designed to fulfill this requirement. (The matter of extraordinary majorities is left open.) Further, if votes are to be equal they must not be coerced; opponents of the party or parties in power must not be subject to arbitrary arrest; free formation and expression of opinion must be maintained; the freedom of assembly and organization for political purposes must be guaranteed, and so on.

Some would leave the definition of democracy at this point; but that won't do. Questions about what forms (fixed terms of office or not, for instance) and what procedures (absolute or qualified majority rule) are constantly arising; and the ensuing discussion is likely to take the form of an argument about what form or procedure is most democratic. It is not a matter of what procedure most accurately fits the definition of formal democracy, as defined above; but rather an appeal is being made to democracy's justifying principles. We need then, and in common usage we assume, a definition of the democratic ideal, one that provides such principles. It refers to a government that is not only democratic in form and procedure but that also has certain objectives, certain goals. It respects above all, equally, the autonomy and freedom (integrally related concepts) of the individuals who comprise the state in question. Many things follow, including most of the rights embodied in our Bill of Rights, as was suggested above. The degree to which this ideal, especially the equality of votes, implies equality of resources is a matter of judgment, but the more nearly this equality obtains the more democratic is the government, other things equal. Avoiding the concept of "social" democracy, my definition of "ideal" democracy is still confined to government, and specifically to the government of a polity.[7] Other implications of this concept of ideal democracy will be discussed as we proceed. Some may say that what I have defined is not democracy per se, but a particular brand of democracy, "liberal" democracy. So be it. It is that form of government and especially its ideals that I shall be justifying.

B. Justification of Ideal Democracy

The life and welfare of its inhabitants must be the starting point for the justification of the state in general and, as here, for a particular kind of state. The state exists for the good of mankind (that portion of it that resides within its jurisdiction), not mankind for the good of the state.

What is this "mankind?" Certain minimum assumptions will be specified. They are, I believe, hardly controversial; but they are fundamental to the subsequent argument. Man is a rational animal. He can think inductively and deductively; he can generalize and formulate abstractions; he can envisage consequences, both by calculation and by reference to experience; he can deliberate, make choices, decisions, and act accordingly. The beings that can do these things are said to be "autonomous," meaning that they are themselves self-conscious causes of their actions. This does not mean that they are the *only* causes, or that they are not themselves subject to causation; but it does mean that the processes enumerated above mediate the lines of causation that affect them and are transformed in the process. We speak of the result as an act of "will."

Not only are human beings rational (and in this sense "autonomous"); they are also moral, in the sense that they have the capacity and the tendency to develop ideas of how they and others ought to behave, a morality, including a sense of justice, a belief in a kind of equality.[8]

In addition to morality, men have needs; not only physical needs but psychological ones as well. The latter include, among others, psychological security, a sense of identity, and a desire for some control of events. For the last one in particular, they require freedom. For a sense of identity they also need a feeling of accomplishment through both competitive and cooperative activity.

Finally, men are social animals. They achieve their self-consciousness and their sense of identity in, and because of, society. They are happy in society, other things being equal, and unhappy without it. Ostracism is a severe form of punishment.

As man values his self, so he values these fundamental characteristics and strives for and values institutions that tend to preserve and promote them. At certain stages of societal development a minimum of physical security is the dominant need, for which a near absolute government appears to be a necessity. But when more favorable conditions prevail and when absolute government rules arbitrarily, oppressively, and in other ways contrary to the needs and desires inherent in human nature, claims for greater freedom and justice develop and eventually come to prevail.[9] The demand for individual as well as group autonomy is at least implied at an early date, as is exemplified by such statements as those by Pericles (as recorded by Thucydides) and by Colonel Rainborough (in the mid-seventeenth century).[10]

It is upon these facts of human rationality, autonomy, and the other characteristics mentioned above that the democratic ideal is justified. For democrats they provide the starting place. The intervening linkage between these facts and the moral claim of right may be variously supplied by the will of God, self-evidence, intuition, what rational persons would agree to, utility, or whatever. My own reasoning in making the move from fact to value is briefly explained in the following section.

C. Ideal Democracy and Individualism

Whether democracy as here defined is "individualistic" calls for consideration partly because individualism is today under attack and even more because addressing this question will cast further light upon the nature and justification of the democratic ideal. It is important here to be extremely careful about the use of the term "individualism." Often it is identified with an atomistic concept of man—with "economic" man or with Hobbesian "political" man. We need not get involved in a debate over the definition. We need only consider certain democratic propositions, without reference to whether they add up to something tagged "individualism." It is implicit in what has been said that humans are held to be *self*-conscious, conceiving of their selves as separate and, in a measure, independent entities. Moreover, the democratic ideal places an extremely high value on the life and well-being of all human beings. It holds that no individual's life or well-being should be sacrificed for the sake of others, living or yet to be born, without some powerful overriding justification. (Some may hold that life, as contrasted with well-being, should *never* be sacrificed for the sake of others. Liberal democrats doubtless divide on this question, depending, for instance, on whether or not they would, under any circumstances, countenance capital punishment or compulsory military service; or on the question of whether cannabalism is justified under circumstances where it is clearly the only alternative to the starvation of all who share those circumstances.) In speaking of both life and well-being I am embracing a continuum that extends from the loss of life through many intermediate points to some loss of liberty, enjoyment, or opportunity for the development of the self. It is also arguable (*pace* Rawls) that in considering what justification is strong enough one must take account of the numbers of potential winners and losers as well as the likelihood that the consequences envisaged will actually occur. On the whole, we are inevitably dealing here with matters of degree.

The supreme value that democracy places on individual autonomy, thriving, and all that contributes to a person's well-being is fundamental. Without autonomy the individual is degraded. It bears repeating that this concept does not mean that the actions of individuals are uncaused. They are caused by the individual's desires, aversions, hopes, fears, goals, and the like, and by his determination, after some calculation and reflection, to act in a certain way. Action resulting from this process, as distinct from reflexive behavior, is autonomous; a being who is capable of such behavior, and knows that he is, is an autonomous individual—a matter of degree once more, but also one of great and intrinsic value. It is good in and of itself. As one writer has aptly described it, following Brandt, it is like the rapturous joy of a child swinging.[11]

Critics of liberal democracy sometimes attack its ideal of individual autonomy as nonexistent and unattainable, because the reigning ideology in a person's society determines his values, and any notion he may have of his own self-determination comes under the heading of "false-consciousness." A full rebuttal of this argument would take me far beyond the limits of this chapter. The chief points to be noted, however, in addition to what has already been said about autonomy, are that it is a matter of degree and that the influence of conditioning factors is by no means denied, but that to hold that these factors eliminate all individual autonomy is a self-defeating argument, undermining the foundation of all rational discourse.[12]

Further, democratic theory, as I understand it, holds that the value of society or of community is not independent of the individuals that compose it; it derives from its constituent individuals. Of course any community has a value for each of its members. Indeed, that value may be an important part of the person's self. The individual is in large measure what he is because he lives in society and because of the nature of the society in which he lives. The individual whose liberty and well-being are objects of democracy's concern is the individual as he is and as he may become; not the individual as he may have been at some prior period, and not (it will bear repeating) an imagined atomistic individual, untouched by those around him. He may feel fulfilled in contributing to it; he may wish to "sacrifice" his own interests (narrowly conceived) for it; he may take an interest in its continuance and its quality beyond his own lifetime; but it is *his* interest. That is all that I mean. I call it "basic individualism," but the tag is unimportant.

Lastly, democracy embodies a strong (but sometimes overstated) presumption in favor of each individual's own judgment about what contributes to his well-being. Several reasons support this presumption. First, the old "shoe-pinches" argument: no one else can know our own feelings, our pains and pleasures, our states of mind, the way we ourselves can. Second, making choices contributes to our development, to our individuality, and to our sense of being real, autonomous persons. (Of course our decisions may prove to have been mistaken, in which case they at least contribute to our education.) Finally, democrats trust the individual because of a strong *dis*trust of what others would decide if they were in positions of unchecked power.

All three of these aspects of individualism are related to the most fundamental elements of democratic theory, the rationality and autonomy of the individual, as defined above.

Along with autonomy and individualism go three closely related characteristics, dignity, self-respect (or self-esteem), and respect for others. Human dignity is that highly valued quality we ascribe to beings who respect themselves and have regard for others, both of which can occur only in society.[13] That these things are good, indeed high-order goods, is hardly denied in theory even by those who deny them in practice.

3. LIBERTY AND EQUALITY

Two of the most fundamental elements of the democratic credo are embodied in what has just been said: liberty and equality. Autonomy itself entails liberty, both political and civil, at the same time that in another sense it flows from liberty. Without the capacity (liberty) to take purposive action individuals could not be autonomous; but if outside forces prevent this capacity from being exercised—if those who have the capacity are coerced into making decisions they can not feel are their own—their autonomy and freedom are diminished. This includes their freedom to decide that certain areas of their lives should be free from intrusion—in short, their privacy.[14] In the absence of a large measure of liberty the capacity of the individual to develop his distinctively human capacities would be virtually nullified. J.R. Lucas has put it well. He writes:

> Freedom is a necessary condition of rationality, of action, of achievement. Not to be free is to be frustrated, impotent, futile. To be free is to be able to shape the future, to be able to translate one's ideals into reality, to actualize one's potentialities as a person. Not to be free is not to be responsive, not to be human. Freedom is good if anything is.[15]

As to equality, it is not just certain individuals or certain kinds or classes of individuals on which democracy sets the highest value; it is the individual person per se. Of course, this does not mean that individuals must all be treated alike. It does mean, however, that their dignity would be violated if they were treated unequally without justification, that is to say in a way that failed to respect and show concern for their dignity and autonomy. Discrimination is invidious unless it passes a severe test. The presumption is always against it and in favor of equality. This is the principle of "presumptive equality." The equality of the vote, the hallmark of democracy, is so not only because it gives each citizen, equally, a substantive power with which to protect and advance his interests (including of course his social as well as his individual interests), but also, perhaps pre-eminently, because it symbolizes that equality of respect to which each individual is entitled.[16] People who are denied this equality feel themselves second-class citizens, and tend to be treated as such.

Whether symbolic equality and equal suffrage is enough to meet the test for democracy or whether the democratic ideal demands that each citizen's "substantive" political power must be equal (requiring equal resources) is a hotly contested point. If the consequence of such egalitarianism would be to diminish production so that even the least advantaged would be made worse off, it is doubtful whether anyone would support it as a requirement of democracy. At the other extreme, if the result would be to make everyone better off, it would probably encounter little opposition, although this is less certain. Philosophers who believe that desert (perhaps measured by effort) should be rewarded might feel it unjust. If this end could be achieved only by increasing inequality, doubtless others would oppose it because they felt that would be inherently unjust. In these hypothetical situations, philosophers' ethical positions might be controlling, but I see no reason to believe that their differences as to ethics would in any way depend upon questions of metaethics. Once more the rival camps of consequentialists and deontologists could readily (and in fact do) find themselves divided on the matter.

4. CAVEAT

In view of what has just been said, it should be apparent that democracy does not require either capitalism or the maximum use of the market. Of course it is arguable that these institutions are essential to the effective functioning of democracy or even to its preservation. It may also be contended that some of the same considerations that justify liberal democracy support capitalism and maximum use of the market as well, and this position may be used either to support the latter or to condemn *liberal* democracy. Likewise, the equalitarian element of democracy is often used to argue that democracy and capitalism are incompatible. None of these arguments is a logical derivation from the concepts, values, and supporting arguments of liberal democracy. These are matters to be settled by investigation, calculation, and experience.

5. Conclusion

A full-scale justification of democracy would require much more than has been attempted here. In the most general terms, it would require a careful consideration of whether the institutions of constitutional and representative government are more likely than any known alternative to achieve the closest possible approximation to the democratic ideal. One of the most central specific questions that would call for analysis and appraisal relates to majority rule: to wit, can it—or indeed *any* voting procedure—do what is required of it—serve as the essential link between the individual's desires, purposes, and welfare, on the one hand, and the results of the voting process on the other? Serious doubts are raised by students of the logic of preference aggregation. To deal with these complicated issues would take me far beyond my present purpose: to illustrate a method of political justification.

Let this much be clear. An effort to make our ethical system coherent throughout and as solidly grounded as reflection and rational thinking can make it is an intellectual enterprise of the highest order. It is also one to which many of our best minds have been devoted in recent decades. Fortunately, it is not a goal that must be accomplished by one who would justify specific political institutions in a way that is satisfactory to those who are willing to accept the justification of our other ethical norms, such as the moral value we place on healthy human life. And certainly it is not a goal that must be achieved in order to prevent the kind of crisis that might threaten the continuance of democracy here or elsewhere. If such a crisis should arise—as certainly it may—it will be because governments have failed to approximate democratic goals or convince their citizens that they are moving in that direction faster than could any alternative form of government.

NOTES

1. James Fishkin, "Liberal Theory and the Problem of Justification," in this volume.

2. Hereafter I shall assume that "he" and its cognates are gender-neutral unless the context indicates otherwise.

3. To be sure, the *extent* of political power they justify is not the same for each of these philosophers, but the reason for these differences is other than their differing metaethical theories, as I shall point out in a moment.

4. Incidentally, insofar as they are *not* the product of rational thought, they are presumably not susceptible to the kind of ratiocination that Fishkin fears will lead to severe legitimacy problems. For a persuasive argument against ideological determinism, see Barry Holden, "Liberal Democracy and the Social Determination of Ideas," in NOMOS XXV, *Liberal Democracy* ed. J. Roland Pennock and John W. Chapman (New York: New York University Press, 1979), chap. 12.

5. This of course is a matter of the form of government only if the form in question is democratic and if it is assumed that democracy calls for a low degree of inequality of incomes.

6. See Jerome Kagan, *The Nature of the Child* (New York: Basic Books, 1984), p. 152.

7. The extent to which either economic or social democracy is a necessary condition for achieving some reasonable approximation to the ideal is also passed over.

8. In stating it as a fact that humans tend to develop a belief in a "kind" of equality, I am recognizing that, in Aristotle's terms, it may be either absolute ("numerical") or relative ("proportionate") equality.

9. Obviously much is left unsaid by this capsule history. It is not meant to imply that political development is either linear or inevitable.

10. Thucydides reports Pericles in his famous funeral oration as having made it a virtue of the Athenians that they valued their private as well as their public life and that they did not "feel called upon to be angry with [their] neighbour for doing what he likes, or even to indulge in those injurious looks which cannot fail to be offensive, although they inflict no positive penalty. But all this ease in our private relations," he continued, "does not make us lawless citizens." *History of the Peloponnesian War*, revised Crawley translation (New York: Modern Library 1982), p. 108. Colonel Rainborough, in mid-seventeenth century England, makes it even clearer. "Every man that is to live under a government," he declared, "ought

first by his own consent to put himself under that government," adding in his next speech that this right to political equality derived from the fact that "the main cause why Almighty God gave men reason, it was that they should make use of that reason, and that they should improve it for that end and purpose that God gave it them." Quoted from the Putney Debates in A.S.P. Woodhouse, ed., *Puritanism and Liberty* (Chicago: University of Chicago Press, 1951), p. 53.

11. Robert Young, "The Value of Autonomy," *The Philosophical Quarterly* 323 (1982): 35–44, 43. This is by no means to deny that it is also instrumental, making our lives "our own" and being conducive to self-esteem. Nor is it to deny that autonomy may be exercised in evil ways, even in ways so evil that the disvalue they cause exceeds their value. Ibid., pp. 43–44.

12. For a compelling treatment of this argument, see Barry Holden's "Liberal Democracy and the Social Determination of Ideas."

13. See my *Democratic Political Theory* (Princeton: Princeton University Press, 1979), p. 84 and materials cited there.

14. See Steven Lukes, *Individualism* (New York: Harper and Row, 1979), chap. 9.

15. *The Principles of Politics* (Oxford: Clarendon Press, 1966), p. 144.

16. Note that Bentham gave priority to this fundamental equality with the phrase "each to count for one and nobody for more than one" and Kant with the dictum that each should be treated as an end in himself and never as only a means.

16

THE ENDS OF ETHICS—
THE BEGINNINGS OF POLITICS

J. PATRICK DOBEL

"Would that be justice, ladies?" asked the just man.
"It would be success, Mr. Low,—which is a great deal the better
of the two."

—Anthony Trollope, *Phineas Redux*

Moralists seldom like politicians and politicians seldom appreciate moralists. But as citizens and governors we pursue moral purposes in political life. Today abortion, environmental regulation and the rights of women and minorities are vigorously fought over in resounding moral cadences. People's concerns are justified in terms of profound moral principles and more than one proponent invokes Charles Sumner's undying creed in his fight to end slavery, "Moral principles cannot be compromised."[1] But we can hear harried contemporary politicians echo the disdain of Sumner's great ally and opponent, William Pitt Fessenden, the Republican leader in the Senate in the fight over Reconstruction, "My constituents did not send me here to philosophize. They sent me to act."[2] We can sense the same tension between Plato's claim that philosophers must become kings before justice can rule and Machiavelli's sardonic yet passionate subversion of moral pieties in political life.

These ill-fitted worlds of discourse and persons are locked together in our persisting attempt to build and sustain a just and enduring political order. Any ideal of the common good requires both the practical reality of common assent and cooperation, and discussion and decision over the content of that good. Any defense of human rights requires both procedure and practice to protect the rights, and discussion and decision on the nature and source of the rights. Any concern with pursuit of interest requires attention to methods of negotiation and adjustment, and discussion and decision on the limits of allowable solutions and ranking of interests.

Political compromise nicely illustrates the inextricable ties between political and ethical claims. When we compromise, we usually agree to accept a morally imperfect solution. Strident allies, opponents and even our consciences express their disquiet with compromise and demand justifications. We must then deploy the best and most powerful reasons available to us. These reasons highlight the three families of reasons we invoke in political life—ethical, political and prudential. Consequently, the examples to illustrate justifications will generally be drawn from real life and possible compromises and their justifications.

I shall examine the importance of and relations among ethical, political and prudential justifications. I analyze the general structure of political justification—the kinds of reasons used, the relations among them and the constraints upon them—and the role ethical reasons play within political life. Although I deal with the general nature of justification, I shall focus upon liberal democracy.[3] First, I survey the nature of political justification and its constraints. Second, I scrutinize ethical principles in political life. Third, I look at political and prudential justifications. Finally, I study the relations among these three families and their constraints. I hope to demonstrate that moralists who would collapse politics into ethics and realists who would banish ethical principles from politics both oversimplify and misinterpret political life. Ethical considerations must weigh very heavily in justifications of political conduct.

POLITICAL JUSTIFICATION

When we justify an action or a belief, we give "good" reasons for what we did or believe. We present reasons to demonstrate that we did the "right" thing or to show an act or belief "makes sense." The goodness of reasons depends upon the appropriateness of the setting and the people we must convince. To say we voted for a bill because we liked the looks of the sponsor would be dismissed as ethically, politically and prudentially irrelevant. Accepting findings from a colleague because he is physically stronger is not acceptable. Political justification involves reasons that identify a situation as suitable for governmental action. This justifies the mobilization of people, resources, law, institutions and ultimately coercive force. Very often ethics leads politics in the sense that if we can demonstrate "harm" or "wrong," then we can motivate people to demand political action.[4]

Justification is an inherently social activity. Even when we justify ourselves before our consciences, we may engage in a raging debate among our own "selves." Most of the time we justify to others. Generally, justification is defensive—to meet questions, doubts or charges. Successful justification requires reference to what we all accept as good reasons appropriate to a sphere of action, or it convinces people to accept new reasons as equally legitimate or better than ones they presently hold. These may refer to ethical reasons—I respected her right; or refer to practical reasons—I cannot accomplish it; or refer to legitmate procedures—I won the election; or refer to symbolic orderings of authority—I possess the office to issue this order.

As a social activity, justification presumes open and free discussion of reasons. The claim that I am bigger or have more power, untempered by legitimate procedures, does not justify, it dominates. No discussion or free assessment has occurred, and we have no reasons to consider the assertion "good." In a similar vein, if our beliefs have been manipulated, then justification becomes a vicious circle. If someone deceives us, then their reasons do not justify because our acceptance presumes both truthfulness and sincerity. Justification can be neither coerced nor manipulated.

On the other hand, "because I said so" can have considerable justificatory power. When a person possesses recognized skill, proven leadership or legitimately gained office, his or her word or pronouncement can serve as a contextually acceptable justification. The skill and authority, however, cannot be closed and must be subject to further appeal, discussion or modification.

For a person's word still constitutes a "reason," not a command or dogma, and reasons can always be open to further reasoning or refinement in order to remain a reason. Consequently, I am not interested in the process of creating reasons or socialization per se; I am interested in the nature of reasons given in an open political society.

As citizens of a liberal democracy, we lead and are led, and hold responsibility, however attenuated, for actions that our votes, money, support and actions make possible. This responsibility and freedom means we must judge and act. We give reasons and evaluate reasons that fellow citizens and governors proffer to us.

Political justification requires uncoerced and unmanipulated persuasion by reasons we and others accept as valid to warrant action or belief. However, in political life, justification is not simply as defensive or ex post facto as I suggested. Politicians must not just answer the question "Why did you do that?" but "Why do you want to do that?" or "Why do you want us to support you when you do that?" Consequently, political justification must become an active form of persuasion to convince individuals not just to accept but to cooperate. Successful political action mobilizes citizens to devote time, energy and money for a cause. If our actions result in changed policy or law, we must convince others who might be indifferent or opposed to accept the change, continue to pay taxes and not disobey the law. Political justification must motivate individuals. Such justifications will depend upon rhetoric that builds a community of belief, explains positions and educates, persuades or convinces citizens.

Conflict inheres in the diversity and heat of political life. I will not examine the possibility of small and deeply consensual associations that might minimize serious moral and political disagreement. The size, classes, diversity and multiple poles of authority of the modern state guarantees that conflict will remain a central aspect of political and social life. Any endeavor to mobilize citizens, change policy, law or attitude and practice runs against the obstinacy of reality—groups and individuals who hold considerable power will often be indifferent or hostile to our proposals or actions. They may have interests that would be harmed or believe our proposals harmful or immoral. A welter of reasons must be offered to justify a political position, to answer a flurry of questions or charges. I will examine the multiple audiences and standard forms of reasons available to present the constraints that shape political justification.

Successful justification means acceptance. The people who accept also determine what constitutes a good reason. In technical endeavors, individuals may share a narrow and widely accepted set of premises and methods. This enables them to pursue "normal" science where they can narrow the range of justification and increase the precision of what counts as a good reason or evidence. They can minimize the emotional or self-interested content of justification and give more weight to impersonal rules of procedure and verification.[5] But politics, even "normal" politics, has no such paradigmatic stability. Political justification is a multifaceted, even Janus-faced, endeavor because of the multiple audiences we must address.

Politicians must mobilize allies. Since a political leader seeks concrete results, she has two different problems. First, she must often yoke together people who want similar outcomes but for different reasons. Anti-abortion leaders must simultaneously satisfy Southern Baptists who trace their opposition to biblical references to life in the womb, and Roman Catholics who base theirs upon a natural law claim about the moral status of potentiality in the fetus. Neither side necessarily accepts the reasoning of the other. On the other hand, allies may hold similar premises but differ about the shape of the solution or the methods to attain the goal. Many environmentalists are committed to preserve resources for the future, but differ profoundly over whether we should use regulation, mediation or market incentives.

Many other potential allies may have to be roused out of their indifference and educated to the reality of the problem. Martin Luther King used his marches to demonstrate to Northern moderates the importance of the problem and provide a good reason to support the movement. Many successful movements organize themselves, and often politicians must not only awake the indifferent, but choose between vigorous pursuit of a goal and maintaining an institutional base that makes long-term success possible. The "radicals" will demand the one, the "moderates" will prefer the other. From 1865 to 1869 the entire Republican Party was committed to freeing black slaves, guaranteeing them civil and political liberty and restoring the shattered union by readmitting "reformed" Southern states. Yet as election defeats made clear, voters resented universal Negro suffrage and delayed admission of Southern states. As the party lost strength, many Republicans distanced themselves from the original "radical" proposals to create a Freedman's Bureau financed by land confiscation and to guarantee Negro suffrage and local democracy by Constitutional and military means. As Senator John Sherman, a conservative Republican leader put it, "It is clearly right that suffrage should be impartial without regard to color. It is easy to convince people so, but harder to make them feel it—and vote it. We will have to carry it because it is right but it will be a burden in every election." All over the country they toned down their rhetoric and increasingly shifted their focus to other issues. The other side of the problem was predicted by radical Senator Benjamin Wade, "I fear its effect will be to make the timorous more timorous."[6]

If persuading squabbling allies were not enough, justifications must be addressed to many indifferent citizens to accept the cause or abide by the results. Here again individuals share different attitudes and premises. Even when they hold common ones, they are "imperfectly shared" terms of an open-ended discussion.[7] An environmentalist might have to awaken latent ethical and religious attitudes toward stewardship of resources and then connect this to activists who may believe that all sentient creatures have "rights." An anti-abortion advocate would invoke the term murder to arouse individuals while pro-abortion advocates would emphasize widely shared beliefs in "free choice." Both sides must address those who feel abortion is "wrong" but are reluctant to legislate a coercive ban or who would limit abortions but would make exceptions for rape or incest and threats to the mother's life. Unlike the early apostles, who could speak one language and be heard by many different audiences in the audience's own language, politicians must sometimes speak different languages to different groups or weave a fabric of justification from different strands.

Finally, political justifications must be accepted by those individuals who oppose our positions, goals or organizations—sometimes all three. The reasons given to such opponents will differ profoundly from those conveyed to allies, the indifferent or the ignorant. Very often we must overtly recognize our opponents' integrity even in opposition and acknowledge their continuing right to think, feel and believe. The openness and fairness of the political order might be emphasized to remind them that they had their say and will have future opportunities. Finally, we may invoke shared loyalty to symbols, rituals and territorial integrity to reaffirm our fellowship even in our conflict. In some cases, we might compromise and accept some of their positions either because they were right or out of respect for their integrity or power. Ultimately they must be persuaded to accept the law, obey it and give financial and human support. We must also persuade them not to take up arms despite a defeat but to fight by established rules. To gain acquiescence from our opponents for our ethically inspired policies remains a central problem and constraint upon political justification and action. Given this problem as well as the diversity among allies and the indifferent, I do not see a simple or neat model of political justification, since success will be inherently contextual.

The cultural tools of justification shape political justification as much as the diversity of audience. These include: the commonsense criteria by which citizens judge, the symbols and rituals of political legitimacy, the methods of power acquisition and conflict resolution and characterizations of citizens' experience and interests. In political life we imperfectly share many judgmental terms of discourse. Some are relatively closed in terms of meaning and application, like murder. Some. like discrimination, are agreed to be wrong but are still very open as to the scope of the term and its exact application.[8] When we apply established terms we characterize actions and imbed them in a web of considered judgments and moral practices that most of us share. We can justify many actions by appealing to commonly shared and understood practices.[9] Here we introduce ethical terms at their strongest and most obvious. But often the issue does not involve the morality of the practice but whether actions are subsumed under a practice. The question of whether abortion counts as murder or neutral free choice does not debate the evil of murder or the desirability of free choice; rather, it concerns the correct characterization of aborting a fetus.[10]

We also possess foundational or symbolic rhetoric and shared ethical aspirations embodied in basic political symbols. "Liberty, equality and fraternity," or "Life, liberty and the pursuit of happiness" provide powerful and enduring terms of shared political heritage. These symbols are deepened by shared history, territorial unity and education. The creation of symbols and agreement upon them enables us to disagree, debate and adopt meanings within a broad historical and cultural continuum. It represents a great historical accomplishment for a viable political order.[11] Such symbols enable multiple audiences to proclaim their loyalty while holding different but related conceptions of symbols and they shape and limit the range of acceptable options while making legitimation of solutions easier for the entire population.

Just as politics compares to science in its broadening of terms and opening of audiences, these foundational terms are the most imperfectly shared of symbols and carry multiple historical interpretations. Additionally, most foundings involve their own compromises, like the American tension between federal supremacy and states' rights. So principles embodied in the symbols may not fit so neatly, as well as having no clear-cut consensual meanings. Liberty and equality, while theoretically compatible, remain poles of competitive discourse and justification in "liberal" "democracies." But to the extent politicians strive to justify their aspirations under the rubric of the terms, the symbols domesticate opposition and justification. When Machiavelli suggested that we should return to the principles of founding to renew a state, he prescribed the requirement of all politicians who seek legitimacy for their reforms.[12]

Shared moral practices and symbolic rhetoric provide us with no determinative outcomes for politics and consequently politicians must utilize accepted methods of exercising power and resolving disputes. These methods legitimize conflict resolution and are strongest when they take on symbolic and ritual power with a population. In a liberal democracy, elections, courts, lawmaking and administrative decisions legitimize patterns of conflict and elicit support from citizens even while shaping the form of the conflict.[13] Justifications cluster around the requirements of gaining power, creating coalitions, passing or implementing laws and gaining peaceful acquiescence.

These conflict resolution procedures can also be defended by referring to the common benefits all sides achieve by agreeing not to eliminate their opponents. But the procedures that replace violent conflict must possess integrity and fairness if they are to carry weight. We may ultimately choose to mute our own political indictments and rhetoric or pull back from demands in the interest of maintaining civility and trust. Such reasoning is often necessary to satisfy the opposition of our shared loyalties and fellowship, and to reassure opponents of further chances for discussion and change. The claims of ritual, law and civility may well shape the urgency of moral justification of reformers. The very power of these reasons informs the justification of those who use civil disobedience to call attention to unjust laws and motivate others to support the cause. Civil disobedience simultaneously affirms loyalty to order and the rule of law while powerfully criticizing the moral failures of that order.

If law and governance are to generate loyalty and obligations, they must ultimately link symbols and rituals to the moral practices and beliefs of most citizens. To be successful across a wide range, justifications must work at different levels and to different audiences. They must touch individual conscience, group loyalties and normal practices as well as public rituals and symbols. Most justifications will possess a patina of coherence but ultimately remain open, contextual and shifting, always reinterpreting to accommodate change, serendipity and various publics.

Finally, justification must link human experience to political goals. Laws, policies and institutions earn their legitimacy over time by providing experienced benefits in the lives of citizens. Politicians must rely upon symbols, rituals and moral practices because these enable citizens to characterize experience. To a great extent symbolic understandings shape experience. But justification requires not just giving good reasons but also characterizing a situation as one that needs political action. Here politicians must actively show citizens what harms are being done or what good is being frustrated that sustained political action could rectify. Politicians may call our attention to a new or hidden experience and portray it as harmful or wrong by our ethical or political understanding. They might recharacterize an experience we have and transform it into a political matter subject to action. They might literally invent a new experience of a type of action and establish it as a political practice. In each case loyalty, understanding and motivation depend upon our experience connecting with the justification offered.

At one level, this is most commonly accomplished by linking political action with interests. Interests may be morally grounded or neutral or derivative of a moral claim such as autonomy, but they possess immense durability and power in personal lives. Interests matter because we experience them as ours and vital to our material and spiritual welfare.[14] Political actions materially affect these concrete concerns. But we may also experience our interests as harmed in ways that seem beyond governmental concern. A job layoff or cancer from exposure to waste may not seem to connect with any characterizations of the type of responsible action subject to political jurisdiction. Justifications will link to interests in order to bring home the human connection between individual lives and political action.

Political justification maps a world and identifies areas of legitimate action. We must distill or create from our experience terms of common reference so that as members of a political community we can understand and accept meanings and actions. Often we need only point to particular disasters, harms or wrongs that once recognized motivate us to act and implicate us in responsibility for them. The great civil rights demonstrations and the ensuing violent attacks upon peaceful demonstrators jolted many Americans and provided the experience and reference necessary to support the enactment of the civil rights legislation of the sixties.

Political justification can also redefine experience. Individuals might well believe that bad luck or God's will gave them cancer or deformed children. But a leader changes their experience when he calls attention to the toxic waste dump that poisoned their water. This connection re-interprets a situation as one justifiably subject to political and legal action. In a similar sense, members of an exploited group may internalize a low self-image and feel impotent at their plight. But leaders can identify this low self-image as a social creation. Courageous individuals can demonstrate its falseness by their success and the group can recover its identity and harness its energies. It can recover its history and cultural nobility and demand changes in the symbols and images of the dominant culture.

Finally, individuals might invent a new action that generates a new experience of themselves and political life. William Connolly explains how the term "boycott" arose to characterize the deliberate and systematic isolation of a particularly ruthless collector of rents for English landlords in Ireland, Captain Charles Boycott. Gradually the practice spread across Ireland and into liberal political life. It summarized and justified an organized effort by disadvantaged groups to refuse to call upon or use the products of an employer whose policies were unduly harsh, in order to punish him or coerce a change.[15] Boycotts identify a new option for individuals in society. This option changes their self-understandings and increases the range of justifications for action, since they can now identify situations where they had been previously powerless as legitimate subjects for political endeavor.

Justification usually conserves. It relies upon established moral and political practices as well as shared symbols. But political life, especially in open societies, seldom sits still. When justifications use symbols with open texture and complex historical genealogy, these justifications can be extended and even transformed. To the extent justification can touch or articulate old and new experience, we come to the borderland between "normal" and "revolutionary" politics.[16] Political violence and terrorism represent the complete failure of justification. Justification presumes giving and accepting uncoerced and unmanipulated reasons. Terrorism and civil war mean that citizens no longer accept symbolic or ritual reasons to acquiesce in the political order. These groups believe that their own experience of harm or injustice is powerful and morally compelling. But their own experience is characterized differently or dismissed by the dominant order—victims get blamed for their victimization, for instance. On the other hand, their voices might simply not be heard, or when heard, ignored. Revolutionary activity represents a breakdown and basic change in the quality but not the kind of political action. Political justification always innovates, extends and re-interprets. It always speaks to several audiences and weaves a fabric of many threads and it uses imperfectly shared understandings in an open textured world. As Burke suggests, reform proceeds within any viable society and justification must expand to encompass new harms, new names for hidden dangers and injured silences now alive with voice. Old forms of symbol may break down or be modified. *Brown vs. Board of Education* finalized a slow, forty-year struggle to dethrone "separate but equal" as a legitimate formula. In a similar way, courts and Congress finally rejected the states' rights formula as an excuse to stop national standards of nondiscrimination.[17] These changes impose immense strains on political order and further undercut our ability to give a nice and neat explanation and weighting of political justification.

PRINCIPLES IN POLITICS

Successful political action results in policy, law and institutions that justify government in sending people to jail, taking their money and restricting their freedom. Government concentrates immense power to enforce its will. It exerts enormous cultural, legal and practical influence on the beliefs, attitudes and actions of citizens. It affects their freedom and life chances; it defends their security and rights and takes large chunks of their earnings. The actions of political life require some ethical justifications to direct and limit them and generate obligations to accept them.

Basic human interests in safety, shelter, freedom, education and earnings are affected for good or bad by government. Institutions of such power and consequence must be justified in very powerful and persuasive terms. As citizens who judge and act, who determine the range of acceptable justifications, we naturally and rightly recur to moral terms to assess both the foundations and daily consequences of such activity. Government makes claims to act on behalf of goods and harms. These claims demand obligations from us to obey laws with which we might disagree. They ask us to sacrifice earnings and freedom for benefits that we do not directly experience. Consequently, we invoke ethical terms along with political and prudential terms to direct, limit or change these institutions. Even foundational rhetoric and symbols incorporate basic ethical claims.

In a liberal democracy government is accountable to citizens in a broad sense. This implicates citizens with responsibility for actions taken on their behalf. In manipulated or viciously circular societies or in societies where political participation is warped by coercion, ethical language plays little serious role. But when governments kill, tax, redistribute and regulate, mere claims of ethically neutral self-interests cannot encompass the goods and harms to fellow humans. This becomes especially true when harms transcend evident material interests and affect human dignity or subvert autonomy. Likewise, calls to include others in the fellowship of citizenry and extend positive civil rights appeal not simply to interest but to duties. Environmental claims on behalf of future generations extend the same realm. I do not deny that other claims figure prominently and sometimes dominantly in political life, nor do I denigrate their power or validity, but I suggest that justifications of obligation, sacrifice for others and distributional claims generally must be made in ethical terms. Additionally, foundational rhetoric and symbols must be capable of incorporating and responding to such ethical claims.

I am interested in political claims articulated on the basis of principles.[18] I am not interested in the source of the principles or even whether they are deontic or consequentialist, for once articulated their moral force remains the same. Most are discovered by seeking a neutral or disinterested point of view and generating duties incumbent upon all rational humans. We might also take commonly shared intuitions and practices and develop a systematic exposition of their detailed ethical requirements. Finally, we might combine an attempt to gain an impartial view with an examination of our intuitions and arrive at principles from what John Rawls calls "reflective equilibrium."[19]

Principles spell out what we ought and ought not to do toward fellow human beings. They serve as very special stops in debates and potent final reasons for action.[20] They frame our ethical obligations and provide independent moral reasons to act. They introduce a set of discriminations and valuations into our lives that both direct and motivate us to act out of duty. The discipline of principles creates a critical distance between unconsidered prejudice and cultural horizons, and the obligations of our humanity. But most principles find their reality in moral practices and internalized rules like "killing is wrong" or "fairness is right." We take such practices as "right as a matter of course."[21]

A number of characteristics of principles are relevant to our consideration of how they influence political justification. First, ethical principles derive from the "moral point of view." This angle of vision militantly drives toward impartiality and universality. All persons must be considered as equal beings. An ethical view disallows idiosyncratic preference for ourselves and requires that we extend the same moral considerations to all. It disallows hypocrisy, for if a principle applies to one, it applies to all. Second, principles are freely chosen or accepted. Unreflected beliefs count only insofar as upon challenge they can be defended in ethical terms to other free and rational creatures. Prejudice does not supersede principle. This reinforces impartiality and universality because all rational beings who possess principles must be admitted to the fellowship of obligation. Third, principles are right and autonomous. Their rightness means that they answer only to other principles or the "requirements of other dimensions of morality such as fairness or justice." Rightness gives principles special status in decisions about actions towards others. Principles serve as trumps in these discussions and supersede most other claims of non-moral interests, idiosyncratic desire or personal prejudice.[22]

Fourth, the principles are also clean in the sense that they are clear and indubitable within their realm. They cut through ambiguity and weigh in with decisive positions and sharp conclusions on rightness or wrongness. Fifth, because principles are right and clean, because they fit our world and characterize it and give it coherence, they demand authenticity. They define our duty and if we have integrity, then we must hold to them with the keenness and purity that they demand. For they anchor our moral self and give it substance against the welter of individual and socially created desires. Finally, principles are imperious. They demand acknowledgment once we hold them and urge us to act accordingly. Imperiousness suffers little contingency or even complexity within its own logic and answers only to other ethical considerations. The imperative power of principles demands positive fulfillment, even when they require only that we refrain from action. The logic of imperiousness discounts sacrifice or obstacles and generates urgency in us to act and impatience with lack of action or progress.[23] Principles might tolerate expediency but only in the terms of William

Lloyd Garrison, the great abolitionist, when he chided Charles C. Burleigh for his unkempt appearance, "Where there is no moral principle involved, it is sometimes wise to sacrifice what is convenient or agreeable to us, that no unnecessary obstacle be thrown in the way of a great or good cause."[24]

Since principles provide strong and independent reasons to act, the strongest principles may warrant immediate and clear actions toward others. This gives principles a decided political role. They obligate us in terms of right and define relevant terms to constitute the ends of politics. These can warrant us to direct government to attain these ends. Paradoxically, they can also define the ends of legitimate government action by justifying limits beyond which political power should not be exercised. Not all principles necessarily warrant political action. We should be grateful to those who benefit us, for instance, does not necessarily generate requirements that the government should mandate that children take care of their parents. But since principles deeply influence how we characterize good and harm and how we defend choice, they constantly generate political concern.

Principles resolve into judgments and give us critical perspective from which to see, analyze and judge. As such, they can give us reasons to accept the moral and political practices of a society. Within the constraints of a political order, principles can direct us to reform and bring the reality and ideals of an order closer. Symbols, practices and rituals can be deepened and expanded when we articulate their implications into principles.

Principles push us to our common humanity and shift the burden of proof onto those persons and practices who would degrade fellow humans. "Reflective equilibrium" or the discipline of impartiality and consistency can subvert pieties and muddled intuitions that support prejudice, hypocrisy and rationalized self-interest. Principled claims interrogate power and require that it be defended with reference to its effect on others. Old orders can not only be subverted, but reaffirmed and reformed, and new ones can be built upon clarified old or new principles.

Principles can transcend the conservative constraints audience places upon political justification. Prophets, witness bearers, saints, agitators and martyrs embody unalloyed commitment to principles and ideals. Their actions can challenge old practices, question complacency and introduce new ideals. Their purity or zeal can demonstrate moral flaws in a political order and call citizens to reform. Lived principles and moral example can create or expand a country's social conscience. William Lloyd Garrison, Susan B. Anthony, Martin Luther King and others crowd and provoke liberal democracy to transcend interest and practice and to reexamine its moral ends.

Principles without power, like prophets, often come to naught. Unconnected to political or prudential skill, principles will often not effect change and sometimes provoke counterreactions that can radically polarize politics and make serious deliberation and stable solutions all but impossible.[25] But at other times, principled rhetoric can challenge superior force and discipline power and discourse. The invocation of shared principles can reveal the hypocrisy of governors and citizens and strip the patina of moral legitimacy from rule and obedience. Conscientious or even self-interested rulers might limit themselves to comport more carefully with the sources of their integrity or legitimacy. These claims can also galvanize the consciences of putative believers and change the terms of political discourse and action.

Principled justifications alone, however, suffer from severe limits in politics. First, the univocal and absolute style they engender can unleash tyranny or tragedy when conjoined with state power. Sure of their rightness and convinced of their enemies' perfidy, unbending prophets or agitators can use acquired state power to enforce their will and disregard moral complexity, personal autonomy and the material or human costs of their vision. The Ayatollah Khomeini, unarmed, inspired the overthrow of a tyrant in Iran. Armed, he led a terror-ridden theocracy. Paradoxically, unalloyed principle in office can also breed the tragic or pious incompetent. Machiavelli jeers at such leaders who act untempered by political or prudential reason, "The fact is that a man who wants to act virtuously in every way necessarily comes to grief among so many who are not virtuous."[26] Such naive rightness not only comes to naught, but betrays the goals of the principles by its own incompetence.

Second, principles generally do not stipulate the exact shape of concrete actions or outcomes required by them. Their general form militates against exact specification except in rare circumstances, and leaves open the exact nature of charged value terms like equality, freedom or dignity. They function better as justifications that influence a concrete action than as determiners of the act. This indeterminancy of outcomes means that a principle such as "all men should be free" and a derivative principle that "slavery is wrong" still leave open the questions of the exact nature of the civil, legal and political freedoms required. Even if we agree on the exact shape of the solution, we must then determine the means to be used, such as the actual extent of the role of the government in enforcing these freedoms.

Third, even if we agree on principles, the shape of the outcome and method, we encounter moral complexity. There may well be other moral principles that must be taken into account. The need to feed individuals in an overpopulated land may conflict with requirements of husbandry of land for future generations. Anti-abortion advocates may come up against claims of self-defense by mothers as well as claims to self-determination. In addition to other principles, we must also respect the autonomy of individuals and respect their voice and values.[27] Even if we find higher-order principles that break deadlocks among principles, autonomy still limits those principles' dictatorial powers. Additionally, the higher-order the principles, the more acute the problem of shape and means becomes.

Fourth, principles gain power by reference to shared understandings or moral practices. They refer to justice, fairness, freedom or equality as terms of moral as opposed to aesthetic or scientific justification. Yet these terms prove slippery. On one hand, because we understand them, they point to established practices and usage. But as moral concepts, they retain an open cutting-edge that yields a critical stance. Individuals reflecting from a practice can generate principles to challenge existing norms by the norms' own terms or with a new and innovative understanding. The perennial debate over whether justice refers to promulgated laws or principles that enable us to pronounce a law unjust reflects this problem.[28]

Finally, principles do not stand by themselves or even in a closed world of mutually referential terms. Their own justification is implicated in other terms of judgment and practice that are relatively open ended. Most ethical terms possess a complex internal structure of characterization and application. The meaning of the term may be relatively closed, like bribery, but still depend upon other principles such as "government power should not be used for personal gain" or "government contracts should be awarded on competence, reliability and price." New problems might arise, as when individuals take jobs in industries they have regulated or purchased from and this introduces new and subtle possibilities of bribery. We might characterize this problem as such and choose to regulate it. We can even disagree over the application of relatively closed terms like the debate over whether abandoning severely deformed or retarded children constitutes murder. Closure remains conventional and subject to extension or re-opening given the elasticity of language, the unpredictability of reality and the creativity of humans.[29]

Principles justify action, but they need not dictate it. They weigh in heavily in political discourse with powerful and autonomous reasons. They perform vital functions of legitimizing, but also of criticizing and calling to reform. Imperious, they demand authenticity and generate urgency, but persons holding them confront complexity and indeterminancy and dangers in application. In politics principled justification must comport with political and prudential justifications that possess power and validity in their own right.

POLITICAL AND PRUDENTIAL JUSTIFICATION

We must not lose moral control of politics. The stakes are too high, the purposes too noble and vital, the means too dangerous. But we should not moralize all political life. The logic of principles possesses real limits and poses real dangers. On the other hand, without principles in political life, we have few resources to question outcomes determined solely by power and skill. Without moral terms, apathy, manipulation or coercion can pass for legitimacy. Discontent must be registered as violent assertions of will or plaints that things "don't work" without any criteria to give "workability" justificatory power.

The ends of politics are pursued in a community with social practices that constitute it. This community needs to be defended and peace needs to be maintained for principles to have any reality. This means the government possesses legitimacy in the use of force and education denied other individuals or groups. In moments of crisis, governors need immense flexibility to succeed in their appointed purposes. The viability and justice of an order, as Hobbes reminds us, depend upon the exercise of power and its domestication. The reality of power and the problem of enemies account for the success of projects like Machiavelli's puncturing of piety in politics. It also explains the glee of realists when they argue that we would have to torture an innocent person in order to discover the whereabouts of a terrorist-planted nuclear bomb about to blow up Cleveland. It should not surprise us that principles should break down in a world where no moral reciprocity exists or when incredible danger stares us in the face. But it should deeply worry us that the requirements of warriors in crises can override cooperative principles and virtues.

Political authority sustains itself by success. Politicians exist in dialogue with citizens' consciences and exercise power with the responsibility to achieve results consonant with the interests and consciences of the citizens. Political ethics, then, is consequentialist and is judged and justified by the quality of humanity, peace and justice in the lives we live. Neither purity of intention, autonomy of will or consistency of commitment matter as much in this dialogue as success in sustaining safety and humane and just social practices.

Politics and prudence justify between the poles of power and success. Principled justifications serve best to define the ends of power and the criteria of success. They also define the boundaries of power and constraints upon success. But political justifications are embedded in political concerns over how to control the exercise of power and coercion and prudential concerns over how to effect results. These concerns present coherent and vital modes of justification which shape the reality of principles and a safe and humane political order.

Successful action in a world confounded by diversity and obstinacy generates a large set of legitimate political and prudential reasons. I designate political reasons as those that refer to the fundamental political choice not to eliminate but to treat with opponents. This family of reasons clusters around claims to establish methods of competition, cooperation and conflict resolution that minimize coercion, keep peace and maintain civility.

They justify tailoring political actions and claims both to cohere with symbols of legitimacy and to abide by accepted processes and rituals of conflict resolution. Each institution of power and coercion may be designed as much with an eye to possible abuses of power as to its immediate effectiveness. During political discussion and conflict, citizens may go out of their way to recognize the right of the opponents to speak and even to acknowledge the legitimacy of their opponents' position and certainly power. These can reinforce both sides' commitments to peaceful resolutions of controversy in ways consistent with civility. Above all, politicians may invoke reasons derived from the desire to minimize the coercion necessary to gain compliance. Actions and rhetoric to avoid driving other citizens to civil war or terrorism in defense of their position fall under these rubrics. When violence must be used in political life, political justifications center around the "economy of violence."[30]

Political justifications converge around maintaining an order that enables us to deliberate and seek goals without resort to coercion. They invoke system-sustaining concerns and difficult-to-measure tradeoffs. These emerge most obviously when politicians seek to maintain civility and terms of discourse even as they battle over deeply divisive issues. These reasons may flow from a principled abhorrence of violence or a respect for human autonomy. But they can also be defended in terms limited to self-interested defenses of freedom or the desire to avoid tyranny while maintaining peace.[31]

Prudential justifications flow from a broader concern with the logic of implementation. The effectiveness imperative would capture its concerns—if we have principled or interested goals worth pursuing, then we should discover the outcomes they require, seek the means to attain them and seek solutions consonant with the goals within the sphere of life in which we pursue them. In liberal democracy and most political orders, goals should be right or consistent with interests and not bring more harm than good into the political order. Accomplishments should be durable, minimally coercive and open to change and adaptation. Obviously this family of concerns overlaps with political justifications, but its range of options and concerns goes far beyond the domestication of force.

Prudence first shapes political goals. Because political ethics depends on consequences and not intentions, it demands that we give concrete shape to the principles. We must see in our mind's eye a concrete sense of what the solution should be given the historical possibilities. For instance, one might believe in the equality of women and believe that an equal rights amendment embodies the best political content of the goals. But others could plausibly and in good faith argue that the principle could be served better and without creating institutions subject to abuse by utilizing statutory means and purging federal and state regulations of sexist implications. Both concretize goals and begin a process of political action and enforcement. Most principles and interests possess a range of consonant outcomes.[32]

Prudence leads us to find the necessary power to attain our goals. This might involve rhetorical appeals to persuade citizens or coalition building among diverse factions or with indifferent individuals who seek other goals. This focus also requires us to gauge how much power we have and acknowledge when we do not have enough. William Pitt Fessenden, the architect of Republican Reconstruction "successes," perfectly summarized prudence's logic, "I have been taught since I have been in public life to consider it a matter of proper statesmanship, when we aim at an object which we think is valuable and important, if that object . . . is unattainable, to get as much of it and come as near as we may be able to do."[33]

To seek durable and right solutions, citizens must acknowledge the real world, its moral complexity and the terms of societal legitimacy. Limitations on resources and knowledge, uncertainty of all sorts and other legitimate moral claims can be invoked to change the shape of a plan or action. The rhetoric of a struggle and public terms of justification might have to be adapted to comport with commonly shared moral beliefs and practices. This enables a policy to be defended in the future and deepens its long-term prospects of acceptance. Finally, prudence dictates that we seek openness in our political gains. Openness to future change enables citizens to rectify mistakes and accommodate unforeseen consequences or new knowledge. It helps ensure that the good accomplished will not be offset by unanticipated harm. In open politics, opponents can abide changes and defeats since they will have a chance to re-form the reforms in the future. Openness also means that small successes viewed as precedents can open the political system to future improvement and can represent considerable gains com-pared to accomplishing nothing.

But neither politics nor prudence necessarily gains justice or humanity. They are limited by concerns to maintain peace, or-der and effectiveness within bounds set by cultures and distri-butions of power. After five years of intense efforts, the radical Republicans barely gained a national guarantee of Negro suf-frage and a skeletal Freedmen's Bureau. Time and time again, great reform bills were vetoed by Andrew Johnson. Moderate Republicans limited proposals by their moral and Constitu-tional commitments to states' rights and the electorate gradu-ally repudiated many of their positions and threatened their party at large. At such moments, principles may stand alone and uncompromising or adapt politically and prudentially; neither position is without costs. Thaddeus Stevens, the relentless abo-litionist congressman from Pennsylvania, distills this quandry in his defense of the great Reconstruction bill, later vetoed, "This proposition is not all that the committee desired. It falls far short of my wishes . . . I believe it is all that can be obtained in the present state of public opinion . . . I shall not be driven by clamor or denunciation to throw away a great good because it is not perfect. I will take all I can get in the cause of humanity and leave it to be perfected by better men in better times."[34] Later, upon the final bittersweet acceptance of a radically weak-ened Fifteenth Amendment and knowing this was its last chance, Henry Wilson sadly remarked, "I have acted upon the idea that one step taken in the right direction made the next step easier to be taken." Perhaps sensing that the next step would take ninety painful and unjust years, he concluded, "I suppose, sir, I must act upon that idea now; and I do so with more sincere regret than ever and with some degree of mortification."[35]

The Ends of Ethics—The Beginnings of Politics

No serious student of political life has claimed that political life in the raw presents a neat and tidy world—that remains

largely for those "who would make a desert and call it peace."
Since political justifications must make sense of this world while
constituting it and sustaining it, we should expect the welter of
reasons and tensions. Political justifications, however, do not
simply resemble a great grabbag in which politicians and citizens can rummage and pull out any reasons with equal weight
at any time. We can sort out the three families of ethical, political and prudential reasons and suggest some relations among
them.

Principled justifications serve a vital and privileged role in
political life. Given the stakes and power involved, we rightly
recur to ethical claims to constitute the foundations of the order and reserve them to question legitimacy. This constitution
provides an initial matrix of meaning that defines the plausible
range of ethically acceptable outcomes and shapes future discussion, claims and innovation. Principled justifications constitute the ends as both goals and stopping points in our political
life. Their limitations even identify the end points beyond which
only humanity, prudence and prayer guide us.

The dynamic of principles and their imperiousness make them
potent forces in political life. Principles remain our basic tools
to challenge, direct and limit the exercise of power by our institutions. This is especially vital when institutional and self-interested influences warp the exercise of power. They provide
strong justification to affirm, but also to reform or reject and
even revolt against the society, and place this vital constraint upon
all forms of noncoerced and unmanipulated legitimacy. The
existence of principles in political life reminds us that our institutions and even social and moral practices remain trustees of
our ethical aspirations and not their ultimate embodiment.

Justification, however, makes no sense unless our reasons are
accepted. Acceptance depends upon our reasons being intelligible and linked to our interests and experience. Even "normal" politics requires great virtuosity in knitting together different assumptions and concrete ends among our allies, let alone
justifying actions to opponents and the indifferent. If justifications are to be reasons, they must be open to criticism and ex-
pansion. They must engage principles, but also be linked to experienced results and symbolic consensus. Accordingly, the
pursuit of ethical goals in political life cannot be reduced to an-

alytic reflection on the implications of intuitions and principles; neither for that matter can it be dictated by the same endeavor. These reflections essentially limit the audience, possess no serious motivational power, dictate without regard to prudence or politics and seldom connect with symbolic modes of justification and understanding. They do not give us the tools to recharacterize experience in coherent and motivating ways. Yet the requirements of political acceptance have profound limits. Audiences begin with very conservative assumptions embedded with prejudice for institutions of problematic justice or humanity. Our reasoning can twist to accommodate these institutions and prejudices and this limits the scope of critical analysis and can freeze out new voices and terms from the political agenda. After a while, a simple concern to play to audiences can cut politicians off from any serious moral benchmarks.

Political reasoning and prudence also possess their own power and react back onto principles. Political reasons typify the activity where we organize our interests and community with power, defend ourselves and resolve disputes with a minimum of violence. Prudence emphasizes that we seek results that affect the quality of humanity and justice experienced by citizens in their lives. These results must be concrete, durable and open. Politics and prudence remind us that in the exercise of power, we must give great justificatory power to preserving social practices and security and to attaining real and livable results. They also remind us that the logic of unalloyed principles can paradoxically breed tyranny and tragedy when joined with official power. Additionally, they identify the problems that arise if all of politics is moralized. Principled rhetoric in its imperious and dismissive strains can polarize and make stable and nonviolent resolution very difficult to attain. But it can also trivialize ethics and debase its effectiveness. If everything becomes a right, cynicism may discredit the proper role of principles in political life. Principled and ethical rhetoric should be used sparingly given its power and limits. It is too easy without politics or prudence to pursue will-o'-the-wisps or hellish utopias in political life rather than serious, stable and desirable solutions.

Political justifications tend to be of three families shaped by one major set of constraints. The ethical demands of principles constitute the ends of political life. Political justifications cluster around the means by which we exercise power and resolve disputes within an economy of violence. Prudential justifications focus on the concrete shape of our goals and the means to attain them as durable social practices. Finally, all these are trimmed by the requirements of acceptance that bends our justifications to connect with intelligibility and experience.

This analysis of the types of reasons and constraints within political justification suggests several broad conclusions. First, no one realm of reasons does sufficient justice to the demands and complexity of political life. Second, each realm limits and enriches the others by increasing the range of concerns from constitutive principles to the organization of power to durable and sensitive solutions. These in turn are shaped by the constraint of audience intelligibility and the symbolic resources of a culture. Third, despite the constitutive priority of principles, no obvious weighting exists among the different realms, nor do any meta-principles suggest themselves as ways to resolve conflicts. Fourth, only an open, accountable and participatory politics can do justice to the three realms. This means that the rightness of our justification will remain inherently contextual and fine-graded. So political justification is ineluctably unsatisfying from a philosophical point of view, but this is true to the reality of politics among autonomous citizens seeking a peaceful, durable and just political order.

NOTES

1. Michael Les Benedict, *A Compromise of Principle: Congressional Republicans and Reconstruction, 1863–1869* (New York: W.W. Norton, 1974), p. 58. I will draw extensively upon Les Benedict's painstaking and powerful book for examples of justifications. The story of Reconstruction and the compromises wrought when principles confronted political and prudential claims forced the participants to deploy the families of justification with great clarity.
2. Ibid., p. 38.
3. Much of this analysis frames the general nature of political justification. The focus upon liberal democracy, however, reinforces the use of compromise examples, since compromise is linked to liberal democracy's moral and practical cores. See Joseph Carens, "Compromise in Politics," in J. Roland Pennock and John W.

Chapman, eds., *Nomos XXI: Compromise in Ethics, Law and Politics* (New York: New York University Press, 1979), pp. 123–141; Bernard Crick, *In Defense of Politics*, 2nd ed. (Chicago: University of Chicago Press, 1972); and J. Patrick Dobel, *Compromise and Political Action*, unpublished manuscript.

4. Even if we characterize a subject as suitable for political concern, we might still argue that it is not serious enough to warrant the risk of governmental power. We might also argue that the task cannot be performed well by government or that government would do more harm than good in trying to accomplish the task.

5. Thomas Kuhn, *The Structure of Scientific Revolutions* (Chicago: University of Chicago Press, 1970). Richard Rorty in *Philosophy and the Mirror of Nature* (Princeton: Princeton University Press, 1979), chap. 7, suggests that even such densely specified communities of discourse as science resemble politics because science possesses no definitive method to adjudicate among various incommensurable paradigms.

6. Les Benedict, *A Compromise of Principle*, pp. 273, 274; passim.

7. The idea of "imperfectly shared" terms of discourse draws upon the work of William E. Connolly, *The Terms of Political Discourse*, 2nd ed. (Princeton: Princeton University Press, 1974, 1983), chaps. 1 and 2.

8. The rest of this section draws very heavily upon the work of Connolly, *Terms of Political Discourse* and Hanna Fenichel Pitkin, *Wittgenstein and Justice* (Berkeley: University of California Press, 1972), esp. chaps. 6–8.

9. D.Z. Phillips and H.O. Mounce, *Moral Practices* (London: Routledge and Kegan Paul, 1970), passim.

10. Moral practices do not form either neat hierarchies or one seamless web. Discussion of an issue might involve reference to many practices that impinge on an issue or characterize aspects of an activity. Abortion discussions might include concern for the innocent and helpless status of the fetus. They might also question the legal and moral oddity of coercively forcing a woman to carry a child to term or introduce demands for compensation for mothers under such conditions.

11. Clifford Geertz, *The Interpretation of Cultures* (New York: Basic Books, 1973), chaps. 8–11, esp., "The Integrative Revolution: Primordial Sentiments and Civil Politics in New States," and "The Politics of Meaning."

12. Niccolò Machiavelli, *The Discourses*, ed. Bernard Crick, trans. Leslie J. Walker, S.J. (Harmondsworth: Penguin Books, 1970), III, 1.

13. Murray Edelman, *The Symbolic Uses of Politics* (Urbana: University of Illinois Press, 1964), passim.

14. Connolly, *Terms of Political Discourse,* refers to interests as a "cluster concept" that links vital areas of life with broader political and moral realms.

15. Ibid., pp. 184–187.

16. I use these terms from Rorty, *Philosophy and the Mirror of Nature,* with some trepidation, since Rorty seems very naive about the difference between intellectual discourse and political change. Several times he hints that the "deliberative process" involved in intellectual paradigm shifts in science do not differ significantly from the shift from the "*ancien regime* to bourgeois democracy, or from Augustans to the Romantics," (p. 327). He questions whether there is really a difference "in kind" between Bellarmine-Gallileo and "Kerensky and Lenin, or that between the Royal Academy (*circa* 1910) and Bloomsbury?" (p. 331). The obvious answer is, of course there is! The political changes used power and violence to silence or eliminate their opponents. Such social beliefs are supported by power and domination and defended with legal violence; their overthrow does not signal a shift in sensibility, gestalt or theoretical acceptability. They entail power, persecution, elimination of opponents and hegemonic education undergirded by self-censorship influenced by power. Rorty's entire book suffers from a serious unwillingness to take the role and danger of power seriously, certainly in politics, but also in his own concerns with scientific shifts. Thus normal and revolutionary take on very different and morally serious connotations that he too cavalierly dismisses.

17. Richard Kluger in *Simple Justice* (New York: Random House, 1968), passim, traces the long and arduous history that lead to the creation of a new formula and the rejection of the old.

18. I am not concerned with virtue as the basis of articulated claims. Virtue simply does not generate the same moral imperiousness or urgency of principles. On the other hand, virtue is probably necessary to give reality to principles. But virtues gain their moral power predominantly from the ethical principles that ground the order in which they are valued. See J. Patrick Dobel, "Justice Versus Virtue," *Commonweal,* forthcoming.

19. John Rawls, *A Theory of Justice* (Cambridge: Harvard University Press, 1971), pp. 20, 48–51.

20. T.D. Weldon, "Political Principles," in Peter Laslett, ed., *Philosophy, Politics and Society* (Oxford: Basil Blackwell, 1970).

21. Phillips and Mounce, *Moral Practices,* pp. 20, 39, 54.

22. This does not always hold for utilitarians. Here the weight of total

utility for an immediate gain always threatens to wash out the underpinnings of any principles the utilitarian may have arrived at.

23. This discussion draws heavily upon Ronald Dworkin, "The Model of Rules I," "The Model of Rules II," and "Justice and Rights," in *Taking Rights Seriously* (Cambridge: Harvard University Press, 1978), pp. 14–80, 150–183; and A. Phillips Griffiths, "Ultimate Moral Principles: Their Justification," in *The Encyclopedia of Philosophy*, volume 8 (New York: Macmillan, reprint edition, 1972), pp. 177–182.

24. Aileen S. Kraditor, *Means and Ends in American Abolitionism: Garrison and His Critics on Strategy and Tactics, 1834–1850* (New York: Pantheon Books, 1967), pp. 223, 224.

25. For a study of the increasingly polarization and escalation of rhetoric prior to the Civil War, see David M. Potter, *The Impending Crisis: 1848–1861*, completed and edited by Don E. Fehrenbacher (New York: Harper Torchbooks, The New American Nation Series, 1976), chaps. 2, 6, 17 and pp. 92–96, 519–520. For an analysis of contemporary issues, see J. Patrick Dobel, "Mail-Order Ethics: The Nature of Irresponsible Campaign Contributions and the Politics They Finance," *South Atlantic Quarterly* (Autumn, 1982): 376–386.

26. Niccolò Machiavelli, *The Prince*, trans. George Bull (Harmondsworth: Penguin Books, 1961), chap. 15.

27. See Arthur Kuflick, "Morality and Compromise," in Pennock and Chapman, eds., *Compromise in Ethics, Law and Politics*, pp. 38–65, for an examination of the implications of autonomy for moral compromise and justification.

28. Pitkin, *Wittgenstein and Justice*, chap. 8.

29. Connolly, *Terms of Political Discourse*, chaps. 1, 2, 5.

30. Sheldon Wolin, *Politics and Vision: Continuity and Innovation in Western Political Thought* (Boston: Little, Brown, 1960), pp. 195–238, coins this term to interpret Machiavelli's concerns to explain and defend the autonomous activity of political life.

31. See Crick, *In Defense of Politics*, for an insightful and provocative defense of this definition of political reasoning. Political justification as I describe it might be considered a special subset of prudence. But force really does pose the fundamental problem for a modern political order, especially where we cannot claim complete agreement and compliance or world peace. A political community must solve the concommitant problems of peace, public safety and peaceful conflict resolution and avoid tyranny in the process before other projects, ethical or otherwise, can be seriously undertaken. I have chosen to treat this cluster of concerns as a separate

but greatly overlapping set of justifications with prudence because of the very central and dangerous role of force in public life.

32. One could argue that prudence alone, without reference to ethical standards or principles, can generate ethical direction for a political order. Prudence can gain such autonomous prescriptive power by invoking the idea of a moral exemplar or statesman. Through imagination or study, we can determine what this person would probably do in a particular situation and have a model for our conduct. However, as I suggested above (note 18), a theory of virtue, even one with cognitive content like prudence so interpreted, remains relative to the moral quality of the context. A citizen or governor might ask what Disraeli or Gladstone, Jefferson or Lincoln would have done. Someone else might ask what Hitler or Stalin would have done.

33. Les Benedict, *A Compromise of Principle,* p. 58.

34. Ibid., p. 182.

35. Ibid., p. 335.

17

JUSTIFICATION, PRACTICAL REASON, AND POLITICAL THEORY

THOMAS A. SPRAGENS, JR.

If human beings are "rational animals" in any robust sense, they must be able and willing to offer justifications—to give reasons—for their political goals and actions. The discipline of political theory seeks to provide an academic habitat for this enterprise of political justification: it is a domain of rational practical discourse about the fundamental purposes, the relevant standards, and the preferred procedures of politics. It is not surprising, then, that talk of the decline or even death of political theory should have been accompanied by considerable confusion and doubt about the nature or even the significance of political justification. These are causally and conceptually related happenings.

It is important for several reasons, then, to arrive at some understanding of the sources of these related confusions and difficulties and to attain some sense of the appropriate strategies for resolving them. Possibly only academics care all that deeply about the health of political theory as a discipline. But the eclipse of the behavioral norms implicit in the conception of the "rational animal" would affect us all. The expectation that

For some provocative arguments and useful bibliographic leads, see John S. Nelson, "Political Theory as Political Rhetoric," in *What Should Political Theory Be Now?* edited by Nelson (Albany: State University of New York Press, 1983), pp. 169–240.

reasons can and should be forthcoming to legitimize our political actions—together with the discourse generated by that expectation—is a significant aspect of civil society. Conversely, the
absence of that expectation and the erosion of the public discourse it sustains eases us back toward the state of nature.

Among the causes for contemporary perplexity about political justification, two would seem to be most important. One is
historical and sociological, and we have little control over it. The
other cause is philosophical and intellectual. That cause we have
the capacity to handle; increasingly, we are gaining the intellectual resources that could enable us to do so.

The relatively intractable historical and sociological source of
the questions besetting political justification is the cultural pluralism of the modern world. In the setting of a relatively ho-
mogeneous cultural environment, political justifications—at least
in the abstract—don't seem all that problematic. If all the participants in a culture inhabit the same meaningful cosmos, if all
citizens are habituated to the legitimacy of their polity's *nomoi,*
then ready reference points are available for political justifications. These common reference points do not necessarily produce political unanimity on policy. But the disagreements do not
extend to cleavage over the relevant standards or to doubt about
the propriety and possibility of providing justifications for the
competing positions. The principals in the Investiture Controversy, for example, were locked in a fierce struggle for control
over an ecclesiastical hierarchy that performed both secular and
churchly functions. Important interests and deep passions were
involved. But neither Henry IV nor Pope Gregory VII nor any
of their adherents would have conceived of denying the existence of relevant norms or the necessity of justifying their actions by reference to them. They offered alternative interpretations of scripture and divergent readings of God's will. But
they all assumed that these touchstones were determinative. And
they shared, in addition, a tradition and a vocabulary of Au-
gustinian and Gelasian concepts and norms that gave additional coherence to the intellectual controversy that attended and
in some respects constrained their battle of wills and interests.

Our contemporary world no longer has this kind of homog-
eneous culture to provide accepted reference points governing political controversies. Western civilization has become plu-

ralistic and fragmented. Christian ideals and beliefs retain their influence in some quarters, but this influence is scattered among discordant sects. In addition, large sections of contemporary Western societies and domains of Western culture have become rather autonomously secular and post-Christian. Moreover, our globe has become much smaller. We can no longer ignore the existence of cultures very different from our own. Some centripetal forces moving us toward a global culture may be at work, but the overriding impression is one of even greater cultural heterogeneity in our political universe—and ever greater difficulty of knowing what coherent and persuasive political justifications might be in these circumstances.

The other major source of contemporary disquiet about political justification is intellectual and philosophical. It is complicated by the cultural fragmentation of our political universe, but it has an independent origin in the vicissitudes of modern philosophy. Political justification is the reflective side of *phronesis*, of practical reason. But modern philosophy has systematically denatured and denigrated practical reason. Even in classical philosophy, practical reason came off looking second best. For all its importance to Aristotle, for instance, practical reason was something of a poor cousin in epistemological weight to its lofty and elegant counterpart of theoretical reason. Practical reason had its autonomy and its profound role to play, but it seemed cognitively imperfect by comparison with the contemplative precision of *theoria*. In the seventeenth century, this epistemic priority of theoretical reason was radicalized. Practical reason lost its autonomy. It lost its claim to genuine cognitive standing except insofar as it could be subsumed under theoretical reason. All aspects or forms of practical reason that could not claim this standing of "post-theoretical praxis" were to be cast aside along with other variants of allegedly empty pseudo-knowledge such as metaphysics.

At the outset, most of the intellectual revolutionaries of the seventeenth century believed this subsumption of practical under theoretical reason to be cause for optimism rather than despair. The more rigorous sifting prescribed for the propositions of practical reason would eliminate only chaff; what remained would be not only epistemologically valid but also sufficient for the guidance of our conduct. Locke, for example, opined that the circumscribed orbit of our genuine knowledge would include "light enough to lead [human beings] to the knowledge of their Maker, and the sight of their own duties."[1] And Descartes, even as he sketched a method possessing the clarity, distinctness, and certain foundations traditionally ascribed to theoretical reason, argued that his universal science would be no purely "speculative philosophy" as "taught in the Schools" but rather "a practical philosophy" by means of which we could "render ourselves the masters and possessors of nature."[2]

Well into the nineteenth century at least, the conception of genuinely theoretical "moral sciences" that would have practical force and relevance remained alive. Increasingly, however, this belief in the possibility of a political philosophy that had both theoretical status and practical impact has lost out to the more skeptical conclusions of a post-Humean empiricism. On this skeptical view, *episteme* belongs to *theoria* alone and practical philosophy does not qualify. No practice is really rational: it is based only on *doxa* and ultimately on feelings, emotions, and interests. Reason—and reasons, or justifications—append to the natural sciences. In the political realm, in contrast, reason is and can only be the "slave of the passions." Some have concluded, then, that the only honest "justification" for a political action is a frank avowal of one's preferences.

Hans Kelsen provides us with the prototype of this outcome. "From the point of view of rational cognition," he writes, "there are only interests of human beings and hence conflicts of interests."[3] Accordingly, when queried about justice, his response has to be a reference to his own important interests. The alleged reference point for normative adjudication—the concept of justice—is really only a pseudo-term, one that fronts for extra-rational desires and interests an honest person will confess upon request: "I cannot say what justice is. . . . I can only say what justice is to me. Since science is my profession, and hence the most important thing in my life, justice, to me, is that social order under whose protection the search for truth can prosper."[4]

Though we can appreciate Kelsen's candor and can be grateful that "his justice" is relatively beneficent, the principles he articulates are unsettling. What would "his justice" have been had he been a sadist instead of a scientist? Would it be entitled to the same respect? And what, in the longer run, would be the implications for political justification of this view? Eventually, it would seem, reason-giving and practical discourse would either die out altogether or else would become transformed into biographical confessions of dubious significance. When asked to justify a political action or recommendation, we could only affirm our personal desires and point out the contingent facts of our individual psyches that led to them. But this "justification" would be adducing causes, not reasons. Those who enjoy personal revelations might be titillated by the explanations, but those seeking rational warrants would not be enlightened.

If this unavoidably brief and partial account of the major origins of our contemporary perplexities about political justification is at all accurate, then it follows that we shall not achieve an acceptable and convincing understanding of political justification unless and until we can first philosophically rehabilitate practical reason. Only if we can recover an appreciation, though no doubt in a somewhat novel way, of the power and legitimacy of practical reasoning will we be able to grasp what it means to "justify"—to give reasons for—political aims and actions. The intellectual achievement of rehabilitating practical reason, of course, would not solve the problems that the cultural fragmentation and pluralism of our contemporary world produce for anyone who tries to offer justifications for actions. These remain as factors that complicate and limit what political justifications can hope to accomplish. At least, however, understanding practical reason can make political justification intelligible; that accomplishment alone would be significant.

The substratum of the unfortunate alternative fates for practical reason offered to us by modern philosophy—i.e., subsume it completely under theoretical reason or strip it of its cognitive standing—is the tacit metaphysics of empiricism. The corpuscular entities that Locke, Hume, and their like-minded descendants saw as populating the world seemed readily amenable to apprehension by *theoria:* they were discrete and unchanging entities that changed spatial location but not form, and their qualities and interrelations could be depicted with the precision of mathematics. The Cartesian metaphysics of *res extensa* assumed a similar corporeal reality, differing only in its insistence that Hobbes's "ghosts" and "phantasms" were also real, even if encapsulated in a distinct spirit-substance *(res cogitans)* of their own.

These fundamentally Democritean premises, whether hegemonic as in Hobbes or in tandem with neo-Platonism as in Descartes, produced three conceptually related problems: the is/ought gap, the ontological homelessness of the human mind, and the incoherence of the whole concept of practical reason.

So long as the "gap" between "is" and "ought" is merely the logical distinction between declarative and imperative propositions, it is of relatively little moment. Respecting the distinction means recognizing that imperatives cannot be simply deduced from a combination of purely descriptive claims. But it is not at all clear, despite Hume's attribution of logical non sequiturs to "every system of morality" he had encountered, that any serious thinker ever suffered from the delusion that he could do so. What is important is not logical deduction but significant bearing; as long as "is" syntax could incorporate statements about human purposes, meanings, needs, and fulfillment, its significant bearing upon—though not its strictly logical determination of—imperatives seemed fairly obvious. It was only when "is" syntax was restricted to descriptions consonant with a corpuscular ontology that the trivial logical gap turned into a perplexity-inducing chasm.

The seventeenth century's turn to corpuscularism similarly rendered it impossible to give a coherent account of the "place" of the human mind and, not accidentally, the nature of time and history. As Alexandre Koyre once succinctly characterized the problem, human beings "lost [their] place in the world" when the closed cosmos became an infinite universe.[5] Perhaps the most striking and even comical manifestations of the anomalous status of the human mind under the new dispensation were Descartes's hypothesis that the pineal gland might be *res cogitans*'s link to the material world and Hume's confession that he could not find his "self" amidst the heap of corpuscular "impressions" that exhausted his mental world.

Since *phronesis* was indelibly linked with human action and with "oughts," it likewise became a cosmic expatriate. Unless it could assimilate itself to *theoria,* it would follow the other members of its conceptual family into the netherworld of unintelligibility. The dilemma of *phronesis* was not necessarily all that troubling to the seventeenth-century revolutionaries, however. It did not mean the end to a belief in rational action. For *theoria*, now contemplating material masses instead of value-laden essences, could be linked with *techne* and thereby given "practical" force. It took a long time for awareness to sink in that this new arrangement, which left *phronesis* in limbo, could both distort and mystify politics: it could distort political actions by reducing them to technical operations, and it could mystify politics by leaving the ends and purposes of these technical operations questionable. At best, the perennial challenge of political justification—"what should be done and why?"—was answered dogmatically by invoking the technological analogy. A political action was justified because it increased human power, a Baconian theme that triumphed, although the critical issues of power for what and by whom were left inadequately addressed.

The first great attempt to solve this complex of philosophical problems and incapacities—together with the potential for moral perversity implicit in them—was made by Immanuel Kant. Kant saw clearly and felt keenly the dangers resident in Hume's heteronomous utilitarianism, although it can be argued that he misconstrued the exact source of the danger. He also perceived, quite rightly, that the only real way to prevent the long slow slide into "emotivism" in ethics and politics was to reconstitute and relegitimize practical reason. Only in that way could political justification be given a rational footing and not be vulnerable to pure subjectivism.

Although Kant's efforts continue to this day to inspire some of the most thoughtful and resolute critics of ethical relativism and utilitarianism,[6] they were not ultimately successful. In some respects, indeed, his way of posing the issue and the weaknesses of his attempted solution have in a perverse way compounded our difficulties in understanding political justifications and the practical judgments that go into them.[7]

The fundamental flaw in Kant's attempt to relegitimize political justification by grounding it in a refurbished account of practical reason was that he began by accepting too many of the premises that had caused the problem in the first place. It could not be said of Kant's moral theory, as it has been said of his epistemology, that he handed Hume's problem back to him and called it a solution. Nevertheless, his account of practical reason was structured and constrained as much as was his account of theoretical reason by his acquiescence in the Cartesian version of the prevailing ontology.

Kant began, as did his spiritual mentor Rousseau, by conceding the corpuscularist and materialist account of the external world. His depiction of the "phenomenal" realm would have satisfied the most resolute mechanist. Unlike the monistic empiricists, however, Kant postulated an internal realm of abstract spirit that was substantively entirely distinct from the external world amenable to natural scientific scrutiny and efficient-causal explanation. As a corollary, he also acquiesced in the is/ought divorce. It was simply that he insisted upon the reality of the "ought" or practical realm within. The necessity of the practical realm's ungroundedness in the exterior world he converted into a moral virtue: if scientific empiricists insisted on the separation of "is" and "ought" to protect the epistemic purity of "is," Kant insisted on the same separation to maintain the moral perfection of "ought." Practical reason had to be pure. Political justification had to be based upon *a priori categorical* imperatives. Nothing less would do.

The excessive demands Kant placed upon morality have deepened the problem of political justification rather than solved it. The counterproductive results of his conscientious efforts occur for several reasons. In the first place, the substantive consequences of Kant's insistence upon moral purity are harmful. Virtue is attenuated in content, even if elevated in moral standing, when it is equated with disinterest and turns into duty *simpliciter*. Virtue similarly suffers from a loss in its loveliness, as its *eros* is distilled into the abstract delight of logical noncontradiction.

The formal consequences of Kant's program have proved even more innocently pernicious than its substantive consequences. Kant accepted for practical reason a standard of epistemic perfection appropriate to and derived from classical *theoria,* just as he accepted for its dictates a standard of moral perfection appropriate to disembodied egos. He stipulated, in addition, that these standards must be met, or else the whole project of rational morality—and of genuine political justification—must be abandoned altogether: "Whoever considers morality real, and not a chimerical idea without truth, must likewise admit its principle as discussed here."[8] When it proved impossible to derive a robustly substantive morality from the only premises Kant would permit, when his quest for a truly autonomous rational will fell through, morality therefore had to collapse back into heteronomy.

When it did so, however, it found itself in a very uncongenial environment. Kant had collaborated in and intensified the moral defoliation of the heteronomous realm. The organic roots of practical reason were no longer there. The moral correlate of Kant's equating all phenomena with automaticity was his equating of all heteronomous passions with selfish "appetites." All natural motivations, physical and emotional, were "drives;" and such blind impulsions did not seem up to generating moral standards. Kant's crude, bipartite ontology had no room on either side for the complex, hierarchic, qualitative, teleological anthropology that permits "prudence" to carry moral weight instead of being, as it was in Kant's hands, a term of opprobrium.

To summarize, then, our contemporary perplexities regarding political justification are at bottom a consequence of modern philosophy's systematic subordination of *praxis* to *theoria*—and the derivative distortion or abandonment of prudence. We seem forced willy-nilly into choosing among several unsatisfactory alternatives. If we accredit the arguments of those who claim to be engaged in post-theoretical *praxis*, we must accept their technical credentials as political justification. If we consent to the positivist debunking of all *praxis* as non-theoretical, we must abandon our demands for political justification as incoherent. And if we insist upon the elevation of *praxis* to a parallel *theoria* of morals, we seem ultimately to reduce political justification to legalistic logical formalism.

Only when we become able to comprehend more adequately the genuine powers and the inescapable limitations of practical reason will we be able to know what we can and cannot expect of political justification. Clearly, this will not be an overnight achievement. We do, however, possess some of the resources necessary to reconceptualizing practical reason and releasing it from its long-standing thralldom to theoretical reason. In the remainder of this chapter, let me mention two of the places we might look for leverage on our problem—one of them rather new and the other more traditional.

The relatively new resource for our attempt to rehabilitate practical reason is contemporary philosophy of science. On its face, this suggestion may seem heretical, even obtuse. It may seem obtuse, because this suggestion seems to blur the distinction between practical and theoretical inquiry. And it may seem heretical, because our conception of science has provided the high standards for genuine *episteme* that have relegated practical reason to its second-class—or worse—cognitive status.

Actually, however, it is precisely because of this latter consideration that recent philosophy of science becomes relevant. One of the principal sources of our inability to come to terms with the cognitive capacities of practical reason has been the stringent conception of scientific rigor characteristic of modern philosophy. We have tended implicitly to acquiesce in the stringent criteria for knowledge that John Locke promulgated in one of his philosophical letters. "With me," wrote Locke, "to know and to be certain is the same thing. . . . What reaches to knowledge may be called certainty; and what comes short of certainty, I think may not be called knowledge."[9] Although Locke himself entertained serious doubts on this score, we have generally viewed "scientific demonstration" as meeting this standard. In the face of such forbidding standards, however, and by contrast with the purported capability of modern science to satisfy them, practical reason has seemed hopelessly incompetent. Only fanatics really believe that the justifications they offer for their political actions amount to certainty. So if Locke is right to say that "what comes short of certainty . . . may not be called knowledge," then practical reason must be a bogus conception and political justifications must fall back into the realm of *doxa*.

What has been called the "received view" of scientific theory[10] carried this high standard, together with the supposition that science lived up to it, until the middle of this century. On this view, affiliated with the philosophy of logical empiricism, scientific theories were internally consistent logical systems that were rooted in unambiguous sensations. It was recognized, of course, that a great deal of what went on in scientific inquiry did not display logical certitude. Scientific investigations often invoked hunches, intuitions, conjectures. But these extra-logical aspects of science were deemed to be part of the "context of discovery," which in turn was clearly distinguished from the "context of justification." It was here, in the area of justification, that precision and certitude reigned. However scientific theories were developed, they were subject to rigorous tests that could confirm—or at least refute—them.

In the past thirty years, however, the certitude has seeped out of scientific justification. The hard line between the contexts of discovery and justification has broken down. And while debate continues over the propriety of speaking of a "logic" of discovery, there seems to be general agreement that scientific theories can be "justified" only contingently and for the time being. The acceptance of scientific theories, and arguments on their behalf, must rely upon acceptance of quasi-metaphysical presuppositions as a point of departure. And decisions by the scientific community about which of two or more contending theoretical frameworks to pursue often depend more upon rationally contestable persuasion rather than upon cut-and-dried demonstration.

Consider, for example, the cognitive tasks confronting a scientist who is trying to decide what course to pursue vis-à-vis rival research programs, to borrow a term made popular by Imre Lakatos.[11] That scientist must try to discern whether recent successes and failures in the deployment of each program amounts to a "progressive" or a "degenerating" theoretical "problemshift." He can rarely rely upon a "crucial experiment" to make that an easy determination. Instead, he must assess both research programs by reference to a variety of criteria, including simplicity, internal consistency, coherence with other theories, heuristic value, and explanatory potency. When these criteria point in different directions, he must decide where the balance lies. Where, as is often the case, some slippage exists between data and theory, he must decide whether these gaps represent trivial counter-instances or whether they instead constitute genuine anomalies. In some instances, one research program may begin to outperform its rival rather consistently across the board, and a new scientific consensus will accordingly emerge around it. In other cases, the balance of competing considerations may be much closer, and highly reputable, experienced, and rationally behaving authorities may continue to adhere to opposing theories. In any case, decisions are rarely simple or instantaneous. As Lakatos puts it, "the idea of instant rationality can be seen to be utopian. . . . [My case studies] show that rationality works much slower than most people tend to think, and, even then, fallibly."[12]

For our purposes, the crucial lesson to be drawn from recent philosophy of science is that scientific justification is a species of intellectual *judgment* and not a species of infallible *demonstration*. Hans Albert summarizes this lesson: "Even in mathematics and logic, fields in which the ideal of certainty was simply taken for granted until quite recently, we have been forced to abandon the idea of absolute justification. The attempt to provide a secure foundation for knowledge is no longer a tenable enterprise. The only rational alternative is to submit our proposed solutions to critical examination, i.e., to evaluate them with a view to possible improvements, to compare them with alternative solutions and to search for new and better solutions."[13]

It is no longer defensible, then, to denigrate practical reason for its failure to achieve demonstrative certitude. If the demand for absolute "proof" is utopian even in the theoretical sciences, the fallibility and ambiguity that practical reason cannot escape need not ipso facto deprive it of its cognitive legitimacy. For the same reason, political justification need no longer be whipsawed between ultimately fruitless efforts to secure foundations in genuinely categorical imperatives or else to confess itself to be a slave of the passions that only pretends autonomy. The alternatives are not so disastrously stark, because the relevant standards are not so impossibly lofty.

Indeed, rather than confronting an abstractly drawn sharp contrast between pure and certain scientific justifications and imperfect and groping political justifications, we can begin to see some real analogies between political judgment and what Stephen Toulmin has termed "scientific jurisprudence."[14] Highly important differences remain, of course, between the theoretical judgments scientists are forced to render and the political judgments political actors must make. Scientists seek truth; political actors pursue the good. Scientists can suspend judgment if they cannot make up their minds; political actors may have to act on insufficient evidence. Scientists have interests and emotions, but the biases these might induce are less pervasive and profound than the biases that sway political judgments. Even here, however, these differences are not the dichotomies we sometimes imagine them to be. Both the true and the good are approached by problemsolving. Scientists can never suspend judgment entirely, however uncertain they may be; they have to make some commitments, however tentative, in order to pursue a given line of inquiry. And only a total ingenue could look at the conduct of science—including cases such as the Velikovsky affair or the search for the structure of DNA—and see there only Olympian disinterest.

Significant political justifications that can be persuasively defended within the broad confines of a given political tradition are structurally rather similar to the arguments of scientists operating within the same research programs. The scientists share a commitment to a basic framework of belief that can be invoked as a reference point in adjudicating disputes over more detailed issues. Within that consensus, they may argue about the best way to interpret a piece of evidence; or they may differ over the proper balance to be struck between competing intellectual values—e.g., simplicity, heuristic value, consistency—in deciding among competing explanations for particular puzzles. The argumentation among adherents of a political tradition assumes a parallel form. The fundamental values and underlying belief system of the tradition provide a reference point for useful discussion. Against that backdrop, however, significant controversies may emerge—and be rationally discussed—over the best balance to strike among competing criteria or over the best assessment of a piece of empirical evidence. One contemporary example of this form of justification is the dialogue among John Rawls, Robert Nozick, Bruce Ackerman, Michael Walzer, and others about the proper interpretation of liberal democracy.[15] Each of these disputants accepts the fundamental belief system and values of liberal democracy. They differ, however, in the interpretation they place on some of these beliefs and values— e.g., over the meaning of norms such as liberty, equality, and toleration. They differ over the proper balance to strike when some of these criteria come into conflict. And they disagree on the assessment of some empirical evidence—e.g., over the empirical relevance of the "Lockean Proviso." Other adherents of the same tradition who deliberate the merits of the arguments will almost surely not arrive at a single determinate judgment. But they can find the reasons offered to be intelligible; they gain insight into the cognitive judgments that shape the competing interpretations; and they may well winnow out some of the less persuasive features of the different views as their precarious footing becomes evident.

Political justifications that take place within an overarching political tradition, in short, are cognitively significant and useful. They are not simple demonstrations. "Crucial experiments" are not available. Unanimity will not result. But those who participate in the discussions can achieve heightened mutual understanding of each other and greater illumination of the complexities and tensions in the tradition they share. Some real progress and narrowing of differences may also result as well. This kind of progress will be limited, however, by the fact that some of the competing criteria being balanced are not simply *indicia* of the good—as simplicity and coherence might be seen as *indicia* of the truth—but are constituents of the good. The tensions among them cannot be resolved, then, but only accepted and possibly compromised.

Political justifications that attempt to reach across political traditions, on the other hand, reveal their limitations more quickly. To follow up our example, the Marxist and classical critics of liberal democratic arguments do not entertain the justifications offered so much as they dispute the relevance of the framework with which these arguments begin. These critiques are less temperate and "rational," because they have less common ground. The same mutual incomprehension and hostility that can characterize disputation across competing research programs in science become evident here, exacerbated by the concrete political conflicts that correlate with the contending viewpoints. Justifications in this context, both political and scientific, can be offered. But, with so much less common ground to build upon, they must be constructed on a much narrower base of premises; and they are less likely to be fully comprehensible, much less persuasive, to parties on the other side of the divide.

Decisions to abandon a political *Weltanschauung*, together with its practical corollaries for action, are structurally—and for that matter, existentially—rather similar to scientific decisions to abandon a particular research program as unproductive. The internal dialectic of justification is complex, often agonized, and takes place over a period of time. Commitment to a framework of interpretation that has proved illuminating and useful in many ways is not easy to relinquish. Rarely are single pieces of evidence or single arguments straightforwardly determinative of such a decision. Instead, a gradual accretion of considerations may slowly loosen the hold of an interpretative framework on both a scientist's or a political actor's mind until he can step outside it into a different one. Arthur Koestler's account of the gradual erosion of his Marxist viewpoint, for instance, resembles in its cognitive dynamics a scientist's gradual determination that a research program to which he has been committed is degenerating and must be jettisoned.[16]

Obviously, this is but a very sketchy account of some of the points of tangency between justification in science and in politics. The two are not identical for several reasons we have mentioned and for other reasons that could be adduced. Nevertheless, the understanding of science is at least heuristically significant for those seeking to understand political justification. Most important, our revised understanding of justification in science makes it clear that the older, neo-Platonic model of scientific justification as tantamount to geometric demonstration is not tenable. At the very least, then, the kinds of "good reasons" offered in political justification need not be disqualified out of hand because they cannot attain this kind of decisiveness. And when we look more closely at the justifications scientists actually offer in opting for particular theories or research programs, it seems defensible to characterize these justifications as differing in species but not in genus from the justifications offered by responsible people for their political actions.

This understanding of political justification—i.e., as meaningful but limited judgments of practical reason—can be bolstered and expanded by looking at the arguments that populate the classic texts in political theory. Here is what was alluded to earlier as a traditional place to look to foster our understanding of political justification—by contrast with the less obvious resource of philosophy of science. The discussions among political theorists are rightly considered, I believe, exemplary concrete embodiments of rational practical discourse. If we attend carefully to the nature of the arguments found there—at what is adduced as evidence and relied upon for criteria—we should be able to gain further insight into the real powers and the equally real limitations of political justification.

In doing so, of course, it is of the first importance not to be misled by a priori assumptions about what *must* be found there or what *cannot* be found there. When commentators survey texts in political theory through the bifocal lenses of logical empiricism,[17] they cut apart the arguments and toss the components into two separate piles of empirical propositions and imperative expostulations. This might be an interesting way to cull old texts for causal hypotheses that can be tested, but it is a sure way to distort and misunderstand the practical judgments in support of which they are marshalled. On the other hand, it can be equally misleading in a different way to arrive at these texts wearing Kantian spectacles that can see only justifications that can assume categorical form.[18]

The classic texts of political theory are a very mixed bag, of course. Any easy generalization about *the* type of argument that is universal or essential to them will be easily refutable. Nevertheless, it is possible to find in these tests a pattern of argument that recurs frequently—a pattern that seems to be an almost unavoidable part of serious attempts at political justification. This pattern of argumentation is fundamentally prudential—though not in the derogatory sense of Kant's lowly and selfish prudence and not necessarily in the stylized form that Aristotle sometimes sought to impose on it. The fruit of the justifications are prudential maxims or recommendations, hypothetical imperatives that resemble "doctor's orders of a peculiarly compelling kind."[19]

So long as we construe "is" statements as exhaustively composed of bald assertions of testable factual claims, and so long as we construe "oughts" as either categorical mandates or idiosyncratic emotive preferences, the "logic" of justification will remain unintelligible. Instead, it is necessary to appreciate the unavoidable hermeneutic component of all but the most primitive empirical assertions about human affairs. And it is also necessary to understand that the ends of prudent actions are not stipulated by the theorist or assumed to be capricious. Rather they are understood by the theorist to be given by "natural," necessary, or nearly universal passions of "normal" people— natural passions to which he can appeal rhetorically.

The political justifications of practical discourse, in short, have never been and could never be genuinely "theoretical" in the contemplative classical sense or in the positivistic sense either. They are instead a combination of hermeneutic vision and rhetorical appeal. The justifying argument interprets the way the political world is and then seeks the listener's acquiescence in the conclusion that certain forms of behavior would be proper and prudent in light of the dynamics and constraints illuminated by the interpretation.

The interpretations are, of course, subject to challenge. They rely upon judgments of several kinds—judgments that are contestable, though not groundless. Since causes don't come labelled as such, even claims about cause and consequence that are important bases for the recommendations may be subject to dispute. Different interpretations of the causes of the Depression and the causes of crime, for example, can lead to very different prudential maxims even if all else is held constant. Similarly, the construction and deployment of hermeneutic concepts such as "alienation," "anomie," "equilibrium," or "happiness" depend upon a whole complex of contestable interpretative judgments. Much of the "great conversation" of political theory, indeed, consists of discussion about the validity and applicability of concepts such as these.

It is also logically possible, of course, for the listener to refuse his assent even if he accepts the theorist's interpretation. The "force" of the argument ultimately depends upon the human emotions of the audience. The arguments would admittedly be pointless if addressed to automatons or amoebae and would probably be unpersuasive to psychotics or intergalactic intruders. Political theorists inevitably appeal to—and justifications depend for their persuasiveness upon—what are deemed to be "normal" human desires and needs. Hobbes's arguments would fall stillborn for anyone willing to respond, "but I like living in perpetual anxiety about the omnipresent possibility of violent death." Plato's arguments would be unavailing against someone willing to exclaim, "what jolly fun to live under the tyranny of a human wolf!" And Marx's stirring admonition to the workers of the world to unite because they have nothing to lose but their chains would not arouse any worker who could honestly reply, "but I love my chains." In fifteen years of teaching political theory, however, I have never once encountered these responses, no matter how logically unexceptionable they might be. Students have protested the recommendations of Hobbes and Plato and Marx, but not by denying the presence or propriety of the human passions to which the theorists rhetorically appeal. Political theorists admittedly depend upon certain natural responses in their audience to sustain the ends of their hypothetical imperatives. And this dependence constitutes a limitation and constraint on the logic of justification. The dependency, however, seems neither scandalous nor crippling to the enterprise.

It should also be said in passing, to forestall potential misunderstanding, that this reading of political justification as prudential argument need not imply the reduction of moral standards to purely utilitarian considerations. The "prudent" is here understood in the broad sense of conducing to the human good; and the human good encompasses not simply the "useful and agreeable," to borrow Hume's phrase, but also the fitting and proper. Arguments on behalf of a scheme of justice, then, assume the same pattern of interpretation cum rhetoric described above. Discourse about justice presumes and appeals to the human "sense of injustice" that Edmond Cahn has memorably depicted in looking at the law.[20] Apart from some such agreement on the part of his audience that it is improper for people to be treated with arbitrary inequity, for example, any theorist of justice would be struck as dumb as Marx confronting lovers of their chains. Assuming assent to the general proposition that people should receive their "due" (absent compelling overriding considerations or constraints), the theorist then must provide an interpretation of human affairs that gives concrete substance to that abstract agreement. And that interpretation will require judgments about such relevant considerations as the sources of wealth, the dynamics of the psyche, and many others—as exemplified by the whole recent critical literature on Rawls's *A Theory of Justice*.

CONCLUSION

This account of political justification, quite obviously, does not amount to a theory of justification in any sense of the term. It is instead a series of suggestions as to what would be relevant to obtaining a more adequate understanding of political justification and why we have heretofore been impeded from looking in the right places.

Political justification is an exercise of practical reason. It is cognitively significant and important, but only within the limits of the human condition. Its nature has been distorted in most of modern philosophy by the dominance of the myth of *theoria*, a myth whose power over us is being dispelled by our more adequate understanding of the growth of scientific knowledge. Political justification is paradigmatically exemplified in classic works of political theory, works that provide us with maxims and admonitions of prudence—in the largest sense of that term. The supporting warrants for these counsels of prudence come largely from interpretative judgments about human nature and affairs. Taken as a whole, these judgments differ in their subject matter but not entirely in their form from those required of natural scientists as they assess competing research programs. The imperative force of the justifications comes from the *conatus* of natural human passions, to which the theorist rhetorically appeals—whether tacitly or explicitly.

We have begun to move out of a philosophical era in which our understanding of political justification was systematically frustrated, just as the functions of practical reason were rendered unintelligible. We can reasonably expect to improve our grasp of the "logic" of justification, if we can call it that, as we gain further insight into the hermeneutic dimension of all knowledge[21] and into the important role of judgment in our cognition of human events.[22] Additional insight may also be gained from a reconsideration of political rhetoric, one that seeks to distinguish the valid features of practical discourse found therein from the corruptions that objectivist rationalists have often seen as its essence.[23]

Although philosophers and political theorists are often portrayed as purveyors of the abstract and the antiquated, their attempt to improve our understanding of political justification is not merely an academic exercise. The public space of a good society is formed around the discourse of political justification. We learn the meaning of political responsibility by acquiescing in the demand that we adduce "good reasons" for our political actions and goals. We also, as the Greeks well understood, both fashion and reveal our political identities in our responsible public speech. We likewise are assisted toward some understanding and tolerance for our fellow citizens as we accept the duty to listen and respond to their own "good reasons" for goals and policies that differ from ours. Through our participation in the disciplined conversation of political justification, moreover, we are assisted toward achievements that are perenially elusive but nonetheless important to a healthy society: namely, a sense of *civitas* and an appreciation of the meaning and legitimacy of "loyal opposition."

For these "good reasons" our enlivened interest in and our enhanced ability to make sense of political justification are developments to be welcomed.

NOTES

1. John Locke, *An Essay Concerning Human Understanding*, I.1.5.
2. René Descartes, "Discourse on Method," in *Philosophical Writings*, ed. and trans. Norman Kemp Smith (New York: Modern Library, 1958), pp. 130–31.
3. Hans Kelsen, *What is Justice?* (Berkeley: University of California Press, 1957), pp. 21–22.
4. Ibid., p. 24.
5. Alexandre Koyre, *From the Closed World to the Infinite Universe* (New York: Harper Torchbooks, 1958), p. 4.
6. See, for example, John Rawls, "Kantian Constructivism in Moral Theory," *The Journal of Philosophy* LXXVII (September, 1980): 515–72; Patrick Riley, *Will and Political Legitimacy* (Cambridge: Harvard University Press, 1982); Alan Gewirth, *Reason and Morality* (Chicago: University of Chicago Press, 1978).
7. Reflecting upon his interviews with students expressing a subjectivistic ethical position, James Fishkin concludes that "subjectivism can be interpreted as the residue left over from a failed Kantianism." See his *Beyond Subjective Morality* (New Haven: Yale University Press, 1984), p. 88.

8. Immanuel Kant, *Metaphysical Foundations of Morals*, ed. and trans. Carl J. Friedrich, *The Philosophy of Kant: Immanuel Kant's Moral and Political Writings* (New York: Random House, 1949), p. 191.

9. John Locke, "Second Letter to Stillingfleet," quoted by James Gibson, *Locke's Theory of Knowledge and Its Historical Relations* (Cambridge: Cambridge University Press, 1960), p. 2.

10. See, for example, Frederick Suppe, "Introduction," in *The Structure of Scientific Theories*, 2nd ed. (Urbana: University of Illinois Press, 1977).

11. Imre Lakatos, *The Methodology of Scientific Research Programmes* (Cambridge: Cambridge University Press, 1978).

12. Ibid., p. 87.

13. Hans Albert, "Science and the Search for Truth," in Gerard Radnitzky and Gunnar Andersson, eds., *Progress and Rationality in Science* (Dordrecht, Holland: D. Reidel, 1978), p. 204.

14. Stephen Toulmin, "From Form to Function," *Daedalus* (106) 1977: 154.

15. See John Rawls, *A Theory of Justice* (Cambridge: Harvard University Press, 1971); Robert Nozick, *Anarchy, State, and Utopia* (New York: Basic Books, 1974); Bruce Ackerman, *Social Justice in the Liberal State* (New Haven: Yale University Press, 1980); and Michael Walzer, *Spheres of Justice* (New York: Basic Books, 1983).

16. See Arthur Koestler, writing in Richard Crossman, ed., *The God That Failed* (New York: Bantam Books, 1952), pp. 11–66.

17. "The view from Vienna was always bifocal." Norwood Hanson, "Logical Positivism and the Interpretation of Scientific Theories," in Peter Achinstein and Stephen Barker, eds., *The Legacy of Logical Positivism* (Baltimore: The John Hopkins University Press, 1969), p. 57.

18. Harold Lasswell and Abraham Kaplan followed the dichotomous approach to political theories in their *Power and Society: A Framework for Political Inquiry* (New Haven: Yale University Press, 1950). Howard Warrender's approach to Hobbes's theory of obligation provides an example of how adopting Kantian assumptions about the requisites of moral theory leads to interpretative constraints that may be misleading. See his *The Political Philosophy of Hobbes* (Oxford: Clarendon Press, 1957).

19. J.W.N. Watkins uses this apt phrase in his *Hobbes's System of Ideas* (London: Hutchinson University Library, 1965), p. 76.

20. Edmond Cahn, *The Sense of Injustice* (Bloomington: Indiana University Press, 1949).

21. For a good recent overview, see Richard J. Bernstein, *Beyond Objectivism and Relativism* (Philadelphia: University of Pennsylvania Press, 1983).

22. For an excellent recent monograph that provides a push in this direction, see Ronald Beiner, *Political Judgment* (Chicago: University of Chicago Press, 1983).

23. Plato set this pattern early on when he identified rhetoric with sophistic demagoguery, even though his own dialectic—with its dialogic appeal to the intellectual assent and noble passions of its audience—incorporated and relied upon some of the essential elements of uncorrupted rhetoric.

INDEX